Archive Matter

T0406695

Liliana Gómez

Archive Matter
A Camera in the Laboratory of the Modern

DIAPHANES

THINK ART Series of the Institute for Critical Theory (ith)—
Zurich University of the Arts and the Centre for Arts and
Cultural Theory (ZKK)—University of Zurich.

Supported by the Swiss National Science Foundation
and the University of Zurich.

Cover image: United Fruit Company Photograph Collection,
Baker Library, Harvard Business School, Box 31

Layout: 2edit, Zurich
Printed in Germany

www.diaphanes.com

Table of Contents

Preface by Jens Andermann 7
Acknowledgments 15

Introduction 19
Archive Matter and Photography 19
Modern Visual Economy and Agriculture 39
The Chapters 47

1. **Camera and Capitalism: the United Fruit Company 53**
   The Corporation and its Photographic Archive 53
   Camera and Capitalism 69
   Slow Violence: Capital, Labor, Technology 90
   The Archive's Chronotope 117

2. **The Crossroads of Science and Discourse Networks 133**
   The Crossroads of Science 133
   Colonialism and Landscaping 146
   Discourse Networks 154
   Company Towns 171
   Imperial Debris 181

3. **"The World Was My Garden" 199**
   The World as Garden 199
   Photography and Botany's Modern Materialities 204
   The Political Economy of Agriculture 229
   Visual Epistemology and Botanical Matter 256

4. **Ethnographic Eyes and Archaeological Views 267**
   The Archaeological Expeditions to Quirigua 273
   The Keith Collection or the Magic of the Company's
      Pre-Columbian Objects 294
   Foundational Images: *The Maya Through the Ages* (1949) 303
   Animated Materiality 318

Epilogue. Upheavals and the Resurgent Photographic Archive 325

Civil Contract and the Materiality of the Image 325

The Banana Massacre and *One Hundred Years of Solitude* 333

The Resurgent Photographic Archive or the Ethics of Seeing 349

The Struggle for Human Rights 370

Bibliography 379

Jens Andermann

Preface

When I go grocery shopping in my New York neighborhood, it's hard to find any bananas not associated with any of the big distributors such as Dole or Del Monte, both U.S.-based, or the Dutch mega-wholesaler Van der Lem BV. All of these have been reliably accused of exploiting child and migrant labor and of intimidating or even assassinating union organizers with the paid assistance of paramilitary groups, as well as of systematically exposing plantation workers to deadly chemicals and of irreparably damaging tropical ecosystems from Central America to the Philippines. Particularly difficult to avoid is a certain yellowish lady in a blue dress, her left arm outstretched in a sexy stage pose while her right hand rests on her hip, and carrying on her head a bowl of tropical fruit in which, apart from bananas, we can discern the shapes of pineapples and mangoes. I am referring, of course, to "Miss Chiquita," the character created—or better, updated—in 1987 by Oscar Grillo, the cartoonist famous for his "Pink Panther" animations, for the corporation then still known as the United Fruit Company but which, in 1990, took on the name of its most recognizable mascot and flagship brand, trading henceforth as Chiquita Brands International. It's this omnipresent merchant of tropical fruit that is the subject of this book, and also the most notorious serial offender in the august company of international wholesalers, from its complicity in the 1928 "banana massacre" at Ciénaga, Colombia, so memorably recounted in Gabriel García Márquez's *One Hundred Years of Solitude*, to the no less violent quashing of the 1954 banana workers' strike at San Pedro Sula, Honduras, which also prepared the ground for the CIA-engineered overthrow of the reformist Árbenz government in neighboring Guatemala that same year,[1] to the more recent US\$25 million settlement the company agreed in 2007 with the U.S. Department of Justice, for illegal payouts made to paramilitary death squads in Colombia.[2]

In fact, just like her company namesake, Miss Chiquita has been something of a shape-shifter over the years, confounding, in her emblematic attire imprinted on the banana skin in the form of a peel-off sticker, associations of gender and of tropical nature, of erotic as well as culinary pleasure, of transnational empire and neocolonial banana republic alike. For, before growing up into a fruit hat and puff sleeve-wearing "Latin" lady, eyelashes and all, Miss Chiquita was, well... a banana—albeit an anthropomorphized and as similarly gendered and racialized one as her humanoid successor. Previous iterations of the sticker featured the puff sleeved dress and fruit hat-attired she-banana, striking the exact same stage pose with her human upper extremities, atop the brand name appearing alternately as "Chiquita Brand Bananas" between 1963 and 1972 and as "Chiquita Honduras" between 1972 and 1987—now also conflating the company name and chief product with its de facto fiefdom, in what Ileana Rodríguez has described as an "instance of feminization of identities and national cultures .... understood as the transposal of the defining conceptual ensembles of gender from one space of knowledge to another; in this case, from the feminine to the national-geographic."[3]

The logo had been created initially by Dik Browne, a U.S. cartoonist best known for his successful "Hägar the Horrible" comic strip, adapting the main character from his own series

1   Kevin Coleman, *A Camera in the Garden of Eden: The Self-Forging of a Banana Republic* (Austin: University of Texas Press, 2016), pp. 202–229.
2   Sam Allcock, "Chiquita to pay \$25m fine in terror case," *ABC Money*, March 15, 2007, https://www.abcmoney.co.uk/2007/03/15/chiquita-to-pay-25m-fine-in-terror-case/ (accessed June 2022).
3   Ileana Rodríguez, "*Banana Republics*: feminización de las naciones en frutas y de las socialidades en valores calóricos," in *La naturaleza en disputa: retóricas del cuerpo y el paisaje en América Latina*, ed. Gabriela Nouzeilles (Buenos Aires: Paidós, 2002), p. 86.

of short animated ads made for the United Fruit Company in the late 1940s, in which a singing and dancing Miss Chiquita starred in the voices of jazz vocalists Patti Clayton, Elsa Miranda, June Valli, and Monica Lewis. In the first of these clips, to the opening beats of a rumba tune, Miss Chiquita—the woman-banana—descends the staircase of an ocean liner we have just seen departing from a lush, palm and banana-lined tropical shore during the opening credits, to proceed directly to a quayside fruit stand and dining table where several bowls carrying smaller-sized (and male-voiced) bananas are conveniently arranged for a quick, non-animated interlude featuring real, profilmic bananas and a pair of female hands, with immaculate red-lacquered nails, preparing a side of baked bananas for a meat and vegetable dish. The song accompanying the clip offers further advice on how to store and prepare the exotic fruit that, we may assume, is being unloaded as Miss Chiquita sings: "I'm Chiquita Banana and I've come to say/ Bananas have to ripen in a certain way/ When they are fleck'd with brown and have a golden hue,/ Bananas taste the best and are the best for you./ You can put them in a salad/ You can put them in a pie/ Any way you want to eat them/ It's impossible to beat them./ But bananas like the climate of the very, very tropical equator/ So you should never put bananas/ In the refrigerator."

Catchy as it may be, the tune is also at pains to hide the fact that, at the time of the clip's first airing in cinemas, public appetite in the U.S. for these strange-shaped, yellow-skinned equatorial berries was not exactly unsatiable—most likely because not many spectators would actually have known when and how to savor them and how to keep them from getting mushy. Even as late as 1947, when the first clip was released, bananas were still more of a luxury item than an everyday food staple in large parts of the U.S.—let alone Europe. Commodities don't grow on trees (or on pseudostems, for that matter)—fruits do. Therefore, to make consumers desire *Musa paradisiaca* (the hybrid cultivar originating from Southeast Asia, from which most commercially available bananas and plantains descend), not just a catchy tune and a good helping of tropical fantasy were in order, but also a sharing-out of at least some of the knowledge accrued in the banana's inter-continental transplantation, mass production, and shipping from harvesting source to retail outlet. The four animated ads, to borrow from Arjun Appadurai's lexicon, were tasked with taking the banana's "commodity career" from its incipient stage of "commodity candidacy" to that of fully-fledged "commodity situation," defined here as the stage "in the social life of any 'thing' in which its exchangeability ... is its socially relevant feature."[4] More simply put, Miss Chiquita had to bring bananas to the masses. She achieved this by, quite literally, imparting a two-pronged consumption lesson, one that combined hands-on, practical (as well as photography-based) advice in the form of recipes on *what to do* with bananas with (animation-based) suggestions on *what to feel* when peeling a banana and biting into the soft flesh underneath.

Teaching consumers how to enjoy bananas—culinarily and ideologically speaking, as actual sweetener and as the catalyst for imaginary flights of (tropical) fancy—required, then, the giving away of some of the archival knowledge patiently and methodically gathered by the United Fruit Company in its circum-Caribbean domains. Knowing how to keep bananas fresh—and how, by baking and frying them, they might still be enjoyed even when past their prime—was information worth sharing with retailers and customers, as a way of making culinary habits more amenable to, and eventually reliant on, the newcomer from the South. Consumption knowledge of the kind divulged in the Miss Chiquita clips is, of course, hardly ever imparted by the object of consumption itself, much less in rhymes and to the beat of congas and maracas in the background. In the case of bananas, as of other trans-hemispheric transplants such as breadfruit, sugar cane, coffee or arrowroot,

4   Arjun Appadurai, "Commodities and the Politics of Value," in *The Social Life of Things*, ed. Arjun Appadurai (Cambridge: Cambridge University Press, 1986), p. 13.

it is a knowledge entangled with centuries-long, violent histories of colonial expansion, extractivism, and slavery; a knowledge often forcibly obtained—along with information on when and where to plant, tend to, and harvest these exotic crops—from the very same populations pressed into service as cheap labor on the plantations appearing first on the Atlantic islands and subsequently across the Americas and the Caribbean from the fifteenth century onwards. As much or even more than the gold and silver mined from the former Aztec and Inca empires in Mesoamerica and the Andes, the plantation machine as a producer not just of surplus capital but of "cheap foods" (including stimulants enhancing the energy of the metropolitan labor force) in formerly unimaginable quantities, whilst relying on the forced labor of indigenous and enslaved African and Afro-descendent bodies, was the springboard of modern capitalism—as a historical as well as world-ecological event, as historian Jason W. Moore has argued, one that we should better start calling by its (ugly) real name of "Capitalocene" instead of the loftier (and arguably misdated) one of "Anthropocene."[5]

Although it has been accorded far less page space in mainstream histories, this botanical, agricultural and nutritional archive collected, organized, cross-referenced and fought over by conquistadors, missionaries, naturalists, plantation administrators, church and crown officials since the earliest days of colonization has arguably had as much or more of an impact on the modern world-system than the nautical and astronomical innovations triggered by European imperial expansion. The banana plantation, and the way in which it remade the polities, economies and demographics of large parts of Central America and the Caribbean, is only one—and arguably the twentieth century's most iconic—iteration of the itinerant "laboratory of the modern" that we could also call the extractive frontier. Having been introduced to South America in the sixteenth cen-

5   Jason W. Moore, *Capitalism in the Web of Life: Ecology and the Accumulation of Capital* (London: Verso, 2015), pp. 53, 171.

tury by the Portuguese, it was only thanks to the accelerated transport routes opened up by steamboats and railroads in the late nineteenth century that large-scale production of the fruit in the Caribbean and Central America for the North American retail market became a viable, and lucrative, prospect. The information about banana skin color as related to ripeness and texture as well as the fruits' resistance to refrigeration technology included in Miss Chiquita's maiden song, in fact, is but a succinct version of the much larger body of archival data that would have been collected, analyzed, and discussed in cigar-clouded boardrooms prior to the implementation of plantations throughout the region, often in a concerted interplay between economic cooptation and geopolitical force exerted by U.S. capital and military power. "Relandscaping" vast portions of Caribbean and Central American land into banana plantations effectively involved the large-scale razing of forests and fields previously submitted to agronomic assessments of soil fertility, and the displacement of local peasant economies for the benefit of export production —thereby also creating the large, newly mobile and half-starved reserve of cheap human labor needed for seasonal harvests. As Héctor Hoyos starkly sums it up,

> the physical layout of the banana plantation itself is a matrix for material transformation: the endless rows of banana trees, shimmering under the equinoctial sun, are a model for dysfunctional human and nonhuman interaction. The story of the domestication of the Asian Cavendish banana could very well inform an understanding of its accompanying worldwide cultural products and human consequences.[6]

If not this entire story, *Archive Matter: A Camera in the Laboratory of the Modern* treats us to one of its key chapters: the entan-

6   Héctor Hoyos, *Things With a History: Transcultural Materialism and the Literatures of Extraction in Contemporary Latin America* (New York: Columbia University Press, 2019), p. 60.

glement—or perhaps better: the assemblage—of the banana's phyto-physiology and materiality with, on the one hand, a modern-capitalist archival circuit of data collection, management, and storage, and, on the other, a "visual economy" re-organized since the mid-nineteenth century around technologies of "mechanical reproduction" of machine-recorded images such as photography and the cinema. In taking us through the networks of science, capital, technology, and politics, Liliana Gómez shows how the "production knowledge" accrued by monopoly producers such as the United Fruit Company stands in a far more complex relationship to the "consumption knowledge" divulged by Miss Chiquita in her post-WWII address to would-be banana buyers than a more straightforward, ideology-critical reading might have it. As we have seen, the commercial clips—once the "real," photo-indexical object lesson on how to make bananas into food has run its course—reverted to *animated* fantasy images invariably drawing on the trope of tropical abundance as related to a hyper-sexualized femininity: it is no accident, of course, that Miss Chiquita's pose on the peel-off sticker almost exactly repeats Josephine Baker's on one of the most iconic production images for "La Revue Nègre" at Folies Bergères, premiered in 1925, where she appeared dressed only in a pearl necklace and a banana skirt.[7] In place of the "real" relations of production, in short, metropolitan fantasy images (to which we should add Busby Berkeley's 1943 musical *The Gang's All Here*, starring a tutti-frutti hat-wearing Carmen Miranda and a troupe of banana-skirted female dancers) offer an "imaginary" vision of inexhaustible abundance and/as (racialized) female sexuality. Yet this "animated," imaginary dream-image is not merely a screen behind which, in the depths of the company archive, the photo-ontological real of transnational capi-

---

7   Alicja Sowinska, "Banana Skirt: The Ambiguities of Josephine Baker's Self-Representation," *Michigan Feminist Studies* 19 (Fall 2005–Spring 2006), http://hdl.handle.net/2027/spo.ark5583.0019.003 (accessed June 2022).

talism in its brutal and exploitative truth is to be found. Rather, as Gómez's in-depth analysis of this previously unseen body of images eloquently shows, the photographic archive is itself haunted by an "animated materiality," and dream-images very much continue to inform its photo-documentary stagings of reality. Just as real historical experiences of chattel slavery and Black resistance returned in distorted, misrecognized fashion to the cabaret stage through Josephine Baker's banana dance, and just as the technological networks underwriting the trans-Caribbean fruit economy inevitably pierced the choreographies of Miss Chiquita and Carmen Miranda, the photo-cinematic matter of the company archive is itself shot through with colonial dream-images and exoticist desire. "Desire" and "knowledge," in fact, are not polar opposites but interwoven with one another, as are "production" and "consumption." Treading a fine balance between exposing the uneven relations of power proper to what Keith Hetherington has suggested to call the dispositives of "agrobiopolitics,"[8] on the one hand, and illuminating the ways in which tropical fantasy informs and underwrites the very make-up of the United Fruit Company's neocolonial plantation machine, on the other, *Archive Matter* puts forth a rich and fascinating object lesson, one that is certain to keep the environmental humanities busy for times to come.

8   Keith Hetherington, *The Government of Beans: Regulating Life in the Age of Monocrops* (Durham: Duke University Press, 2020), pp. 14–15.

Acknowledgments

To Vincent and Younes

When in 2006 I started to visit the photographic collection of the United Fruit Company at the Harvard Business School, in a very precursory phase of this project to be materialized only at a much later moment, and began to follow the ongoing conservation process, I noticed that during these procedures there occurred an erasure of material traces, written fragments, or pencil notes. This erasure or loss took place within the materiality of both the photographs and the albums, as photographs were removed from the albums, losing their original inscription and context, and even being grouped together differently: the material conservation instead followed a pragmatic logic that seemed to oppose the inherent materiality of the pictures and albums and thus their meaning. Facing the archive's relationship to the future, these archival images found their echo in the reoccurrence of transfer, storage, cancellation, and modification. I needed to make a decision, and I opted to select and include some of my own copies and reproductions of pictures and album pages that I had made that time of the initial beginnings of the project and that no longer correspond to the pictures as we find them in the United Fruit Company photographic collection today.

Thus, the archive constellation I discuss in this study is conceived around some of these lacunae that continue to haunt the Company photographic archive as imperial debris. This dimension is materialized in a manifold and contradictory way, appearing in the archive as struggle and friction, horizon and transgression, requiring a reading of the images beyond any regional conception. It is in this dimension that the archive becomes a privileged site of witnessing that necessarily claims a contemporary perspective for its reading, notably with regard to the special place this photographic archive holds in the geocultural history of the Caribbean. Despite the singularity of this photographic archive, the archival images are still carefully enclosed within the Harvard Business School. Although there has been an initial, timid attempt at partial digitization of some of the pictures, the need persists to open this collection up to a wider public outside of an institutional space. As a figuration of recording the past and the contested present the archive makes visible the hitherto unseen or overlooked. Accordingly, a future reclamation, reception, and possible re-appropriation of the photographs might emerge, permitting alternative narratives and new political subjectivities.

This project had a fruitful beginning when I was a visiting scholar at Columbia University, at the Institute of Latin American Studies and the Center for the Study of Ethnicity and Race (CSER), between 2008 and 2010. I would like to express my deepest gratitude to Claudio Lomnitz for his encouragement, his intellectually sharp and always inspiring and human comments on the development of this project since its very inception and during the long and often difficult material research. At Columbia, I could also count on a continuous and stimulating dialogue with Michael Taussig and many other colleagues in the Anthropology Department and CSER as well as with the students there. Also at that time, I started to visit the Carnegie Mellon University, to search for photographic material at the Hunt Institute for Botanical Documentation. I would like to express my gratitude to Angela Todd who helped me navigate through the abundant archival material there. I also would like to thank Aviva Chomsky, with whom I have been in dialogue over the United Fruit Company for a long time and who truly inspired me and helped sharpen the approach to the photographic archive.

At a later moment, I had the opportunity to continue and deepen this project and thus dedicate myself to the first drafts of the book into which the research project had by then progressed, when I was at Harvard University, with a research fellowship in the Romance Languages and Literatures Department and Department of Art History and Architecture, between 2013 and

2016. I met great and supportive colleagues in both departments: my deepest thanks go to Thomas Cummins, Sergio Delgado Moya, June Erlick, Robin Kelsey, Malcolm Rogge, Rainer Schultz, Doris Sommer and Dell Hamilton, who as an artist works herself on the United Fruit Company. The staff at the Harvard Archives was greatly supportive and very helpful. I would like to thank the Special Collections and Archives at the Baker Library at Harvard Business School for all these years of support.

For reading and commenting on parts of the project at different stages, I would like to thank Lisa Blackmore, Thomas Bremer, Kevin Coleman, Juan Duchesne-Winter, Isabel Exner, Ana María Gómez Londoño, Sarah Gónzalez de Mojica, Daniel James, Jairo Moreno, Gesine Müller, Irina Podgorny, Ori Preuss, Wolfgang Schäffner, Sven Schuster, Jessica Stites Mor, and Ines Yujnovsky.

The research and book project found its final shape through a third intellectual constellation at the University of Zurich, when I first discussed it with Jens Andermann, Svenja Goltermann, Philipp Sarasin and Jakob Tanner at the Forschungsstelle für Sozial- und Wirtschaftsgeschichte. At the University of Zurich, this research project was then accepted as Habilitationsschrift in 2016. My sincere gratitude goes to Jens Andermann who with his intellectual generosity, curiosity, and sharpness helped find me the final form of this book project.

The book's language was rigorously shaped by my copy-editor Kate Wilson, with whom I have not only shared a long professional relationship but a true inspiration for thinking with archives. I thank her a lot for her patience and commitment to the text.

During different phases of the project, I could count on the generous financial support of the DAAD (German Academic Exchange Service), the DFG (Deutsche Forschungsgemeinschaft), the Martin-Luther-University Halle-Wittenberg and the University of Zurich, where I held the SNSF professorship (Schweizerischer Nationalfonds) until 2021. Without this generous support the research and the book would not have been possible.

Finally, I would like to share a personal note: during this time from the beginning of the research, the conception of the project, the writing and the final materialization of it as a book, my two children were born. These magical and great moments of the beginnings of their lives are entwined with the realization of this project. Many times, it was they, demanding their own time, who kept me away from the desk and the intense writing, in a fruitful way. I am deeply indebted to them for their patience, unconditional love, and care, which helped me keep confidence in writing this book. I dedicate this book to them.

Kassel, June 2022

Introduction

> Thus, since photographic archives tend to suspend meaning and use; within the archive meaning exists in a state that is both residual and potential. The suggestion of past uses coexists with a plentitude of possibilities. In functional terms, an active archive is like a toolshed, a dormant archive like an abandoned toolshed. (Archives are not like coal mines; meaning is not extracted from nature, but from culture.)[1]

Archive Matter and Photography[2]

In one of the albums of the large United Fruit Company Photograph Collection, we find a picture bearing the caption "Natives and huts – Escondido River – Nicaragua, 1891." It seems to be one of the oldest pictures contained in the corporate photographic albums. Bear in mind that the United Fruit Company was only formally established as a transnational corporation for tropical fruits in 1899. This photograph—or the picture of the album page—both fascinates and irritates on different levels. It captures a sort of bird's-eye view of a group of workers and their living environment in the midst of a banana plantation. As indicated in the caption, the picture shows "natives and huts," as well as the "Escondido River – Nicaragua," a geographic location. It shows the laborers, many of them dressed in white clothing or in simple working clothes, standing in a group in front of their "huts." We also see seven girls or young women in

---

1   Allan Sekula, "Photography Between Labour and Capital," in *Mining Photographs and Other Pictures, 1948–1968. A Selection from the Negative Archives of Shedden Studio, Glace Bay, Cape Breton*, ed. Benjamin Buchloh and Robert Wilkie (Halifax: Press of the Nova Scotia College of Art and Design, 1983), p. 197.
2   See my discussion in Liliana Gómez-Popescu, "Epilogue: Archive Matters," E.I.A.L. *Estudios Interdisciplinarios de América Latina y el Caribe*, Special Issue *History through Photography*, 26:2 (2015), pp. 95–103.

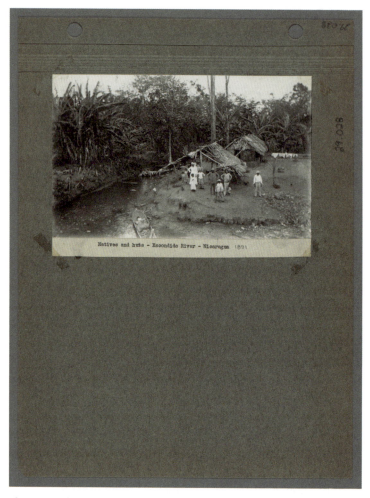

Fig. 1.1: "Natives and huts – Escondido River – Nicaragua 1891," Gelatin silver process on paper, United Fruit Company Photograph Collection, Baker Library, Harvard Business School, Box 29.

white dresses, standing up in an orderly group to the left side of the image, while the men and boys are grouped together on the opposite side. Behind them, we see a "typical" kitchen and a "hut" of that time. The critical viewer is immediately aware that black people in Nicaragua were not natives at all. Rather, they had migrated with the companies to the Central American Caribbean and later the Pacific coasts, following work dynamics in a time when transnational companies experimented with new forms of labor. The demand for it was high in this region, especially in the labor-intensive agricultural business, which suffered from a chronic lack of working hands. Gigantic modern infrastructure projects, such as the construction of the Panama Canal, meant that migratory labor flows were steady and ever-increasing. The end of the nineteenth century was a dynamic and busy time of migration, particularly from the West Indies to the Isthmus of Darién, from which the fruit companies profited the most.[3]

The caption further irritates in the way it assigns meaning to the photograph that became part of one of the most significant corporate photographic archives of the twentieth century, that of the United Fruit Company. However, the photographer's gaze, or perhaps the gaze of the person who later collected this photograph for the Company archive, is made explicit in the registration of the image in the album with the caption, which remains both opaque and omnipotent, while at the same time it lacks information. These added captions often become the errata in the production of the photographs, misleading or misinterpreting the depicted views and thus disguising the encounters for which the photograph becomes the event. So it is that the people depicted in the photograph became what the Company had imagined them to be: the natives. Through the camera and the caption they become disciplined and controlled laborers at the margins of an ever-expanding capitalism. Nevertheless, this photograph, recovered with the archive, becomes an important matter in the way it seems to give voice to those whose

3   These flows have been analyzed and discussed as ethnic segregation and racial politics in particular by Philippe Bourgois, *Ethnicity at Work. Divided Labor on a Central American Banana Plantation* (Baltimore and London: The Johns Hopkins University Press, 1989) and Aviva Chomsky, *West Indian Workers and the United Fruit Company in Costa Rica, 1870–1940* (Baton Rouge: Louisiana State University Press, 1996).

collective memory has been forgotten, and to the omitted histories of extractivism, hitherto invisible, but resurging through this corporate photographic archive. "Whatever judgements it imposes can always be contested," Ariella Azoulay reminds us of photography.[4] In another context, Jacques Derrida observes that "the archive [...] will never be either memory or anamnesis as spontaneous, alive and internal experience. On the contrary: the archive takes place at the place of originary and structural breakdown of said memory."[5] What he diagnoses, that the archive takes place at the place of structural breakdown, is pertinent for the complicit yet complicated relationship between history and photography, problematized by this photographic archive.

In this book I will follow an understanding of photography as history to argue that it is this collapse as matter of the archive that is configured by the resurgent United Fruit Company photographic images. As art historian Clément Chéroux underlines, regarding the recurrent attempts to methodologically relate photography with history, the photograph as a medium seems to have the capacity to reflect on history, rather than being a medium of history itself.[6] This may be a powerful discovery in itself as it implies conceiving of the photographic image as a historical reflection that could spark a history through photography. Yet, the non-convergence of photography and history has only recently been discussed, in terms of the "invisibility of the visible" in the discourse of history.[7] While the history of photography is flourishing, history through photography seems to be poorly explored. So, it is in the light of this com-

---

4   Ariella Azoulay, *Civil Imagination: A Political Ontology of Photography* (London: Verso, 2010), p. 219.

5   Jacques Derrida, "Archive Fever: A Freudian Impression," *Diacritics* 25:2 (1995), p. 14.

6   Ilsen About and Clément Chéroux, *Fotografie und Geschichte* (Leipzig: Institut für Buchkunst, 2004). See also Liliana Gómez-Popescu, "Towards a History through Photography: An Introduction," *E.I.A.L. Estudios Interdisciplinarios de América Latina y el Caribe*, Special Issue *History through Photography*, 26:2 (2015), pp. 7–16.

7   About and Chéroux, *Fotografie und Geschichte*, p. 97.

plex relationship between photography and history that the United Fruit Company photographic archive must be read, and urgently reclaimed. In this sense, this study foregrounds the complex relationships between history and photography, and thus the diverse epistemic, political and cultural contexts in which these images were being produced. What Derrida points out is that the archive takes place where no such memory is possible or materializable anymore. As a negative figure, within the collapse, the archive seems to contour the suppressed, marginalized and thus the optical unconscious—here with regard to the Company photographs—of capitalism. I will argue that the relationship between history and photography is defined by the archive as a place of consignation, negotiated by the photographic images that may nevertheless become powerful enough to articulate counter-semantics and alternative narratives of civil imagination, and to resist the power regimes, in the way Azoulay has suggested.[8] Accordingly, I intend to study this political-ontological dimension of photography that is irreducibly tied to the archive.

With regard to the material turn, particularly in the context of studies of photographic archives, the purely visual content of photographs has been abandoned "in order to consider them as material objects."[9] Significantly, the turn recognizes the importance of materiality for the production of meaning. Following this, while studying the Company photographic archive, my focus is less on the visual content, but more on the material practices that embed the archive into a visual economy and thus a broader process of knowledge production. In this context, Elizabeth Edwards has pointed out that "ideas about the sociability of objects suggest that objects," such as archives and photographs, "are not merely the stage settings for human

8   Azoulay, *Civil Imagination*.
9   Costanza Caraffa, "From 'Photo Libraries' to 'Photo Archives': On the Epistemological Potential of Art-historical Photo Collections," in *Photo Archives and the Photographic Memory of Art History*, ed. Costanza Caraffa (Munich: Deutscher Kunstverlag, 2011), p. 36.

actions and meanings, but integral to them."[10] Consequently, I adopt her reading of "'mattering' as opposed to 'signifying,' that is, to follow the idea of historiographical 'significance' not in terms of representation or a signifying discourse, but through 'that materiality and thingness' of the material trace rather than on its 'textuality and content'."[11] Therefore the relationship between the archive and its "outside" is best described as the conception of the archive as *media a priori*, in the way this photographic archive pre-organizes and pre-registers the complex cultural encounters of the bio-contact zone of the United Fruit Company and the transformation of the agricultural land into a productive media-discursive landscape. Due to its order as a media dispositive of the political, the archive contains the potential to be contested at every moment, making it a site of political struggle.

It is not known why or under what circumstances this one photograph was taken and included in the album. The opacity that surrounds the origins of the image is a powerful feature of the many United Fruit Company photographs and, more generally, poses a true challenge when it comes to discussing the photographs as source material. However, rather than looking at what the image presents, I underscore another aspect here in order to examine the tensions between facts and meanings raised by the photograph. It is noteworthy that the picture was collected and stored in the Company photographic archive. This was laborious work and it was done consistently throughout almost the entire life of the corporation. These epistemic practices of collecting, storing, and ordering items may be called archival processes, and these further define the photographs as a part of civic practice, as Azoulay suggests.[12] This is to emphasize that the archive matters as an authority for the meaning

10   Elizabeth Edwards, "Photographs: material form and the dynamic archive," in Caraffa, *Photo Archives and the Photographic Memory of Art History*, p. 49.
11   Ibid., p. 50.
12   Azoulay, *Civil Imagination*.

of the images. Furthermore, these photographs were embedded in the United Fruit Company's social practice of corporate communication. Because of this, the Company photographic archive becomes a primarily political matter that defines the photographs' tension between facts and meanings. This is why Alan Trachtenberg trenchantly reminds us that:

> Ordering facts into meaning, data into history, moreover, is not an idle exercise but a political act, a matter of judgment and choice about the emerging shape of the present and future. It may be less obvious in the making of a photograph than in the writing of a history, but it is equally true: the viewfinder is a political instrument, a tool for making a past suitable for the future. [...] The sacrifice, for better or for worse, is for the sake of testing and exemplifying a way of reading photographs, not as pictures alone or as documents but as cultural texts. The value of photographs as history lies not just in what they show or how they look but in how they construct their meanings.[13]

The United Fruit Company archive is the point of departure for this book's reflections about the constructions but also the contested meanings of photography and thus about how the camera both depicts and configures the Caribbean as a laboratory of the modern. As archives emerge, they are resurgent, may change over the course of time, mold space anew, or revise history. By their nature archives are Pandora's box, the outcome of opening them necessarily unknown, bringing the possibility of detournements. They move, translate, make tangible and may irritate, unsettle, provoke, subvert, or reconstruct. Because archives may be active, as concoctions or made things they become matters in their own right. As Allan Sekula powerfully suggests, archives are "toolsheds" whose use remains to be evoked, revived, and critically investigated. As archives may fall into abeyance, and their "toolsheds" become neglected,

13 Alan Trachtenberg, *Reading American Photographs: Images as History, Mathew Brady to Walker Evans* (New York: Hill and Wang, 1989), pp. xiv, xvi.

25

they are "in transit and in translation" and are no longer a stable space of storage. Rather, they are an "engine of circulation," a performative act that "mobilizes different media" and is "mobilized by them."[14] More specifically, as political matter the photographic archive becomes resurgent, reclaiming civil power, and thus defines the main conceptual concern of this study. The powerful photographic archive of the United Fruit Company embeds, bears witness to, and at the same time conceals, manifold imperial struggles, violent ecological degradation, and the contestation and resistance that the Caribbean has experienced since the arrival of this omnipotent modern transnational corporation. It also raises potential questions of historical justice and accountability that may rely on the visual as testimony to this long process of environmental degradation and attacks against personhood, abuse of labor, migration and forced displacement, systematic contamination, exhaustion, human rights violations and toxic injustice.[15] Moreover, the archive powerfully articulates a place of reclamation, inasmuch as its photographic images become files that interlock the past with the present, marking a space between memory and the law. Knowledge is still linked to judicial power, and by taking evidence and storing it in private, you are controlling it. The archive is therefore also about withdrawing evidence from the public sphere.

In this book I will discuss the varied visual material as archive matter, following the different epistemic contexts of the images of the United Fruit Company photographic archive. This archive makes tangible an emergent visual field that helps unfold the corporation's involvement with the production of a

14   Marianne Hirsch and Diane Taylor, "The Archive in Tansit. Editorial Remarks," *E-misférica* 9:1–2 (2012).
15   For the use of this term, see the discussion in Susanna Rankin Bohme, *Toxic Injustice: A Transnational History of Exposure and Struggle* (Oakland: University of California Press, 2015), where she reconstructs the context of legal claims made by former laborers—including those of the United Fruit Company—against transnational corporations.

modern political space. Moreover, this archive offers insights into new processes of media exploration and the development of modes of visualization that constitute tools in the making of a modern media-discursive landscape, that of the Caribbean. The important and hitherto overlooked photographic archive of the United Fruit Company sheds light on the modernization processes and the transformation of the Caribbean into a laboratory of the modern. As archives matter, media scholar Cornelia Vismann underlines, also "societies grow aware of the secret power of files."[16] Similarly, archival images act as files, as is, to some extent, the case of the United Fruit Company photographic archive. As access to the United Fruit Company's written corporate files is still being denied, or those files no longer exist, the visual becomes vested with a particular authority, situating the Company photographic archive within a culture of corporate bureaucracy. This book therefore enquires into the workings of the photographic archive and its visual economy, how these related to governmental agencies, and to knowledge production as part of the constitution of the laboratory of the modern. As photographic archives seem to reflect a form of latency, they are residual remnants of institutions that are no longer immediately relevant or have simply not yet been destroyed.[17] As Vismann further notes, "Once the archives grow out of bounds and more files are hoarded than circulate, files no longer control themselves," so an "action in the realm of the real" is required "that is not restricted to the level of the signifier."[18] This action is the "ordered segregation" or "destruction of files"; a rationale that may explain why the photographic archive of the United Fruit Company has become accessible only "posthumously," after the United Fruit Company ceased to exist as a legal entity, becoming the present-day Chiquita Brands. The United Fruit

16 Cornelia Vismann, *Files: Law and Media Technology* (Stanford: Stanford University Press, 2008), p. xiv.
17 Knut Ebeling and Stephan Günzel, eds., *Archivologie. Theorien des Archivs in Wissenschaft, Medien und Künsten* (Berlin: Kunstverlag Kadmos, 2009), p. 20.
18 Vismann, *Files*, p. xiv.

Company photographic archive, its collected albums, never cir-culated widely outside of the Company and related fields of sci-entific knowledge. When I started to investigate this archive, I was told that it had, to a large extent, been destroyed in the early 1970s due to a lack of storage space and a lack of awareness of the potential importance of this visual archival material. Acts such as "transmitting, storing, canceling, manipulating, and destroying—write the history of the law," Vismann reminds us, and I wish to add, also write the genealogy of the visual economy and its contestations, which rely significantly on the resurgence of archival images.[19]

I therefore understand the archive not as a place of storage, in which we simply locate or revisit facts, but rather as an active process that provokes a permanent redeployment and continu-ing transformation of the facts.[20] Processes of institutionaliza-tion become meaningful therein, inasmuch as they vest author-ity in the images that determine knowledge and its production, materialized in the archive. Because of its nature as a media dispositive of the political, the archive contains the irreducible potential of actualization and reclamation, as is the case of the United Fruit Company photographic archive. In this context the institutional processes that determine the preeminent role of the archive and its photographs are shaped by private or corpo-rate and public or governmental actors. Moreover, because these photographic archives disclose the embodied institutional and bureaucratic practices of the corporation or the State, they con-stitute, by definition, administrative-technical authorities.

Photographs are marked by an irreconcilable friction that "encodes them with contradictions that continue to be intelli-gible": that is because this intelligibility is "rendered possible in part by the persistence of bureaucracy as a recognizable form

---

19 Ibid.
20 See the discussion by Knut Ebeling and Stephan Günzel, "Einleitung," in *Archivologie. Theorien des Archivs in Wissenschaft, Medien und Künsten*, ed. Knut Ebeling and Stephan Günzel, p. 18.

of social production."[21] The very fact that the United Fruit Company collected so many photographs—about 10,000, reflecting a period of more than seventy years, between 1891 and 1962 in the midst of the Cold War—to make them into a photographic archive, not only indicates the importance of the bureaucratic undertaking in the production of the images' meaning, but also gives account of the long-lasting global-local encounters of the Company in the Caribbean. The archival images not only suggest that the Company's economic advancement enabled the incorporation of the Caribbean into the orbit of Western knowledge, but even more so they reveal that vision became the primary sensory modality that advanced this very incorporation into a laboratory of the modern.

In historical and media studies, there has, since the 1960s, been a critical approach to the medium of photography: concerning image production, an historical and institutional analysis of the meaning, status, and effects of photography has superseded the art-historical discourse of aesthetics.[22] Following Michel Foucault's concept of discourse, which also allows a novel approach to the social praxis of photography, this shift has brought the significance of the institutional network behind the production of these images into focus. Accordingly, the paradigm of representation has been replaced by an imperative of contingency of knowledge.[23] Moreover, the way Foucault conceived the archive went beyond representation, stimulating a non-teleological conception of historical temporality. He inspired a productive discussion that started to focus on the codification of knowledge and

21   Robin Kelsey, *Archive Style: Photographs and Illustrations for U.S. Surveys, 1850–1890* (Berkeley: University of California Press, 2007), p. 18.
22   See John Tagg, *The Burden of Representation: Essays on Photographies and Histories* (Minneapolis: University of Minnesota Press, 1993); Trachtenberg, *Reading American Photographs*; Lili Corbus Bezner, *Photography and Politics in America: From the New Deal into the Cold War* (Baltimore: The Johns Hopkins University Press, 1999).
23   Ebeling and Günzel, "Einleitung," in *Archivologie. Theorien des Archivs in Wissenschaft, Medien und Künsten*, ed. Knut Ebeling and Stephan Günzel, p. 17.

history.[24] Following this, art historian John Tagg significantly revoked the idea of photography as a record of reality and questioned any documentary traditions of photography. Neglect of the history of the image and of image production not only poses a critical challenge to the traditional history and theory of photography, but, even more so, implies a new focus on the role and meaning of images and their knowledge codification in modern social regulation. Accordingly, an image analysis that is aware of the emergence of the mighty modern State and the corporation reoriented the debate on photography beyond the field of the history of art. In this context, the effects of the epistemic entanglement of perception, power, and difference become matters of concern.[25]

One of the main concerns of this study is the entanglement of knowledge production and the modern visual economy of the archive in this specific context of the United Fruit Company's expansion of corporate capitalism, which is also manifested in the many politico-spatial struggles and upheavals in the Caribbean.[26] So I favor the understanding of the de-ontologization of the images against the predominant tendency of affirmation of their physical relations, and their role as evidence, stressing instead their immanent cultural and "verbal" relations with history. Consequently, I deal with the image as relation, following what Walter Benjamin conceived elsewhere: he understands representation not as an expression of something essential or

---

24 Ibid., p. 23.

25 This also significantly reoriented the field of visual anthropology. Elizabeth Edwards and Christopher Pinney have discussed this entanglement as the relationship between history and photography, examining the British colonial system, its expansion towards India and Africa, and specifically the role of photography in the institutionalization of anthropology. See Elizabeth Edwards, ed., *Anthropology and Photography, 1860–1920* (New Haven and London: Yale University Press with the Royal Anthropological Institute, 1992), and Christopher Pinney and Nicolas Peterson, eds., *Photography's Other Histories* (Durham: Duke University Press, 2003).

26 I adopt here the concept of modern visual economy as elaborated by Deborah Poole, *Vision, Race, and Modernity: A Visual Economy of the Andean Image World* (Princeton: Princeton University Press, 1997).

archetypal, but rather as a symptom of something displaced. Accordingly, the study adopts the position that images of the past are not simply objects of knowledge, but rather they are media of or relationship to knowledge.[27] This is particularly pertinent for my discussion of these archival images, because they attain legibility from within the present: as files they obtain "a value as testimony [...], not simply because they inform us, but because they are able to oblige us to relate in a time-critical and non-aesthetical way to what they represent, to what we see."[28] This is what resonates throughout this study, and is further discussed through the photographic archive in the following chapters. To this end, the visual material of the United Fruit Company is studied as a significant element of a cultural, that is, discursive and media production of the Caribbean as a space of expansion of a modern capitalism. This is no longer determined by an aestheticization of the landscape, but rather mobilized by a series of visualization strategies that are bound to the emergent knowledge production, in for example economic botany, archaeology or tropical medicine, as part of a media-discursive network, within which photography played a central role.

Some of the relationships between the archive and photography have also been outlined by Allan Sekula, as "archival ambitions and procedures" that started to define a correspondence with photographic practices.[29] I closely follow this relationship between the corporate archive and its photography, in order to grasp the related production of value and the emergent regime of value in the convergence of a "uniform logic of representation" and a "uniform logic of exchange," which are both bound to the

27   Walter Benjamin, "Theses on the Philosophy of History," *Illuminations* (New York: Schocken Books, 1969), p. 255.
28   Milena Massalongo, "Bild und Zeugenschaft. Erkenntnis und Gedächtnis im Zeitalter des Zeugen," in *Nachleben und Rekonstruktion. Vergangenheit im Bild*, ed. Michael Hagner and Peter Geimer (Munich: Wilhelm Fink, 2012), p. 193, my translation.
29   Sekula, "Photography Between Labour and Capital," p. 194.

capitalistic production of space.[30] This is particularly true for the
United Fruit Company photographic archive, which incorporates this logic as its hegemonic discourse, notwithstanding that
archives always have the potential to revoke their subordination.
Sekula maintains that "archives are not neutral; they embody
the power inherent in accumulation, collection, and hoarding
as well as that power inherent in the command of the lexicon
and rules of a language."[31] Yet, as photographic archives, they
also embed the residual and future meaning allowing for different potential uses that may, at some point, shatter this hegemonic discourse. In the case of the United Fruit Company, I will
show, this "archive has to be read from below, from a position
of solidarity with those displaced, deformed, silenced, or made
invisible by the machineries of profit and progress."[32] I therefore
ask: How do the archive and its images serve to legitimate and
re-inscribe power relations? But also: How is this photographic
archive being contested and resisted?

I conceive the United Fruit Company photographic collection and its albums as nothing less than an archive. I will discuss
that archive as an epistemic figure and the archive's correlation
with its "outside," by identifying a series of visualization strategies that transform the Caribbean into a laboratory of the modern. As I examine the photographic archive of the United Fruit
Company, I advance this theoretical understanding against the
backdrop of the archive's own materiality as a modern corporate means of communication and as site of contested political
struggle, situated at the unstable limit between the public and
the private, as Derrida reasoned with regard to "archive fever."[33]
Understanding this relationship to its "outside," the archive
seems to be a performative act. I will examine that relationship
by advancing two theses: first, the "representation" of planta-

---

30 Ibid.
31 Ibid., p. 197.
32 Ibid., p. 202.
33 Derrida, "Archive Fever," p. 57.

tion economy as landscape that defines the archive's outside; second, the Company's projection of a chronotope envisaged as an eternal transition towards modernity, a promise of modernization itself, that aims to transform the Caribbean into a productive media-discursive landscape. As I attempt to outline the institutional entanglement of the United Fruit Company, looking at the diverse epistemic contexts in which the photographs were being produced, I also consider the archive as figure of thought. In its double nature, as a concept and a material reality, I seek to grasp the projection of the chronotope of the United Fruit Company into the Caribbean. So, I aim to unfold the different visual strategies and practices that have constituted the archive, since, as Ann Laura Stoler comments, "Those epistemic practices were not just recorded in the [...] archive, but developed and worked through the genres of documentation that civil servants were required to make."[34] Derrida, who was concerned with the agency or instance of authority over the institution of the archive, points out that the archive is always also the place of contestation for the political.[35] While archives are contested in a manifold and controversial way, in the case of the United Fruit Company photographic archive, it seems that a "Material force was engraved in phantasmagoric scenarios of potential revolt that called for militias readied with arms."[36] Archives seem to bear witness to the fear of revolt that is implicitly and almost invisibly concealed in them. More so, the images clamor to be reappropriated by those once visually presented as marginalized, making the archive a site of potential decolonial empowerment, in the way the images resurge and are vested with authority to reclaim. Following this, the archive, in its relation to this embodied political force, may transcend its once intended specific purposes. Stoler has warned in this context that:

34   Ann Laura Stoler, *Along the Archival Grain: Epistemic Anxieties and Colonial Common Sense* (Princeton: Princeton University Press, 2009), p. 4.

35   Ebeling, *Archivologie*, p. 29.

36   Stoler, *Along the Archival Grain*, p. 2.

As such, documents in these colonial archives were not dead matter once the moment of their making had passed. What was "left" was not "left behind" or obsolete. [...] these colonial archives were an arsenal of sorts that were reactivated to suit new governing strategies. Documents honed in the pursuit of prior issues could be requisitioned to write new histories, could be reclassified for new initiatives, could be renewed to fortify security measures against what were perceived as new assaults on imperial sovereignty and its moralizing claims.[37]

Archival practices certainly correspond to the desire of documentation. Indeed, at first glance, this may be the very nature of an archive. The United Fruit Company, certainly, deployed the pictures as documents, inasmuch as the corporation aimed at documenting its operations abroad, particularly in the Caribbean and Central America. Yet, documents have a mediating role, often overlooked, "because it's easy to see them as simply standing between the things that really matter, giving immediate access to what they document."[38] As the pictures were collected and stored by the United Fruit Company between 1891 and 1962, the pictures have also become documents, that altogether form an archive constituted by a "set of practices, institutions, and relationships,"[39] whose function does not primarily lie in storing information, but in having a share in internally organizing the corporation and its future spatial relationships, its "outside."

Again, in a different context but no less relevant for my discussion, Derrida once observed that "There is no archive without a place of consignation, without a technique of repetition, and without a certain exteriority. No archive without outside."[40] Significantly, he conceives the fundamental relationship between

37   Ibid., p. 3.
38   Matthew Hull, *Government of Paper: The Materiality of Bureaucracy in Urban Pakistan* (Berkeley: University of California Press, 2012), p. 12.
39   Richard Bolton, *The Contest of Meaning: Critical Histories of Photography* (Cambridge, Mass.: MIT Press, 1989), p. xvi.
40   Derrida, "Archive Fever," p. 14.

the archive and its place of "consignation" or "registration" as a constitutive one that describes the archive's epistemic correlation with its outside, that of a "*hors-texte*." He specifies that "'text' implies all the so-called 'real,' 'economic,' 'historical,' social-institutional structures, in short, all possible referents."[41] Now, with regard to the United Fruit Company photographic archive, I read "text" in this broader sense. I ask: What correspondence does exist between the archive, the United Fruit Company photographic archive, and what seems to be outside of it? Derrida speaks of the archive as *arkhe*, the "consignation" referring both to the history and the law, as commencement and also as commandment, that coordinates two principles in one. He further stresses that "[...] there where authority, social order are exercised, in this place [...] order is given."[42] While he offers a long and reasoned rereading of the Freudian psychological twist, proposing, following Freud's unconscious, an explicit project of archiviology, I prefer to scrutinize some of the constitutive relationships of the United Fruit Company photographic archive. It therefore becomes significant, as Derrida distinguishes, that:

> [...] the technical structure of the archiving archive also determines the structure of the archivable content even in its very coming into existence and in its relationship to the future. The archivization produces as much as it records the event. [...] This should above all remind us that the said archival technology no longer determines, will never have determined, merely the moment of the conservational recording, but rather the very institution of the archivable event.[43]

This relationship between the archive and its outside, determined by how the "archivization produces as much as it records

---

41 Jacques Derrida, *Limited Inc.* (Vienna: Passagen-Verlag, 2001), p. 228, my translation.
42 Derrida, "Archive Fever," p. 9.
43 Ibid., pp. 17–18.

the event," seems pivotal for conceiving the United Fruit Company photographic archive as a sort of speech act and, further, the projection of a chronotope that as a figure describes the laboratory of the modern. What Derrida explicitly had in mind is an interplay between the economy of memory and its medium or media bearer; that is, to think of the materiality of the archive as something that, on the one hand, defines the functioning of its economy, and, on the other, determines the single event to be stored. He conceives of the determination of meaning through a media structure, though, without reducing sense to its bare medium.[44]

Let me unfold this broader historical context behind the archive as modern means of documentation and thus as media structure. As widely recognized, significant new impulses and new forms of documentation emerged at the turn of the nineteenth century to reorganize large corporations. The project of a photographic archive seems to complement a "written archive," as the centrality of writing, and its relationship to formal organization, was recognized in Western social thought before the middle of the eighteenth century, and was later theorized by Max Weber as bureaucracy "or rule by writing desk."[45] Through the archival practices of collecting, ordering, storing and preserving for a potential future, the United Fruit Company photographs have become documents that have a mediating role within a "politics of immediation" that "may be a tactic of power and authority."[46] Notably, these images were collected in albums assembled for this purpose by the Company's later created Department of Public Relations. This type of activity can certainly best be captured as an "internal machinery of corporate public relations" that aimed at demonstrating the "progressiv-

---

44 Mercedes Bunz, "Die Ökonomie des Archivs – Der Geschichtsbegriff Derridas zwischen Kultur- und Mediengeschichte," *Archiv für Mediengeschichte* 6 (2006), pp. 34–35.
45 Hull, *Government of Paper*, p. 11.
46 Ibid., p. 13.

ism" and "'humanity' of large-scale bureaucratic enterprise."[47] These emerging modern corporations presented themselves as a new form of business organization that required new internal communicational means and systematic management. However, with regard to internal communication the photographic archive seems to reveal the relationship between the Company's divisions abroad and the headquarters in Boston, and it unveils a hegemony of vision. Most of the archival images were sent from the divisions to the Company's headquarters, in order to inform, in minute detail, about the operations abroad. The images often accompanied the new modern means of business communication, such as the memorandum. This is remarkable as, by its very nature, the "memorandum gives directions, makes recommendations, but, above all, it is a means of transmitting information within the large bureaucratic structures organizing virtually all work in modernity," making it an irreducible documentary element.[48] The archive matters because of its function of making, assembling, and organizing the photographs as "documents" and preserving them materially. This is to emphasize that the archive becomes the authority when it comes to the images' meaning, since it is embedded in the social practices of the United Fruit Company's corporate communication. Both the memo, as a new genre of organizational and communication means, and the pictures, are filed to form an archive, defining the paper coherence of bureaucracy in a large modern corporation.[49] However, "Bureaucratic writing is commonly seen as a mechanism of state control over people, places, processes, and things. But the political function of documents is much more ambiguous," the anthropologist Matthew Hull reminds us.[50] So archival matters seem to outline "a practical attack on the problem of words and things, an attempt to make discourse into

---

47   John Guillory, "The Memo and Modernity," *Critical Inquiry* 31:1 (2004), p. 114.
48   Ibid., p. 112.
49   Ibid., pp. 114–115.
50   Hull, *Government of Paper*, p. 5.

actions definable through the trustworthy material order open to the witnessing of members of the Company. [...]. It was precisely the materiality of graphic signs [and of photographs]," we are reminded by Hull, "that made them useful as a palpable sedimentation of the real";[51] and "[...] such documents often become mediators that incorporate aspects of the people, things, and processes they were designed to control from a distance."[52] In this study, as I follow how the photographs circulated or did not circulate, changed, or ceased to exist, the archive is not simply the storage of information or fact, but rather it matters, because it shapes the discourses and media-discursive networks it mediates. The archive is therefore also the site of political and social struggles. The photographs of the Company archive speak of the resistance and contestations in this contact zone, both against and within the formation of the Caribbean as a modern political space. This reading is underscored by Thomas Richards when he points out that "Today we routinely assume that no power can possibly exist without its underlay of documents, memoranda, licenses, and files."[53] The agent is no longer simply the nation or the State as was characteristic of previous centuries, but also the corporation, which became an authority so powerful that it reorganized spaces and knowledges, as did the United Fruit Company. Richards suggests with regard to the uncontested meanings of the imperial archive that the

> idea of an imperial archive was an early version of today's fantasies of a world unified by information. Today it is easy to see that, all by itself, information cannot possibly possess all the powers attributed to it. Like power, information does not exist in a vacuum. It has to be made and used. Data has no inherent function and can just as easily lend itself to open societies as closed ones.[54]

51 Ibid., p. 8.
52 Ibid., p. 21.
53 Thomas Richards, *The Imperial Archive: Knowledge and the Fantasy of Empire* (London: Verso, 2003), p. 8.
54 Ibid., p. 73.

Reading the archive along these lines, from within these contestations and as a political concept, it becomes urgent to understand that the archive is not just bound to its enclosed manifold and ambivalent information, but rather to a media-discursive network, in which the United Fruit Company photography plays a central role.

Modern Visual Economy and Agriculture

One of the main theses of this study is that the archive, which I will discuss in the following chapters as an epistemic figure, is constitutive of the formation of the landscape not simply as a "tropical" aesthetic, as it used to be for the British and French plantation economy in the eighteenth and nineteenth centuries, but rather as a media-discursive materiality that made of the Caribbean a powerful laboratory of the modern. I will study this shift through the visual-material and thus technological-discursive interventions of the United Fruit Company and its photographic archive. To this end, I mobilize Deborah Poole's concept of the modern visual economy, to better grasp the knowledge production and employment of visual strategies through photography as a means to transform this space into a laboratory of the modern, by looking at economy as the organization of the production of images, and their circulation, and thus overlapping the question of circulation with one of an economy of vision.[55] I do not ask what a specific image means, but rather "how images accrue value," that is, I expand this question to the representational function of the image as its "use value."[56] That is to say, with Poole, that "images also accrue value through the social processes of accumulation, possession, circulation, and exchange."[57] I adopt Poole's suggestion to shift our attention

55 Poole, *Vision, Race, and Modernity*, pp. 9–10.
56 Ibid., p. 10.
57 Ibid., p. 11.

from the image to the archive, and to understand the intersection of vision and power and its accrued value of capitalist accumulation, in order to identify the features of the modernization of the space of the Caribbean.

I would like to expand on the modern visual economy: it is beyond doubt that the archival images configure a crisis that is linked to the relentless material alteration of landscape and the violent modern transformation and contamination of the environment. Yet most of the photographs do not escape landscape conventions, so to speak, but rather adopt and reformulate them. Landscape meant to address the land as potential real estate and as a site for investment and development.[58] This figuration of crisis seems to unfold both on the level of representation and as the historical obliterating of resistance to the radical alteration and degradation of landscape. As suggested by Sekula, landscape has also been understood as "the notion of a photographically mathematicized nature [that] took on an explicit economic character."[59] This is because "the meaning and value of the photograph ultimately resided in its exchangeable character, its inclusion within this global archive which translated all signs, all visions, into relations of formal (and mathematical) equivalence."[60] By establishing a regime of value following the capitalist production of space the "connection between photographic representation, quantification, and commodity exchange" is promoted.[61] Once we define the United Fruit Company archive's hegemonic discourse in this way, it becomes crucial to recognize the technique of photography as a means to submit "the world to a uniform logic of representation, just as the global market economy established a uniform logic of exchange."[62] Early readings of photography

58   Joel Snyder, "Territorial photography," in *Landscape and Power,* ed. W. J. T. Mitchell (Chicago: Chicago University Press, 2002), p. 187.
59   Sekula, "Photography Between Labour and Capital," p. 219.
60   Ibid.
61   Ibid.
62   Ibid.

understood it as a "system of communication that mirrored the logic of commodity fetishism"; that is, because the exchange value revoked the use of commodities, so that "the very form of the photographic sign came to eclipse the contingency of its referent," as Sekula underlines.[63] Nevertheless, what these archival images certainly configure as crisis are the limits of an historical world, the margins of an era. From within this relationship the images have to history, another space emerges: that of exhaustion, that is the subversion of the consistency of meaning. The violence exercised on the transformation of the landscape is thus constantly displaced and becomes only tacit and tangible as an expenditure of the images' meaning. From within this displacement, we sense the violence embodied in this radically altered environment, and in the degradation of personhood as an irrational moment of the disproportionate, the immense, and the unlimited, as contested by the many upheavals experienced in the Caribbean, and the resurgent photographic archive.

It has been recognized, in another context, that photographic archives became what Jens Andermann describes as a "heterotopian model for national development, not least because it facilitated a stage for performances of citizenship through orderly visual consumption."[64] The United Fruit Company photographic archive unquestionably imagined and projected visually the Company's economic expansion, inasmuch as it staged the "spatial dimension [...] of value as negotiated, and performatized, in the course of things and actions travelling from one place to another."[65] The United Fruit Company photographic archive helped establish regimes of value which, following Arjun Appadurai's conception, "[...] are never self-enclosed but by necessity *transcultural*, as they are always already mediated through

63   Ibid., p. 220.
64   Jens Andermann, "Tournaments of Value: Argentina and Brazil in the Age of Exhibitions," *Journal of Material Culture* 14:3 (2009), p. 349.
65   Ibid., p. 335.

(intervened by) another—or *an Other's*—evaluation. Value [...] emerges as a contested, political relation as things travel from the site of production to those of exchange and consumption, all of which are unevenly invested with power-knowledge [...]."[66] Accordingly, regimes of value that emerge with the circulation of commodities, bodies, and knowledge always refer to the exchange between cultures. Following Appadurai, they are relevant for discussing how objects or photographs circulate within time and space manifesting the ways "in which desire and demand, reciprocal sacrifice and power interact to create economic value in specific social situations."[67] Accordingly, "Economic exchange creates value. Value is embodied in commodities that are exchanged. Focusing on the things that are exchanged, rather than simply on the forms of functions of exchange, makes it possible to argue that what creates the link between exchange and values is *politics* [...]."[68] In this vein, I argue that there is a significant material correspondence between the archive and the Caribbean as a transformed landscape, that is determined by the production of value, formed by the exchange between cultures in an asymmetrical power-knowledge situation. We can speak of that relationship as a politics of value. Since the Company pictures define the visual consumption and production of the landscape as the archive's "outside," they bind it to the exchange between cultures and eventually to the production of value. This might be one reason for looking at the social dimensions of a tool or thing, as proposed by Appadurai. Correspondingly, material culture is explicitly related to epistemic practices.[69] Material artifacts, such as the archive, not only mediate this cultural contact, but also reflect it, making it palpable and potentially causing a productive rupture in the habitualized modes of perception.

66   Ibid., p. 334.
67   Arjun Appadurai, ed., *The Social Life of Things: Commodities in Cultural Perspective* (Cambridge: Cambridge University Press, 1986), p. 4.
68   Ibid., p. 3.
69   Ibid., p. 12.

Let me further expand the historical context of the modern visual economy to situate the images and their role in the making of the modern landscape, as they are in particular used in economic botany and agriculture as primary fields into which the United Fruit Company photographic archive intervened. A focus on visualization outlines a valid new approach to modern knowledge production, as recent literature has widely discussed the visual in transmitting, producing, and authorizing knowledge.[70] The visual has also always played a significant role in making empire or any other colonial undertakings viable. This has been studied recently by the art historian Daniela Bleichmar, who specifically describes the enterprise of knowledge production during the Spanish Enlightenment, looking at the Spanish Royal botanical expeditions between 1777 and 1803 both to Spanish America and the former colony of the Philippines.[71] She argues that the Spanish empire, in its desire to collect and produce knowledge, became effective because of systematic visualization and extensive practices of making visible, transmitting, translating and communicating scientific knowledge as natural history. This visualization echoed the ongoing institutionalization of botany that, *vice versa*, supported the formation of an "authorized" visual culture that was integral to an imperial knowledge machine. Along with this, let us say, changes in the apparatus of perception and knowledge production, whereby the visual complemented the "lettered order" and the collected material thing, led to the formation of botany's modern discourse network, which started to rely significantly on the visual, reinstating vision as the primary modality

70   See Peter Galison and Caroline A. Jones, eds., *Picturing Science, Producing Art* (London and New York: Routledge, 1998); Michael Lynch and Steve Woolgar, *Representation in Scientific Practice* (Cambridge, Mass.: MIT Press, 1988), and Bernardo Bolaños and Mario Casanueva, *El giro pictórico. Epistemología de la imagen* (Rubí, Barcelona, Mexico: Anthropos/Universidad Autónoma Metropolitana/Unidad Cuajimalpa, 2009).
71   Daniela Bleichmar, *Visible Empire: Botanical Expeditions and Visual Culture in the Hispanic Enlightenment* (Chicago: Chicago University Press, 2012).

of modern knowledge. With regard to the scientific expeditions to the Americas, in which visualization always constituted a significant epistemic activity, the image became a complementary and even a primary tool for describing, analyzing and recording the new and as yet unseen. It is this particular visualization of nature and landscape that enhanced a new production of space and territory. The visual became inextricably interwoven with a new practice of spatialization, which in turn stimulated the creation of a visual culture that necessarily demands an immanent spatial analysis.

Now, questioning the United Fruit Company photographic archive, it becomes pertinent to examine the archive against the backdrop of the epistemic entanglement of visual economy and agriculture. The political economy of agriculture is one of the main epistemic contexts in which the many thousand photographic images of the United Fruit Company were being produced, and that defines the appropriation of nature as it was molded into the radically altered modern landscape of the Caribbean. The transfer of knowledge through the transplanting of "tropical" crops such as sugar, banana, sisal, tobacco, cacao or coffee, together with the search for raw materials, determined the beginnings of an accelerated globalization around 1880 that continued well into the twentieth century. Economic botany, tropical medicine, archaeology, engineering and geodesy formed part of the scientific appropriation of the world and laid the foundations for an effective expansion of global capitalism. In this context, the corporations that guaranteed food and natural energy resources in the Global South significantly shaped transnational exchanges such as the transfer of knowledge or the circulation of technologies. The Caribbean in particular, having experienced various superimposing colonial and imperial systems, the Spanish, the French, the British, the Dutch and others, is an example of the materialization of exchanges *par excellence* and thus the divergent material regimes defined by geopolitics centered on agriculture and on the search for raw materials, territories, and commodities. From this perspective, the Caribbean shares all the features of a laboratory of the modern, defined by an eternal transition towards modernity; a transition that was distinctively marked by the experience of colonization. Moreover, in this context, transnational corporations no longer simply acted in the interests of the nation, as had been characteristic for the nineteenth century and the colonial regimes, but became increasingly important in shaping this emergent modern political space, in accordance with their own interests. After the Spanish-American war of 1898 the United States efficiently integrated the Caribbean into its sphere of political, economic and cultural influence. It was at this point and to this end that transnational corporations took on a significant new role, becoming a predominant political force. The significant role of the United Fruit Company in shaping this new geopolitical relationship and, correspondingly, the new geocultural configuration of the Caribbean and Central America, through the creation, development and exploitation of science, communication and transport media, and their related discourse networks, will be explored in this study, following a close reading of its resurgent photographic archive. The Company photographic archive in its own right has been hitherto greatly neglected, and preference is still given to its political history.[72] Yet I argue that an analysis of the photographs and their related epistemic contexts and discourse networks helps to fill

72   To name but a few major studies on the social, economic and political history of the United Fruit Company: Chomsky, *West Indian Workers and the United Fruit Company*; Stephen Schlesinger and Stephen Kinzer, *Bitter Fruit: The Untold Story of the American Coup in Guatemala* (Garden City, N.Y.: Doubleday, 1982); Steve Striffler and Mark Moberg, eds., *Banana Wars: Power, Production, and History in the Americas* (Durham: Duke University Press, 2003); Stephen Kinzer, *In the Shadow of State and Capital: The United Fruit Company, Popular Struggle, and Agrarian Restructuring in Ecuador, 1900–1995* (Durham: Duke University Press, 2002); Marcelo Bucheli, *Bananas and Business: The United Fruit Company in Colombia, 1899–2000* (New York: New York University Press, 2005). An exception is the study by Kevin Coleman looking at the visual culture of the United Fruit Company, *A Camera in the Garden of Eden: The Self-Forging of a Banana Republic* (Austin: University of Texas Press, 2016).

some of the blind spots of the cultural and thus media history of the Caribbean as it exists today.

It is noteworthy that since the 1990s a new focus on transatlantic knowledge circulation has emerged, with a transnational perspective that has significantly reshaped questions concerning the nation or the State, but also inquiring into imperial expansions and the knowledge cultures involved that quintessentially fostered the modernization of the Caribbean and Latin America.[73] Against the backdrop of globalization, questions started to focus on the transnational entanglement of culture, science, economy and politics, and the differentiations of the reciprocal and dynamic exchange processes. Consequently, this perspective revoked the schematic dualism of metropolis and colony, center and periphery, relating to the turn that was already defined by earlier postcolonial studies that shed new light on the complex processes of the independence of nations, the formations of de- and neo-colonization in the twentieth century and the phenomenon of globalization. Edward Said formulated a critique of the order of Western knowledge that he understood as an epistemological prerequisite for imperialism.[74] As has been acknowledged recently, the success and efficiency of Western expansion including that of the United States are not only due to military but also biological components.[75] Conceiving this discourse of economic utility as part of the hegemonic discourse of the photographic archive, this study examines the

73   See for instance the discussion in Aviva Chomsky and Aldo Lauria-Santiago, eds., *Identity and Struggle at the Margins of the Nation-State: The Laboring Peoples of Central America and the Hispanic Caribbean* (Durham: Duke University Press, 1998); Ricardo Salvatore, ed., *Culturas imperiales. Experiencia y representación en América, Asia y África* (Rosario: Beatriz Viterbo Editora, 2005); Gilbert M. Joseph, Catherine C. LeGrand, and Ricardo D. Salvatore, eds., *Close Encounters of Empire: Writing the Cultural History of U.S.-Latin American Relations* (Durham: Duke University Press, 1998).
74   Edward Said, *Orientalism* (New York: Pantheon Books, 1978).
75   See Lucile H. Brockway, *Science and Colonial Expansion: The Role of the British Royal Botanic Gardens* (New Haven: Yale University Press, 2002), and Alfred W. Crosby, *Ecological Imperialism: The Biological Expansion in Europe, 900–1900* (Cambridge: Cambridge University Press, 1993).

photographs while discussing the epistemic premises of botany and agriculture that became constitutive parts of the scientification of the "Tropics."[76] It further reflects upon photography in the way it helped advance the expansion of capitalism into the Caribbean. In this, photography and space became intrinsically linked, shaping the field of economic botany and enabling the material alteration of the environment and the emergence of the Caribbean as a media-discursive landscape. Subsequently, the study examines the visual as a means of modernizing the Caribbean and discusses the corporate archive's own visual strategies against the backdrop of the modern botanical machine, which over time became increasingly bureaucratic and consolidated in its interplay with the US Department of Agriculture, linked both to governmental bureaucracy and the private corporation of the United Fruit Company. Following a close reading of the photographic archive, this study offers, for the first time, a discussion of the United Fruit Company as an important agent of modern science of the twentieth century.

The Chapters

The first chapter "Camera and Capitalism: the United Fruit Company" focuses on the emergence of the United Fruit Company photographic archive. Adopting the conceptual pair of camera and capitalism, it discusses some of the relations between photography, labor and capital that shaped the modern visual economy of the United Fruit Company.[77] As the expansion of a modern capitalism advanced into the Caribbean and

---

76 See Londa Schiebinger, *Plants and Empire: Colonial Bioprospecting in the Atlantic World* (Cambridge, Mass.: Harvard University Press, 2004).

77 I wish to thank Kevin Coleman for the ongoing discussion on the complex relationship between capitalism and the camera, and his initiative to bring this understudied relationship to the forefront. See Kevin Coleman and Daniel James, "Capitalism and the Limits of Photography," *Photography & Culture* 13:2 (2020), pp. 149–156.

Central America at the end of the nineteenth century and until the middle of the twentieth century, it was the technology of photography that helped imagine the abundance of production and consumption and ideologically form the modernization of space, that remained concealed in the violent transformation of land into a productive monocultural tropical landscape. The chapter discusses this visual economy and the photographs of the United Fruit Company that mirror the entanglement of capitalism and a "new vision," linked to the production of value. Whereas theories of capitalism have tended to omit reflections upon photography, this chapter discusses the camera and its role in the capitalistic production of space. It builds on the idea that the Company's use of the camera helps understand capitalism's redefined relationships, articulated in labor, capital, and technology, and hence the historical development of capitalism, and the construction of a capitalist dominion over nature and human labor. The Company uses the camera to discipline through photography. Vision redistributes power in space as a concerted distribution of bodies, surfaces, and gazes that are subjected to a new field of visibility, that radically reordered both people and landscape. The modern belief in man's independence from nature seems to emanate from this thunderous violence, inscribed as foundational act in the corporate photographic archive, becoming a *media a priori* to discuss the relationships between history, capitalism, and photography, as effective ideological documents that helped to establish this modern visual economy.

This relationship is further discussed in the chapter on "The Crossroads of Science and Discourse Networks" that explores the spatial figure of the enclave, as it materialized in the company towns and plantations of the United Fruit Company that became the spaces *par excellence* for a global technological communication. Discussing the company towns as neuralgic nodes for establishing and advancing modern technological and media networks, I work, in this chapter, with the photographs as photographs, while at the same time using them as documents of changes to the real landscape. The chapter explores the Company's long engagement with institutionalization and research in tropical medicine, unfolding the Company as a significant, but overlooked global agent in the modern sciences. It examines the related photographs as part of the production of a modern and political space, and as infrastructure that accommodated the capitalist production of space, for which these pictures became an administrative regime. However, the pictures also disclose some contradictions within the Company's own narratives: on the one hand, these photographs mirror the Company's prejudices, self-consciousness and cultural constructs of a society; on the other, they deconstruct these biases and the construction of alterity and differences that hierarchizes capitalist space. By looking at the internal workings of the United Fruit Company and thus at the materialities of other media, such as the Company's radio and railroads, depicted systematically in the Company archive, the chapter advances the concept of discourse networks. It argues that the company towns were material networks, processes and techniques that led to the establishment of an effective global communication of technology and science, into which the production, circulation and reception of the photographs were embedded. Along these lines, the chapter subsequently charts the Caribbean as a laboratory of the modern, mirrored clearly in the company towns and plantations as material modernities, encoded both as utopian and dystopian realms.

The chapter "'The World Was My Garden'" draws upon the relationship between knowledge production in botany and the visual economy, and discusses the historical context of botanical expeditions and the scientific routes to the "American Tropics." It centers on the explorer-botanist Wilson Popenoe, a key figure in botanical sampling and plant research hired by both the United Fruit Company and the US Department of Agriculture. By studying Popenoe's scientific route and deploying the concepts of collecting, drafting and grafting as modern "cultural techniques" or technologies of land colonization, this chapter analyzes the relations between knowledge production and photography in botany, against the backdrop of increasing institutional entanglement between the US and the Global South. Introducing the concept of visual epistemology, the chapter offers a detailed analysis of vision and visualization in knowledge production in economic botany from a broader perspective. It examines the technologies, processes and procedures of "landscaping," as elaborated by Jill Casid, through which the Caribbean underwent radical man-made transformations, becoming a monocultural productive landscape. In this chapter I aim to advance the modern "landscape" in the light of landscaping; that is, the transformation of landscape into an aesthetic, economic, political or scientific space, through the transplantation and circulation of plants, seeds, machines, commodities and bodies. I approach the way that photography becomes a novel media technology that determines a new visuality shaped by an increasing institutional entanglement of bureaucracies, by addressing the wider question of the Anthropocene as a fundamental concern that is ultimately constitutive to the United Fruit Company photographic archive.

The chapter "Ethnographic Eyes and Archaeological Views" relates to this context, yet focuses on the United Fruit Company as an agent that advanced the related collections of archaeological and ethnographic artifacts, intrinsically linked to the capitalist expansion into the Caribbean. In May 1946, ethnologist and photographer Giles G. Healey, who at the time was engaged in making a film of Mayan ruins and the living Maya by and for the United Fruit Company, *The Maya Through the Ages*, "discovered" Bonampak in Chiapas, Mexico. By looking at Healey's ethnographic photographs and at his film, this chapter explores the discursive boundaries between history and photography and at the way these pictures circulated within a modern visual economy. It discusses Healey's filmic narrative as a cultural self-legitimation of the Company, and goes on to examine the idea of the relationship between the human and the non-human, that is "nature," as negotiated by the camera, and the modes of perception and representation relevant to the Company's self-image. In order to situate the Company's broader cultural-ideological engagement and thus the production, circulation and reception of images, the chapter draws upon the long-time agency of the United Fruit Company in archaeology, and discusses the famous archaeological expeditions to Quirigua, Guatemala, between 1910 and 1914, with the related Minor Keith foundational collection of archaeological artifacts at the American Museum of Natural History in New York and the Brooklyn Museum. Focusing on the Company's collecting and photographic practices, it speculates on how photography makes new spaces accessible for the extraction of natural resources, forming a cultural legitimation of the Company. In this way it critically examines the ambivalent nature of the photographs, and the Company's deterministic and self-legitimating use of the images, and its relationship with material culture through the artifacts.

This study concludes with the discussion of "Upheavals and the Resurgent Photographic Archive," and from a perspective of resistance to and counter-narratives of the United Fruit Company. In the context of the expansion of modern capitalism, the massacre became a topos for socio-political upheavals, narrated and profoundly remembered in Latin American literature. To this end, this epilogue re-reads the photographic archive against recent legal initiatives to condemn the crimes against humanity committed by Chiquita, the successor of the United Fruit Company. It argues that the archive itself encloses an overlooked series of photographs of upheavals and resistance that today clamor for accountability and provoke a powerful counter-discourse to the unspoken historical and environmental injustice done by the United Fruit Company. To do so, it centers on the discussion of the relationship between literature and a series of photographs that reflect the archive's silences and ideological omissions, as residues that attest to the (in)visibility of the banana massacre in 1928, as retold by Gabriel García Márquez in *One Hundred Years of Solitude*. It discusses how literature conceptualizes crisis and violence and examines how photography appears to be a layer of self-reflection in a literary mediality, as a counterpart against which literature demarcates its own limitations and possibilities, thus becoming a counter-semantic of historical oblivion. This epilogue focuses on two different but intertwined theoretical moments, the photographic in literature and the relationship between photography and history. It concludes with a discussion of the latter as the book's primary concern, bringing up the question of the ethical use of photography. Finally, the book's argument of photography as a visual means for the capitalistic production of space, reaches a conclusion about the historical agency of the photographs to create reality, and the use of the archive's powerful imaginaries to effectively bring the Caribbean into modernity; and *vice versa*, that these photographs have had an aftermath that helps scrutinize this reality and modernity, thus forming an historical judgment.

Chapter 1

Camera and Capitalism: the United Fruit Company

The procedure of iconization makes us forget the fact that a
photograph is a document produced in an encounter, in what I
call "the photography event." This takes place with the mediation of the camera, and is repeated, directly following the first
event or apart from it, mediated by the photograph. The second event takes place in the encounter with the viewer who, as
emerging from the archive fever, enables us to question turning the archive photographs into dead pages, stable references
of concepts or categories that served to file them and subsequently stuck to them like a second skin.[1]

The Corporation and its Photographic Archive

In a private letter sent from Cuba, "Guaro, Oriente," in 1919,
United Fruit Company employee Everett Brown writes to his wife
in Massachusetts: "I am going to send you some pictures soon.
Some of the boys have cameras and they take to order for any one
that wants them."[2] As an intimate letter disseminated outside
of the banana zone and the company towns to reach loved ones
back home in the United States, this is one of the very rare documents that speak of the photographic practices in the United
Fruit Company divisions from the perspective of the subjective
experience of everyday life in the plantations. This letter bears
witness to the fact that Company employees were themselves
amateur photographers, who recorded their lives in the different

1   Ariella Azoulay, "Archive," in *Political Concepts*, http://www.politicalcon-
cepts.org/archive-ariella-azoulay/ (accessed October 2021).
2   Everett C. Brown, "Guaro, Oriente, Cuba, Aug. 21, 1919," in *Everett C. Brown
Papers, 1919–1921,* Special and Area Studies Collections, George A. Smathers
Libraries, University of Florida, Gainesville.

divisions in the Caribbean and Central America. These pictures offer stories of their lives abroad, unconsciously mirroring an extractive view and the fabricated self-vision of employees in the American "Tropics." Nevertheless, these photographic practices also seem to stabilize the hierarchical order that the Company had established as a global corporation through its many guises and increasingly technical operations. Moreover, the camera turned out to be the privileged device for the proficient organization of a new kind of cultural encounter. It eventually became the mechanical counterpart in structuring the emergent modern political space. With regard to any technological apparatus once it is brought into the contact zone, Michael Taussig reminds us:

> Vis à vis the savage they are the masters of these wonders that, after the first shock waves of surprise upon their invention and commercialization in the West, pass into the everyday. Yet these shocks rightly live on in the mysterious underbelly of the technology—to be eviscerated as "magic" in frontier rituals of technological supremacy. [...] Taking the [photographic] machine to the jungle is to do more than impress the natives and therefore oneself with Western technology's power [...]; it is to reinstall the mimetic faculty as mystery in the art of mechanical reproduction, reinvigorating the primitivism implicit in technology's wildest dreams, therewith creating a surfeit of mimetic power.[3]

This cultural encounter, asymmetrical as it may be, becomes mediated by the technological device, the camera, that seems to create "a surfeit of mimetic power." Significantly, though, the photographic images Everett Brown speaks about in his letters do not become part of the photographic albums of the United Fruit Company. Instead, they seem to have circulated very privately, for example by being sent to the employees' families. Most likely, these pictures were collected in family albums and stored as private family photographs, reminders of their time

---

3   Michael Taussig, *Mimesis and Alterity: A Particular History of the Senses* (New York: Routledge, 1993), p. 208.

abroad. This communicative but private exchange of images certainly delimits the photographic archive of the United Fruit Company. I argue here for understanding these private pictures as an articulation of the boundaries of the Company archive, inasmuch as they offer a glimpse into the everyday life of the divisions, so carefully concealed by the Company archive's own visuality. In this sense, the written fragments, such as the few letters sent by former Company employees, may form a private written archive, and as such are significant found pieces.

Let us then take a closer look at the United Fruit Company photographic albums. On the back of one picture, we read "No. 8. Taken September 29th, 1922 – Quirigua Hospital, Front View. United Fruit Company Guatemala Division." This is most likely the picture's original caption, as captions used to be typewritten directly on the back of the pictures. The caption contains information on what is presumably the exact date of the picture being taken, as well as a short explanation detailing the view, and naming a specific place. Through these time-space coordinates, the picture is framed and given a precise context, inscribed in the narrative of the United Fruit Company's archive. Moreover, on a different level, "No. 8" refers to a numerical order or even a systemic organization of the breathtaking amount of pictures that the United Fruit Company collected and carefully glued into the many albums. Indeed, this attempt at enumeration through a sort of precise numerical and at times chronological order gives those images a serial logic that aimed at an overall coherence, while they also speak of the Company's desire to number, name, and classify their photographs. Furthermore, through this meticulous archival procedure, the Company establishes a process of reification: through naming they make visible what belongs or should belong to them. Accordingly, this framed gaze appropriates, and the corresponding written elements become part of a corporate visual economy. Notably, photography and words in the form of inscription through the captions have an entangled history as a type of communication through which a photograph becomes a distinct social object.[4] The captions or the written text create the conditions for the possibility of registration that makes the collected photographs documents of the corporate archive.[5] With regard to photographic archives, Elizabeth Edwards observes:

> What kind of visibility should be afforded to the photograph? [...] Should labels be placed on the back, or apprehended in one visual artifact? What did this mean for the viewer? These choices were material performances of moral, scientific and subjective desires, without which this archiving project cannot be understood. [...]. Labels are thus not merely a descriptive or a discursive framing, rather their spatial relations with mounts marked out the contained space of useful disciplinary knowledge, aligning and cohering disparate approaches. They also embody the potential for expanding or contested knowledge, expressed by layers of surface markings, from the laying down of photographic chemical to additions and crossings out in captions as users add comments, reattribute in a material palimpsest of disciplinary knowledge held, literally, in the hands of the users.[6]

But who really were these users? Who mounted the many photographic albums? Why did these pictures circulate from the different divisions to the headquarters in Boston to be carefully collected, stored away and become part of the corporate records? On the back of that same picture there is a hand written pencil note that indicates: "Eng. Dept Boston Album." This note bears witness to the photograph's social biography, how the picture passed through many hands. It gives insights into the archival practices that define the album photographs as a collective work. The caption contains an important piece of information about the internal circulation of the album photographs: "Eng. Dept"— read as either "for" or "from" the Engineering Department

4   Tiziana Serena, "The Words of the Photo Archive," in *Photo Archives and the Photographic Memory of Art History*, ed. Costanza Caraffa (Munich: Deutscher Kunstverlag, 2011), p. 60.
5   Ibid., p. 64.
6   Edwards, "Photographs: Material Form and the Dynamic Archive," pp. 51–52.

of the Company. These specialized departments were always kept on site at the divisions abroad. The caption contains the important message "album," indicating a collective project of documenting, of collecting, of making an artifact, namely, the photographic album. Also, there is apparently a third layer of inscription advising "do not mount" and informing us about the photograph's size, another pencil note, which most likely belongs to a layer added much later by an archivist and does not belong to the same time moment as the album's original creation. Art historian John Tagg once metaphorically called this writing the "pencil of history," identifying it as an inscription reflecting an intimate and constitutive relationship between the archive and the photograph.[7] Yet, besides the fact that the captions may have been added only at a later moment, we are prudent enough to recognize that they frame our view and guide us in the way we look at the pictures today. The pictures become interrelated with their captions or, to be more precise, the captions interfere with the images' meaning, as they become part of the distribution of the sensible and, moreover, the political that delimits the "visible and the invisible, the audible and the inaudible, the sayable and the unsayable," as Jacques Rancière once put it.[8]

In a different album we find another sequence of writing that embeds the images within some of the corporate practices. The photographs are assembled as a series that aims to show agricultural operations in the Costa Rica division of Monteverde in 1945. The pictures speak of the different processes and techniques of handling abaca fiber, another material good the Company was dedicated to producing, showing the different stages of the production process that are described through handwritten notes that accompany the pictures as captions, thus "documenting" the agricultural and technical processes of production. In these notes, we read "extra copy on dup. file," giving us a sense of the

---

7   John Tagg, "The Pencil of History," in *Fugitive Images: From Photography to Video*, ed. Patrice Petro (Indianapolis: Indiana University Press, 1995), pp. 285–304.
8   Jacques Rancière, *The Politics of Aesthetics* (London: Continuum, 2004), p. 3.

Fig. 2.1: (*above left*): "Crushed abaca junks entering decorticator machine"; (*above right*): "extra copy in dup. file Stripped fiber transferred from delivery end of decorticator machines & hanking & grading rope conveyors"; (*below left*): "dried abaca fiber Monte Verde, 1945"; (*below right*): "extra copy in dup. file abaca bales"; Black & white prints, Photographer Foto Roa. United Fruit Company Photograph Collection, Baker Library, Harvard Business School, Box 61.

archival practices and the use of the pictures that were sent back to headquarters. Bits of information inside these written fragments indicate and remind us that these photographs are embedded in a social practice of establishing and managing visual data. Because the pictures were disseminated between the different and specialized departments of the Company, these archival practices played a decisive role in establishing a corporate image economy, advancing control through the visual, that only became possible because of the archival practices that, to some extent, seemed to organize the internal workings of the corporation. The photograph names the photography studio, "Foto Roa," most likely located in a nearby town. Notably, this note reflects transforming cultural dynamics in the division abroad and the use of cameras in the banana zones, mirroring the vibrant and pulsing company towns and their urban environment as a modernization of cultural life.[9] The pictures, nevertheless, are carefully composed, revealing an explicit aesthetic take on labor. The technical quality of the picture is high, if we consider the camera's focal point, the composition of the image and the well-controlled exposure time: the image is a *mis-en-scène* of a hegemonic narrative controlling labor. Edwards suggests that the "photographs and the archive are dynamic forces within the networks of non-humans and humans which themselves constitute social processes. They exercise a form of agency as powerful and active players in that it is not the meanings of things *per se* (here what a photograph is 'of') which are important, but their social effects as they construct and influence the field of social action."[10]

The following picture reflects how photography was used with the purpose of "documenting" the ongoing, modernizing processes of construction and buildings, such as company towns and labor camps. The caption informs us about an index of photographs, an attempt to organize the photographic archive *vis-à-vis* the abundance of photographs. In addition to the Company's business and economic expansion further into the Caribbean, the simultaneous establishment of a new orbit of knowledge became equally important: a new language and a social imaginary were introduced to make this knowledge apparatus work efficiently, as performed by the pictures' captions. I argue that the photographic archive helped make this bureaucratic corporate apparatus work. Yet, the photographic archive also conceals the Company's fears of and desires for modernization. On the one hand, as Edwards reminds us, the "process of archiving [is] a form of narrativising in itself."[11] On the other, we sense that

9   For a further discussion about the use of the camera and some innovative rural-urban photographic practices, and about the subversion of established hierarchical orders in the fruit companies' contact zones, see Kevin P. Coleman, "A Camera in the Garden of Eden," *Journal of Latin American Cultural Studies* 20:1 (2011).

10   Edwards, "Photographs: Material Form and the Dynamic Archive," p. 51.

11   Ibid., p. 52.

Fig. 2.2: "#637 (Aerial View) Northern half of Isabel Farm with labor batey in foreground and Villa Isabel rice district in background. November 1948, Dominican Republic. Letter 12/30/48." Gelatin silver process on paper, 8 x 10 inches. United Fruit Company Photograph Collection, Baker Library, Harvard Business School, Box 19.

the photographs and image series forming the archive are narratives in their own right, of modernity and of a radical environmental transformation, that can be read as both utopia and dystopia. As utopia, they belong to the fantasies of economic expansion, envisaged as a chronotope of an eternal transition towards modernity, a promise of modernization itself. As narratives of the dystopic, the images bear witness to the processes of modernization and what has been called a "'modern/colonial world system'" that is accompanied by "constant production cycles of marginalities."[12] A chronotope that is both a form of narrativizing the archive, and the very space of projection the archive envisages. It may be of singular importance to recall

12   Hermann Herlinghaus, *Violence Without Guilt: Ethical Narratives from the Global South* (New York: Palgrave Macmillan, 2009), p. 13.

that at the time of writing, the papers, files, memos, and other documents of the "written archive" are still classified by the Company, or have simply been lost. Significantly, only the photographic collection, as the visual archive, has been released. Is this because pictures are perceived as being more ambiguous about what they speak of than written text? Is this because the idea persists that the visual is less concise and less clearly political here? It is certainly plausible, at least with regard to the Company photographic archive, that "Documents honed in the pursuit of prior issues could be requisitioned to write new histories, could be reclassified for new initiatives, could be renewed to fortify security measures against what were perceived as new assaults on imperial sovereignty and its moralizing claims."[13]

The United Fruit Company archive as an attempt at modernization is situated at the liminal space of the contact zone. Importantly, Mary Louise Pratt discussed the contact zone as "the spatial and temporal copresence of subjects previously separated by geographic and historical disjunctures, and whose trajectories now intersect,"[14] where the camera is used as a media device through which a gigantic flow of data is generated and organized, thus advancing the management of the Company's new spatial possessions in the Caribbean. Accordingly, its archive became a privileged site for visually enclosing information: the Company's enterprise of knowledge. With regard to modern media devices, which led to a novel knowledge production, as a condition for making the European expansion toward the New World possible, Wolfgang Schäffner suggests that "cultural encounters or contact zones, which occur on travels, conquests and colonization, presuppose the production and administration of a topographical space."[15] In order to successfully realize such an expansion, the management of gigantic

13 Stoler, *Along the Archival Grain*, p. 3.
14 Mary Louise Pratt, *Imperial Eyes: Travel Writing and Transculturation* (London: Routledge, 1992), p. 7.
15 Wolfgang Schäffner, "Verwaltung der Kultur. Alexander von Humboldts Medien (1799–1834)," in *Interkulturalität. Zwischen Inszenierung und Archiv*, ed.

flows of complex data becomes urgent, the chains of operation of this are to be conceived from within a *media a priori* established long before that expansion.[16] The camera in the contact zone becomes just such a *media a priori*, in so far as it facilitates the production and administration of a topographical space, visually structuring a space of knowledge, through which the newly accessed spaces are incorporated into the orbit of Western knowledge. This conception of a media history of the conquest of America as part of a project of colonization, and of colonizing regimes in the context of European-American cultural encounters has been only recently acknowledged; and the case of private global agents, such as the United Fruit Company, and their role in the enterprise of knowledge *vis-à-vis* a media history of cultural contacts has been almost entirely overlooked. Yet, the Company's photographic archive and the use of the camera in this bio-contact zone are part of what has been conceived as *media a priori* in the production and administration of a topographical space, advancing the control of the newly accessed spaces. Thus, I situate my conception of the archive as epistemic figure necessarily in the context of a media-anthropological turn. Schäffner further points out that:

> [...] the history of European knowledge production about other cultures was not a result of immediate contact by individual travelers, scientific explorers, or colonizing armies. Rather, reports of other cultures are products or respectively parts of complex data transfers, which presupposes a homogeneous space as well as an archive, in which cultural differences can be registered and located. [...] That means that cultural knowledge is an effect of media-technical production, transfer and storage, an effect of remote actions, which define differentiation as boundaries of cultures.[17]

Stefan Rieger, Schamma Schahadat and Manfred Weinberg (Tübingen: Narr, 1999), p. 353, my translation.
16   Ibid., p. 354
17   Ibid., p. 254, my translation.

The Company's photographic archive seems to belong to these effects of remote actions in the way it reflects, negotiates, and conceals knowledge about complex bio-contact zones, of which the Company's enclaves are a prime example. In her conception, Pratt emphasizes contact, which she understands in terms of an interactive and improvised dimension of the colonial encounters, a dimension which has generally been neglected, giving preference to the imagined aspects of conquest and dominance. She underlines how subjects are constituted through their interrelation, emphasizing here co-presence, interaction, and cultural entanglement often taking place within an asymmetrical power relationship.[18] Bringing both positions together, as they formulate two different but intertwined perspectives, the *media a priori* become equally important in describing these encounters to the extent that the subjects of encounter are not exclusively operational. The complex intercultural interferences are determined by both moments, that of media dispositives and that of the performative nature of the encounter, because dispositives are never entirely regulative.

In another context, Beatriz Jaguaribe suggests something similar about the camera and modernity:

> Yet if we have become overly visible, contemporary hypervisibility traces its roots to the singularly modern belief in appropriating and desire to appropriate the world by means of the gaze. The modernization of cultures and societies was linked to an increasing secularization of the invisible. [...] Their use of a visual rhetoric that defines scenarios, excludes or includes protagonists, and, most crucially, evokes pedagogies of the gaze allows us to glean signs of becoming, modes of *making visible* imagined modernities and communities.[19]

18 Pratt, *Imperial Eyes*, pp. 6–7.
19 Beatriz Jaguaribe and Maurício Lissovsky, "The Visible and the Invisibles: Photography and Social Imaginaries in Brazil," *Public Culture* 21:1 (2009), pp. 175–176.

Fig. 2.3: "Group of Natives taken at Juan Vicente. Preston 1925." Gelatin silver process on paper, 8 x 10 inches. United Fruit Company Photograph Collection, Baker Library, Harvard Business School, Box 44.

In the Company archive, the images remain ambivalent in their meaning: they are part of a visual economy, which appropriates and corresponds to the imperial gaze, and of a side (sight) effect of making potentially seen the thus-far invisible. This imperial gaze can be perceived in these pictures. The second one in particular shows the modern project of "colonization" as an attempt at social control through the regime of labor and corresponds to a mode of visualization of labor as a future resource for exploitation. This self-perception of the Company, qualifying the gaze as an imperial one, is overwhelmingly present in the photographic archive. In other words, sharing the insights of a racist discourse of labor and labor colonization, the images visually reassure and self-assure the Company in its politics of exploitation. In this ritualized reading, the imperial gaze is mirrored as "white supremacy" and represents the Company's

Fig. 2.4: "No. 1233. Colonization of Cuban labor, Laborers' families. Preston. August, 1928." Gelatin silver process on paper, 8 x 10 inches. United Fruit Company Photograph Collection, Baker Library, Harvard Business School, Box 44.

business philosophy. The picture captioned "No. 753. Barracon Scene – Preston Division, Cuba" certainly unites both: the imperial gaze upon the laborers, that is, the colonization of labor, as well as an ethnographic gaze, which remains more ambivalent, by "documenting" laborers in front of their houses and following a modern visual rhetoric of social engineering.

Similarly, in another album, assembled and labeled as "Ecuador," we find a few very interesting pages, dated from 1949. The Company was clearing and making accessible new territories further south, because of the extensive space required for banana cultivation. The Company was constantly on the move, bringing with them migrant laborers and technological resources, forming an ever-increasing orbit of knowledge. For example, these pictures show most likely Company employees photographing

Fig. 2.5: "No. 753. Barracon Scene – Preston Division, Cuba." Gelatin silver process on paper, 8 x 10 inches. United Fruit Company Photograph Collection, Baker Library, Harvard Business School, Box 44.

themselves with "Colorado Indians." Further, this photograph series clearly aims to document the ongoing survey of new territory to be incorporated into the banana plantations. It imagines and delimits a chronotope or what I will refer to as the archive's correlating spatial-temporal structure, the archive's "outside." In minute detail, the pictures mark the different stops on the Quito-Ambato road and the Quito-Quininde road, mapping the trajectory with detailed geographical descriptions along the roads: we start to see landscapes that are marked by the pace of a projected future modernization of the space. Moreover, this image series shares the visual rhetoric of scientific travel and exploration, framed by both an imperial gaze and a scientific appropriation. The camera guides the viewer into a vast terrain that would eventually become a modern technological enclave: a new banana plantation. As the imperial gaze coalesces with a

Fig. 2.6: (*top row from left to right*): "Colorado Indians at Santo Domingo de los Coloradoz. ECUADOR Sept. 1949"/"Colorado Indians at Santo Domingo de los Colorados. ECUADOR Oct. 1949"/"Colorado Indians at Santo Domingo de los Colorados. ECUADOR Oct. 1949"/"Near Quito – ECUADOR Sept. 1949"; (*middle row from left to right*): "ECUADOR Sept. 1949"/"Salcedo Indian near Pelipeo ECUADOR Sept. 1949"/"Indian near Pelipeo ECUADOR Sept. 1949"; (*bottom row from left to right*): "ECUADOR Sept. 1949"/"ECUADOR Sept. 1949." Black & white prints; United Fruit Company Photograph Collection, Baker Library, Harvard Business School, Box 33.

geographical framing, this image series shows how the camera is used to visually imagine an economic appropriation and subsequent future spatial engineering of the enclave. Certainly, the archive as epistemic figure correlates here with its "outside," that is, the enclave. Moreover, this correlation becomes significant, because it reflects the chronotope as an eternal transition towards modernity.

This ordering and projecting of space is also manifested by the material organization of the photographic albums, which forms the internal organizational logic of the archive: we find labels that attempt to classify the pictures according to "topoi," such as PLANTAIN, PLANTING BANANAS, PLANTING RICE,

Fig. 2.7: (*top row from left to right*): "Dead Lake below Quito Ambato Road –
ECUADOR Sept. 1949"/"Dead Lake below Quito Ambato Road – ECUADOR Sept.
1949"/"Shack at Kilo. 163 Quito- Quininde Road ECUADOR Oct. 1949"/"Over-
night Shelter Quininde River at 45 Kilos from mouth. ECUADOR Sept. 1949";
(*middle row from left to right*): "Balsa raft crossing of Rio Blanco near Kilo 166
– Quito-Quininde Road. ECUADOR Sept. 1949"/"Balsa raft crossing of Rio
Toachi near Kilo. 149 – Quito-Quininde Road. ECUADOR Sept. 1949"/"Across
Countryside to Volcan Turgurshua ECUADOR Sept. 1949"/"Volcan Turgurshua
ECUADOR Sept. 1949"; (*bottom row from left to right*): "Quininde River at 36
Kilos from mouth. ECUADOR Oct. 1949"/"Crossing Blanco River at Kilo. 191
Quito-Quininde Road. ECUADOR Sept. 1949"/"Balsa raft crossing Blanco river
at kilo. 186 Quito-Quininde Road. ECUADOR Sept. 1949"/"Crossing Blanco
River at Kilo. 166 Quito-Quininde Road. ECUADOR Sept. 1949." Black & white
prints; United Fruit Company Photograph Collection, Baker Library, Harvard
Business School, Box 33.

ROLLING STOCK, S/S BOATS, SPRAY, SUGAR, WATER SUPPLY,
WHARVES. This peculiarly random list may seem miscellaneous, however it reflects the organization of these new spaces
in terms of their economic profitability and technological management, that is, the creation and management of a topographical space. In this attempt to order and classify, we can observe
the Company's desire to give coherence to the vast quantity

of pictures they collected. The Company seems to have imagined the photographic albums, the archive, as a homogeneous space, organized through the visual. But the captions are often false or misleading, indicating different geographical places or simply reflecting an ignorance on the part of those involved with assembling the albums. So it is that within the archive the ethnographic gaze is naturalized and subsumed by the rhetoric of a bureaucratic technicality. Yet, this gaze defines the Company's self-reflection, inasmuch as the images reflect complex interferences in the cultural encounters between the Company, the photographer, and the photographed.

Camera and Capitalism

> What is meant, historically, to seek the truth of technical processes by means of pictures? And what is meant that since the middle of the last [19th] century, technical processes that were increasingly subject to mechanization were increasingly represented by mechanical means, by means of photography? In short, what role has been played by scientific picture-making in the historical development of capitalism, in the construction of capitalist dominion over nature and human labour?[20]

In the midst of resurgent discussions about capitalism, the camera or photography seems to play a significant and often overlooked role in reflecting upon the production of space. It is the technology of mechanical reproduction *par excellence*, and it has shared, since its invention, the common features of this new capitalist space. Yet, because theories are fickle things, the paths of capitalism and photography do not explicitly intersect; instead, they seem to encounter each other only at a time when photography was understood as a model of historical reflection. Understanding capitalism and the camera as a sort

20   Sekula, "Photography between Labour and Capital," p. 203.

of conceptual pair, I will focus on the emergence of the United Fruit Company photographic archive in order to speculate on the relationships between capital and labor, and capital and photography, in more detail.[21] One underlying assumption is that the Company's use of the camera helps reveal how capitalism redefined some of the fundamental relationships, articulated as labor, capital, and technology, and hence sheds light on the historical development of capitalism. Yet, the United Fruit Company pictures certainly conceal the violence and labor unrest, as well as any other transgressions that took place in the divisions abroad. They make the labor-intensive nature of the agricultural operations unseen—these ideological or phantasmagorical operations seem to be the very nature of both photography and capitalism.

The United Fruit Company collected photographs between 1891 and 1962, forming a photographic archive. Entangled within a complex network of emerging and newly constituted institutions pertaining to global governmental and corporate activities in the fields of science and technology, this archive represents an extraordinary source for discussing the specific use of photography as a capitalist production of space. Moreover, the photographic archive reflects the visual as a means of modernizing the Caribbean, as the archive provides the double perspective of camera and capitalism, embodied by the United Fruit Company, and is thus inscribed into a political economy of the visual. Just as the use of the camera seems to correspond with the expansion of modern capitalism, so photography quickly redefined the visual and modern processes of social regulation that were a part of the capitalist production of space. This was significant, as corporate photographic archives were constitutive in the visual reorganization of space and became a means to foster a radical environmental transformation of the Carib-

21   See Kevin Coleman and Daniel James, *Capitalism and the Camera: Essays on Photography and Extraction* (London: Verso, 2021); Coleman and James, "Capitalism and the Limits of Photography."

bean. Photography seems to tell us about the importance of the United Fruit Company as a large and powerful corporation, and about the ideological workings of these pictures in these transformations.

Two main circumstances become relevant for conceiving the United Fruit Company photographic archive as an extraordinary source of pictures. Firstly, the Company represents a mighty global corporation which geo-politically reorganized spaces through its agricultural and technological operations in the Caribbean, making it a testing ground for the modern. It not only reshaped agricultural industry and created a monocultural landscape, but also became a major agent in the making of modern sciences in the United States. Secondly, the photographic archive covers a long period of the United Fruit Company's existence as a corporation, depicting and creating divergent image worlds that acted upon the production of modern capitalist space. The United Fruit Company photographic archive is significant as it is one of very few corporate collections of more than 10,000 pictures taken during the period of American big business from the last decades of the nineteenth century and running well into the Cold War era of the 1960s, depicting the Company's manifold agricultural activities and the implementation of a new form of agro-imperialism. These activities were seemingly embedded in a complex, emerging and expanding institutional and political network supported by a new corporate culture. With the United Fruit Company photographic archive at hand, I aim to rethink capitalism through the camera and the role of photography in helping establishing the "aesthetico-political field" shaped by the capitalistic production of space.[22]

Unlike other photographic studies of large corporations that centered on pictures as constitutive of corporate image worlds and self-identities, the United Fruit Company and its pictures have been looked at mainly from the perspective of publicity and

---

22   See the discussion in Rancière, *The Politics of Aesthetics*.

corporate communication. For instance, David Nye frames the incorporation of the American company General Electric as a powerful complex that significantly shaped the modern world.[23] He points out that corporations have a tendency to meticulously control the past, inasmuch as they "edit archives, control access to papers, underwrite favorable works, destroy evidence (more often through neglect than by design), and lay down a barrage of favorable publicity that tells customers and stockholders how they ought to be understood."[24] This is certainly true when it comes to discussing the United Fruit Company photographic archive; but what are the archive's wider meanings?

The United Fruit Company started to collect photographs as early as 1891, before it was even properly formed as a corporation; that formally happened later, in 1899. These first pictures may also be read as images of the Company's cultural self-legitimation, inasmuch as they imagine the potency of the future corporation as a regional developer. As pictures they resonate with two major developments of that time: first, the rise of American big business along with the creation and internal development of the corporation as a novel business model; second, the technological refinement and development of the practice of photography, in particular between 1890 and 1930. In the 1930s new technologies emerged, such as smaller cameras and the less costly reproduction of color pictures in magazines, which reshaped the representational needs of corporations and federal agencies alike. In this double perspective of camera and capitalism, it was the United Fruit Company that became the corporation *par excellence*, employing diverse media, media strategies, and technologies, making it a global player in business, technology, science, and geopolitics to this day. The United Fruit Company certainly reflects some of the mechanisms and ideological functions of photography in forging a new corporate visuality in

23   David E. Nye, *Image Worlds: Corporate Identities at General Electric, 1890–1930* (Cambridge, Mass.: MIT Press, 1985).
24   Ibid., p. 3.

the violent transformations of labor and land, as embodied by a capitalist mode of space production.

As with many archives, the United Fruit Company archive kept the pictures in an inconsistent order, and many of the earlier pictures seem to have been included only at a later date. This reflects a retroactive collecting practice, part of the corporation's attempt to assemble an archive and control its past. However, from the 1920s on, the pictures became part of a simultaneous and steady collecting process and thus became documents, inasmuch as they accompanied internal corporate communications, such as memos and letters. Interestingly, Nye underscores in his study that the "images objectify the corporation's values, presenting in concrete terms its conceptions of both economic and social relations." They often seem to express a "contradictory pattern of concerns," and "these contradictions are as important as the specific content of the images themselves," as they "record the failure of corporations to express a unified vision." Accordingly, corporations do not "construct a coherent social reality, even in the imaginary world they visualized."[25] The very archive thus reflects the network of interrelations and oppositions, and raises questions about the practice of photography in corporate communication. Yet, we might even detect a certain lack of awareness of the corporate photographic archive in its moments of disorganization, and later in the 1970s "the archive eventually fell into neglect because few in the corporation could understand it."[26]

The United Fruit Company seems to reflect the authenticity of the picture, not in its connection to the reality depicted, but rather that the photograph seems to be "the 'relic' of a communication situation in which the photograph had the function of a visual message."[27] Significantly, both the photographer

25   Ibid., p. 5.
26   Ibid., p. 153.
27   Jürgen Hannig, "Photographs as a Historical Source," in *Pictures of Krupp: Photography and History in the Industrial Age*, ed. Klaus Tenfelde (New York: Philip Wilson Publishers/Palgrave Macmillan, 2005), p. 270.

and the viewer are "tied into the system of cultural norms and individual or group-associated valuation and behavior patterns that constitute the visual 'viewing consensus' within a society, and into the context of their objective social and economic circumstances."[28] In this context, photography's realism seems to be grounded on "social conceptions of significant reality," as suggested by Jürgen Hannig with regard to the Krupp photographic archive.[29] Interestingly, we read in the United Fruit Company Annual Reports, a specific site of reproduction and circulation of these archival pictures, how the corporation aimed at orchestrating itself:

> BUILDING A BANANA DIVISION: The Company's extensive plantations have been developed in lands previously covered by tropical jungle. For the most part, prior to development they were uninhabitable swamps because it is the deltas and bottom lands that have the deep rich soils in which bananas thrive. In order to prepare the unproductive lowlands for cultivation, it is first necessary to send field parties into the swamps and jungles for the basic surveys. Detailed plans are then assembled by agricultural, engineering, and medical experts. The conversion of jungle forests into thriving plantations is a tremendous task requiring large-scale use of machinery and the investment of large sums of capital.[30]

This glamorous description of the conversion of the jungles into cultivated lands by the mighty business of banana production reflects the dominant language of the annual reports to the United Fruit Company stockholders. At the same time, it highlights that this vigorous enterprise is scientifically backed, imagining a new expertise related to agricultural business abroad. In contrast to industrial photography, as has been studied in

28 Ibid.
29 Ibid., p. 72.
30 United Fruit Company, *Twenty-Sixth Annual Report to the Stockholders of the United Fruit Company* (Boston: United Fruit Company, 1948), p. 19.

the cases of General Electric or Krupp, it is significant that the major operations here are abroad, in the circum-Caribbean. This global dimension of agricultural business is of pivotal importance when it comes to discussing visual culture in the social conceptions of a significant reality, inasmuch as the pictures participate in the environmental conversion by giving contours to the imagery of this conversion. What they outline along with things, people, land and goods is a chronotope that is imagined as a modern homogeneous space to be appropriated, first, visually, and then materially, through the conversion of land into an agricultural landscape. What is at stake in the United Fruit Company's photography is ultimately the formation of a modern time-space that is materialized in labor, the production of commodities and, furthermore, a regime of value determined by accumulation and exchange that backs this conversion, and reaffirms the epistemic relationship between the camera and capitalism. So, it seems, paralleling industrial photography, as is the case with Krupp, that the "final cause of this image production is therefore the value alone [...]. The purpose of bare value accumulation puts its means, the concrete products, in exchangeability and degrades their sensual appearance to a pure effect."[31]

So, two main regimes characterize the formation of this chronotope of a new time and space, related to the Caribbean's conversion into a laboratory of the modern: first, the visual, and, second, the spatial. The latter is related to the transformation of autonomous agrarian and manual work into dependent employed industrial work that fosters a need for discipline. The conflictive nature of this and the drive for discipline is, without a doubt, present in the United Fruit Company photographic archive, albeit concealed, invisibilized, and sometimes even harmonized. As a leitmotif, the pictures of the Company archive imagine modernity and reflect a belief in capital and technology.

---

31   Reinhard Matz, *Industriefotografie. Aus Firmenarchiven des Ruhrgebiets* (Essen: Museum Folkwang, 1987), p. 88, my translation.

To this extent the corporate visuality reveals its premise of presenting the company as up to date, to sketch out the image of its modernity and with it to identify its productive efficiency. The pictures of the Company archive do not so much reflect a "window open on to the world as a safe let into the [albums], a safe in which the visible has been deposited."[32] They reveal an "image of the safe in which the visible has been deposited [and which] initially applies also to the industrial company's behaviour: it was and still is the unrestricted lord and user of the store of pictures which it has had deposited in its treasury."[33] This lieu of enunciation defines the ambivalent and conflictive nature of the images, inasmuch as it allows for the negotiation of the limit between the public and the private, as with the emergence of a private corporation the public sphere has been radically reorganized promoting private interests. Despite the fact that these corporate pictures reproduce the hidden ideology of the capitalist production of space, they also allow for a future reclamation bringing to light the dynamic, non-irrevocable relationship between the photographer and the photographed, in this case, the laborers. The chronotope is realized as "site and sight" and as a precise time-space configuration of the modern, shaped by the epistemic entanglement of the camera and capitalism.

This relationship between the camera and capitalism reframes the question of representation, as it is shown in the pictures through labor and technology. Moreover, I adopt the conceptual pair of camera and capitalism to discuss a series of more fundamental questions on the relationship between "nature" and culture, which are both radically remodeled in the course of violent transformations of environment, community and personhood, placed at the center of the Company operations, becoming the main concern of the corporate photographic archive. It is thus the relationship between agricultural land-

---

32 Ulrich Borsdorf and Sigrid Schneider, "A Mighty Business: Factory and Town in the Krupp Photographs," in Tenfelde, *Pictures of Krupp*, p. 161.
33 Ibid.

scape or the capitalist production of space and the radical environmental change, captured in the photographs, that is central to this study. Accordingly, it is the photographic archive that quintessentially remains bound to the knowledge production of a new capitalist order, which I discuss through the lenses of the camera and the production of value that emanates from the uneven pair of labor and capital, the two main forces inherent to the corporate photographic archive.

Written corporate archival sources of the United Fruit Company, that could complement or make the photographic albums speak, are, however, scarce or simply do not exist anymore. It is therefore of special interest that this visual material is being released to the public, for it unfolds a particular kind of media history mostly overlooked in the sphere of entrepreneurship and the expansion of a modern capitalism, but also relevant for questions of environmental justice and human rights.[34] An important feature is that some of these archival pictures seem to have been taken by professional photography studios in the nearby towns of the different divisions, a common practice that emerged with the development of company towns. Moreover, these photographic practices tell us about the aesthetic take inherent to the pictures in the way they not only model our vision, but also mirror the Company's ideology and will to control the photographed people and land. The photographers seem to have been hired to depict and document the Company's operational, industrial-agricultural and extractive practices and facilities, as well as the workforce.

Nevertheless, a significant portion of the pictures was apparently taken by amateur photographers, most likely the employees of the Company themselves. Overall, the preeminent will of the Company to photograph, collect, and depict is of major importance as it becomes clear that the photography is related

---

34 Philippe Bourgois, "One Hundred Years of United Fruit Company Letters," in *Banana Wars: Power, Production, and History in the Americas*, ed. Steve Striffler and Mark Moberg (Durham: Duke University Press, 2003), pp. 103–144.

to the Company's inherent social practice. In the reasoning of Pierre Bourdieu, photography becomes the very expression and thus symptom of social relations. Following this, it seems to be too narrow to discuss the meanings of photography only on the level of the photographer's intentions or the modes of expression. Rather, it becomes crucial to discuss photography from the viewpoint of surplus meaning or the production of value, which is given unintentionally and within a psychic and material space, inasmuch as photography participates in the symbolism of an epoch or a class. Following Bourdieu's argument and his distinction between amateur and artistic, or commercial, photography, it is significant that the artistic take always redefines *a priori* every photographed object as an artistic feature, as the artistic purpose of the picture lies in the artistic grasp of the photographed object and not in the object itself. Contrarily, amateur photography is determined by places and moments, because it follows a principle of its existence and its limitations that comes from outside of itself, in the form of a given social system of rules and schemes.[35] As a consequence, aesthetics and representations that are largely unconscious perform a specific function. Further, the social system, somehow expressing divergent interests, is also not entirely absent from the pictures that embed a professionalized view, directed towards something with a particular objective. The inherent social reality is certainly reflected in all the Company pictures, regardless of their secured authorship. What therefore becomes important in the case of the industrial-agricultural pictures of the United Fruit Company is that the question concerning authorship is not of primary interest. Rather it is the question of the production of value that is necessarily related to the social system of rules and, further, to the symbolic. This is underlined also by what has been critically articulated against a naïve understanding of documentary photography:

35   Pierre Bourdieu, *Photography: A Middle-brow Art* (Stanford: Stanford University Press, 1990), p. 8.

If the camera is increasingly being regarded as a pictorial technique in keeping with industrial production [...], then this development reflects the as yet very uncertain experience of the individual as the productive agent, no longer having the scope that is traditionally ascribed to him. [...] In this way the finished work can no longer be seen as the realization of an idea or reproduction of reality already worked out in the mind of the photographer, the explanation of which might be found in the question of what the author in fact wanted to show us. On the contrary, the work must be understood as the result of a multiplicity of effectualities which are latent in the mind of the photographer. [...] If, correspondingly, we try to understand a photograph as an overdetermined product [...], we should try to ascertain the meanings produced along with the photographs and we should do this in a symptomatological analysis of the specific aesthetic form of these photographs, that is, an analysis of the very differences from the given reality effected by the photographs themselves [...].[36]

Though not all photographs related to the United Fruit Company were collected for the photographic albums, they circulated in specific circuits and discourses that were aimed at reaching professional audiences, such as the Company's stockholders, had a scientific purpose in the fields of agriculture, economic botany, tropical medicine, and even archaeology. Pictures were also produced and distributed as simple illustrations and included in pamphlets distributed for the United Fruit Company annual meetings—a common practice among the emerging corporations forming a new visual corporate culture. In 1900 the new media of the annual report series surfaced as a communicational means, though until 1920 it did not include photographs at all and relied mainly on statistical information about the Company's business performance. Only later were more and more visual illustrations and photographs included, depicting the Company's business activities in the divisions

36   Reinhard Matz, "Gegen einen naiven Begriff der Dokumentarfotografie," *European Photography* 6 (1981), p. 11, my translation.

abroad. However, as underscored by Nye in his study, in a similar vein, the "photographs did not serve as mirrors of reality or as pictures of an older social reality that was slipping away. Rather they provided corporate stability at moments of transition. [...]. In all these cases photography served not to objectify already existing social relations but to visualize new ones. It assisted the development of a pluralistic corporate ideology in which [the corporation] legitimized varying interpretations of itself."[37] With regard to the United Fruit Company, an economy of image production became particularly important with the circulation of the annual reports to the stockholders, dating from 1948 until the dissolution of the Company; an image economy that is characterized by a new type of highly illustrated report. Although the annual report of 1925 already included photographs for the first time, as illustrations of the Company activities and operations, it was not until 1948 that the design of the annual report significantly changed to include the image. It is true that the Company visually underlined economic and agricultural advances, which evidenced the capitalistic production of space, working consciously on its self-representation and self-image as a modern and globally expanding corporation. The annual report of 1948 and the ones that followed assertively included more and more pictures that visually orchestrated the Company's agricultural operations and improvements, serving as visual arguments for the corporation's economic performance and legitimation of the radical environmental transformation and extractive practices in Central America and the Caribbean.

As pointed out by Allan Sekula, the "official pictures, [are] matter-of-factly committed to the charting and celebration of progress. [...] Industrial photographs may well be commissioned, executed, displayed, and viewed in a spirit of calculation and rationality. Such pictures seem to offer unambiguous truths, the useful truths of applied science."[38] Indeed, the pictures

37 Nye, *Image Worlds*, pp. 155–156.
38 Sekula, "Photography Between Labour and Capital," p. 201.

of the photographic archive partake in the visual rhetoric of applied science, inasmuch as they visibilize economic performance as a simple "matter-of-fact." In the rhetoric of evidence, they imagine the Company's story of tropical business success that was depicted as the peaceful conversion of the "unproductive" tropical jungle into the productive and efficient cultivation of agricultural land. The images thus underscore the economic activities, and, when included in the annual report, make the corporation visually viable to the stockholders. Moreover, corporate photography here serves the interests and expectations of the stockholders, as manifested in the published Company annual reports, following a discourse that stresses efficiency and industrial-agricultural rationality. It is also a notable feature of the photographic archive that it both shapes and reflects this corporate visual culture, despite the fact that most of the images were not circulated beyond it, as the majority seem not to have been published. To this extent, the pictures of the Company archive are of particular interest as they negotiate a liminal space between and radical transformation of the private and public spheres, shifting towards serving the Company's private interests, but also pre-configured as a potential public space of a future reclamation and revision. An archive *per se* is situated at this unstable limit between the private and the public. The Company archive thus articulates a social space that is mediated in the way the pictures were published and circulated or, indeed, not circulated. Accordingly, two different types of photographs are important to characterize this photographic archive: the one is more specifically related to the practice of the amateur photographer, who does not capture and thus differentiate the object with an artistic take; this is the bulk of pictures in the archive. The other can be clearly characterized by a specific, sometimes scientific, and often corporate interest. Yet, by forming a photographic archive, both types are indifferently intermingled, giving contours to a corporate practice that defines the nature of this archive. In the context of modern capitalism, labor and capital correspond as an uneven pair. As a corresponding part, the visualization of labor in the archive seems to stress "the dignity of work, the need for cooperation and efficiency, and the benevolence of the company."[39] Yet, as contradictory force to capital it bears the potential for an articulation of resistance and appropriation other than the pictures' purpose to imagine the glamorous corporate world of profit and success. However, the discourse of capital also insinuates an ambiguity into the Company photographic archive, in the way it reflects both conflicting energies and attempts at harmonization, thus invisibilizing the pictures' conflictive nature and the distinctively recognizable rhetoric of a corporate modernism as the "picture-language of industrial capitalism."[40] On the one hand, Sekula suggests in his study that "increased sales depended upon industry's ability to aestheticize itself to the public."[41] On the other, there is an overtly visible rhetoric of another related modern discourse to which many of the pictures irreducibly belong: that of science, forming a part of the so-called industrial-academic-military complex. Moreover, the photographic archive suggests the industrial and industriousness are an integral part of natural history, and, more specifically, economic botany and tropical medicine, in which the United Fruit Company became an important player, as well as the corresponding radical environmental changes that the Caribbean has undergone. Notably, the pictures were collected specifically for the photographic archive, assembled by the Company's Department of Public Relations that was also involved in other public relations projects affecting the visual production of imagery.[42] This type of activity can best be captured, Sekula suggests, as an "internal machinery of corporate public relations"

---

39 Ibid., p. 259.
40 Ibid., p. 203.
41 Ibid., p. 259.
42 With the creation of the Department in the 1940s this was a common practice, as evidenced by the Annual Reports. In that time Vice-President Edmund Whitman supervised the Department and even sponsored the creation of the first and only movie by the United Fruit Company, *The Maya Through the Ages* (1949).

that aimed at demonstrating the "progressivism" and "'human-ity' of large-scale bureaucratic enterprise" such as the corpo-ration.[43] Moreover, to take up Sekula's argument, it becomes urgent to examine "photography, as a cultural practice, [that] could signify both the domination and preservation of nature. The camera could preserve remnants of a pre-industrial world, while embodying the very essence of technological progress."[44] Nevertheless, the United Fruit Company archive assembles het-erogeneous pictures, mostly ordered geographically, according to the different divisions in Central and South America and the Caribbean. Its photographic albums communicate the Com-pany's main operative activities, scientific research, and experi-mental stations, and show how tools and machinery circulated between the different divisions, and how ships and railroads served as crucial networks in a time-sensitive fruit business. Archives seem to be always internally organized to become distinguishable as such. Accordingly, archives follow a kind of chronology, a diachronic or sequential order that reflects its tax-onomic order. In most cases the archives' organization results in an alternation between the two forms, and the archive eventually becoming necessarily inconsistent with either order. This is true in the case of the United Fruit Company photographic archive. Because of the complexity of collecting and organizing knowl-edge, inconsistency may even be the prevailing characteristic of the archive, namely that it mixes different forms of organiza-tion, thus constituting an incongruent space of representation, and, moreover, a space of negotiation of representational mean-ings. Sekula coined this organizational attempt as being "torn between narration and categorization, between chronology and inventory."[45] So we find that Company albums have different and overlapping orders following geographical logics, such as the divisions with their different plantation names; thematic logics,

43   Sekula, "Photography Between Labour and Capital," p. 235.
44   Ibid., p. 218.
45   Ibid., p. 197.

according to subject matter such as "Abaca," "Bananas," "Palm Oil Plants"; or referring more precisely to agricultural operations like "Spraying" and "Irrigation" or building activities such as "Railroads," "Bridges," "Housing"; other categories include "Welfare," or more generally "Recreation," and some are simply labeled as "Miscellaneous." Other images depict activities in the United States, such as a series of meticulously documented building processes at the Weehawken Interchange Terminal in New Jersey and the Revere Sugar Refinery near Boston that constitute entry figures for organizing the abundant photographic material. Yet, the United Fruit Company photographic archive makes two aspects pivotal: first, the fact that the technical processes captured by the photographs depict agriculture as a highly industrial sector, whilst at the same time invisibilizing the mechanical means employed to advance the idea of industrialization and modernization. Second, the scientific practice of picture-making conceals the very idea of and thus invisibilizes this "construction of capitalist dominion over nature and human labour."[46] The photographs' primary function seems to divulge seeing as knowing, that is to say that their intervention has an epistemic dimension, making effective the capitalist dominion over nature.

Sekula further underscores that the nature of seeing through photography became related to utilitarian machines, such as the famous Panopticon, where there "was total and perpetual surveillance," while the "inmates were forced to assume that they were watched continually" without being able to verify if there were watchers in the central observation tower.[47] This certainly favors a reading of the archive from the perspective of the corporation's omnipresence, becoming a total institution that aimed at socially controlling the laborers. In this original context of the corporate archive, the very idea of omnipresence becomes real as a panoptical view shared by the main addressees, the man-

---

46   Ibid., p. 203.
47   Ibid., p. 221.

agement and the Company employees and, in another context, the stockholders when they glance at the annual reports. It also seems that "While the image becomes the bearer of fragments of scientific truth," related to the capitalistic dominion over nature, "it also serves as a generalized *sign* of science, an emblem of the power of science to understand and dominate nature."[48] The photographic archive seems to foster this modern and industrial logic that correlates with the emerging corporate visual culture and imperial gaze, that is, the dominion over nature. In the interstices of visualization and knowledge production, "photography came to supplant hand-drawing, painting, and engraving," which in previous centuries had dominated visualization in the fields of landscape, botany, and agriculture, "as the dominant form of visual culture."[49] In Sekula's case of the "mining photographs, however, [the pictures] present a nature that had *already* been radically altered by organized human energies. They introduce another spectre, because it raises the issues of practice, proves to be embarrassing for idealist historiography."[50] Similarly, the United Fruit Company photographs make visible the "organized human energies" and make them unseen in the way they altered the natural and human environments and, significantly, the radical transformation of space. This dimension of hidden environmental violence is an important source of upheavals and struggles, which the photographs negotiate on the level of (in)visibility. As a dissonant narrative or counterarchive this is also discussed by Kevin Coleman[51] and myself[52]

48   Ibid., p. 205.
49   Ibid., p. 222.
50   Ibid., p. 228.
51   Kevin P. Coleman, "The Photos That We Don't Get to See. Sovereignties, Archives, and the 1928 Massacre of Banana Workers in Colombia," in *Making the Empire Work: Labor and United States Imperialism*, ed. Daniel E. Bender and Jana K. Lipman (New York: New York University Press, 2015), pp. 104–136.
52   Liliana Gómez-Popescu, "La Masacre de las Bananeras: la imagen fotográfica y la literatura," in *Imaginando América Latina: historia y cultura visual, siglos XIX a XXI*, ed. Sven Schuster and Óscar Daniel Hernández Quiñones (Bogotá: Editorial de la Universidad del Rosario, 2017), pp. 23–57.

with regard to the infamous, but invisibilized, banana massacre in the Colombian Caribbean in 1928, a topos of the socio-political upheavals in the history of Latin America. Sekula observes that modern industrial documentation with its technological, economic, and ideological conditions fully surfaced only at the end of the nineteenth century. "Modern," in this sense, refers to "any system of documentation in which pictures are made available for circulation in mechanically-reproduced form."[53]

Around 1900 the photograph became one of the dominant forms of visual culture, and was able to subsume "previous modes of static visual representation."[54] It was around that same time that photographic archives and collections were emerging as forms of image inventory and as visual repositories for many newly established institutions, such as governmental agencies or corporations, while becoming modern means of organizing visibility and thus contested sites. Industrial documentation has been acknowledged as a result of the so-called second industrial revolution and the "emergence of [a] monopoly form of capitalism," valid for the United States between 1880 and 1920.[55] Moreover, it characterizes a particular phase during which US corporations broadly and rapidly expanded as global corporations into Latin America.[56] However, this accelerated global expansion is to be understood as a turn within the logic of capitalist space production that is increasingly determined by vision. Industrial photographs aimed to narrate "capital improvements, to illustrate catalogues of industrial equipment, and ultimately to intervene directly in the labour process."[57] This latter is of primordial significance: it negotiates and controls labor movements and unrest, and the very acts of resistance that were frequently experienced in the United Fruit

---

53   Sekula, "Photography Between Labour and Capital," p. 232.
54   Ibid., p. 234.
55   Ibid.
56   See the study by Emily Rosenberg, *Spreading the American Dream: American Economic and Cultural Expansion, 1890–1945* (New York: Hill and Wang, 1982).
57   Sekula, "Photography Between Labour and Capital," p. 234.

Company divisions abroad. The United Fruit Company photographs can be read, taking a cue from Sekula, as "operational" documents. They foretell and "document" the environmental transformation the Caribbean undergoes with the operations of the Company. Photography functions here as a media dispositive, backing a larger discourse network, and I will discuss this in the next chapter. A significant number of the pictures aim to promote the many leisure facilities and newly realized modern buildings in the divisions abroad, though they only show a "restricted range of sociality."[58] They constitute an inventory of new agricultural tools and machines, outlining the imaginary of industrial mechanization and the nature of the agricultural operations of the Company, by adopting an industrial aesthetic.

The relationships between camera and capitalism are manifold. One particular mode is related to the carefully reworked visual representation of the workforce and labor, as is the case with regard to the photographed laborers on the plantations and divisions, mostly in the acts of harvesting or constructing heavy infrastructure, but always visualized as a workforce. On the one hand, as operational documents the pictures seem to re-inscribe the reified power relations of the Company, embodied as a discourse of "race" and labor. On the other, they might articulate a potential discourse of possible reclamation and resistance, inasmuch as they make visible "imagined modernities and communities," the unseen laborers of the United Fruit Company divisions.[59] Some "family portrait" pictures make visible the laborers, however, these are indiscriminately mixed up with those others that document the different agricultural operations. As Sekula underscores in his study, "The family, still the unit of social reproduction, is itself reproduced," forming a hidden but powerful discursivity and representational meaning in the images.[60] Moreover, the overt stasis of pose in these portraits

58   Ibid., p. 262.
59   Jaguaribe and Lissovsky, "The Visible and the Invisibles," p. 176.
60   Sekula, "Photography Between Labour and Capital," p. 256.

Fig. 2.8: "Steamshovel at work at Las Delicias, Colombia." Gelatin silver process on paper, 8 × 10 inches. United Fruit Company Photograph Collection, Baker Library, Harvard Business School, Box 32.

becomes garishly visualized: the pose represents "a group of managers or [laborers] standing self-consciously in front of the camera. For the [laborers] it was a momentary break. For the managers it was a momentary performance as [laborers]."[61] However, a second stasis is made visible here, that of the poses as movement. These visualized poses are neatly organized arrangements of the laborers and their families, mostly grouped together in their settings and surroundings, and the pictures reproduce the social and moral hierarchies of the time, corresponding to the attempt to document the diverse forms and modes of social welfare in the divisions.

In the larger discursive context of camera and capitalism, photography seems to be an image technology used by the United Fruit Company to incorporate the Caribbean into an

---

61   Ibid., p. 257.

Fig. 2.9: 1927, "Completed Fulton Tandem – Central Preston, Preston, December 13, 1927." Gelatin silver process on paper, 8 × 10 inches. United Fruit Company Photograph Collection, Baker Library, Harvard Business School, Box 45.

orbit of Western knowledge. All United Fruit Company photographs are informed by a new form of modern space that is reorganized by vision as a privileged sensory modality. As pointed out by Sekula, "photography was seen as a reward, a token of managerial approval, as well as a pedagogical instrument. The *operational* value of the photograph was supplemented by an *ideological* function."[62] Accordingly, these photographs belong to what has been framed as a "central archive or 'information bureau'," adopting the image within the idea of scientific management as a "specialized form of representation, intended for the manager and engineer,"[63] understanding this as the archive's primary function that helped forge the division of manual and intellectual labor. In this sense, as an articulation of

62   Ibid., pp. 248–249.
63   Ibid., p. 239.

the laboratory of the modern, "scientific management" became a novel and efficient form of business organization and a constitutive part of modern capitalism. The photographer thus mediates between capital and labor, "acting as kind of middle-man in the unequal traffic in representations."[64] And with this "notion of conflict of representations in mind"[65] we need to examine how the United Fruit Company pictures negotiate and mirror the echoed and contested meanings of the archive's ambivalent nature.

Slow Violence: Capital, Labor, Technology[66]

Slow violence "creates and sustains the conditions of administered invisibility" that result in the production of "unimagined communities:" extractivism [...] is also a mode of representation that incessantly manufactures emptiness and renders native communities of resource-rich areas (humans as well as more-than-humans) into "virtual uninhabitants" [...] whose statistical removal precedes and makes possible their always already imminent physical disappearance, their status as disposable lives.[67]

Both mining industries and agricultural monocultures form part of the paradigm of extractivism, within which the United Fruit Company is a special case of interest. As previously argued, its photographic archive both makes seen and invisibilizes the embedded slow violence of the radical transformation of the landscape into productive land. This transformation is realized through a series of employed knowledge dispositives that re-

64   Ibid., p. 251.
65   Ibid.
66   I borrow the term "slow violence" from Rob Nixon, *Slow Violence and the Environmentalism of the Poor* (Cambridge, Mass.: Harvard University Press, 2011).
67   Jens Andermann, "Memories of Extractivism: Slow Violence, Terror, and Matter," *Journal of Latin American Cultural Studies* 29:4 (2021), pp. 5–6.

order the capitalist production of space. In this section, I delve into the environmental violence inherently linked to extractivism in regions of high biodiversity that constitutes the photographic archive itself, to further unfold the entanglement of the camera and capitalism, which fosters the various extractive practices. While knowledge dispositives more generally organize territory and space, the use of pictures in particular speaks to us about modes of visualization and invisibility, referring to both knowing and seeing as two distinct but inextricably intertwined epistemic practices. Photography is introduced as image technology and visual device "as sites of both knowledge and power."[68] As pointed out by Jonathan Crary, with the diffusion of photography, film and later television, a "vast hegemonic organization of the visual [...] becomes increasingly powerful in the twentieth century."[69] Further, as recently elaborated by Kevin Coleman and Daniel James, discussing on the one hand the birth of photography as a new technological medium with the capacity to mechanically fix images, and on the other Karl Marx and Friedrich Engels's "philosophical-historical accounts of the division of labor, primitive accumulation, and commodity fetishism," the question about the intrinsic connection between photography and capitalist accumulation resurfaces.[70] As a conjunction, it seems to push for a global extractivism into the regions of high biodiversity, but also to foster the extraction of human labor and global resources. Coleman and James ask: "And might photography play a role in refusing capital's infringements upon [...] planetary life?"[71] In another context, Jens Andermann warns us that:

> [...] once technologies such as the civil and military use of nuclear
> fusion, deep-sea drilling, or the transgenic modification of crops and
> animals have irrevocably enmeshed social and political issues with

---

68   Jonathan Crary, *Techniques of the Observer: On Vision and Modernity in the Nineteenth Century* (Cambridge, Mass.: MIT Press, 1990), p. 7.
69   Ibid., p. 4.
70   Coleman and James, *Capitalism and the Camera*, p. 1.
71   Ibid.

geophysical phenomena, "natural catastrophes are no longer separable from their technological, economic, and political implications or repercussions" [...]. We can no longer distinguish between natural disasters and historical catastrophes, [...] given that the new regime of radical immanence under which we now live has put to rest the concept not only of nature but, therefore, also that of the human itself as at least partly removed from the natural realm.[72]

Following this, I wish to point out that the United Fruit Company photographic archive lingers on the limits between what has been perceived as natural disaster, in the form of its extractive agricultural monoculture, through vast banana plantations and other tropical fruits and commodities, established in the Caribbean and Central America, and a historical catastrophe, as it has rendered whole "communities of resource-rich areas (humans as well as more-than-humans) into 'virtual uninhabitants'."[73] This rendered modern space between biopolitics and extractivism is defined by a new quality in the circulation of commodities, knowledge, science and technologies, plants and fruits, which I discuss through the lens of the visual economy of Company photography. However, the photographs also embody narratives that might subvert "capital's infringements upon [...] planetary life,"[74] where, perhaps, alternative regimes of vision may become possible. It is precisely these two poles, that of an imperial gaze and extractive view, and that of a space for alternative narratives for the empowerment of the photographed, that define my reading of the photographs of the United Fruit Company archive.

Take for example the picture with the caption "Group of Haitian Cane Cutters, Preston Division." It shows a group of cane cutters standing in a sugarcane field. The caption indicates that they are from Haiti; Haitians working in the cutting and harvest-

72 Andermann, "Memories of Extractivism," p. 13.
73 Ibid., p. 5.
74 Coleman and James, *Capitalism and the Camera*, p. 1.

ing of sugar cane in Cuba. *Preston*—the name refers to Andrew Preston, founder of the Boston Fruit Company (1884), which in 1899 was incorporated into the United Fruit Company, founded by Minor C. Keith and Andrew Preston—formed part of the Cuba division and was an important plantation for the United Fruit Company. What is made visible in that image, what is invisibilized? How does it belong to the extractive view? On one level, the photograph speaks of the circulation of workers in the Caribbean, a space that has been defined by flows of migration. On another level, it speaks of the Company's interest in documenting their business activities and the production processes for the different fruits. Yet, it also speaks of the Company's will to organize and order this space through vision and particularly photography. It is quite characteristic that, during this period, photography conquered the territory of the workplace and was effectively introduced into the context of production and industry, as it (re)produced an aesthetics of labor, forming different tropes of a visual discourse. In the photograph, the Haitian cane cutters have stopped cutting, and are looking towards the Company's anonymous photographer, as the image seems to follow a visual logic of ceasing the harvest to pose as movement. All the workers seem to have stopped swinging their tools, the machetes. One person is chewing a piece of cane, providing a counterpoint to the group through this casual, momentary action. It seems that the image expresses an overall extractive vision of the Company, but it also expresses the idea of labor control. However, photographic images, like this one, also form part of a narrative of possible re-appropriation that will define, in the words of Arcadio Díaz-Quiñones, the self-recognition and self-representation of the different peoples of the Caribbean, by generating categories that belong to modes of subjectivation shaped by the aesthetic and the political.[75] This image does not simply represent the

75   Arcadio Díaz-Quiñones, "El 98: La guerra simbólica," in *Culturas imperiales. Experiencia y representación en América, Asia y África*, ed. Ricardo Salvatore (Rosario: Beatriz Viterbo Editora, 2005), p. 181.

Fig. 2.10: "Group of Haitian Cane Cutters, Preston Division." Gelatin silver process on paper, 8 x 10 inches. United Fruit Company Photograph Collection, Baker Library, Harvard Business School, Box 44.

laborers, it represents the laborers as determined by their labor in the sugar industry, with sugar cane, a crop of significant economic and commercial interest, becoming part of the discourse of capital and the production of value that define the image's meaning. The photograph mimics the aesthetics of labor in the industrial-agricultural world, while belonging to the order of the production of the "tropical" landscape.

Yet, as Krista Thompson observes in her study of the picturesque as a trope for representing the *New Jamaica* at the beginning of the twentieth century, the link between the fruit companies and the production and circulation of these new images was significant for the arranging of the landscape according to a visual grammar. In this grammar the picturesque was an important trope for marking the "Tropics" as an ordered, civilized and manageable landscape, promised by the fruit companies in order to obtain effective economic expansion, which would determine the circulation of bodies and commodities. At the same time, the fruit companies' images are composed according to this visual grammar, she argues, precisely in order to divulge and legitimate the violent processes of environmental transformation, making the processes of extraction that underlie them unseen. Through visual markers, such as the palm or banana tree, the images participated in the naturalization of the plantations and the harmonization of the physical and economic landscape of the islands.[76] We read these picturesque narrations by the Company's first official biographer, Frederick Upham Adams, as he looked out over the banana plantations in the Jamaican Blue Mountains:

> [...] below these dizzy altitudes tumbles a sea of hills, a tumult of smaller mountains without plan or order, and twisting about them sprawls a bewildering labyrinth of valleys lacking seeming end or purpose, but all of this anarchy of nature is subdued and mellowed by the glittery fronds of the palm and banana [...].[77]

The ideological discourse and visual language are inscribed into the photographs of the Company archive. The aesthetics of the album images adhere to the visual grammar that defines the tropicalization of the Caribbean and the naturalization of the environmental and economic landscapes of the fruit plantations, in particular with regard to "tropical" trees and fruits such as banana and coconut palm, the products of economic botany, thus invisibilizing monoculture as violent extraction. The banana tree as a visual marker of both the tropical and the plantation became a figure of ordering space that helped to imagine the modernization of the Caribbean. The aesthetics

---

76   Krista A. Thompson, *An Eye for the Tropics: Tourism, Photography, and Framing the Caribbean Picturesque* (Durham: Duke University Press, 2006), p. 86.
77   Frederick Upham Adams, *Conquest of the Tropics: The Story of the Creative Enterprises Conducted by the United Fruit Company* (Garden City, N.Y.: Doubleday and Page, 1914), p. 130.

served to order the rural and remote wild into a "tropical" landscape, and to include the Caribbean and Central America within the North American hemispheric orbit of knowledge. Further, it seems that the inscribed visual grammar of the images in the archive, which principally serve to form a record, an inventory, an internal documentation of the operations and processes of production, circulation and consumption of the fruit, also defines the self-perception and fantasy of the corporation.

Blending biopolitics and extractivism, another image from the photographic albums, "Shipping Coconuts, Jamaica 1926," provides an interesting example. It shows four laborers and, it would seem, a child. This time, a regime of control, that of supervision, defines the narrative of the image. Women are seated in a warehouse selecting the coconuts. The image suggests an instantaneous moment because the women do not interrupt their labor activity; the moment is more intimate and less distant. This is, without a doubt, because the supervisor, the only person standing, dominates the visual composition of the image. These two images articulate the conjunction of a visual and racial discourse. In so doing, the images form part of a new type of photography which I call corporate photography, and further form a corporate image archive.

However, in the realm of the images' discourses there seems to be another imagery: photography plays a particular role in narrating the features of alterity, helping to project the modern Self outside itself.[78] The Company photographic archive speaks to us of these workings, of re-appropriating discourses and constructions, and through an effectively "administered invisibility" the production of "unimagined communities."[79] Photography also effectively participates in the exploitation of new spaces, in the extraction of resources and labor, by establishing a new visual regime for accessing raw materials, and appropriating territories and bodies. Following this, the Company photographic

78   Herlinghaus, *Violence without Guilt,* p. 13.
79   Andermann, "Memories of Extractivism," p. 5.

Fig. 2.11: "Shipping Coconuts, Jamaica 1926." Gelatin silver process on paper, 8 x 10 inches. United Fruit Company Photograph Collection, Baker Library, Harvard Business School, Box 51.

archive speaks to us of this (in)visibility, of the radical environmental transformation of landscapes, the inherent ecocide, and the capitalistic production of space that has profoundly shaped the modernization of the Caribbean. Here corporate photography also outlines a space of fantasy and desire: the circumstances in which a photograph speaks for itself reflect the ideological operations that participate in making the cultural seem natural.[80] Photographs reflect the aesthetic relationship human beings have with history and are therefore an important historical source. In their interior they seem to capture a contested site and counter-memory capable of subverting the

---

80   Abigail Solomon-Godeau, "Wer spricht so? Einige Fragen zur Dokumentarfotografie," in *Diskurse der Fotografie. Fotokritik am Ende des fotografischen Zeitalters*, ed. Herta Wolf (Frankfurt am Main: Suhrkamp, 2003), p. 72.

hegemonic vision and extractive view. The photographs of the Company's archive reflect the imagery of abundance: They imagine the abundance of the endless banana plantation, and ultimately, the unending labor force, ever-available bodies that made the economic expansion of the Company possible at all. They show the boats loaded with bananas and other fruits, the radiotelegraph, trucks and rail networks that form part of the Company's modern infrastructure. It is therefore important to read these photographs in their primary discursive context of economic expansion and the capitalistic production of space.

The cultural imagery through which this expansion and extraction takes place recalls the figure of abundance that has interrelated the European and American continents in their dynamics of exchange for centuries, that is, the first allegory of the American "imagined community," as underscored by Julio Ortega. This figure seems to clarify the discursive context of the Caribbean not only in terms of economic expansion, but also in terms of how this expansion is perceived, narrated and fictionalized.[81] The United Fruit Company photographic archive reflects this overall cultural imagery in the realm of perceptions, the production of a modern environment and the extractive view in a particularly interesting way. As we shall see, this archive gives us an exceptionally lucid idea of how photography as image technology participates in the different knowledge and related scientific discourses that advance economic expansion inscribed into the imagery of abundance. Furthermore, the camera played a crucial role in the integration of the Caribbean and Central America into an aesthetic and political regime that is configured by one particularly mighty emerging global player at that time, the United Fruit Company. This aesthetic and political regime, as in the encounter of the camera and capitalism, certainly found its manifestation in the idea of disciplining through photography. "Photography derives its illustrative objective quality not from

81   See the discussion by Julio Ortega, "The Discourse of Abundance," *American Literary History* 4:3 (1992), pp. 269–385.

its greater correspondence with the reality of things, but from its correspondence with the social definition of the objective view of our world," Jürgen Hannig underlines with regard to the pictures of Krupp: "Photography's realism is not based on the visible things, people and action depicted, but on social conceptions of significant reality."[82]

Moreover, as Georges Didi-Huberman argues elsewhere, we can therefore state that "photography fulfills a similar function as the image and memory do; and so it has their enormous *epidemic force*."[83] Because of this epidemic force, photography not only seemed to have ensured the modern transformation of the Caribbean, but also enabled the Company's global economic expansion. Accordingly, the relationship between camera and capitalism can be defined here by the nature of photography as *media a priori* that enables the establishment and advancement of capitalism in the form of the corporation as a powerful complex that radically shapes the modern world. Two main visual fields emerge here: the first is related to the broad theme of labor, the second is more intimately linked to technology. It is thus significant that the majority of the pictures embody both, labor and technology. Yet, at the center of the Company's archive are the agricultural-technological complex and its operations in the banana business abroad. Labor is only represented to a lesser extent, due to the fact that the labor-intensive agricultural business took place in complicated socio-political situations in the host countries and often caused open conflict, labor unrest and transgressions. The images carefully conceal this violence. But as "photography fulfills a similar function as the image and memory do" its "enormous *epidemic force*" with regard to the conflictive labor relations that are concealed is nevertheless present in the photographs.[84] Read carefully, these pictures, albeit

82   Hannig, "Photographs as a historical source," p. 272.
83   Georges Didi-Huberman, *Bilder trotz allem* (Munich: Wilhelm Fink, 2007), p. 42, my translation.
84   Ibid.

very subtly, disclose these conflictive relations, and in this sense, reality is visualized as peaceful, just as nature's transformation into agricultural land is presented harmoniously. Moreover, the photographs divulge an overt rhetoric that frames this form of labor as non-conflictive. What they also visually suggest is that agricultural business is labor-intensive and not entirely replaceable by technology. Importantly, labor and technology belong to each other; this too is part of the archive's social conception of a significant reality. While technology was replacing more and more manual labor, "Industrial technology [at least up until the 1960s] had not yet become a second nature to people."[85] Rather,

> [photography] creates an exaggeratedly modern image of technology and the world of work. It was not the heroic machine operators, but the workers in the [plantations] and those moving loads who represented the bulk of the workforce even in companies then at the leading edge of technology. Physical exertion and manual labour were the norm, the operation of machine the exception.[86]

This becomes true when looking at the type of pictures that share both, labor and technology, inasmuch as they depict labor-intensive operations such as the installation of heavy infrastructure as prerequisites for the cultivation of bananas and tropical fruits. This aspect of the involvement of a modern heavy industrial infrastructure is often overlooked when considering the business of the fruit companies. The innovation and success of companies, such as the United Fruit Company, lies in the up-to-date technologies that grounded the discourse networks of tropical botany with regard to this particularly time-sensitive fruit business. To communicate this idea, fostering territorial advancement, photography played a significant role in promoting this transformation of nature into reliable productive land.

---

85 Ulrich Wengenroth, "Photography as a Source of the History of Labour and Technology," in Tenfelde, *Pictures of Krupp*, p. 90.
86 Ibid.

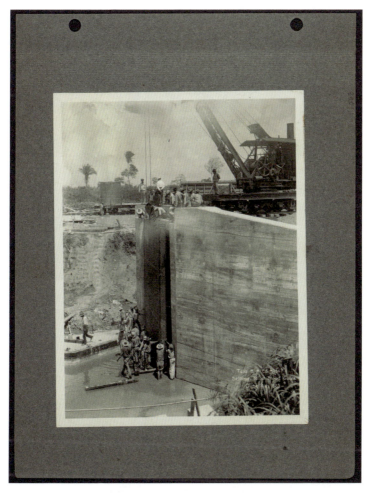

Fig. 2.12: "Tela R.R. Co. #154. Setting Toloa Flood Gates, June 14th 1925."
Gelatin silver process on paper, 8 x 10 inches. United Fruit Company Photograph Collection, Baker Library, Harvard Business School, Box 11.

That this radical environmental transformation is quintessentially violent and destructive is present in these photographs
only on the level of a mighty and eventually sublime conversion. As such, the following images focus on the work in progress of a heavy infrastructure realized by visually subordinated
laborers: looking at these images we remain fascinated by the

Fig. 2.13: (*no caption*). Gelatin silver process on paper, 8 x 10 inches. United Fruit Company Photograph Collection, Baker Library, Harvard Business School, Box 32.

(in)visibilized forces that seem to tame nature, by the powerful technologies digging into the sacred ground, and by the epidemic force these pictures communicate of the past. As such they share the visual rhetoric of the work in progress that has always depicted and imagined the region since the construction of the Panama Canal as the utmost laborious undertaking.

It is nevertheless striking that some of the photographs depict technologies as rather primitive working techniques, that show the operation of ditching a canal as not at all a mechanized work. Looking thus at the photographic albums, it becomes quickly clear that we find a wide range of different, not always up-to-date, technologies in the unevenly developed United Fruit Company divisions in the Caribbean, bearing witness to the different phases and manners by which the land was transformed into plantations. However, on the level of visual rhetoric, labor is represented as being part of technology and determined by it: what is seen is technology, not labor. The industrious work implied by this kind of field operations is

Fig. 2.14: "San San drainage project. #334 – view spur 16, quarry, showing rock uncovered. 9/19/27." Gelatin silver process on paper, 8 x 10 inches. United Fruit Company Photograph Collection, Baker Library, Harvard Business School, Box 28.

invisibilized as the visual focus is on the mighty technologies that make this conversion a significant reality. The Company carefully controls the visual in order not to partake morally in this environmental transformation, but rather to represent itself as a facilitator of technologies.

Although a major characteristic of industrial and corporate photography, the representation of labor was not explicitly intended. Rather, "it cannot be supposed that it was the intention of either the [...] firm or of photographers working for other steel and mining companies to make a record of working conditions in heavy industry. Working people, if they even appear, in the picture, are incidental."[87] More precisely, forced labor is not visibilized at all and remains deliberately unseen, although it seems that it constituted an important part of the United Fruit

87   Axel Föhl, "On the Internal Life of German Factories – Industrial Architecture and Social Context at Krupp," in Tenfelde, *Pictures of Krupp*, p. 161.

Fig. 2.15: (*no caption*). Gelatin silver process on paper, 8 x 10 inches. United Fruit Company Photograph Collection, Baker Library, Harvard Business School, Box 27.

Company work force. Along with other industrial or corporate photographic collections, the United Fruit Company pictures provide primarily "more information about the development of the industrial architecture and the history of technology than about the working conditions in industrial circumstances."[88] We do not gain "unfiltered glimpses into the world of work," but rather we witness a purposefully administered invisibility, that conceals the inherent slow violence against laborers and the environment.[89]

These pictures belong to the visual field of modern technology: some depict the theme of water works in the broadest sense, that of loading ships and harbor construction, of canal infrastructure including pump stations and irrigation related

88   Ibid., p. 180.
89   Ibid.

Fig. 2.16: "Agricultural Department: Guaro. Disc Rolling Machine: Pin Roller, making pins for Truss Wheels. November 10, 1927." Gelatin silver process on paper, 8 x 10 inches. United Fruit Company Photograph Collection, Baker Library, Harvard Business School, Box 45.

to the banana business; others belong to sugar cane operations in Cuba and depicts heavy technology, facilities and machinery.

These pictures certainly bear witness to the technological transfer that took place in the Caribbean and Central America with the aim of visually promoting the technological nature of agricultural business abroad. This modern technology becomes a visible marker of the capitalist production of space being part of the "extractive theft": "Under such circumstance, visible reminders of theft through modernity's infrastructural invasions—by oil pipelines or massive hydroelectric dams or toxic tailings from mines —foment rage at the life-threatening environmental degradation combined with the state's failure to provide life-enabling public works."[90] In particular this picture

90   Nixon, *Slow Violence*, p. 42.

(Fig. 2.16) depicts technology as a costly artifact, as in the sugar industry it indeed was. This series is certainly a showcase for the imagery of abundance made possible by technology for extracting the wealth of the earth. Still, the focus on technology hides something else, namely that the sugar industry remained bound to a colonial form of slavery, as it demanded considerable *main-d'œuvre*. Yet, the colonial past is present in the pictures only in a residual form: the pictures articulate a repressed "reality" that forms part of the social conception of a significant reality made visible here. In other words, what is suggested is the idea of optimization of work through technology that cancels out manual work and finally subordinates the laborer. Inscribed into a discourse of rationalization, the pictures suggest a disciplining through work and photography that necessarily represses the conflictive nature of this kind of transformation of the workforce.

Yet, what does it mean to be looked upon while working? As most of the album pictures suggest, the laborers pose and have a break from whatever they were doing, often gazing at the photographer, often in a carefully arranged pose. At the same time, the photographer intervenes in the working scene and eventually controls the laborers through his gaze, inasmuch as he depicts them in relation to their work. For example, Fig. 2.15 shows an industrious scene at the harbor, loading recently arrived bananas from the railway car to the waiting banana freighter. It visualizes an extremely time-sensitive operation realized basically by manual work. Some of the photographed laborers, including what appear to be overseers, look at the photographer, so that their gazes meet and pose for a moment; they are aware of being looked upon. It becomes pertinent to acknowledge photography's fundamental characteristic here as a modern technology: "Because of its instantaneous way of representing, photography can express little of the time dimensions of discipline. Yet all the more, because of this, it articulates the pervasion of discipline."[91] These momentary

91   Matz, *Industriefotografie*, p. 111, my translation.

glimpses into work or simply being supervised visually at work by arbitrary moments of a potentially powerful present gaze relate to what Michel Foucault has developed elsewhere as disciplining through seeing and as the operative principles of the famous Panopticon. Vision redistributes power in space, inasmuch as the power is automated and de-individualized, because "Power has its principle not so much in a person as in a certain concerted distribution of bodies, surfaces, lights, gazes; in an arrangement whose internal mechanisms produce the relation in which individuals are caught up."[92] Foucault emphasizes: "He who is subjected to a field of visibility, and who knows it, assumes responsibility for the constraints of power; he makes them play spontaneously upon himself; he inscribes in himself the power relation in which he simultaneously plays both roles; he becomes the principle of his own subjection."[93] One of the critical fields of intervention is that of labor. Significantly, this constitutive relationship between photography and labor describes a fundamental structure of the Company's archive, although as structure it is never present, nor fully visible. Inasmuch as it determines the relationship between men and things, men and men, we become aware only of its effects. The pictures undeniably remain silent about it. Yet, in the context of the study of industrial photography, some findings also become relevant for the United Fruit Company photographic archive. These concern the structural similarities between photography and industrial work, inasmuch as both photography and labor determine space according to the same principle of disciplining it.[94] This becomes pertinent for the United Fruit Company plantations and divisions whose spatial organization might have been determined by a kind of omnipresent vision. Following this, one of the main theses of this study is that the

---

92   Michel Foucault, *Discipline and Punish: The Birth of the Prison* (New York: Vintage Books, 1979), p. 202.
93   Ibid., p. 203.
94   Matz, *Industriefotografie*, p. 111.

photographic archive plays a pivotal role in the spatial organization of the plantations, while becoming a constituent component, insofar as vision and space correlate in the modernization of the Caribbean. It is important to emphasize that "The new organization of the spheres of authority was intended to ensure control. However, an overview and proper insight were needed—literally so. Photography [...] seemed particularly valid for this purpose."[95] The photographic archive reflects this capitalist production of space, through the different themes and subjects introduced in the inherent order of the photographic albums. So it is that "Within the framework of photography the relationship between disciplining and seeing/being seen is less mediated by a backlash and more by the ongoing influence of its product as image."[96] This spatial organization seems to become effective because it is visually already articulated and projected onto the future: what we perceive today looking at these pictures is thus the epidemic force of this projection. The United Fruit Company photographic archive orchestrates technology as a marker of modernization while suggesting how the abundance of nature, land and resources of South America and the Caribbean can be tamed by that same technology, materializing the very idea of modern progress and the imperial desire for economic potency. Depicting this mighty technology brought to the regions abroad, the corporate archive visually suggests what has become a business credo, that man is able to dominate and domesticate nature peacefully, changing grounds and river channels, clearing dense vegetation for the sake of a vast agricultural business, digging, cutting, erecting, extracting, building. From this thunderous environmental transformation thus emanates the modern belief in man's independence from nature.

This environmental violence is also captured by two other related pictures. Both images depict everyday scenes and even-

95   Alf Lüdtke, "The Faces of the Workforce. Portraits of Labour," in Tenfelde, *Pictures of Krupp*, p. 67.
96   Matz, *Industriefotografie*, p. 112, my translation.

tually feature the carefully veiled working conditions: the first (Fig. 2.17) depicts a payday at La Cruz farm office in Puerto Libertador in the Dominican Republic (1948); the second (Fig. 2.18) shows a group of women picking out lumps at the cleaning machine in the Limon Cacao Plant. This latter is one of the rare photographs showing women at work in agricultural operations, characteristically sorting or cleaning fruits inside the Company facilities. The first picture gives a snapshot of how the salary was received. It depicts a heterogeneous crowd of people gathered together in a moment of waiting, reflecting a common scene, inasmuch as the Company used to pay its on-site laborers every fourteen days, often using a pay-car to reach remote locations in the newly emerging divisions. Nevertheless, it is remarkable that the scene is depicted at all, because other historical sources suggest that paydays used to be conflictual and often violent, with clashes among the laborers. Yet, as "corporate photographs express an often contradictory pattern of concerns,"[97] this picture together with a few others represents the fissures and incoherence of the Company photographic archive. The other picture showing posed female workers, who gaze at the photographer whilst taking a break, transmits a calm and orderly impression of a clean workplace. It visualizes what has been widely discussed in other studies, namely the composite of the United Fruit Company workforce: it bears witness to women with diverse ethnic backgrounds, Hispanic, mestizo, and Indigenous. The position of the one and only male laborer in this scene suggests a hierarchical work relationship, at least between him and the female workers, inasmuch as he seems to control the final and quality sensitive selection of the cacao beans; he supervises the work of the others. Interestingly, Matz observes in his study of industrial photography and corporate archives that: "Such representations would have pointed— were it possible through photography—to the immediate hazardousness or the monotony, the corporeal and nervous burden

---

97   Nye, *Image Worlds,* p. 5.

Fig. 2.17: "#3 Pay day at La Cruz Farm office. Pto. Libertador. March, 1948."
Gelatin silver process on paper, 8 x 10 inches. United Fruit Company Photograph Collection, Baker Library, Harvard Business School, Box 40.

of industrial labor, they would have emphasized the corporeal and psychical marks of the humans. However, even there where these traces of stress become visible, they are covered by concentration and zeal."[98] The picture does not offer any glimpses of the real working conditions of these laborers; it remains silent and obscure. Yet it raises some questions: what does it tell us about the relationship between the workers, and between the workers and the photographer? How does the image reflect this complex situation of the Company and its workforce in a highly politicized contact zone at a time characterized by political coups and US Cold War policies towards the Latin American countries? What does it tell us about the material and psychic sedimentations in the bio-contact zones?

98   Matz, *Industriefotografie*, p. 53, my translation.

Fig. 2.18: "#705 Another view of the cleaning machine in the Limon Cacao Plant. Showing women picking out lumps of placenta as the beans pass from the machine to the bags. Limon, Costa Rica." Gelatin silver process on paper, 8 x 10 inches. United Fruit Company Photograph Collection, Baker Library, Harvard Business School, Box 67.

With regard to the pictures' social conceptions of a significant reality, there is another theme that is of particular interest: Among the photographic albums is one labeled "Recreation," which assembles pictures showing representations of social welfare, such as recreation, schools, churches and sports facilities. This theme is pivotal as it outlines the life of United Fruit Company employees in the contact zone abroad: the pictures depict social welfare work, but they also imagine the internal social order through the disciplinary measurements of leisure and welfare. As a programmatic complex it seems to correlate with the "risky" nature of the work of the Company employees sent abroad, characterized by deprivation, being far from a US American cultural environment. The album "Recreation" outlines the cultural boundaries, exclusion and internal marginalization of different Company social activities. As scholarship has

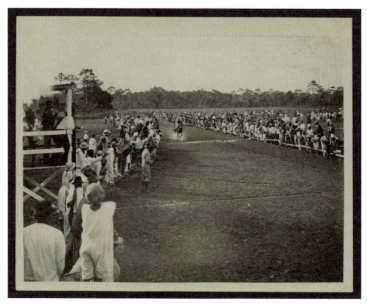

Fig. 2.19: "#245. Horse Racing, Blair Park, Guabito. Panama, 1924." Gelatin silver process on paper, 8 x 10 inches. United Fruit Company Photograph Collection, Baker Library, Harvard Business School (olvwork714043).

paid little attention to the role of the representation of welfare in this context, this photographic series is of special interest: it reveals not only an ideological discourse and the politics of white supremacy, but also the conflictive and disciplining nature of modern labor, inasmuch as the visual representations became effective means to control labor unrest and the emergence of labor unions, tested ever since the emergence of the mass industrial labor sector. The pictures argue for cultural legitimation and a peaceful public image of the United Fruit Company's presence in the Caribbean. They form an integral part of the Company's self-presentation, inasmuch as many of this type of pictures circulated in the Company annual reports and other corporate media. The pictures depict a broad range of leisure and sports facilities provided for Company employees in the different divisions, giving visual contours to a modern enclave.

Fig. 2.20: "No. 6793 – Corner of Classroom for Girls – Truxillo – April 8, 1927."
Gelatin silver process on paper, 8 x 10 inches. United Fruit Company Photograph Collection, Baker Library, Harvard Business School (olvwork713975).

Most of the facilities were exclusively reserved for white
employees, though some were also used by other ethnic groups.
So it is that leisure and recreation, more generally, structure
and order cultural time and space in the divisions, inasmuch
as they regulate the time beyond work. Significantly, two main
arguments are visually made here: first, that social welfare matters for the Company, this is a political message; second, that
there is no cultural dispossession in the divisions abroad, this
is a message about enclosing and culturally differentiating the
contact zone. Yet, this latter argument is also supported by the
fact that most of the leisure and welfare activities and specific
cultural events are carefully segregated spatially from the rest
of the divisions. Access is exclusive, and as defined by a hierarchy this space is distinct and distinguishable: it is about the
visual reproduction of the one's own space against the other,
necessarily outside of the enclave, as an internal marginaliza-

tion. Moreover, this welfare series discloses a social conception of a highly hierarchized modern space as a reality that is thus made significant. As such, the Company photographic archive reflects and acts upon the emergent modern corporate space.

Two types become relevant for the visual representation of social welfare: first, the representation of "atmospherically resonant everyday situations" that "spontaneously recorded momentary impressions of the course of everyday life"; and second, the "creative approach demonstrated by the other iconic tradition," that is, that "In appearance and composition it is dominated by the photographer's strong interest in arrangement and in achieving an unambiguous, intense pictorial effect. The arrangement of the people and the distribution of the pictorial space are carefully calculated."[99] Both moments certainly describe this welfare series. In all these pictures space is carefully visually composed and the constitutive violent nature of this exclusion and of the Company's hierarchy remains concealed. The picture series that represents the social institutions of the United Fruit Company, such as schools or churches, argues for an imagined and desired *mission civilisatrice* or civilizing mission as a Westernization of the Indigenous, West Indian, and native workforce. They form part of the colonizing discourse that aims to include the Caribbean into the orbit of Western knowledge: this time it is the global corporation that "civilizes" and "modernizes." The pictures that portray these key social institutions in the company towns and divisions as discipline and order underline the Company's cultural self-legitimation and self-image. The Company's violent rule abroad and its strict policy of ethnic segregation and exclusion are purposefully hidden and eventually the opposite visual message is adopted: the productivity and steady capacity of the Company business even allow "natives" to gain modern knowledge and enjoy welfare and wealth. However, with regard to the social

99   Heinz Reif, "'The worker's well-being and domestic happiness'. Works Life Beyond the Factory Gates in Photography at Krupp," in Tenfelde, *Pictures of Krupp*, pp. 107–108.

conception of a significant reality, it becomes true that the visual representations of social welfare, and because these pictures circulated and were included in a specific thematic photographic album, are constitutive of an economic exchange that creates value.[100] This visual economy of the images manifests a new regime of value that is embodied in the photographic archive. Yet, as Reif reminds us, "Each photograph depicts a cropped image of reality which always remains ambiguous, cannot be made unequivocal in its meaning despite all the arrangements, creative works and captions, and inevitably contains a large number of details that interfere with the unambiguous iconic message being aimed for, and partly even contradict it."[101]

The meaning of the images is not unequivocal, but rather remains open and is not exclusively controlled by the photographer or the Company's intentions. Indeed, it may even undermine some of the desired effects. This fundamental aspect of the nature of photography becomes significant in the context of the bio-contact zone, as it may also allow for perceiving social inequality, environmental injustice and abuse of human rights. Modern, unimagined communities are visibilized and eventually made seen, as has been observed with regard to the social documentary photography of the 1930s, inasmuch as it "assumes and encourages photography's 'privileged status as a guaranteed witness of the actuality of the events it represents'."[102] These kinds of potential side effects of "documentary photography" that are neither wished for nor intended by the United Fruit Company and its photographers were carefully controlled. Nevertheless, they remain as incidental meanings. This relationship between the corporation and its photography contours a social practice of making the Company's self-representation and self-image viable. Perhaps a major characteristic of corporate photographic archives is "The set of albums

100 Appadurai, *The Social Life of Things*, p. 3.
101 Reif, "'The workers' well-being and domestic happiness'," pp. 108–109.
102 Corbus Bezner, *Photography and Politics in America*, p. 9.

and the patterns of company publicity work developing from the signal efforts by the company management to make the 'social legibility' [...] of the firm stand out as distinctive in the modern medium of photography, to stabilize it by means of a restricted, homogeneous supply of pictures and to make it effective as a complex message in selected circles of recipients."[103] Furthermore, this relationship may be characterized, on the one hand, by a "forced formation of tradition, that is the consistent historisation of a specific works memory by means of safeguarding sources, the documentation of things that were disappearing."[104] On the other, it is defined by a visual economy that seems to inform a more intimate social legibility and eventually determines photography's participatory power of agency in business. Affirming this, it becomes pivotal to look at the pictures' afterlife in order to avoid the self-reproductive perspective of a carefully fabricated view of the Company. It cannot be overestimated that the United Fruit Company photographic albums were released as a gift in 1979. They still remain the most significant and comprehensive archival source, and this is because the information they offer is visual.[105] The question concerning the depiction of social welfare by corporate photography, again, proves to be tricky, inasmuch as photographic distinctions or "documentary realism" seemed to be determined by "wider sociological-historical conditions."[106] Interestingly, what was accepted as "docu-

103 Reif, "'The workers' well-being and domestic happiness'," p. 115.
104 Ibid., p. 116.
105 There are a few United Fruit Company written archival sources and materials, such as those rescued by Philippe Bourgois, comprising in particular letters and correspondence. There is also significant United Fruit Company written documentation located in Cuba, known as the archive of Banes, which comprises managers' office files (1930–1958), land documents, annual reports (1939–1944, 1951–1959), production statistics (1901–1959), and lists of payrolls (1903–1959) that are known as the archive of "central" Guatemala, which also includes private correspondence (1937–1960) and sugar operations (1931–1953). See details in Oscar Zanetti and Alejandro García's *United Fruit Company: un caso del dominio imperialista en Cuba* (Havana: Editorial de Ciencias Sociales, Instituto Cubano del Libro, 1976).
106 Corbus Bezner, *Photography and Politics in America*, p. 14.

mentary realism" "underwent sometimes violent and occasionally subtle transformations during the 1940s and 1950s, when America entered one of its most repressive political climates of the century. [...] the parallels between the decline of documentary work and the rise of more formally engaged photography relate to clear, real, historical events in time."[107] The pictures of the United Fruit Company photographic archive challenge this understanding, as they remain ambiguous and often involve the perceiver of the images in different and contradictory ways.

The Archive's Chronotope

Let me conclude this chapter with a return to one of the most explicit figures of the photographic archive: the chronotope. Derrida defines the meaning of the archive as always both spatial and temporal.[108] In his reasoning, against a logocentrism that punctuates the idea as truth and not its literal materialization, Derrida demonstrates that *meaning* cannot primarily be related to mental content, but rather that its significant substance is always an effect of the material.[109] He underlines the simultaneity of content and form against a philosophical model that conceives form only on a secondary level. This understanding becomes pivotal for my reading of the photographic archive, as it helps reflect the relationship between the archive and its outside, defined by two premises: first, spatialization, and, second, temporality. In the following I shall discuss this relationship of the United Fruit Company archive as a projected chronotope, that is, the imagined eternal transition towards modernity as a promise of modernization itself. The archive configures this chronotope, inasmuch as it projects a new relationship of time and space: the creation and management of the

107 Ibid., p. 14–15.
108 Bunz, "Die Ökonomie des Archivs," p. 30.
109 Ibid., p. 39.

topographical space is efficiently applied through a *media a priori* that belongs, nevertheless, to the re-imagination and projection of a new time-space relation in resonance with a simultaneous technological media development. It is useful here to briefly introduce Mikhail Bakhtin's conception of the chronotope, taking a cue from his literary theory. Bakhtin originally conceived the chronotope on different levels for the formulation of a chronotopical analysis of literature. For the discussion of the photographic archive, two of these conceptual definitions seem particularly fruitful: first, the chronotope as a cultural theoretical category, and, second, the chronotope as a narratological category, used for the analysis of the form-content of literary texts.[110] Yet, the archive's chronotope can best be grasped following the first conception of a cultural theoretical category, inasmuch as it describes the archive's entanglement with its "outside." Bakhtin distinguishes between the real (or external) and the literary (or internal) chronotope, where the first refers to the cultural historical circumstances, which define the spatiotemporal order that structures the human perception of the world.[111] This is pivotal for understanding the chronotope as a projected time-space of the photographic archive: the archive seems to reflect a certain correspondence of an internal and external chronotope. Moreover, the photographic archive embodies the chronotope of spatiotemporal order that mirrors the specific historical and cultural circumstances of the plantation economy: the archive's chronotope corresponds to the cultural historical circumstance of a spatial and temporal order, that is, the modernization or conversion of the Caribbean into a modern space. This correspondence can be characterized in the way the archive's chronotope materializes the specific time-space of a projected future development: the plantation economy becomes landscape. Further, the chronotope reflects the correlation of the camera and

---

110 Mikhail Bakhtin, *Chronotopos* (Frankfurt am Main: Suhrkamp, 2008), pp. 205–207.
111 Ibid., p. 205.

Fig. 2.21: (*no caption*). Gelatin silver process on paper, 8 x 10 inches. United Fruit Company Photograph Collection, Baker Library, Harvard Business School, Box 52.

capitalism as a form of the production of time and space. For his part, Bakhtin conceives of the categories of time and space as forms of actual, and not transcendental realities, that is, as conditions of possibility of perception.[112] He makes this aspect particularly productive for the cultural working of the archive. This idea becomes relevant when conceiving the photographic archive's share in the cultural conversion of the plantation economy into a peaceful and productive landscape. This is possible because the photographic archive as a *media a priori* organizes our vision of the space as the archive's outside.

This picture (Fig. 2.21) shows how "nature" is appropriated by man, and more specifically, by a white male United Fruit Company employee. The image depicts "nature" becoming a measured, viewed and documented terrain that will be

112 Ibid., p. 8.

inserted into a future economic circuit. The camera captured a scene: the imperial gesture of measuring with scientific or technical devices, while bringing the site into sight. Another man is standing beside the group in a posture that suggests either supervising or giving orders, which it seems the others are following. The viewer is directed by the eye of the photographer who captures the scene. The tool the one man is using is a tripod with a theodolite, a precise instrument for topographic measurements, which was commonly used in the exploration of terrains to extract new space for the banana plantations. Also, the careful viewer notices two white marks that indicate precise points inside the image—marks that were only added later while the photograph was being processed. The marks draw the attention to two real points in the terrain to be measured via the theodolite. This picture eventually discloses the chronotope: first, by the inscription of precise measurement into the space, which we read as a sign of dominating the space through technology; and second, by a media operation through which men dominate space through time, projecting a future spatial transformation. Since the photographic archive gives contours to the visual appropriation of "nature," it is the chronotope of a new time-space, framing a modern political space, that gains its momentum here. This visual representation of landscape not only organizes the photographic archive's dominant narrative, that of the extraction, but also makes the eventual realization of the projected plantations possible at all: the archive's internal chronotope corresponds with its external one. Further, the archive as a cultural operation predominantly works on the topographical space itself.

According to Bakhtin's reading, the chronotope as a narratological category helps reveal the temporal and spatial organization of the "plot" while determining the content. Certainly, the procedure regarding time-space in literature differs greatly from that of the photographic archive. Nevertheless, we find a similar materialization of time in space and in the archive: the archive reflects and suggests a specific imagination of a modernization, envisaged as a chronotope that corresponds to the emergence of a modern political space, as experienced in the Caribbean with the emergence of the plantation economy. Looking at the many photographs, organized and kept in the albums, the chronotope seems to be a configuration of a specific time and space further realized as the Company's enclave, which reflects the real space of the plantation economy. Within the chronotope, time becomes concretely visible and manifested as the possibility of a scenic unfolding of events: captured in the many photographs that make visible the built infrastructure; the new facilities brought to these places; and the circulation of machines, commodities, and bodies. The chronotope outlines the plantation economy as a productive landscape, into which the United Fruit Company's new territories are to be transformed. This conversion of the landscape is realized as site and sight and as a precise time-space configuration. The pictures of the archive envision and narrate this veiled conversion as agricultural improvement in making unseen its related slow violence, and in doing so, they imagine a sort of modernization: this landscape eventually becomes the chronotope, inasmuch as it promises the eternal transition towards modernity. From within the chronotope as both cultural-theoretical and narratological category, we may describe the photographic archive as constitutive of the modern configuration of space and time, that is, of the Caribbean as a laboratory of the modern. The United Fruit Company photographic archive plays its part in the construction of a hegemonic visual and discursive space, which is realized and stabilized by the interplay of a multitude of political, academic, and economic agents. This archive thus plays an undeniable role in the iconographical, scientific, and geopolitical appropriation and exploration of the Caribbean as a transnational economic space and a space of knowledge.

At this point, again following Derrida's reasoning, I wish to return to some of the features of the archive. Particularly important here is his observation about the materiality of the archive and its place of consignation, that is, the correlation between the archive and what seems to be outside of it. What becomes pertinent for the understanding of the archive directed towards the future is the concept of history as explored by Derrida: the material storage of content with its external spatialization becomes relevant as being constitutive of the archive. More importantly, it is the technique of repetition that determines the archive's economy. If the archive preserves, it must be materially spatialized. This becomes even more pertinent since with this spatialization the archive is repeatable: In fact, it is this very repetition that we conserve.[113] Both spatialization, as defining the archive's embeddedness within what is outside of it, and temporality are constitutive to the archive. Here it becomes significant how the archive intersects with what seems to be outside of it, on the level of time and space, and more precisely how it works on history and "nature." The "strong emphasis on nature and its broad definition, covering human nature as well, carries the risk that events represented in the album will be ascribed to human nature, thus erasing historical agency," Marianne Hirsch noted elsewhere.[114] This gesture of "erasing historical agency" certainly always frames "tropical nature" as an existing state of nativeness: pictures showing native trees and crops along with "native people" as objectified nature, carefully concealing nature as cultural landscape. Moreover, nature seems to have become the primary object of the United Fruit Company's intervention, as it is related to the idea of productivity and thus included in the realm of the production of value. This might be obvious, as agriculture by definition is the technique of transforming "raw" nature into a rationalized landscape. The pioneering work of the United Fruit Company came to be known as a radical environmental transformation of vast terrains, realized through the effective use of agricultural technologies. This was possible because, within an ideological

113 Bunz, "Die Ökonomie des Archivs," p. 36.
114 Marianne Hirsch, *Family Frames: Photography, Narrative, and Postmemory* (Cambridge, Mass.: Harvard University Press, 1997), p. 57.

discourse, "nature" became void of the idea of any historical agency defining the archive's imperial and thus modern ambition and the pictures' representational meaning: the codification of the plantation economy as the "natural tropical" landscape and as a discourse of landscape.

The following picture (Fig. 2.22), with the caption "A Typical landscape, Banes, Cuba," like many others, manifests a gaze that captures and extracts from nature as landscape. This particular emphasis on landscape is a feature that many images share, including the following image (Fig. 2.23): it shows a very narrow path down into an impressively high mountain valley. The view is guided towards a tiny white bridge at the end of this path, on which the eye finally rests. Nature is seen as abundant, and the human traces seem insignificant, almost lost. However, the attentive viewer notices a telegraph or electrical line along the way: an important trace of the infrastructure installed in order to create and manage this framed topographical space. It is this kind of visual manifestation of terrain wrested from nature that depicts how the Company takes possession of space, making it a sign of the visual order of landscape, gently manifested as persistent visibility. Further, that extractive view helps transform the perception of nature into a concept of landscape. Embedded within a typical iconographical language of framing the landscape—which we may recognize from the landscape iconography of previous centuries—this type of photography shares what colonial discourse has already installed to recreate the colonization of nature through an extractive view.

These pictures not only determine the major theme or *leitmotif,* so to speak, of the codification of the plantation economy as landscape, but also outline a projection and desire for transformation. From within this framework, that which has not been previously perceived as landscape becomes visible, stabilizing a hegemonic cultural order by geoculturally reconfiguring the Caribbean. Landscaping, Jill Casid reminds us, thus describes the creation and transformation of landscape into an economic, political, and aesthetic hybrid space that is characterized by transplantation, the circulation and transfer of plants, seeds, machines, commodities, bodies, and representations, which can therefore be rationalized as a "landscape of utility," an improved, peaceful landscape, of productive cultivation, and as a chronotope.[115] With regard to the United Fruit Company, the visual ideology elaborated was based on the assumption of landscape as a primary object of geopolitical transformation. In the context of this media and thus geocultural transformation, photography came to be the privileged means because of its ability to incorporate the transformed and extracted spaces into a new orbit of knowledge, determined by the circulation of commodities, plants, and bodies. The archive became a primordial and irreducible technique for ordering this space. The Company's economic and spatial expansion are witnessed through these archival images; the archive thus became the *media a priori* for the creation and effective projection of this chronotope.

This can also be explored through this photograph showing a banana plantation (Fig. 2.24). As we are most likely unfamiliar with the social biography of plants, we might assume that the coconut tree or the banana plant are native to the island of Jamaica or Central America; however, this view only seems familiar because of the visual *mis-en-scène* through the photographs, giving nativeness to the plant and the landscape. This suggestive and manipulating gesture that most of the pictures manifest invisibilizes the violent transformation of the environment and social space created with the plantation economy: the photographic archive conceals the contested meaning of this transformation, as we still "[...] may be hampered by the indexical and iconic aspects of photography, by the fact that photographs tend to be read as mimetic representations of what is rather than as wishful constructions of what might be."[116] So it is

---

115 Jill H. Casid, *Sowing Empire: Landscape and Colonization* (Minneapolis: University of Minnesota Press, 2005).
116 Hirsch, *Family Frames*, p. 57.

Fig. 2.22: "A Typical Landscape, Banes, Cuba." Gelatin silver process on paper, 8 x 10 inches. United Fruit Company Photograph Collection, Baker Library, Harvard Business School, Box 41.

that the viewer of the photographic albums is never confronted with this violence, as it is concealed by a visualization that makes the visible a wishful, manageable, and projected space.

Among these pictures, we find photographs that show the Company's facilities as given instances within a naturalized order and as visual markers of a new order of landscape. Thus, the depicted landscape becomes part of a visual reification, inasmuch as the pictures are collected and assembled for the archive. The archive seems to be a heterotopic space through which the possession, appropriation and extraction of spaces are realized and thus projected. Further, the creation and management of the topographic space is predominantly realized visually, punctuating vision as the dominant sense that organizes the emergent modern political space. This imagination of spatial extraction and its resources became meaningful only because of the representation of the modern plantation economy as landscape, or let

Fig. 2.23: "Road to Newcastle – Jamaica." Gelatin silver process on paper. United Fruit Company Photograph Collection, Baker Library, Harvard Business School, Box 51.

us say the reality effect of the archive: the plantation economy in the Caribbean as a peaceful and productive landscape, belonging to a narrative of space, ideological discourse and a geocultural order, to which the archive corresponded as an organizational means. With regard to the role of photography, since colonialism went out of fashion, the expansionist debate resolved around other means of control, such as tutelage under theoretically independent protectorates, or governmental encouragement of private connections, especially economic ones: it was understood that the extension of American know-how and the expansion of trade and investment could best proceed without formal colonialism.[117] It became clear that with the invention of photography, the visual world was reorganized or reinvented, and it seemed that knowledge was reconstituted through vision

117 See the discussion in Rosenberg, *Spreading the American Dream.*

Fig. 2.24: (*no caption*). Gelatin silver process on paper, 8 x 10 inches. United Fruit Company Photograph Collection, Baker Library, Harvard Business School, Box 31.

thus conforming the modern hegemony of vision. Accordingly, mimetic machines like photographic cameras in the bio-contact zones became the new means for advancing this capitalist economic expansion without formal boundaries promoted explicitly by transnational corporations. Thus, the Caribbean became a privileged site and testing ground for the modern.

As observed elsewhere, the eye appears to be the "organ of tactility," through which we relate to the world.[118] Yet, the camera as a media device has primarily been associated with the idea of copying, or of mimesis, as Taussig describes, "To get hold of something by means of its likeness."[119] Interestingly, he further observes that "Here is what is crucial in the resurgence of

118 Taussig, *Mimesis and Alterity*, p. 20.
119 Ibid., p. 21.

Fig. 2.25: "No. 425. 'Tacky' party given by Mrs. Doswell in Club. Santa Marta, March 27, 1926." Gelatin silver process on paper, 8 x 10 inches. United Fruit Company Photograph Collection, Baker Library, Harvard Business School, (olvwork713810).

the mimetic faculty, namely the two layered notion of mimesis that is involved—a copying or imitation, and a palpable, sensuous, connection between the very body of the perceiver and the perceived."[120] Amid the pictures taken by the United Fruit Company, we find some that clearly could be related to practices of self-portrayal, working at the archive's unstable limit between the private and the public, between oneself and oneself. These are a significant image series: photographs depicting casual scenes, family portraits, and photographs of the many laborers, hierarchically positioned next to the timekeepers or overseers, reflecting a sort of self-assurance on the part of the Company about its undertakings in the American "tropical" jungle. Nonetheless, the picture (Fig. 2.25), like the one that follows, reflects

120 Ibid.

the complex play of representation, between the two poles of alterity and mimesis, bearing witness to a self-reflexive moment on the part of the photographer.

The picture mirrors the Company's perception of the other that was made part of a carnival play at Mrs. Doswell's party: it shows a group portrait of a masquerade party in a private setting within the Company's social world. In particular, two persons give contour to the contact zone as it seems to have been perceived by the Company: one boy or young man sits on the left side of the second row, wearing an oversized hat that was typical of the overseers or timekeepers, imitating a hyperbolically enlarged colonial costume. The other person is a white woman sitting in the first row on the right side of the image. She has her face colored in black. Mirroring the other with a carnivalized gesture, the outside of the labor camp is converted inside this more private sphere of a social gathering, thus stabilizing the cultural enclave: the racial divide is visually marked at the unstable limit between oneself and oneself. The photographic practices viewed here are part of these social practices of leisure time that reproduce the Company's hierarchical order: the pictures show white American families that came to the contact zones. What they instantly seem to frame is the question of representation and self-awareness, articulated as the play of alterity and mimesis, to which these photographic practices become significant. Rightly, Taussig argues:

> To ponder mimesis is to become sooner or later caught, like the police and the modern State with their fingerprinting devices, in sticky webs of copy *and* contact, image *and* bodily involvement of the perceiver in the image, a complexity we too easily elide as nonmysterious, with our facile use of terms such as identification, representation, expression, and so forth—terms which simultaneously depend upon and erase all that is powerful and obscure in the network of associations conjured by the notion of the mimetic.[121]

121 Ibid.

Fig. 2.26: "Story and pictures of Escuela Agricola Panamericana." Gelatin silver process on paper, 8 x 10 inches. United Fruit Company Photograph Collection, Baker Library, Harvard Business School (olvwork713717).

Undeniably, the photographic images reflect here both "copy *and* contact," while they conceal the question of representation as something of being-involved-with, that is, a sensory engagement. This intimate material relationship is related to my argument for conceiving the archive as a performative act. Taking this idea further, we ask: How does photography participate in social exclusion by reproducing a visual regime? How does "race" as visual technology become effective in determining a moment of reification inscribed in the power relations of the United Fruit Company? "What are the politics of photographic truth?"[122] Fig. 2.26 shows another group portrait of white Company employees and some white women. A large white man is positioned amidst the group, in accordance with the accepted posture of (division) manager, framed by two small dark col-

122 Bolton, *The Contest of Meaning*, p. xvi.

ored women who are carrying baskets of tropical fruit on their heads. The two dark colored women disappear as individuals, as their only function seems to be to frame this central person. The careful viewer becomes aware that this image visually enforces the hierarchical social order of the plantation economy and thus the enclave. In the intimate fissure of "copy *and* contact, image *and* bodily involvement of the perceiver in the image,"[123] a crucial distance is kept through the image captions. It seems that by giving the pictures these captions for the purpose of classification, the limit between the self and the other is restored: the images function here as means of stabilizing the hierarchized racial constructions underpinning "white supremacy." Nonetheless, they also tell us something else that is best grasped as the "unconscious strata of culture [...] built into social routines as bodily disposition."[124] This configured alterity, the materialized idea of difference, has become "the mythology of color built into the cultural apparatus of work and bureaucracy organized to construct the [Panama] canal [which] surely took it to a higher level."[125] The "cultural apparatus of work and bureaucracy" was later incorporated into the American banana companies: as is known, the United Fruit Company profited significantly from labor brought from the West Indies to this part of the world, an "'excess', drawing on the rich imaginative resources that colonial history offers border culture."[126] Moreover, these social routines are embedded in what "fits only too well with European racism as instituted by almost four centuries of the African slave trade and the massive infusion of anti-black sentiment."[127] For "frontier" towns or border zones, these complex cultural encounters have to be considered within a cultural apparatus of bureaucracy, such as that of the United Fruit Company, to sense how cultural orders

123 Taussig, *Mimesis and Alterity*, p. 21.
124 Ibid., p. 25.
125 Ibid., p. 145.
126 Ibid.
127 Ibid.

were visually stabilized, particularly through the corporate photographic archive. Let me thus turn again to some of Taussig's observations, developed within the conceptual pair of mimesis and alterity. In particular with regard to the physiognomic aspects of visual worlds, he engages with a new anthropology of signification, in which, conceptually, materiality has an essential role: meaning is articulated materially and related to the senses to be grasped as co-presence of subjects in the contact zone. Senses, in particular sight, are involved with what later came to constitute the photographic archive. The Company was engaged with shaping and molding the contact zone, while they used vision as a primary modality to stabilize the cultural order between oneself and the other. Accordingly, the archive defines the meaning of the photographs not only as an effect of the material but also within the performative, from which meaning emerges as an open situation. Having said this, it becomes pertinent to underscore again the photographic archive's dual nature as it advances, on the one hand, the plantation economy and the economic expansion of the United Fruit Company into the Caribbean, crafting it as a homogeneous modern space. On the other, the archive remains an open semiotic site of contestation that clamors for an act of political re-appropriation.

Chapter 2

The Crossroads of Science and Discourse Networks

The Crossroads of Science

The plantations are an example of system and immensity, all the more impressive because of their setting of primeval jungle. In the transformation within a few years of a riotous wilderness of huge trees, palms, vines, ferns and other tropical growth into a vast tract of cultivated land, there is a succession of steps which can scarcely be comprehended by those familiar only with farming operations in the temperate zone. The surrounding country is first thoroughly explored as to its fitness for cultivation. Then comes the clearing away of forest and brush, the digging of the main drainage ditches, the building of houses, railroads and tramways and finally the planting. Then follows the gradual development and extension until vast areas are pouring their product methodically and regularly into the holds of the steam-ships at the loading ports. [...] The Company on its plantations has built towns and villages, some of which are of considerable size; and in these towns has installed laundries, bakeries, electric light and ice plants, water works, sewerage systems and all other utilities and conveniences of a modern community in the North. [...] The districts where our plantations are located have to be sanitated, and extensive sanitary measures maintained at all times to protect the communities and keep conditions healthful for employees and their dependents. Through the areas owned or operated by the Company flow streams and their tributaries, with adjacent swamps and ponds, all possible breeding places for mosquitoes. Along the railway lines borrow-pits were made in the earlier days of construction, some of which have been drained or filled with great difficulty. In many instances it is necessary to keep these pools of water constantly larvicided. When the obstacles to be contended with are taken into consideration, the magnitude of the work of sanitation and caring for the sick and injured can be thoroughly appreciated.[1]

It is a recurrent narrative, a much repeated self-image: the United Fruit Company saw itself as a modern corporation bringing health and wealth to the Caribbean and its Central American divisions by envisioning a more economically efficient region. Situated at a crossroads of the sciences the Company imagined its new territories abroad "as a laboratory of hygiene and modernity," in which "American medical officers were indulging in a form of magical thinking, creating sympathetic associations in the hope of changing the world."[2] As underscored by Warwick Anderson, "the laboratory was an appealing representational space, but also seemed to allow a manipulation of the scale of things, so that macro may become micro and then magnified again."[3] This idea of colonial undertakings also describes the interventions of the United Fruit Company in its expansion towards the South. "Obsessed with systematic documentation and marshalling of fact" the modern corporation aimed to demonstrate "the power of bureaucratic intervention and technology" and of science to transform the environment and land into a productive modern landscape.[4] Without a doubt, as indicated by the concept of "colonial pathologies,"[5] the American "Tropics" became a testing ground of the modern, backed by progressive corporate bureaucracies as well as a scientific network that aimed to advance botany, agriculture and tropical medicine. As a conceptual framework for the discussion of the United Fruit Company, tropical medicine, although

1 United Fruit Company, *Annual Report* (Boston: Medical Department, United Fruit Company, 1922), pp. 72–73.
2 Warwick Anderson, *Colonial Pathologies: American Tropical Medicine, Race, and Hygiene in the Philippines* (Durham: Duke University Press, 2006), pp. 5–6.
3 Ibid.
4 Ibid., p. 7.
5 Ibid.

an ideological construction,[6] was linked to the development of "civic bacteriology," whose activities, from "mapping biological difference onto a 'tropical' territory to mapping human difference and civilizational potential in the new American possessions" became significant in stabilizing the highly hierarchical relationship between the metropolis and its "colonial territories" abroad.[7] This is also true with regard to the contact zone of the United Fruit Company divisions in the Caribbean, ordered as it was by previous colonial powers as a laboratory of hygienic modernity. This contact zone subsequently delimits the frontier that "provides the setting within which the problem of discipline magnifies the savagery that has to be repressed and canalized by the civilizing process," as punctuated by Taussig in another context.[8] Following on from this, as an anxiety, the discourse of otherness finds its correspondence and projection space in the "Tropics." As Anderson describes in relation to Homi Bhabha:

> The sense of menace—"a difference that is almost total but not quite"—could shade into an obsession with mimicry, "a difference that is almost nothing but not quite." In [...] public health programs [...], such figures of paranoia and narcissism, expressed in terms of potential for contamination or as gradations of civic virtue, are held in tension with each other.[9]

I will follow this idea of contamination and the fear of menace in the discourse of the "Tropics" through a series of materials that mirror the laboratory of the modern as representational space. Moreover, in the light of an epistemic violence, the subsequent spatial control and hierarchical organization of the divisions was backed by the scientific discourse of "tropicality"

---

6   Stephan Besser, "Pathographie der Tropen: Literatur, Medizin und Kolonialismus um 1900," (Ph.D. diss., Amsterdam School for Cultural Analysis, 2009), p. 22.
7   Anderson, *Colonial Pathologies*, p. 3.
8   Taussig, *Mimesis and Alterity*, p. 156.
9   Anderson, *Colonial Pathologies*, p. 5.

that reproduced the "environmental otherness" upon which the economic expansion of the United Fruit Company was grounded.[10] Consequently, I return to its photographic archive, but also to the Annual Reports of its Medical Department. The pictures are not understandable if stripped of their main purpose of transforming the Caribbean into a productive and tropical landscape, whose conversion is furthermore realized by a preeminent spatial figure that characterizes this modern political space: the enclave. In their interlocked epistemic relationship, the spatial figure of the enclave and photography describe a mutual process that advances this conversion ascribed to the visual and the spatial. This conversion is backed by the discourse networks of the plantation that, in a similar vein to colonial expansion, are situated at a crossroads of the sciences.

Let me thus turn again to the Company photographic archive. The caption of one picture states "New swimming pool at Hospital Point. Costa Rican Div. Dec. 1923": the picture shows a single concrete wall bordering the sea, whose horizon dissolves in the background of deep gray. Technically deficient, the image shows a technicality: a sort of bulwark or a bulkhead that seemed to be newly erected at the sea, against "nature." It shares with the other pictures of the photographic albums a common language, that of documenting the technical advances in the "Tropics" against major natural threats, such as floods, storms, and other kinds of wild natural eruptions. Moreover, the caption imagines the very modernization the Costa Rica division seems to have experienced; it envisions the installation of modern infrastructure, such as hospitals, as a ground-breaking technical achievement brought to the region. While the visual language remains "documentary" and even neutrally technical, the visual unfolds a complex and complicated relationship between man and "nature" while articulating what is at stake in the undertak-

---

10   See also David Arnold, *The Problem of Nature: Environment, Culture and European Expansion* (London: Blackwell, 1996), p. 143.

Fig. 3.1: "New swimming pool at Hospital Point. Costa Rican Div. Dec. 1923."
Gelatin silver process on paper, 8 x 10 inches. United Fruit Company Photograph Collection, Baker Library, Harvard Business School (olvwork713973).

ings of the Company. Moreover, the visual language of technicality erases any signs of undomesticated and wild "nature."

The pictures included in the Annual Reports of the Medical
Department of the United Fruit Company or the photographic
archive become instrumental in visually stabilizing the plantation economy as a discourse, whose workings, looking at the
tension between technology and the idea of "nature," I address
in this chapter following the question of the instruments of
landscaping and the discourse network. The images play very
subtly on the imaginary of the contamination of the "Tropics,"
by involving a highly technical visual language through which
the abundance of natural resources as a promise of wealth is
domesticated and made economically viable. Yet, this discourse
is principally realized with the circulation of civilizing goods and
through urbanization. Accordingly, the company towns are to
be conceived as neuralgic nodes for establishing and advancing

modern technological and media networks. The company towns are in this sense material networks of processes and techniques that led to the establishment of a global communication of technology and science, in the institutionalization of which the United Fruit Company played a significant role. Specifically, tropical medicine and health helped to reorganize the Caribbean and most notably the Central American divisions and plantations.[11]

How does the visual help shape this discourse of the "Tropics"? How does it participate in establishing the plantation economy? To grasp the visual in the context of a corporate culture challenges the idea of "nature" and the "Tropics" alike in a manifold way. Both the visual and the spatial become the terrains where menace and fear of contamination are most persistently manifested, so they are meticulously controlled by specific scientific discourses. In their particular discourses of botany, agriculture, and tropical medicine, they are preeminently at work in the material networks created by the United Fruit Company, sustaining the violent and lasting transformation of the Caribbean into a laboratory of the modern. As Jill Casid highlights within a colonial regime, landscaping techniques became critical instruments in the spatial "conversion of the colonial landscape machine into a vision of picturesque intermixture,"[12] displacing this fear of contamination and menace onto the visual. This was certainly true for the seventeenth and eighteenth century British Caribbean. By the end of the nineteenth and beginning of the twentieth centuries, under the influence of the United Fruit Company and with the emergence of the "Tropics" within the discourse of tropical medicine, landscape and the idea of intermixture certainly acquired a different and highly critical meaning, expanding the fear of contamination to the spatial and political. This fundamental change in the perception of the "Tropics" and of their discursivity, no longer

11   See Charles Morrow Wilson, *Ambassadors in White: The Story of American Tropical Medicine* (New York: Henry Holt and Company, 1942).
12   Casid, *Sowing Empire*, p. 9.

a sole discourse of potential and abundance, is due to a change occurring in another terrain: that of science. Significantly, around 1890, tropical medicine and the idea of tropical disease powerfully revived the fear of contamination and menace. This first emerged in the European colonial nations and later in the United States, and it defined a new form of knowledge and discipline, but more importantly a form of control over the population and the newly acquired territories abroad. Around 1900 the concept of the "Tropics" obtained a decidedly pathological connotation while generating particular figures of knowledge and a different field of meaning.[13] Moreover, as punctuated by David Arnold, in his discussion of the concept of tropicality, it is clear that the discourse of abundance, through which the Americas always have been imagined and narrated, allowed for the incorporation and appropriation of the "Tropics" through at least three significant processes: first, the control of natural resources; second, the mobilization of non-white labor; third, the mastery over "tropical diseases."[14] He emphasizes that:

> Despite sanitary and medical advances in the nineteenth century, disease remained in the European mind one of the defining characteristics of the tropical world. The emergence of "tropical medicine" as a medical specialism by the 1890s and 1900s served both to celebrate Europe's growing sense of mastery over the tropics and the abiding idea of tropical difference. The very idea of "tropical diseases" and "tropical medicine," always difficult to justify in purely epidemiological terms, since few diseases are in fact unique to the tropics, epitomized the way in which medical science in the imperial age gave its own endorsement to the idea of tropical otherness.[15]

It is true that tropical medicine played a crucial role in the advance and spread of the United Fruit Company divisions, but

13   Besser, "Pathographie der Tropen," p. 10.
14   Arnold, *The Problem of Nature*, p. 163.
15   Ibid., p. 153.

also in the discursivity of the "Tropics" as a distinct and other space to be made economically efficient. To this end, for medical and scientific research, the Company established its own Medical Department with specialized medical personnel sent to the divisions overseas, initiating a series of research activities and communication in the fields of tropical medicine and health.[16] One of the significant publications promoting tropical medicine, thus stabilizing the fear of contamination at the same time as advancing the modern idea of scientific progress, making effective tropicality as an "environmental otherness," was without a doubt the publication of a series of Medical Department Annual Reports between 1912 and 1931. These publications served to inform the medical scientific community at home about different kinds of diseases, not only tropical ones in a strict sense, but also other curiosities or pathological abnormalities occurring in the divisions, while at the same time promoting modern medicine, health, and sanitation as primary corporate achievements.[17] Yet, the Annual Reports remain highly ambivalent and tropical medicine seems to be only an elusive concept here. Significantly, malaria in particular was framed as the major tropical menace to the white Company employee and as such became the emblem of tropical disease to be controlled and conquered in the divisions. The biased medical research favoring malaria as the tropical disease, following corporate interests and manifesting a racialist attitude, is also

---

16   In 1924, the United Fruit Company organized a significant international conference on "tropical America" and health in Kingston, Jamaica, attended by leading figures in the fields of health and tropical medicine. See the *Proceedings of the International Conference on Health Problems in Tropical America*, published by the United Fruit Company in 1924.

17   With regard to the Company medical policies the discursive construction of the "infectious bodies" of the natives and the West Indians follows a bacteriological turn, which is manifested in the emphasis on eradicating malaria and other diseases with drug therapies rather than with broader health measures. The living conditions of the majority of the laborers in the labor camps did not profit from these measures, which principally served the company towns. This certainly reveals, again, the Company spatial policy of hierarchies and segregation materialized in the spatial configuration of the company towns and labor camps.

critically discussed by Aviva Chomsky, when she notes that a large part of the research and health budgets were spent on the few white employees who suffered mostly from malaria, while the other laborers principally died of pulmonary diseases.[18] Besides the fact that the Company medical policies were part of a paternalistic program, "medical policies geared toward maintaining economic efficiency [...] often made the work force anything but contented" and were not at all effective.[19] Chomsky critically points out that "to combat malaria effectively would necessitate a kind of social change that went far beyond the paternalistic benevolence of company policy."[20] This attitude certainly reveals the Company medical policy to have been a highly colonial one, principally serving the Company's own interests and not those of the inhabitants in the respective countries abroad.[21] Yet, malaria as the paradigmatic tropical disease is an interesting lens through which to understand the uneven development of the highly spatially hierarchized and segregated divisions.[22] The Annual Reports quintessentially promote the cure of malaria and help consolidate the image of the United Fruit Company as an important agent of research in tropical medicine. Following strategic interests, the Company appointed the well-known expert and leading figure in tropical research William Edward Deeks as general manager of the Medical Department, a circumstance that helped stabilize the

18   Chomsky, *West Indian Workers*, p. 96.
19   Ibid., p. 94.
20   Ibid., p. 101.
21   It is thus important to underline here that some of the models of tropical medicine in nineteenth-century Latin America had a different impact on the native population's health by seriously involving social change as a prerequisite for controlling tropical diseases. By adapting European models of tropical medicine, the informal Bahian Tropicalista School of Medicine in particular favored comprehensive health measures for a broader Brazilian population. However, generally models of tropical medicine diminished or even denied the connection between socio-economic circumstances and "tropical disorders." See Julyan G. Peard, *Race, Place, and Medicine: The Idea of the Tropics in Nineteenth-Century Brazilian Medicine* (Durham: Duke University Press, 1999).
22   See Chomsky, *West Indian Workers*, p. 100.

discourse of tropical medicine and health. Tropicality in the form of tropical medicine thus became an effective dispositive to help transform the "Tropics" into an economically viable and aesthetic landscape. Moreover, tropical medicine was subsequently converted into a landscaping technique.

The success in controlling malaria, in order to limit the loss of labor days and to make the plantations economically more efficient, was principally linked to sanitation, which was also a side effect of other agricultural measures in technically preparing the terrain for plantation; these measures were already part of primary Company policy.[23] This is visually evinced as the main argument and became the imaginary of the modern chronotope, thus becoming the Company's master narrative. Ultimately, the Annual Reports remain ambivalent about explicit Company policies for the treatment and prevention of malaria. They are of a hybrid nature, promoting research in tropical medicine, reporting about the building activities for the modern hospital infrastructure, and simply depicting spectacular cases of more common diseases that are based on clinical histories, lengthy pathological descriptions, and sensational photographs that relate to a hygienic discourse.

Overall, it is of primary importance to understand the United Fruit Company's undertakings in tropical medicine, the vast institutionalization, and the establishment of a scientific network within the conceptual framework of tropicality.[24] Revealingly, it was the United Fruit Company photographic archive

23   Ibid., p. 103.
24   The institutionalization resulted in the establishment of departments of tropical medicine such as at Harvard University and Tulane University. It is noteworthy that in 1913 Harvard University appointed Richard Pearson Strong (1872–1948) as the first professor for tropical medicine, who was later engaged in several expeditions to South America and Africa, some of them financially and logistically supported by the United Fruit Company. His papers suggest that he was a key figure in bringing together corporate interests with academic and scientific ones. He was the foremost authority in the field of tropical medicine in the United States. See John Farley, *Bilharzia: A History of Imperial Tropical Medicine* (Cambridge: Cambridge University Press, 2003), pp. 128–130.

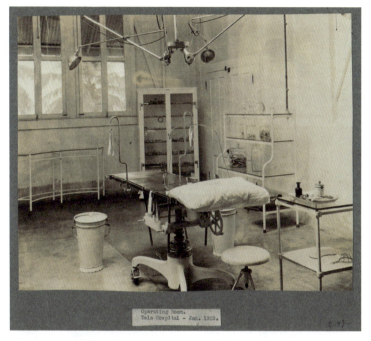

Fig. 3.2: "Operating Room. Tela Hospital – Jan. 1923." Gelatin silver process on paper, 8 x 10 inches. United Fruit Company Photograph Collection, Baker Library, Harvard Business School (olvwork729540).

that indexed the emergent transformed landscape and became itself a tool to integrate the new territories into a modern political space. Moreover, it is the visual that determines an efficient mode of colonization of "tropical land" while making seen the "tropical landscape." It reproduces the very idea of tropicality, that is the representation of the "Tropics," corresponding to a colonial or imperial imagination and experience that could best be described as a pathographical imagination and Western construction of the Other, while emphasizing the idea that the "Tropics" are related to a geographically defined space that was constituted, to a large extent, by its visual and written representations, and specifically by the natural sciences, here geography, climatology, natural history, botany and medicine. The "Tropics" started to be perceived principally as a distinct

Fig. 3.3: "Hospital ward-second class, Tela, Jan. 1923." Gelatin silver process on paper, 8 x 10 inches. United Fruit Company Photograph Collection, Baker Library, Harvard Business School (olvwork729535).

space of knowledge and science. Expanding on Edward Said's concept of Orientalism, it is thus significant that the natural sciences had a prominent role in making the Caribbean the "Tropics," furthering Western forms of othering that yielded considerable geopolitical and cultural entities as objects of an imperial will to knowledge.[25] Significantly, the concepts of both Orientalism and tropicality emphasize the spatiality of these constructs and their discursive character.[26] It is therefore pertinent to join with Arnold in highlighting the related idea of environmental otherness as, in his words, "one of the principal manifestations

25   Said, *Orientalism.*
26   Besser, "Pathographie der Tropen," p. 12.

of environmental otherness in European thought since the fifteenth century has been in terms of a developing distinction between temperate and tropical islands, and that the complex of ideas and attitudes that we will here call 'tropicality' represents environmentalism in one of its most influential and enduring forms."[27] The discursive construction of the "Tropics" disregards their feature as human made cultural landscape, a feature that is particularly stressed by the natural sciences. Human inhabitants of these (island) terrains have the tendency to be invisibilized and made unseen by an exuberant abundance of "tropical nature" that is depicted as alien space or the environmental other. It thus becomes important to pay attention to these discursive scientific constructions of the Caribbean and the specifically scientific dimension of tropicality and, subsequently, the epistemic and aesthetical waywardness of the disciplines and discourses involved, in the case of the United Fruit Company, such as botany and agriculture, archaeology, even urban planning and tropical medicine.[28]

Against this backdrop, this chapter seeks to examine the Caribbean as a transformed geopolitical and knowledge space and thus aims to scrutinize its conversion into a "tropical landscape" that takes place through a series of techniques and landscaping practices deeply rooted in the discourse networks of the plantation. It subsequently charts the Caribbean as a laboratory of the modern, mirrored clearly in the company towns as material modernities, encoded both as utopian and dystopian realms. On the one hand, the United Fruit Company photographs that depict and document the company towns and plantations as a utopian fantasy, imagine a capitalistic economic expansion envisaged as a chronotope of an eternal transition towards modernity. On the other, the images relate, as narratives of the dystopian, to the very processes of modernization that radically reorganize these material modernities through

---

27   Arnold, *The Problem of Nature*, pp. 141–142.
28   Besser, "Pathographie der Tropen," p. 13.

capital and labor. Following the idea of the "colonial archive of land," the chapter seeks to discuss the enclave as a significant spatial and more importantly epistemic figure that corresponds to modern space-time compression and to what have been called discourse networks, but also to the imperial will to knowledge. Significantly, it was the leviathan of the United Fruit Company that pushed the limits of the production of space and capitalism correlating with a modern space of knowledge further into the Caribbean by governing it as the testing ground of the modern.

Colonialism and Landscaping

Looking at the Company photographic archive, on the level of the visual, the photographs belong to the order of landscape, as framing of the plantation economy as landscape seems to be the tendency of the United Fruit Company photographs. As suggested by Jill Casid, the "material practices of transplantation and grafting were part of the ordering and articulation of the Plantation as discourse, that is, these technologies were also codes that reworked these island terrains, endeavoring to resignify marks of transplantation, clearing, deforestation, disindigenation, private property, enclosure, discipline, and monoculture."[29] With these landscaping practices of transplanting machines, plants, and commodities the United Fruit Company meticulously evolved the discourse of plantation in a manifold way. The photographs served as a means to visually frame the plantation economy as a naturalized and tamed landscape. Accordingly, landscaping is a material practice that helps develop "site and sight," into which, Casid argues, are inscribed the technologies of drafting and grafting, cultural techniques that conceal the violent environmental transformation of the modern plantation regime. Casid further observes with regard

---

29   Casid, *Sowing Empire*, p. 2.

to the British colonization of the Caribbean that: "This landscape was to be both the producer and the emblem of imperial power as natural possession through the mythic reimaging of the plantation machine turned homely farm, bringing in its wake not destruction of the indigenous environment but rather agricultural improvement and an effect of pleasing 'variety'."[30] Indeed, most pictures in the Company photographic albums imagine this transformation of land into landscape and in so doing, they envision modernization. Landscape as "a cultural medium," as Mitchell notes, "has a double role with respect to something like ideology: it naturalizes a cultural and social construction, representing an artificial world as if it were simply given and inevitable, and it also makes that representation operational by interpellating its beholder in some more or less determined relation to its givenness as sight and site."[31] Landscape as an evolved site through sight becomes thus a meticulously worked artifact both on the level of representation and material transformation. So landscape is a significant material modernity. In her study Casid illuminates:

> The instruments of colonial relandscaping were not limited to the plow, the hoe, the mill, and the sugar refinery. The reproductive and disseminatory technologies of print and their artifacts—the descriptive and natural histories, topographical maps, drafts of plantation terrain, illustrations of botanical cuttings, and scenic landscape views—worked to produce imperial power as colonial landscaping and were in turn critical instruments in the conversion of the colonial landscape machine into a vision of picturesque intermixture.[32]

She examines this double procedure through the material and the visual, or what is principally the representational, which

---

30 Ibid., p. 8.
31 W. J. T. Mitchell, ed., *Landscape and Power* (Chicago: Chicago University Press, 2002), p. 2.
32 Casid, *Sowing Empire*, p. 9.

helps to effectively transform land into a landscape and make the site through sight. This apparently peaceful transformation, in particular on the level of representation, conceals and displaces, in the Freudian sense, the violence at work. Accordingly, in the making of the colonial and thus imperial landscape not only do machinery and other technological innovations become important means to help transform the Caribbean into this tropical landscape, but also, and even more so, this transformation has to be effectively imagined and mediated, to which end novel representational techniques and means appeared on the scene: they helped establish the plantation as the main regime of the colonial machine. Botany, agriculture, and tropical medicine as decidedly modern sciences became thus strategic knowledges that helped realize the material transformation of the Caribbean. The United Fruit Company was particularly instrumental in tailoring the new fields of modern natural sciences through an emergent corporate-academic complex. Botanical and agricultural material transformations were an effect of previous centuries of the plantation regime, and had been occurring since the sugar plantations of the French and British Caribbean in the seventeenth century. The Company undeniably relied on these technologies, proven efficient in terms of the exploitation of soil and resources. Casid points out that "ideologically and discursively, plantation was often used as a synonym for colony":[33]

> Materially, the construction of the sugar plantations, on which the economy of the British Caribbean islands was based, involved a vast deforestation, the clearing of the undergrowth, and the burning of any remaining roots. This process termed both simply "clearing" and "plantation" made of an overwhelming percentage of the island of Jamaica, for example, the virtual tabula rasa required by the British agriculturalist argument for the right of possession taken from the Roman legal principle of *res nullius*. [...] Plantation and colony were

33   Ibid., p. 7.

interchangeable precisely because effective colonization with "justification" depended on disindigenating, transplanting, and relandscaping the British West Indian island such that the land was made empty and then (re)possessed by its ostentatious cultivation, its agri-culture.[34]

This discursivity or discourse of plantation relates to what Arnold has framed as environmental otherness. It is part of the long experience of transferring and transplanting a manifold variety of grafts from Europe, Asia, Africa and the South Pacific to the Caribbean —a long experience that favored the installation and perfection of the Company's agricultural machine. Likewise, the plantation as a spatial organization became central to the "colonizing" enterprise of the United Fruit Company, which played a particular role in the birth of big business in the United States at the turn of the nineteenth century. Following this, the company town became a significant modern "material technology" in making the plantation viable. Significantly, the formation of two spatial figures, the company town and the enclave, became constitutive of the realization of the plantation as discourse. They became part of the Company's media technologies, brought to the Caribbean islands, which had become the primary "tropical" battleground in the competition of colonial and imperial powers, in particular after the Spanish-American-Cuban war of 1898.

Materially and discursively, "Sowing seed may hold out the promise of regrowth from the soil wherever the winds of dispersion have cast one. But historically it has also been the means of taking possession. In the scene of the founding imperial gesture of sowing seed, to plant was to make colonies."[35] More than just a metaphor or a symbolic act, "sowing seed" is a material practice that involves a complex process of technological and cultural transfer, but also abets an environmental otherness. "Sowing seed" is certainly one of the core material practices deployed by the United Fruit Company, which expanded and

34   Ibid.
35   Ibid., p. xvii.

perfected the modern instruments of landscaping into a rationalized agricultural machinery that invisibilized the industrialized and even violent nature of this transformation. As a constituent and correlative part of botany and agriculture, tropical medicine started to appear on the scene as a landscaping technique, becoming a means for organizing space and for the control of the social body following a highly ideologized rationale. The discursive and material practices, nevertheless, articulate "relations between 'man' and nature and between leisure and work, the rights of property, the founding of nations and empires" and make cultivation and farming metaphors for civilization.[36] Furthermore, this "metaphorical impetus" relates to a geopolitical implication, that is, the imperial seizure of territory and space. Accordingly, the company town is to be conceived as an instrument of imperial landscaping and as a part of the modern spatial reorganization that reflects the emergence of a modern political space. Ascribed to a larger discourse network, company towns are tangible material and spatial articulations and neuralgic nodes in the establishment and advancement of modern technological and media networks. As part of modern landscaping and, moreover, as cultural technique, photography has had a crucial role to play in the representational and even pictorial traditions of landscape. So it is that the Company pictures, of the photographic albums and the Annual Reports of the Medical Department, provoke questions such as: What is the means of photography in imagining landscape, and more specifically the built environment of the company towns and the plantations? How do these pictures manifest the material and technological practices of the Company, and even help constitute them? How do they work as instruments of landscaping?

The company towns in the 1920s and even before were already a cosmopolitan hub, where different people from very distinct areas and for very different reasons crossed the Isthmus of Darien. Not only did the fruit companies generate a flow of

36   Ibid., p. xxii.

people and commodities, but other corporations and governmental personnel also intermingled with them. Since the Americans took over the construction of the Panama Canal, they specially designed spaces that allowed all kinds of leisure activities and amenities. By exposing leisure the pictures promote the inhabitability of the "wild" nature of the "Tropics," erasing visually the imaginary of its menace and contamination altogether, while turning it into a homely land. The unfamiliar, so to speak, remains sealed in the visuality the picture manifests: a visuality that has rendered "nature" domesticated. Pasture grass offers to the eyes an ordered ground, which banishes the "tropical" and all other menacing elements, such as the jungle, onto a distant horizon. Not surprisingly, many of the album pictures adopt a visual language that reassures the viewer's eye and orchestrates the absence of wild nature, concealing the industriousness and the violent nature of the plantation. Moreover, historically, the audience "was exposed continually to stories and pictures romanticizing the frontier and inflating the promise of wealth and self-sufficiency that lay just beyond the frontier."[37] This is particularly so for the Company pictures that were disseminated in the Annual Reports of the Medical Department, showing the leisure facilities for the white American employees.

As argued, the images' predominant discourse is that of landscape, and more precisely that of improving land through agriculture, reproducing the discourse of plantation. In his study, the art historian Joel Snyder brings up a very interesting concept of photography when it comes to discussing landscape. He develops the idea of territorial photography as a type of picture that emerged in around 1870, specifically in the context of survey photography, with the photographer Timothy O'Sullivan when he was exploring the American West. Furthermore, Snyder understands territorial photography as an evolvement, a pictorial discontinuity of a landscape photographic tradition of the nineteenth century. Taking a cue from Snyder, the United Fruit

37   Snyder, "Territorial Photography," p. 190.

Company pictures can also be conceived as "generally descriptive photographs" and were probably taken to "give a sense of the area."[38] Their hidden intention articulates a desire for an encyclopedic recording of everything the camera could capture: the company towns, the building activities, plants and the fruit processing operations, infrastructure, people and things while articulating a collective gaze and displaying the technological nature of agricultural business as modern materiality. Ontologically, Snyder reminds us, photography "was [...] consigned or elevated to the realm of the factual, the material, the physically real."[39] He notes that "By the mid-1860s, photography had entered into popular culture, characterized as a utilitarian medium primarily useful for purposes of documentation because of its contingency upon nature and natural processes."[40] To a certain extent the United Fruit Company photographic practices mirror this understanding of photography, as for the purpose of documentation, deploying it as a utilitarian medium. But the photographs significantly also project a would-be territory; they delimit a new space, while at the same time realizing this space in the moment of its projection. Interestingly, Snyder observes:

> O'Sullivan's photographs work not so much to delineate a territory of potential American States as they do not define a very difficult kind of territory—one that we would now call a field, a discipline—that could properly be investigated only by the new elite [...]. O'Sullivan's illustrations provide visual, photographic proof of the unknown character of the land and imply the need to gain power over it by coming to know it. The job is to probe the territory, subject it to scientific examination, thus understanding what it can tell us about its past and how it can be used in the future. [...] O'Sullivan's photographs thus introduced their audience to a new domain—it is not a geographic region but *the territory of modern science and its attendant professionals*. These pic-

38   Ibid., p. 192.
39   Ibid., p. 181.
40   Ibid.

tures are territorial, but they adumbrate a territory unapproachable in terms of representational schemes that are the common property of the propertied [...]. They work the beginning of an era—one in which we still live—in which expert skills provide the sole means of access to what was once held to be part of our common inheritance.[41]

Although the photographs from the Company photographic archive did not circulate widely, some pictures were explicitly circulated in specific contexts predestinated to reach expert eyes. As such, the Annual Reports of the Medical Department become a significant medium to visualize and articulate this new territory of modern science, a territory subjected to scientific examination. Brought together, the photographic archive and the Annual Reports envision the utopian dream of modernization, of a scientific and technological progress still to come. But, in the "territory" of tropical medicine and health, it becomes clear that this scientific progress is only imagined for the white employees, leaving the others on the verge of poverty and malnutrition. The Company photographic archive thus shares the adumbration of a "territory unapproachable in terms of representational schemes that are the common property of the propertied"—in this respect they differ from what Casid has observed with regard to the representational means of images, because they avoid the picturesque as one of the dominant representational schemes of framing landscape. But they share the idea of progress that was "understood in terms of ownership and industrial development of the land and its resources."[42] In this regard, the United Fruit Company photographic archive remains ambivalent and elusive, as it seems that the meaning of its images was at stake in the different discourses outside it, in "the territory of modern science and its attendant professionals."[43]

41   Ibid., pp. 199–200, my emphasis.
42   Ibid., p. 188.
43   Ibid., p. 199.

Discourse Networks

> There are quite a lot of Spaniards and various nationalities on
> board. Colon is the center of the universe as far as shipping is con-
> cerned, one gets a boat to almost any part from here on Panama.[44]

It is certainly true that the Isthmus of Darien has always been a
busy contact zone, ever since the Spanish conquest. Moreover, by
the turn of the nineteenth century it had become a cosmopolitan
and global one, perceived also by United Fruit Company employee
Everett Brown, who wrote about it in his letters to his wife. Significantly, the Caribbean and in particular the Atlantic coast of the
Isthmus of Darien experienced early the hub of naval outposts,
botanical experiments, and migration flows and thus became one
of the modern compressed time-spaces in the circum-Caribbean.
These geographical and even more so geopolitical circumstances
shaped the company town as a privileged figure of the capitalist production of space. Furthermore, they favored its establishment as a nodal point, at an infrastructural level. This not only
enabled the development and deployment of modern technological inventions, such as the telegraph or the early radio that
coalesced around the building of a modern harbor network, but
even more so fostered entrepreneurial innovations. Focusing on
the material and technological transfers I discuss the discourse
network in this particular historical setting, which grounded the
production of space of the company town and the plantation.
With regard to the monocultural plantation as a long-lasting bio-
geographical intervention and the company town as an urban-
agricultural one, it is important to recall that the very beginnings
of the banana trade were rooted in them being understood as a
technological improvement and rationalization of landscape.
They were significantly enabled by another technological inter-

---

44   Everett Brown, "Sept 12, 1920, on board SS Ulloa, at dock, Colon," in *Everett C. Brown Papers, 1919–1921*, Special and Area Studies Collections, George A.
Smathers Libraries, University of Florida, Gainesville.

vention, that of the railroad, which could best be captured as an effect of transmission, or what is referred to in Friedrich Kittler's media history as *Übertragung* or *Rückkopplung*.[45]

In his study, Friedrich Kittler makes a very different point about the relationship between nature and technology when discussing the phonograph, which he conceives, alongside innovations such as the typewriter, to be one of the major modern technical inventions of the turn of the twentieth century. Accordingly, both technologies are groundbreaking, inasmuch as they provoke a radical reorganization of the senses and knowledge production. As modern media they not only extend our "nervous system" but complement it, and radically change the perception of our senses and ourselves vis-à-vis the world. Thereby, the phonograph and, I add, the photographic camera as novel media technologies and sensory apparatuses transform the very senses of listening and seeing and with them the undertakings of knowledge production. Kittler conceives transgression/transfer (*Übertragung*) very literally or even materially. He affirms: "Acoustics arises from physiology, technology from nature."[46] Consequently, transgression describes a principle that allows us to focus on the question of how discourses are shaped by technical media. Kittler thus calls attention to the identifiable formations of discourse, which he understands as discourse network, that is: "The term *discourse network* [...] can also designate the network of technologies and institutions that allow a given culture to select, store, and process relevant data."[47] I argue that discourse networks become primarily relevant when addressing the concern about imperialism, as they reflect the complex dimension of the cultural. In his study, Kittler identifies two exemplary epochal thresholds that defined new discourse networks, the first around 1800 and the second around 1900, both linked to

45   Friedrich A. Kittler, "Aufschreibesysteme 1800/1900. Vorwort," *Zeitschrift für Medienwissenschaft* 6 (2012), pp. 117–126.
46   Friedrich A. Kittler, *Discourse Networks, 1800/1900* (Stanford: Stanford University Press, 1990), p. 44.
47   Ibid., p. 369.

the emergence of novel technical data storage and technological innovations. With these discourse networks a paradigm shift of knowledge production occurred that was altered by and even dependent upon the new media technologies.[48]

Without entering into the argument on how the Foucauldian discourse analysis is turned into a media-technological one, an ongoing debate which is centered on the technological formation of discourse as discourse network, I wish, nevertheless, to stress two operational procedures that fundamentally characterize discourse networks and that become relevant for the United Fruit Company's implementation of modern science in the Caribbean: first, transmitting and, second, storing. Again, Kittler describes three basic media-functions, namely, transmitting, storing and processing data. The first refers to communication and telecommunications as media's capacity to overcome long spatial distances, the second refers to the surmounting of time, and relates to formations of tradition and cultural continuities.[49] These two operational procedures are relevant for my argument, as the discourse network of the plantation relies upon these two fundamental operations: transmitting and storing. Whereas the procedure of storing is related to the photographic archive itself, I expand now on the procedure of transmitting in order to discuss it as a material process and thus media materialization. Transmitting as a material practice also describes the railroad as the very foundational undertaking of the Company's banana production, and, henceforth, the materialization of the chronotope as eternal transition towards modernity. Railroads in Central America, most notably in Costa Rica, are conceived as the beginnings of the story of the banana business. This was conspicuously the work of Minor Cooper Keith, who was then engaged with the construction of railroads,

---

48   Geoffrey Winthrop-Young, *Kittler and the Media* (Cambridge: Polity Press, 2011), pp. 58–59.
49   Hartmut Winkler, "Prozessieren. Die dritte, vernachlässigte Medienfunktion," in *Media Theory in North America and German-Speaking Europe* (Vancouver: University of British Columbia, 2010), p. 1.

in a moment when the Costa Rican government was gloriously failing, technically, as an entrepreneur, following a number of attempts going back as far as the 1840s.[50] It is told that Keith primarily began his business in Costa Rica with his brother-in-law Henry Miggs in 1871, when he was invited to work with him on the contract for the construction of the railroad from San José to the port of Limón. After several setbacks and major financial difficulties, he was able to finally finish the railroad construction in 1890. This is considered to be a kind of foundational act of the banana business, and Keith entered it formerly in 1899 as the founder of the United Fruit Company merger with Andrew Preston and Lorenzo Baker from the Boston Fruit Company. Keith then became Vice-President of the United Fruit Company and mainly took over the overseas business in Central America, while continuing with the railroad projects. The narrative trope of making nature accessible through the mediation of technology is important here. In this case, railroads were the primary technology that reconnected the American continent. As an efficient technology the railroad became the very condition of the possibility to advance industrial capitalism into remote and previously inaccessible lands and to advance an imperial colonialism. This foundational fiction, retold many times, reproduces the mythical beginnings of the success story of the bananas of the United Fruit Company.

However, alongside the technological foundations of the banana trade, a quintessential aspect continues to be overlooked. I focus here on the operational procedure of transmitting (data) and discuss it against the backdrop of what Kittler conceived as *Übertragung*, that is, one of the basic functions of media. Interestingly, media-functions are defined by the concurrence of heterogeneous (historical) moments, to which technical apparatuses as well as symbolisms, institutional circumstances,

---

50   Watt Stewart, *Keith and Costa Rica: A Biographical Study of Minor Cooper Keith* (Alburquerque: University of New Mexico Press, 1964), pp. 2ff.

Fig. 3.4: "#6358. Truxillo RR Co. Aguan Canal Project, Construction of Headgate, 1925." Gelatin silver process on paper, 8 x 10 inches. United Fruit Company Photograph Collection, Baker Library, Harvard Business School, Box 14.

practices and forms of knowledge belong.[51] This is certainly valid for the concurrence of heterogeneous moments in the specific historical constellation that determines the railroad as a medium, when technical apparatuses and novel technologies, such as the photographic camera, made new lands accessible and enhanced Keith's entrepreneurship. This case is not unique to Costa Rica, it mirrors a media effect that reshaped the entire American continent and determined inter-American relations at the beginning of the twentieth century. At the center of these relationships were new discourse networks, based upon novel communication and telecommunication apparatuses. In the case of Costa Rica and Keith, the railroad became a medium to foster the discourse of the banana plantation. It remains note-

51   Joseph Vogl, "Medien-Werden: Galileis Fernrohr," *Archiv für Mediengeschichte* 1 (2001), p. 122.

worthy, with regard to the biology of the fruit, that the banana as a very delicate and perishable fruit could only be turned into a natural commodity because of this media network, as it is based on the reciprocity between 'nature' and technology and, moreover, on a technologized nature.

This relationship of "nature" and technology is also visually manifested in the Company photographic archive and is defined by the discourse of science, first and foremost of tropical medicine, botany and agriculture, but also archaeology. Yet, the photographs in their ambivalence and elusiveness play on this constant tension between what is to be conceived as technology and what is ideologically articulated as "nature." I expand on the concept of transmission here as a basic function of media that describes the workings of the landscaping techniques and eventually of territorial photography within the discourse networks of science. Wolfgang Schäffner reminds us:

> Beyond the routes of the old roads that organized colonial space, a large part of the territory remained, for centuries, a "*terra incognita*" or "lost world". This lack of communication between the many "parts" of the continent gave rise to different technical and scientific projects that aimed to explore them and integrate them into the different national territories [...]. On the one hand, the engineers—many of whom came from Europe—proposed enormous projects to install, in collaboration with European companies and the new Nation States, rail roads and telegraphs, the most important means of communication of the nineteenth century. On the other hand, there were the scientists, who went on their expeditions to travel these unknown areas and, in that way, collaborate in the development of the territory.[52]

In a similar fashion, banana production after its experimental initialization was stabilized within the discourse networks

---

52   Wolfgang Schäffner, "Los medios de comunicación y la construcción del territorio en América Latina," *História, Ciências, Saúde – Manguinhos* 15:3 (2008), p. 812, my translation.

Fig. 3.5: "No. 6652 – Engineer's Camp Cars on Siding at Kilo. 82.0, Mendez Farm Truxillo Railroad Company, Nov. 6, 1926." Gelatin silver process on paper, 8 x 10 inches. United Fruit Company Photograph Collection, Baker Library, Harvard Business School, Box 14.

of science. As medium the railway not only connected parts of the national territory that previously did not communicate with each other, but also in the case of the United Fruit Company facilitated the overcoming of long spatial distances that delineated a so far unknown transnational space, literally disconnecting the coastal parts from the capital of the interior. This could happen because the banana business and with it the use of the railways were entirely controlled by the Company. Spatially, vast terrains were reconnected to form a new territory suitable for banana production that rapidly and voraciously required more and more land. This may seem, at first glance, to be a trivial observation, but it is not: the railroad became here a kind of media-event. The railroad was possible because of the very occurrence of a diverse range of historical moments, which it simultaneously stabilized and reinforced, such as the availability of land for potential monoculture banana production, the corporation as a novel institutional framework, and the banana as an emerging natural commodity on the newly established global market. Moreover, this new media subsequently enabled the circulation of scientists who enhanced a new knowledge production along the routes in the diverse related disciplinary fields while creating new circuits:

> The telegraph networks that connect everyone in an instant create the simultaneity of a territory, the disappearance of distances for the communication of information, and the strange effects of the incongruence of time in this new telecommunication pace. Although the telegraph lines are physical installations that cover enormous distances, they create the paradox that those same lines dissolve the distances of metric space through the speed of their transmission. In this way, the lines of communication of objects and people reduce space to straight lines.[53]

Around the time of the initiative of railroad construction in Costa Rica and subsequently in Santa Marta, Colombia, the United Fruit Company became involved in the discovery of another means of communication that quickly evolved as a strategically important technology and, henceforth, became an important corresponding medium: the radio. This is depicted in the Company photographic archive, but also imagined as a technological rationalization within the Medical Department Annual Reports. The many pictures show the technological achievements and technical transfers the Company realized and constantly advanced. Moreover, they orchestrate and display the diverse technical apparatuses and technological installations made in the divisions, relevant not only for the agricultural operations but also for other communication processes. As a foundational and hence technological fiction, the pictures speak to us about the use of media and orchestrate these technological achievements as an overcoming of space and time, thus outlining the Company's chronotope of the modern.

---

53 Ibid., p. 816, my translation.

Fig. 3.6: "Radio station office and operating room, Santa Marta, Colombia, Dec. 17, 1925." Gelatin silver process on paper, 8 x 10 inches. United Fruit Company Photograph Collection, Baker Library, Harvard Business School (olvwork717365).

These pictures represent a type of picture series that meticulously documents diverse technical apparatuses. They show the radio station office and operating room in the Colombian division of Santa Marta, in 1925, and the room's interior with the installed radio, which represented the highest standard of radio technology of that time. The images capture the radio station towers and antennas, focusing thus on the technicality of landscape, and remind us of the primarily technical features of the company towns. Moreover, they reflect the material transformation of land into a technological artifact altogether, molding this previously cleared "natural" land into a viable and single constituent of the mechanization of nature, by both delineating it spatially and reconnecting it to the outside with technical artifacts such as cables, towers, antennas, fences and buildings. Space is literally traversed by the new communication media, while it is simultaneously abstracted by it, as it seems that the fundamental characteristics of space, distance, and extension are rapidly overcome. As the pictures show, the material transformation, which reflects this fundamental media operation of transmitting, is highly technological and manifests another operation here: that of speed and acceleration. This latter operation stabilizes media as media, both railroad and radio, within their effects, functions, social and material practices and in their roles as specific cultural techniques. Yet, the pictures also become "documents" of a visual self-assurance and promote the narrative of a technical reification of the plantation.[54] We read in the United Fruit Company Annual Report:

> As long ago as 1904—the very infancy of Radio—the United Fruit Company was pioneering in Inter-American Communications. Starting with two small stations located in Costa Rica and Panama, the system rapidly expanded through the Middle American area and aboard vessels of the Great White Fleet. The general public early began to make use of it too. This growing public demand led to the organization in 1913 of the Tropical Radio Telegraph Company, wholly-owned subsidiary of the United Fruit Company. Today, stations of Tropical and its affiliates dot the Middle American area on the east and west coasts and in the capital cities, maintaining direct connection with associate stations of others in South and North America, as well as all ship stations of the Company's fleet and the Company's own stations in Boston, Miami and New Orleans. Today, the parent Company has in Tropical America the required facilities for fast communication between the Americas, both by radiotelephone and radiotelegraph. It is significant that this subsidiary, originally designed

54   It is important to conceive the Great White Fleet or the ships as *media*, on which the Company heavily relied and which it developed into a modern transportation means even for touristic purposes in the Caribbean. In the Annual Reports the Company frequently praised the development of the Great White Fleet. See United Fruit Company, *Annual Report* (Boston: Medical Department, United Fruit Company, 1948), p. 22. Furthermore, the ships seemed to be frequently used in military missions during the Cold War and to have significantly supported the transfer of communications and materials.

purely for Company service, has now become an important medium of instantaneous communication in the public service. Not only does the system permit the parent Company to coordinate its operations on almost a split-second basis of timing; but in providing these same facilities for the governments and peoples of the three Americas, it is making a decided contribution toward continued expansion of trade and cultural relationships in the Western Hemisphere.[55]

As has been addressed by previous historical studies,[56] the Company's radio activity founded the technical operations of banana production, while pioneering in the early radio business in Central America and the Caribbean. This was possible because of the Company's institutional involvement, which has been mostly overlooked when it comes to discussing the radio as a novel technology that was linked with fruit production. From within this institutional-scientific entanglement, as a prefiguration of the Cold War military-industrial-academic complex, and the emergence of a new modern political space, the enclave became a privileged spatial figure that corresponds to the discourse networks of science. In this context, the radio and the railroad are key technologies that enabled the processes of transmission and subsequently helped establish the modern plantation as a discourse. Moreover, both the railroad and the radio telegraph system are media in a historically situated context, and both were systematically installed by the United Fruit Company. The railroad was a material medium that allowed for operations of tropical fruits and other freights, organized through different but intertwined processes in a complex network of specialized subsidiaries. Meanwhile, as it channeled

---

55   United Fruit Company, *Annual Report 1948*, p. 22.
56   Adams, *Conquest of the Tropics*; R. Mason, "The History of the Development of the United Fruit Company's Radio Telegraph System," *Radio Broadcast* 1 (1922); Charles David Kepner and Jay Henry Soothill, *The Banana Empire: A Case Study of Economic Imperialism* (New York: The Vanguard Press, 1935); Christina S. Drale, "The United Fruit Company and Early Radio Development," *Journal of Radio and Audio Media* 17:2 (2010).

Fig. 3.7: "Radio station towers and antennas, Santa Marta, Colombia, Dec. 17, 1925." Gelatin silver process on paper, 8 x 10 inches. United Fruit Company Photograph Collection, Baker Library, Harvard Business School (olvwork717370).

primarily information data, the radio was a technical means that facilitated, first and foremost, a direct communication between the different United Fruit divisions and the United States. Second, this media apparatus later became to a certain extent a form of commercial wireless service to the public, giving the region, particularly Central America, a highly developed international communication structure. Yet, this media apparatus was not used for broadcasting services and programming (as happened in the US at that same time), because this was not the primary corporate interest.[57] The early radio telegraph system and later the wireless one, once it was working as a reliable 24-hour communication technology, served primarily as media for internal communication and thus processed data within the

57   Drale, "The United Fruit Company," p. 208.

165

Company's units, becoming a technical means for the banana business. Importantly, the fundamental feature of this type of business is the timely coordination of the different and interrelated fruit processing operations, of picking, transportation to the ports, and shipping on time to the United States or Europe, before the delicate fruit would perish. The Company thus targeted first and foremost time and space, to which these technological innovations principally correlate.

The Company was involved with leading engineers and scientists and was constantly in search of pioneering techniques in early telegraphy technology, which it tested on and expanded into the divisions in the Caribbean and Central America.[58] The Company created the subsidiary Tropical Radio Telegraph Company to establish radio and telephone services on so-called "Fruit Company Territory." As early as 1904, the United Fruit Company had established limited telegraph and telephone exchanges between some of its division headquarters and plantations.[59] As key technologies, both the railway and the radio or telegraph became an early and integral part—as conditions of possibility—of the banana business, though both technologies were sensitive and vulnerable means in the territory of the "Tropics." Here, again, the topos of "wild" and "dangerous" nature is flamboyantly at work in the historiographies of both the railroad and telecommunications. Both technologies became media that realized the basic function, that of transmitting, thus becoming a crucial operation of the Company. In 1941, the Tropical Radio chief engineer Charles Harris proudly states that the Company's "system [...] comprises nineteen owned shore stations in Central America and the West Indies and approximately one hundred ship stations. It is handling approximately 7.600.000 words of paid public message traffic, 1.500.000 words of Press transmissions and approximately 182.000 minutes of radiotelephone

58 Mason, "The History of the Development of the United Fruit Company's Radio Telegraph System."
59 Ibid.

calls."[60] However, as Roy Mason underscores with regard to the use of this kind of technology in political operations, "during the period of the Nicaraguan revolution and for a considerable time thereafter, the Colon-Port Limon radio route was one of the fastest and most accurate telegraphic routes in the world."[61] Interestingly, he goes on to say:

> It was during this period that the Company made it a standard require-
> ment of its service for all receiving operators to transcribe radio mes-
> sages directly on the typewriter. Although used in wire telegraph
> offices for a long time previous, typewriters had not up to this time
> been considered essential as a time-saving factor in the receipt and
> delivery of radio messages. So far as known, this is the earliest adop-
> tion of typewriters as standard equipment for a ship or shore radio sta-
> tion, and the United Fruit Company was the first to make compulsory
> the use of the typewriter by radio operators.[62]

The technical apparatuses and novel technologies, both the typewriter and the radio, significantly helped establish a new business in the case of banana production. They connected, accordingly, sound and writing into shared and even corre-sponding material practices. And yet, at this early time of radio technology it seems that the written word was still more reli-able than the spoken, as unreliable as the early telegraphic ser-vice used to be, suffering frequent physical threats by torrential downpours, washouts, floods and delays because of "unmerci-ful static [which] rendered [the stations] nearly useless for most of the year" in the "Tropics."[63] When the Company started to opt for the wireless radio technology, land lines were nevertheless often maintained by governments, and old-fashioned transmis-sion systems were kept between the divisions, such as local mes-

---

60   Cited in Drale, "The United Fruit Company," p. 205.
61   Mason, "The History of the Development of the United Fruit Company's Radio Telegraph System," p. 387.
62   Ibid.
63   Drale, "The United Fruit Company," p. 199.

sengers, which frequently substituted for the new wireless radio transmission. It is remarkable, though, that listening and writing seemed to be the most sensitive and secretive material practices of the United Fruit Company, in the face of ongoing technological advances. They were the nucleus of the development of high technology delimiting a field of control. These very processes of transmitting seemed to be directly linked to reading and listening as primary sensory practices that complimented that of seeing, as evinced by the Company's use of photography. Literally, the Company kept the written and spoken word as a private and corporate secret. This is because the Company relied on the word being kept secret in a situation of complicated institutional entanglement, involving different players, such as the US Government, the military, scientific and industrial entities, in order to maintain its tactical advantage and dominance both in Central America and the United States.[64] Moreover, it is the word—and the image—that is the material to be most carefully processed, transmitted and stored. Accordingly, both technologies, the railroad and the radio, became the primary media of discourse networks that fostered the expansion of a corporate capitalism, correlating with the now technologically possible compression

---

64   Christina Drale depicts this entanglement against the backdrop of the Company's business strategy, which supersedes the core business of banana production towards a strategic diversification to dominate core markets, such as telecommunications, to this day. The Tropical American Telephone Company did not just disappear, but was bought out many times and transformed by various other companies: "The dominance of United Fruit in early Central American radio development and its alliance with the U.S. radio cartel gave it a strong tactical advantage in the tropical fruit industry leading to its supremacy in the world banana market and its elevated influence on the Central American political economy. Its emphasis on business applications and point-to-point transmission also meant that broadcast radio in this region would follow a slow evolutionary path over many decades rather than a rapid, corporate sponsored diffusion as it did in the United States and other developed nations. A slower indigenous development of broadcast radio in Central America may have been in its best long-term interests. Had the United Fruit developed its own programming network, it would have been very difficult for local interests to compete effectively and the fruit company would have had yet another tool of influence in the 'Fruit Company Territory'." Drale, "The United Fruit Company," p. 208.

of space and time and allowing for the imagined and realizable chronotope of an eternal transition towards modernity.

I thus conceive the discourse network as the founding principle of the plantation. Against the backdrop of the material transplantation and the technological grounds of the materialities of this network, which convert the plantation into a "real" and physical machine, the representational, the imaginary, and even the ideological should be reconsidered. Let me recall, at this point, some of the main characteristics of discourse networks. As discussed in recent media studies, Kittler refers explicitly with this term to Foucault's concept of discourse, focusing thereby on the channels through which discourses are made and received. Subsequently, he focuses on the practices that underline an understanding of the cultural *a priori*, focusing on what came before, the prior reification of apparatuses and substances "to allow access to the verbs and operations, from within which the nouns and artifacts first originated."[65] Accordingly, cultural techniques, sciences, and art forms are entangled in a "'co-determining network of historical relations' [...], that does not put any of its components as transcendental or ahistorical, but rather [...] offers in their interconnectivity the possibility of a reciprocal stabilization."[66] What is brought into focus by such a methodological and henceforth conceptual approach are the "'cyclical chains of the translation process between signs, persons, and things,' or 'the chains of operations [that] precede the media concept [...]'."[67] We find thus a "constant medial >translation/transmission< performance between the involved entities."[68]

Kittler's *Discourse Networks* can be understood as a rereading of Foucault's discourse analysis in *Archaeology of Knowledge*, which seems to describe the "systems as systems, that is,

65   Schüttelpelz cited in Matthias Koch and Christian Köhler, "Das kulturtechnische Apriori Friedrich Kittlers," *Archiv für Mediengeschichte* 13 (2013), p. 158, my translation.
66   Ibid., p. 159, my translation.
67   Ibid., p. 158, my translation.
68   Ibid., p. 159, my translation.

to describe them from the outside and not merely from a position of interpretive immanence."[69] Kittler's point is that "Archeologies of the present must also take into account data storage, transmission, and calculation in technological media."[70] I underline this aspect for my overall argument and relate it to the entanglement of media, persons, codes and things that determines the United Fruit Company's production of space, that is best described as a media knowledge complex. This definition of cultural techniques and how they work becomes particularly relevant for the understanding of the media materialities that characterize the undertakings of the United Fruit Company and how it fostered novel technologies and a seemingly efficient organizational apparatus for channeling information. Accordingly, discourse networks here may describe an analytical perspective. Interestingly, discourse networks require permanent work and stabilization. So, there is a constant exchange within the reciprocal relationships of the network between the human and non-human actors.[71] With regard to the United Fruit Company, it is clear that the company town as a spatial figure is stabilized as a constituent within this network of technical artifacts and apparatuses, people and capital. Moreover, it is stabilized as a media materiality within the Company's discourse networks, through which the necessary permanent exchange of constant and reciprocal interrelation takes place. Returning to this initial understanding of the plantation as a discourse, in a Foucauldian sense, I can now advance the following argument: the plantation could only work within this discourse network. Moreover, the very material processes of transplanting and transferring are constituent parts of the chains of cultural operation that stabilized the plantation as a discourse and helped convert the Caribbean into a laboratory of the modern, which the Company reproduced as a capitalist complex.

69   Kittler, *Discourse Networks*, p. 369.
70   Ibid.
71   Koch and Köhler, "Das kulturtechnische Apriori," pp. 163–164.

Company Towns

"We break into the wilderness and make things ready for civilization," writes the United Fruit Company employee Everett Brown
in a letter to his wife Ethel, telling about his fantasies and his
desire to join the Company.[72] As a sort of *en route* writing,[73] he
shares with his loved ones his feelings and states of mind, such
as his quarrels, but even more so he bears witness to the routes
he follows, meandering across the Caribbean between 1919 and
1920. These are rare and singular written documents; as intimate
letters, they give glimpses into the fissures and discontinuities
of the imagined chronotope of the United Fruit Company. Not
only does Brown give an account, from a subjective point of view,
of the internal workings of the Company and of the making of
(neo)colonial subjectivities, including himself as an employee,
but he also materializes his very subjective fears. This "wilderness" is domesticated by the implementation of a fictitious and
projected chronotope, outlined by routes, railways, the company
towns, and the labor camps that become the spatial configuration of the transformation of "nature" into land, and land into an
improved agricultural landscape. "At present the valley is virgin
forest," Brown notes, "but in a few weeks' time the land will be
planted with bananas and the trees all cut. In 18 months more
you may eat some of the bananas from this very section."[74] The
letters were sent from the divisions and plantations of the Company, from Cuba, Panama, and Costa Rica, to Swampscott in
Massachusetts, meticulously following the routes that are related
to the radical transformation of the Caribbean into a modern
space. In the first critical study of the United Fruit Company,
Charles Kepner vividly observes, establishing herewith a recur-
ring trope in the historiography of modernity and more precisely
that of the Western relationship with technology and "nature":

72 *Everett C. Brown Papers, 1919–1921*, May 29, 1920.
73 Brita Brenna et al., eds., *Routes, Roads and Landscapes* (Surrey: Ashgate, 2011).
74 *Everett C. Brown Papers, 1919–1921*, May 29, 1920.

171

On other plots of land active centers of human habitation had sprung, not Caribbean towns, but bits of New England and Jamaica, transplanted to Central American shores. Near the seaports many acres were cleared for the company's employees. Less pretentious cottages are variously located, some in slightly residential sections, others facing sooty railroad yards. Railroad shops, roundhouses, freight yards, wharves, lighthouses, water works, sewerage systems, commissary stores, storehouses, electric light plants, bakeries, laundries, schools and churches, hotels, clubhouses and athletic fields are included in the physical outlay of these mushroom towns. Most conspicuous and appealing in the division headquarters are the eleven hospitals, some of which are plain wooden buildings, but others of which compare favorably on architecture with medical centers in the United States and Europe. Behind the larger buildings are long lines of stereotyped labor camps, small, plain and solid, which in most of the company's establishments are painted yellow. Throughout the banana districts are farms, each of which contains a similar long line of connected labor camps and an individual camp for the foreman. Separated from these camps by green screens of tropical foliage is the bungalow where the *mandador* (overseer) and his timekeeper reside. The fruit companies are not only producers of bananas and builders of cities but also operators of transportation and communication systems.[75]

The genealogy of the company town as a spatial form of capital and labor within the production of space has been studied quite extensively, because as a new spatial and urban form it began to expand into large remote and mostly rural areas that became industrialized in the second half of the nineteenth century in the Americas. Understood as an urban formation within a corporate regime, the many company towns quickly became symbols not only of industrialization but also of an urbanization process that started to shape these remote rural areas, which hitherto had lacked any kind of infrastructure. Moreover,

75   Charles David Kepner, *Social Aspects of the Banana Industry* (New York: Columbia University Press, 1936), pp. 17–18.

the company town quickly became an emblem of a modernization process that reorganized labor and capital through space and subsequently reshaped social relations by implementing a novel spatial and organizational apparatus. Based on modern principles of efficient spatial organization, tested already elsewhere as urban and architectural elements, as domestic and vernacular architectures following an ideological consensus on a rigid spatial organization shaped by modern ideas of social hygiene and labor control that belonged to the very idea of industrial capitalism; in the Americas, at least, company towns were the other face of the Southward advance of industrialism. As both spatial form and modern figure, the company town and the plantation intertwined and molded the material and environmental transformation of the Caribbean and Central America. As "'deliberate efforts to shape the built environment in particular ways,' [...] the so-called logic of capitalism was to create powerful symbols of modernity that would both impress the outside world and 'civilize' the locals—in most cases, rural peoples. In these 'spaces of transnational interaction,' industrial capitalism not only transformed peoples and landscapes but also had to adapt to local circumstances."[76] In their study of company towns in the Americas, the historians Oliver Dinius and Angela Vergara frame the company town this way:

> Company towns played a similar role [...] in the economic and social history of all parts of the Americas. They pushed the frontier of industrial capitalism into new areas. Mining, logging, and railroad towns, in particular, became outposts of industrial modernity connecting remote and sparsely settled areas to urban centers and strengthening their integration into the nation-state. Not unlike trading posts or military forts in earlier stages of the colonization of the Americas, they brought more land, more natural resources, and more people (i.e.

76   Oliver J. Dinius and Angela Vergara, eds., *Company Towns in the Americas: Landscape, Power, and Working-Class Communities* (Athens: University of Georgia Press, 2011), p. x.

workers and consumers) under the control of European colonizers and their descendants. [...]. Conceiving of company towns in terms of their place on the frontier embeds them in the larger narrative of European colonization in the Americas and emphasizes the spatial dimension of industrial development.[77]

They propose a concept of the company town as a contact zone, which became "an important element of inter-American relations in the twentieth century and reinforced their neocolonial character."[78] Though company towns were tested and endorsed long before the banana industry reached its height with the United Fruit Company, their typical spatial character was developed further and perfected by this transnational corporation. As early as 1905, the urbanization of the Caribbean by the United Fruit Company had already given significant shape to the built environment, at least on the Caribbean coasts of both the Atlantic part of Central America and, to a lesser extent, the island terrains. This urbanization process was uneven, due to different historical constellations: some parts around the Panama Canal, such as Panama and Costa Rica, but also Cuba and Jamaica, had already experienced considerable urbanization in the spatial form of company towns, but also earlier plantations of a more agro-urban character that were subjected to modern industrialization related to the sugar industry.

I wish to expand the concept of instruments of landscaping towards the complex form of early urbanization or the urban-industrial built environments, enhanced by a systemic material and technological transfer, which is not limited to machinery, technical plans or drafts. With this material and technological transfer an intrinsically intertwined cultural transfer is made that is related to the knowledge of manufacturing and later industrial techniques that further significantly transformed the Caribbean. The company town became an infrastructural

77 Ibid., pp. 4–5.
78 Ibid., p. 4.

complex and thus a nodal point of an advancing capitalism that materializes as the constitutive interrelationship between routes, roads and the making of landscape.[79] Accordingly, the company town is a significant constituent of the discourse networks, inasmuch as it advances the technical making of sensory media.[80] So the company town not only refers to a single monopolistic urban entity, a single identifiable town, but, more significantly, is a sign of a network of towns that facilitates and enhances an infrastructural complex allowing for technological transfer and innovation. Correspondingly, the emergence of the company town as a spatial-medial form correlates to the development of the technology of an industrial capitalism expanding towards the Global South.

Along the routes of the railways and ships the enhancement of a modern urbanization took place, which shaped the newly accessed land, transforming it into a recognizable and "healthy" landscape. The company towns and ports become the nodal points of a continuously advancing infrastructural network, which built up the plantation as discourse.[81] Moreover, it is the ship, the radio and the railroad that made the company town work as a nodal point and literally materialized the network by introducing a new sensory apparatus and deploying novel technological means, through which the global was connected with the local, thus incorporating the Caribbean into an orbit of Western knowledge.

Health authorities, following the routes of the United Fruit Company, thus encountered advanced sanitation works, upon which the company towns were founded. They visited the modern towns of Port Limón in Costa Rica; Bocas del Toro in Panama, with its singular and symbolic quarantine island, an

79   See Brenna, *Routes, Roads and Landscapes*.
80   Friedrich A. Kittler, *Grammophon, Film, Typewriter* (Berlin: Brinkmann & Bose, 1986), p. 79.
81   See also *Quarantine Tour of Central America and Panama by Health Authorities as Guests of the United Fruit Company*, 1906.

Fig. 3.8: "Birichiche and Palomas – Toloa Canal. Tela, 1924." Gelatin silver process on paper, 8 x 10 inches. United Fruit Company Photograph Collection, Baker Library, Harvard Business School, Box 11.

emblematic spatial figure of modern urbanization following the principles of hygienization; the Panama Canal Zone; Bluefields in Nicaragua; La Ceiba and Puerto Cortés in Honduras; Belize; Puerto Barrios; and Livingston in Guatemala, before returning to New Orleans. These spots, which had already existed before the creation of the United Fruit Company routes, were developed as new economic poles. They became visibly interconnected and defined as nodal points within an efficient system of circulation and transportation, in order to enhance the expansion of the world market in bananas. Yet, as the historian John Soluri has shown with regard to the interior of Honduras, company towns bore witness to an entirely different situation and reflected divergent states of urbanization and thus modernization, with different standards of housing and neglected and segregated labor

Fig. 3.9: "Standard 6-room labor camps salvaged and reconstructed in Tela, 1924." Gelatin silver process on paper, 8 x 10 inches. United Fruit Company Photograph Collection, Baker Library, Harvard Business School (olv-work729886).

camps and other facilities.[82] Moreover, at least until the 1940s most company towns were very unevenly developed and mirrored different stages of urban development, so that it is difficult to speak about the company town of the United Fruit Company, but rather about different types of company towns, labor camps, and plantations that admittedly shared similar spatial principles of organizing and reinforcing social segregation in order to implement an effective control of labor.

Furthermore, the spatial figures of the company town and the plantation are intertwined with a modern sensory apparatus that reconnects and re-channels the different senses in a

82   John Soluri, *Banana Cultures: Agriculture, Consumption, and Environmental Change in Honduras and the United States* (Austin: University of Texas Press, 2005), pp. 154–155.

Fig. 3.10: "Standard (2) room camp. 20'x 24'. February 1921." Gelatin silver process on paper, 8 x 10 inches. United Fruit Company Photograph Collection, Baker Library, Harvard Business School, Box 27.

novel form, allowing for a new spatial order. Accordingly, media reflect here the material and epistemic processes of spatial production, which is related to the technologies of the telegraph, the railroad, and photography. I argue that the industrial and corporate capitalism of the United Fruit Company could only succeed because of this novel transmedial sign system. In this context of company towns, photography as a modern drafting media joins "the other features of colonial landscaping— the marks of enclosure, private property, fortification, and confinement."[83] Whereas Casid underlines in her study, with regard to the landscape paintings of the seventeenth and eighteenth centuries, that in "the idiom of the picturesque landscaping, these lines and incisions, barriers and blocks become

83   Casid, *Sowing Empire*, p. 12.

Fig. 3.11: "Labor Camps Urraco, Tela R.R., 1921." Gelatin silver process on paper, 8 x 10 inches. United Fruit Company Photograph Collection, Baker Library, Harvard Business School (olvwork729888).

merely little intermittent dots and things of beauty,"[84] it is clear that the pictures of the Company photographic archive seem to betray the aesthetics of the picturesque altogether. Most pictures that show the company towns emphasize a technical language and thoroughly conceal or naturalize the poverty of the living conditions of the laborers. Plantation economy as landscape invisibilizes cane fields and other plantations, "produced by disindigenation and lethal labor."[85] On the level of the images' discourse, though, it "is not black slave labor [or posterior slave-like labor forms] but the plantation system's ordering and arrangement of the forcibly relocated and 'intermixed'

84 Ibid.
85 Ibid.

Fig. 3.12: "#12 Close-up Farm 35, Camp 6, Tela, 1924." Gelatin silver process on paper, 8 x 10 inches. United Fruit Company Photograph Collection, Baker Library, Harvard Business School (olvwork729805).

plants and people that 'all together contribute to make a landscape' out of the [...] plantation."[86] Significantly, the United Fruit Company organized its plantation system through differentiated spatial figures, which alongside the company town—designated for the upper ranks of the division, for managerial and white employees and specific staff, such as engineers, medical doctors and other scientists—elaborated the figure of the labor camp, or enclave, to make the discourse of plantation work. Thus, these three main spatial figures, the company town, the labor camp and the plantation, organized the chain of cultural operations that linked the crops, plants, commodities, people and machinery along with the material practices that belong to the Company's discourse networks.

86   Ibid.

Fig. 3.13: "" #6716 – Aerial View Madre Farm – Nov. 1948 – Looking South from northern boundary- unplanted Maguaca farm on right and Julian in foreground. DOMINICAN REPUBLIC, Sept. 28, 1949." Gelatin silver process on paper, 8 x 10 inches. United Fruit Company Photograph Collection, Baker Library, Harvard Business School, Box 40.

Imperial Debris

> The cultivated lands of the company are yearly encroaching on the untamed jungle; the variety of products is ever increasing. A highly organized company, applying modern inventions, is today making tropic jungles contribute to the world's food supply.[87]

In the context of the modern configuration the enclave certainly is a special figure for the Company's organization of space and time. At this point I return to my initial concerns about the enclave as an epistemic figure that correlates to the environmental changes

87   Victor M. Cutter, "Caribbean Tropics in Commercial Transition," *Economic Geography* 2:4 (1926), p. 507.

taking place in the Caribbean. I refer to the enclave as epistemic figure not only in the sense that it characterizes the socio-economic space of the plantations developed in the Caribbean through slavery, as observed by Chomsky when she refers to the plantation as institution.[88] But even more so, the enclave as an epistemic figure describes the very formation of the emergent modern political space, which reflects a rising corporate colonialism at the turn of the twentieth century that reproduces and reorganizes the previous relations of labor and race.[89] This modern political space may, furthermore, be characterized by a geocultural reconfiguration of the Caribbean and by what I conceive as a new form of knowledge production that reorganizes and simultaneously reproduces social hierarchies. Likewise, these hierarchies are defined by a spatialization, which is determined by a new institutional entanglement, in which the United Fruit Company had a significant impact. Accordingly, in terms of a territorial organization, also in the sense Snyder suggests with regard to "the territory of modern science," a newly reproduced type of space emerges at that same time, that is, the functional-technological enclave, which backs the efficiency of the United Fruit Company's expansion. The enclave as epistemic figure therefore may describe this new knowledge order, embodied in the photographic archive.

The historian Jason Colby rereads the organization of the space in the United Fruit Company divisions of Costa Rica and Guatemala between 1904 and 1912 as a crucial phase of the installment of what he frames as corporate colonialism.[90] Accordingly, he reconstructs the different means of this spatial organization and labor control vis-à-vis the many upheavals and riots the Caribbean had experienced since the construction of the Panama Canal and the establishment of the Canal Zone,

---

88   Chomsky, *West Indian Workers.*
89   Jason Colby, *The Business of Empire: United Fruit, Race, and U.S. Expansion in Central America* (Ithaca: Cornell University Press, 2011), p. 79.
90   Ibid.

attracting thousands of workers from the Caribbean. This control of labor is organized along racial lines, mainly between the majority West Indian workers and the Hispanics who were contracted later, as argued by the anthropologist Philippe Bourgois in his study of the labor forces in Costa Rica and Panama.[91] Yet, Colby makes an interesting argument here, that the mechanisms of labor control elaborated in the Canal Zone, with which the US Government was inextricably entangled, were echoed by the United Fruit Company in the first decades of the twentieth century, when contracting many of the same laborers. The discourse of race and racism was reinstated and perfected in order not only to mobilize the workforce, but even more so to operate a racial policy of labor control and to fashion social control in the newly incorporated Central American nations. This happened in a manifold and complex way, to which the specific medical policies of the United Fruit Company and, more generally, the elaborated discourse of tropical medicine corresponded.[92] Moreover, this was also framed by at least two larger contexts: on the one hand, national politics, which reproduced and even reified the existing State racism against the West Indian laborers, and on the other, a semi-official US racial policy that propagated the ideology of social stability through a politics of race.[93] Drawing upon the dyad of race and empire and against a backdrop of transnational racial tensions in the US, Colby quotes Department official and former US minister to Costa Rica Lewis Einstein:

> "A justifiable fear exists that with the problems of internal order confronting us and the difficulty of assimilating the millions of [im] migrants at home, any further extension of our responsibilities in the direction of bringing new people, the great majority of whom are inferior in civilization, within our control ought strenuously to be resisted." Despite this reluctance, Einstein argued, the combination

91   Bourgois, *Ethnicity at Work*.
92   Chomsky, *West Indian Workers*, p. 89.
93   Colby, *The Business of Empire*, p. 80.

of American investment and racial disorder in Central America required a firm hand from Washington. "[T]he heterogeneous nature of [the region's] population, apart from Costa Rica, and the existence in other countries of a majority of Indian and Negro Indian blood" inevitably spawned instability, he explained, which in turn threatened U.S. enterprises, including not only the Panama Canal, but U.S. owned railroads, mines and "banana plantations... close to the coast."[94]

Colby rightly draws attention to the alliance between labor control and racial hierarchy as a principle of the United Fruit Company's organization, which I would like to stress as the foundation of the formation of this modern political space, to which the enclave corresponds as both spatial and epistemic figure. An embodied racism can be observed in the many internal communications of the United Fruit Company's management and among the lower-class employees in an openly discriminating way.[95] Historical documents and internal corporate records bear witness to the tensions between the Company and some of the British authorities that this eventually caused, as racism was overtly manifested against the West Indians, who were British subjects. Colby observes that "the racialized structure of the company's labor system ensured that black workers would see racial and class grievances as one and the same."[96] He further concludes that the period between 1904 and 1912 "witnessed the critical formation of U.S. imperial culture" in the context of Dollar Diplomacy and the Monroe Doctrine, to which a racial labor policy corresponded, founding herewith a corporate colonialism.[97] Constitutive of the formation of this modern political space, I argue, is the spatial and hence epistemic figure of the enclave.[98] One of the key categories that describe the efficiency

94   Ibid., p. 86.
95   Colby, *The Business of Empire*; Bourgois, *Ethnicity at Work*.
96   Colby, *The Business of Empire*, p. 112.
97   Ibid., p. 117.
98   In his study, Colby quotes original sources of internal communication between Victor Cutter and British authorities and other communication. Although

of the United Fruit Company's economic expansion is "race," which is inextricably interlinked to the labor regime. Deborah Poole argues in her study of the visual economy of the Andes for conceiving "race" as visual technology.[99] This is relevant also for the United Fruit Company's hierarchical and hegemonic organization and, henceforth, the production of space that was constitutive of emergent corporate colonialism: As visual technology "race" participates in the spatial order of the United Fruit Company towns, labor camps, and plantations. As Étienne Balibar remarks elsewhere, corporate colonialism's production of space is based upon "a variable combination of a continuous external exclusion and an internal marginalization,"[100] two corresponding processes mirrored clearly in the Company's racial and thus spatial hierarchy.

To outline the visual economy, the production of the images and the discursivities that define their effect, meaning and status, I recall what Ann Laura Stoler critically highlights in her studies. She observes that an important change in the forms of power and knowledge took place through a transformation of the discourse of European identity in the nineteenth century, created through the emergence of the concept of "race." European self-perception depended on the formation of the perception and determination of the Other, and as such, speaks of how the European was constituted in the mirror of colonialism. This is certainly also true of the dynamics in the realm of the

these aspects of labor race-relations have also been discussed by Aviva Chomsky (1996) and Philippe Bourgois (1989), Colby makes an interesting argument here. He underlines that a labor policy along racial lines must be considered against the backdrop of international relations, while stressing the important and active role of the United States government. Accordingly, the United States allowed for testing the United Fruit Company's labor policy in Central America at a time when the United States faced major labor struggles and racial tensions at home. Colby thus identifies a transnational entanglement that favored and backed the United Fruit Company's labor policy and thus the political interventions in Central America and the Caribbean that became the testing ground of the modern.

99   Poole, *Vision, Race, and Modernity*.

100   Étienne Balibar and Immanuel Wallerstein, *Rasse – Klasse – Nation. Ambivalente Identitäten* (Hamburg: Argument-Verlag, 1990), p. 55, my translation.

US empire. "Race" has become part of a broader discursive economy and therefore represents an episteme. Two questions thus become relevant that help understand the function and nature of the United Fruit Company photographic archive: To what extent does "race" define a knowledge regime embodied in the archive? What is its visual discourse and what alternative regimes of vision are possible, when it comes to a reading of the images today? In her analysis of a visual modernity, Stoler observes that European bourgeois identities were formed in a context of debates about "race," gender and sexuality in the colonies. In this way, the ambivalences and the fears resulting from the colonial experience were constitutive of the modern project and of cultural and social formations in Europe and later in the United States. Following on from this, "race" becomes part of an administrative regime, and as visual technology shapes the practices of normalization of the modern State. Thus "race" as a discursive economy constitutes transnational spaces that rewrite this racial difference, defining the philosophical and cultural comprehension of otherness, and with it, US American self-recognition. In this sense, the image is also a device in which perception and representation coincide with the modes of perception and representation of that time.

With regard to the United Fruit Company's photographic archive, many pictures flamboyantly evidence the material organization of the agro-urban enclaves of both the plantation and the company town and depict the environmental transformation of space, mirroring the Company's social and labor hierarchy. Consider this picture (Fig. 3.14), "No. 602. A Product of our Schools: being employed by the Company as a timekeeper." It unquestionably corresponds to the very discourse of labor following racial lines while reflecting "race" as a visual technology in the way it both reiterates a racial hierarchy within the Company and enhances the idea of modern productivity and discipline through labor. This particular picture suggests that social mobility is possible, when "being employed by the Company." Yet, this suggested social mobility corresponds to a meticu-

Fig. 3.14: "No. 602. A Product of our Schools: being employed by the Company as a timekeeper." Gelatin silver process on paper, 8 x 10 inches. United Fruit Company Photograph Collection, Baker Library, Harvard Business School (olvwork713949).

lously elaborated labor regime. The Company's intervention was indubitably aimed, on the one hand, at social relations. But, on the other, social mobility certainly did not correspond to an everyday experience in the plantation, so that the image must be read rather as a corporate promotional narrative and as the Company's self-legitimation. Furthermore, social mobility through labor for West Indians was simply not envisaged.[101]

In terms of territorial organization, I have argued that the emergence of modern political space is accompanied by a politics of the enclave, which was fostered by the Company and characterized the first half of the twentieth century. More generally, the enclave is defined as a principle of sovereignty. It is a closed area surrounded by territories that belong to a different

101 Colby, *The Business of Empire*.

regime or order. For instance, the case of nineteenth century economic development in Colombia, and the formation of a national economy as part of the project of the modern nation, makes it clear that poles of development were implemented in the landscape of the regions to be "civilized": there were systems of intensive and extensive production such as the agro-industrial plantations and the installation of the infrastructure necessary for the expansion and stability of an urban commercial system, through ports, canals, military bases, and prison systems.[102] The enclave was configured as an enclosed space. This is true also for the United Fruit Company when the enclave became a constitutive part of corporate colonialism. Moreover, with the implementation of the labor camp—one of the United Fruit Company vocabularies referring to the newly introduced space—spatial segregation is reproduced, reified and perfected. In this process, the enclave became the privileged form. Taking a cue from Margarita Serje's regional study of nineteenth century Colombia, which outlines some of the main characteristics of the spatial figure of the enclave, the enclave deployed by the United Fruit Company is principally a testing ground of the modern and henceforth has evolved as an epistemic figure. Let me recall some of the findings by Serje, relevant for my reading of the corporate enclave in the Caribbean:

> Behind an enclosure fence with watch towers, the spaces are organized and the hierarchical distances in the camp are carefully maintained. They transcribe the system of divisions of the society that generates them: class, race, gender. The camp is spatially organized based on the old and mythical system of opposites: whites and natives, foreigners—according to the country of origin of the corporation involved—and nationals, administrators and laborers. The system of differences is reflected in the zonal organization of the camp where carefully delim-

102 Margarita Serje, *El revés de la nación. Territorios salvajes, fronteras y tierras de nadie* (Bogota: Universidad de Los Andes, Facultad de Ciencias Sociales, Departamento de Antropología / CESO, 2005), p. 212.

ited areas appear for laborers, foremen, administrators, high-level employees, and special guests; each with their recreation sites, commissaries, offices, etc. with the finish and comfort (or the absence of these) corresponding to each rank. Its viability depends on a disciplinary system, which reproduces, and at times exacerbates the system of segregation. These disciplinary systems have, in some cases, reached disgraceful extremes. In this way, the enclave is brought into effect through what has been characterized by some as the setting up of real "independent republics" under the reign of those who exploit a given territory and its inhabitants. This characterization is not an exaggeration if one takes into account the way these companies function in the exploitation of oil, mining and agro-industrial undertakings, with which they paradoxically aim to achieve development and national integration.[103]

This type of enclave can be characterized by the implementation of an omnipresent power and the suspension of legal regulations and national sovereignties, which seems to define the key characteristics of the United Fruit Company's politics of enclave. Significantly, the enclave correlates to the radical transformation of space and society, which the Caribbean and Central America had experienced after the abolition both of slavery as a predominant form of labor and of colonialism. Moreover, it correlates to a new type of work measured in salary, which was then massively introduced and which became an integral part of important infrastructural and agro-industrial undertakings that intensively extracted natural resources, reproducing similar spatial segregation patterns that were the foundations of the emergent corporate colonialism. As further observed by Serje, this transformation produced a new spatial and eventually demographic order, particularly in rural and remote areas.[104]

It is of significance that the photographic archive of the United Fruit Company depicts how the corporation organized the lives of the laborers and employees in the labor camps,

103 Ibid., p. 213, my translation.
104 Ibid., p. 215.

showing the hierarchical order of space. Violence becomes tangible most notably in the spatial hierarchy the great majority of the pictures reflect, showing how the Company experimented with the development of different types of housing for different sections of the labor force. This hierarchy is embodied in the photographic archive's order, in the way the pictures are arranged to imagine technological progress, and in the way the many thousand pictures make seen different types of housing: standard housing, manager's housing, superintendent's housing, overseer's housing, timekeeper's housing, engineer's housing, family housing, and laborer's housings or barracks. The images obscure the violence on which this spatial hierarchy is founded, and make it disappear altogether, while orchestrating a technicality and eventually the modern material accomplishment promised by the discourse of plantation.

Labor camps were organized according to a social and racial taxonomy adopted from colonialism, which the Company reproduced and elaborated as labor policy and as modes of domination in order to control the labor force. Labor camps, devoid of all the technical improvements the company towns for the white employees had experienced since their early erection, particularly in the region around the Panama Canal Zone, reflected this spatial hierarchy within the new urban order of the Company as left-over space, as something disassociated or discharged. This is also underscored by Chomsky when she discusses the Company's medical policies and the social causes of diseases among the laborers, pinpointing a discrimination and segregation of health, "For as on the United Fruit Company plantations, the 'conditions' of white managers and black laborers were very different, and these conditions affected their morbidity and mortality rate much more than did their race."[105] Accordingly, the discourse of hygiene, embodied in the enclave's spatial organization, defined the "left-over" spaces as something dangerously infected and as vectors for disease, reiterating the idea of the

---

105 Chomsky, *West Indian Workers*, p. 112.

"infectious Tropics." The spatial logic that was linked to the politics of the enclave was projected onto the bodies of the laborers, defining the imaginary of the space as contaminated, contagious and menacing. The politics of the enclave, I argue, correspond to the emergent discourse of tropical medicine of that time, to which the United Fruit Company became an important agent. It is of primary significance that the Company's expansion of corporate colonialism was founded on this spatial and thus epistemic figure of the enclave. With its establishment a new form of commodity circulation was introduced in the division, which enhanced the dominance and control of the laborers. The Company increasingly generated commercial circuits for the employees' and laborers' needs, as framed by John Williams:

> [The commissaries] put the white man's necessities of life before the native. He can not only buy cheap calico and the machete, but can purchase luxuries, thus raising his standard of life. It is not long before the native population is working regularly in order to secure needed wants. The proposition is then to create wants—and the once lazy tropical population will eventually strive to possess these wants.[106]

This is also reflected in the letters by Everett Brown, who describes how segregation is not only evolved spatially and along racial lines, but furthermore through the intrusion of a type of commodities, which further enhance the social divide consolidating a "white supremacy" through signs of modernity and luxury, and conversely, a degradation of the "rest" by a reinforced exclusion through the inaccessibility of this consumption. Deliberately, the Company implemented a politics of increasing indebtedness among the laborers by controlling their consumption. Brown notes: "The policy of the Company is to keep things first class and give men the best things and treatment. When

---

106 John L. Williams, *The Rise of the Banana Industry and Its Influence on Caribbean Countries* (Worcester, Mass.: Clark University, 1925), p. 46.

Fig. 3.15: "Quepos. Showing commissary site at foot hill to right and hospital site on top of same hill. 1939." Gelatin silver process on paper, 8 x 10 inches. United Fruit Company Photograph Collection, Baker Library, Harvard Business School, Box 23.

it gets to the head of the office [...]."[107] Brown himself, though, seems to have had a different experience: as a white lower-class employee he could not participate in the many amenities of the company towns and frequently complains about it in his letters.

According to Foucault, the biological limit of the modern in a society is revealed when gender, and the individual as a simple living body, become a political strategy.[108] In a similar vein, Hannah Arendt observed that *homo laborans* and his biological life have come to be the center of the modern political space, a characteristic that seems to be important in the new spatial order and the enclave of an emergent corporate colo-

107 *Everett C. Brown Papers,* Feb. 5, 1920.
108 Michel Foucault, *La naissance de la biopolitique. Cours au Collège de France, 1978–1979* (Paris: Éditions du Seuil, 2004).

nialism.[109] The functional-modern enclave reflects this changing economic value of the workforce. Moreover, it makes visible
the practices of hierarchy and difference, the inclusion and
exclusion of laborers, and reflects an important spatial figure of
a new ordering of the territory and of the discourse of the plantation in the way it determines the circulation of bodies, knowledge, and commodities: the enclave as labor camp is the new
paradigm of the modern political space. This reading of the
paradigm brings us to understand the enclave, which has generally been studied from the economic perspective, as a place of
direct foreign investment, in a different way, as a figure of modernization. The enclave describes the processes of social regulation and, in particular, the modern processes of industrialization and urbanization of the "Tropics" by the fruit companies.
Further, this spatial ordering is based on the biological life
of the workforce and the racial reproduction of the Other, as
evinced particularly clearly by the intervention of tropical medicine and hygiene. Following on from one of my entry points,
that of the role of photography in modern social regulation, the
spatial order converges here with the discourse of race. Moreover, "race" as a visual technology, clearly reflected in the Company photographs, participates effectively in this modern spatial ordering. The United Fruit Company photographic archive
raises these questions about the enclave and the discourse of
race as corresponding parts that best define the expansion of a
corporate colonialism. As interlocked components they form a
regime that works on social regulation through a hierarchical
spatial order.

The discourse of race and the enclave as a spatial figure
have been the object of analysis in other contexts too. I refer
briefly to the study by Ann Laura Stoler of the colonial discourse
and the relationship between the metropolis and the colonies

---

109 Hannah Arendt, *Elemente und Ursprünge totaler Herrschaft. Antisemitismus, Imperialismus, Totalitarismus* (Munich: Piper, 1986).

Fig. 3.16: "Christmas Toys put on display, Retail Dry Goods – December 8, 1926." Gelatin silver process on paper, 8 x 10 inches. United Fruit Company Photograph Collection, Baker Library, Harvard Business School, Box 27.

of the British Empire.[110] She calls our attention to the white women who accompanied their husbands employed in the colonies. In the discourse of colonialism they play only a marginal role; however, in certain circumstances they were tasked with maintaining a white and Western lifestyle. Stoler argues that it was these women who enhanced the face of colonial society by imposing racial domination. The European, and in my case the US American women, whose number began to grow around 1912 as they accompanied their husbands to the United Fruit Company towns,[111] brought with them racial and racist conceptions, but they were also the operators, putting these concep-

110 Ann L. Stoler, "Making Empire Respectable: The Politics of Race and Sexual Morality in 20th-Century Colonial Cultures," in *Imperial Monkey Business: Racial Supremacy in Social Darwinist Theory and Colonial Practice*, ed. Jan Breman (Amsterdam: VU University Press, 1990).
111 Colby, *The Business of Empire*, p. 115.

tions into practice, stimulating class distinctions and favoring new racial antagonisms.[112] According to Stoler, the colonizers put the white women into a position of bearers of a redefined corporate or colonial morality,[113] in order to reduce the turnover of white personnel, but more significantly to prevent the feared racial intermixing. White women reflected the rationalization of a colonial order and a corporate policy of preventative measures against the "racial degeneration" of white employees in moral terms, signifying a regulation of relations within the enclave. Likewise, Stoler in her study observes that new employees in the colonies received courses in how to "manage" the natives while their wives were educated in colonial propriety and domestic administration.[114] It has been widely acknowledged that in colonial contexts more generally, racial order was determined by gender politics and a redefinition of the division of labor. The exclusive policies of colonialism are demarcated not only by external limits, but also by internal frontiers that specify internal conformity and order within colonial societies; the categories of colonizers and colonized are underwritten by a racial difference that is constructed in terms of gender. Stoler points out that these redefinitions emerged, particularly during the crises of colonial control, precisely because they questioned authority and dominion within the Western metropolitan communities. This is certainly paralleled in the case of the United Fruit Company, in a time when labor unrest and racial tensions were the order of the day in the United States. Furthermore, similar gender politics may have existed and defined the spread of corporate colonialism with the objective of maintaining a politics of racial segregation through a spatial hierarchy, in order to exercise social control both in the "colonies" and at home. After all, the company towns and the plantations were dominant masculine cultures, which female laborers only visibly entered

112 Stoler, "Making Empire Respectable," p. 45.
113 Ibid.
114 Ibid., p. 58.

much later, as domestic servants, plantation laborers or in the maintenance of the plantation infrastructure.

The United Fruit Company photographs depict a masculine working environment, only making the laboring woman visible in an ambivalent way. Nevertheless, the Company's politics of gender is tangible in the case of the wives and families who accompanied the white employees, and the other white women sent from the United States to the different divisions to work in the company's schools and hospitals. The photographs of the Annual Reports of the Medical Department and the United Fruit Company photographic archive reflect "race" as visual technology through which a modern social regulation in the divisions and at home is achieved. Moreover, as both media technologies and modern imaginaries they articulate and reify the Company's racial fantasies and fears of racial intermixing that are subsumed by the plantation economy as discourse of landscape. I return once again to the spatial and epistemic figure of the enclave, as one of the main features of the laboratory of the modern. It has been discussed elsewhere how the production of space and "nature" under historical capitalism generated an "uneven development" of landscape.[115] Historical capitalism can be characterized by the existence of "permanently differentiated zones, territories, climates, and peoples."[116] Accordingly, this characteristic of a "permanently differentiated zone" best describes the enclave as a spatial figure. Significantly, spatial differentiation is reproduced and imagined with the photographs: they are tools of commodifying landscape by helping to transform land into an economically viable landscape.

And yet, like the enclave and the photographs, these representations are traversed by other potentially subversive narratives, inasmuch as they are articulations of an imperial debris. Imperial ruins are the leftover material infrastructures we wit-

---

115 Neil Smith, *Uneven Development: Nature, Capital, and the Production of Space* (Athens: University of Georgia Press, 2008).
116 Edward Said, *Yeats and Decolonization* (Derry: Field Day, 1988), p. 12.

ness today as fragments of the structures of the plantation economy in the Caribbean. Stoler remarks that "such infrastructures of large and small scale bear what captivated Walter Benjamin, the 'marks and wounds of the history of human violence.' It is these spatially assigned 'traces of violence', more than the 'deadening of affects' to which we turn."[117] By focusing on the materiality of debris, she suggests, the "logic of the concrete" may be unlocked, as "ruins can be marginalized structures that continue to inform social modes of organization but that cease to function in ways they once did."[118] This is true with regard to the United Fruit Company plantations in the Caribbean today. I argue that the spatial figure of the enclave reflects this kind of imperial debris, in the way it materially corresponds to the organization of a modern plantation economy, being shaped by the transition from slavery into a post-slave labor regime at the heart of colonial and corporate capitalism. Stoler astutely asks: "What happens when island enclaves [...] become repositories of vulnerabilities that are likely to last longer than the political structures that produced them?"[119]

In the context of corporate capitalism, the enclave can be thus conceived as a form in organizing space and time on the plantation. I argue for conceiving it as an epistemic figure to describe the formation of a modern political space. Accordingly, the functional-technological enclave emerges as a type of new spatial phenomenon of a territorial organization, that is, a space characterized by the capitalist production of space. The Company photographic archive evidences the material organization of the agro-urban enclaves and the plantation, while embodying the violent environmental transformations that correlate with the violent implementation of the social and labor hierarchy. Today, the enclaves remain as leftover structures

117 Ann L. Stoler, *Imperial Debris: On Ruins and Ruination* (Durham: Duke University Press, 2013), p. 22.
118 Ibid.
119 Ibid.

and are part of an imperial debris, while articulating "new deformations and new forms of debris [that] work on matter and mind to eat through people's resources and resiliences as they embolden new political actors with indignant refusal, forging unanticipated, entangled, and empowered alliances."[120] So it is that on the level of psychic sedimentations the photographs that envision and bear witness to the enclave materialize a visual imaginary that carves out the contours of the modern political space. This perspective focusing on the imperial genealogies of the present allows for working "through the less perceptible affects of imperial interventions and their settling into the social and material ecologies in which people live and survive."[121] Stoler goes on to stress that this means looking "at 'imperial formations' rather than at empire per se [...] to register the ongoing quality of processes of decimation, displacement, and reclamation."[122] In this sense, visual and material leftovers, such as these photographs and the enclaves ask for reclamation by generations to come in order to overcome discrimination and racism. Moreover, beyond the discourse of the Tropics, this kind of potential and powerful renewed reception of visual and material leftovers seems to avoid the reproduction of the fixed structures that come with focusing exclusively on Empire, Capitalism or Plantation.

120 Ibid., p. 29.
121 Ibid., p. 4.
122 Ibid., p. 8.

Chapter 3

"The World Was My Garden"

> Farming is a material activity that spans the gap between pre-
> modern societies and our contemporary world. It is very obvi-
> ously a materially rooted domain of knowledge, embedded
> in social networks. [...] What kinds of knowledge and whose
> knowledge were inscribed in [...] agricultural texts which have
> come down to us in such abundance, and in the farming land-
> scapes whose distinctive features we can track over two millen-
> nia? Agriculture is a domain of knowledge where it is impos-
> sible to separate ideas about matter from the struggles with
> matter that generate them. Nor are the knowledge and tech-
> niques politically neutral. The norms of good farming are a very
> powerful instrument for ordering society.[1]

The World as Garden

The metaphor the "world as garden" relates to two overarch-
ing arguments, which are what is at stake in this chapter. The
first is the material transformation of the world symbolically
and geopolitically into a "garden," describing a complex process of conversion that is bound to the primary human activity
of environmental and thus cultural alteration, which I discuss
as the representation of the plantation economy as landscape.
The second is the conversion of the "natural" world into a commodity that is grounded in material circulation conceived as
"exchange as a source of value," related to the political economy

---

1   Francesca Bray, "Science, Technique, Technology: Passages between Matter and Knowledge in Imperial Chinese Agriculture," *The British Society for the
History of Science* 41:3 (2008), p. 321.

of agriculture,[2] and to what has elsewhere been dubbed "science-monde" and "économie-monde."[3] Following the rationale of the inventory of the world as a *mise-en-valeur* of the terrestrial globe, it becomes pertinent to discuss this complex conversion of the world into a garden through botany and agriculture, as passages between matter and knowledge. Whereas Arjun Appadurai focuses on the economic exchange within a social and cultural context, in which the exchange of things is primarily and necessarily situated in what he concisely terms the "social life of things," looking at the different temporal life phases of the things that become commodities, I examine how the commodification of "nature" is chiefly created by the exchange and the scientification of botany and agriculture, in which the United Fruit Company was a major global actor partaking in new discourse networks. More generally, botany has been widely discussed within the conception of colonialism.[4] Accordingly, what has been emphasized is the relationship between the scientific study of nature—the institutionalization of a network of botanical gardens or tropical experiment stations—and the plantation economy, which sparked the inventory and the mobilization of plant resources from across the entire globe, and was linked to a profound and long-lasting alteration of the "agricultural map of the world."[5] There was a radical transformation of the world into a garden, which I conceive as the effects of the politics of value and the capitalistic production of space that laid the groundwork for the emergence of a modern political space.

2   Appadurai, *The Social Life of Things*, p. 56.
3   Marie-Noëlle Bourguet and Christophe Bonneuil, eds., *De l'inventaire du monde à la mise en valeur du globe : botanique et colonisation, fin 17e siècle – début 20e siècle* (Saint-Denis: Société française d'histoire d'outre-mer, 1999), p. 7.
4   Paul Carter, *The Road to Botany Bay: An Exploration of Landscape and History* (New York: Knopf, 1987); Bourguet, *De l'inventaire du monde*; Janet Browne, "A science of empire: British biogeography before Darwin," *Revue d'histoire des sciences* 45:4 (1992); Roselyne Rey, "Espèces, espaces : la biogéographie sans frontières," *Revue d'histoire des sciences* 45:4 (1992); Brockway, *Science and Colonial Expansion*; Schiebinger, *Plants and Empire*.
5   Bourguet, *De l'inventaire du monde*, p. 10.

So, as "science-monde" and "économie-monde" coalesce, it is recognized that:

> if it is justified to say that natural history has contributed to the development of the *économie-monde*, by helping to "transform" natural objects—plants—into objects for consumption, merchandise, one can show that this process of transformation, far from being an element outside the sphere of scholarly knowledge, was, on the contrary, an integral part of the dynamic that has led to the development of naturalist research [...]. It is clear that, far from being simple preconditions, the extraction, circulation, accumulation, and finally appropriation of samples is inscribed at the very heart of natural history, constitutive of its practice and its construction as a science. Thus, to go beyond the too simple and unidirectional interpretative model of botany as a "tool of empire," and study the interconnections between naturalist practices and the commodification of nature—or, to put it another way, between the formation of a *science-monde* and the formation of an *économie-monde*—undeniably constitutes a more promising line of research.[6]

That said, it is important to bind this fundamental, reciprocal relationship between science and economy—or the capitalist production of space—to the exchange that creates value, in order to better grasp the expansion of the United Fruit Company and the conversion of the Caribbean into a laboratory of the modern. I consider some aspects of the social life of things as commodities, as proposed by Appadurai with regard to the "regime of value," this being the main feature of the transcultural contact, before moving on to my main concern. Subsequently, this conversion is to be conceived as a primarily cultural one, for "the economy as a particular social form 'consists not only in exchanging *values* but in the *exchange* of value'," that is, "exchange is not a by-production of the mutual

6   Ibid., pp. 25, 27–28, my translation.

201

valuation of objects, but its source."[7] Correspondingly, Appadurai argues for examining "the things themselves, for their meanings are inscribed in their forms, their uses, their trajectories" in order to follow "the human transactions and calculations that enliven things" and the relationship of culture to commodities.[8] He conceives the politics of value as inherently bound to the politics of knowledge; that is, framed differently, the very idea of knowledge production is bound to geopolitics, for it concerns the spatial history of botany and particularly the emergence of economic botany. Whereas commodities are seen as "typical material representations of the capitalist mode of production,"[9] I focus here on the materiality that shaped the "natural object" both as a scientific object and as a commodity in its specific circumstances of exchange. My aim is to explore the conversion of the world into the garden, realized materially and culturally, against a backdrop of the political economy of agriculture, the exchange and making of plants into natural commodities and technical artifacts, in the context of the United Fruit Company's knowledge production and, moreover, the significant institutionalization of US economic botany during the first half of the twentieth century. However, the peculiarities of knowledges "that accompany relatively complex, long-distance, intercultural flows of commodities" become pivotal for the study of commodities and their circulation; insofar as commodity is used here as an analytical concept. This is pertinent for my study, too, for "Commodities represent very complex social forms and distributions of knowledge,"[10] through which the Caribbean is quite efficiently incorporated into a Western orbit of knowledge. Indeed, economic botany and agriculture become privileged fields of geopolitical intervention. Ultimately, Appadurai further distinguishes two sorts of

---

7   Appadurai, *The Social Life of Things*, p. 4.
8   Ibid., p. 5.
9   Ibid., p. 7.
10   Ibid., p. 41.

knowledges here: "the knowledge (technical, social, aesthetic, and so forth) that goes into the production of the commodity; and the knowledge that goes into appropriately consuming the commodity."[11] It is noteworthy that both knowledges precisely describe the interventions through economic botany and agriculture of the United Fruit Company and, furthermore, the workings of the discourse networks involved. "Knowledge at both poles has technical, mythological, and evaluative components, and the two poles are susceptible to mutual and dialectical interaction," Appadurai affirms.[12] Relating this to my concern with the conversion of the world into a garden, two main cultural techniques emerge once again—drafting and grafting—that involve this trait of knowledge at both poles: these determine a sort of discourse network of botany. As discussed in the previous chapter, this is a network of techniques and institutions that allow for storing and processing relevant data, while articulating the passages between matter and knowledge particularly clearly. Following this, the conversion of world into garden has a primarily cultural feature: understanding the plantation economy in terms of a modern capitalistic mode of production, it becomes pertinent, once again, to acknowledge that "capitalism represents not simply a techno-economic design, but a complex cultural system with a very special history in the modern West" and that "in this formation commodities and their meanings have played a critical role."[13]

In the following I draw upon this relationship between knowledge production in botany and materiality. Herein the cultural transfer determines a quintessential feature of the newly emerged agricultural commodities of a modern global market, which led to a series of spatial and geocultural configurations in the Caribbean in the course of the plantation economy regime and what later evolved from it. To this end, I

11   Ibid.
12   Ibid.
13   Ibid., pp. 48–49.

consider some aspects of the historical context of the botanical garden at Soledad as a tropical experiment station and as chronotope *par excellence*; the botanical surveys of agricultural explorations, such as those undertaken by Wilson Popenoe, who was notably hired by both the United Fruit Company and the US Department of Agriculture; and the discourse networks of agriculture. Significantly, the passages between matter and knowledge relate to visual and textual inscriptions of agricultural knowledge that made the lasting conversion of the world into a garden possible. This conversion is grounded on two epistemic figures: the archive and the enclave, that is, the enclosed space, the botanical garden or the materially engineered space of the plantation. From the vantage point of the political economy of agriculture, I will discuss this conversion by looking at the varied visual inscriptions of agricultural knowledge and in particular the photographic archive of the USDA. I will speculate on two aspects: first, the relationship between photography and botany, as an articulated passage between matter and knowledge, and, second, the formation of a visual epistemology in the light of botanical knowledge production grounded on vision as a primary sensory modality. By focusing on these material and epistemic practices, I aim to disclose the visual inside the different chains of cultural operation that transform the "natural" artifacts into commodities within the institutionalization of economic botany.

Photography and Botany's Modern Materialities

When exploring the visual and material inscriptions of botanical and thus agricultural knowledge we have an emblematic example in the figure of the German artisan and botanist, Rudolf Blaschka. Blaschka undertook extensive field trips in Jamaica and the United States to collect plants. The first was undertaken in 1892 and the second in 1895, when he carried out comparative botanical research in world-acclaimed botanical gardens from Missouri to Jamaica, whose *raison d'être* was for medical, economic and scientific purposes. These field trips, each lasting several months, seem to have been crucial for Blaschka's work on his glass botanical models, that later became the world-renowned Glass Flowers, which today constitute the Ware Collection at the Harvard Museum of Natural History. For Blaschka these field trips meant an opportunity to study plants in their "native" habitat, which were then classified as economic or tropical botany. This circumstance was of primary importance, in that the field trips resulted in a series of field drawings that articulate a particular visuality of botanical knowledge. I ask: Is visuality here an articulation of materiality? What does materiality offer as an analytic focus, and what questions does it raise?

Concerning the idea of materiality and the passages between matter and knowledge, it seems that the Blaschka drawings reveal some of the underlying scientific practices of visualization in the field and of recording as an epistemic practice that corresponds to that of collecting material specimens. As a prehistory to the Glass Flowers, which disclose a very specific materialization, mimicking nature, it seems important to emphasize this prior and thus fundamental epistemic practice of visualization as an articulation of materiality. Although modern science and specifically botany have a long visual history, and their scientific illustrations or images have been widely and popularly admired for their aesthetic value,[14] in the specific case of Blaschka's Glass Flowers the drawings have been rather overlooked. Interestingly, Blaschka had "a very small camera" on loan from the Botanical Museum, but he regarded the use of it as a waste of his time. "'Photographs are totally unnecessary to our studies,' he reported [...], 'since I could much rather draw than toil with

14   Martin Kemp, "'Implanted in Our Natures': Humans, Plants, and the Stories of Art," in *Visions of Empire: Voyages, Botany, and Representations of Nature*, ed. David Philip Miller and Peter Hanns Reill (Cambridge: Cambridge University Press, 1996), p. 197.

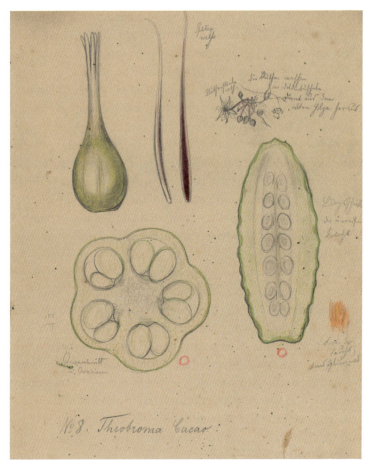

Fig. 4.1: "No. 8. Theobroma Cacao," 1893. Pencil and colored pencil on paper, 21 x 17 cm; Rudolf Blaschka, CMGL98005. Courtesy of the Rakow Research Library, The Corning Museum of Glass, Corning, New York.

boring photography'."[15] As photography was dismissed as a visual technology in his botanical field studies, in the following I will have a look at the field drawings, which Blaschka crafted

15   Cited in Susan M. Rossi-Wilcox and David Whitehouse, eds., *Drawing upon Nature: Studies for the Blaschkas' Glass Models* (Corning: Corning Museum of Glass, 2007), p. 27.

in situ and which meticulously depict the plants and flowers of the West Indies that he collected as reference specimens for the glass models.

At the turn of the twentieth century, photography was widely acclaimed and used in botany, while both media, the hand drawing and photography, were deployed simultaneously and often in a competing manner in botanical fieldwork. Moreover, photography was recognized as a basic research tool in the natural sciences, provoking its use in botany:[16]

> As an observational classificatory science, botany had come to rely heavily on pictures, the inspection of which provided both sensory enjoyment and rational pleasure. This appeal of the visual both to the senses and to the mind was overtly recognized and utilized by promoters of science in their task of persuading private, independent individuals to occupy their time with the pursuit of scientific botany.[17]

What is stressed here relates to the understanding of a complex and broad process of knowledge production in the context of the formation and differentiation of the modern natural sciences. Yet, with the perspective of pleasure and allurement the visual becomes both the underpinning and the prerequisite for communication, dissemination and knowledge production in botany. This broader perspective seems to be relevant, inasmuch as it conceptually reframes visualization as constitutive of scientific knowledge and as an articulation of the passages between matter and knowledge. Subsequently, visualization in botanical knowledge production necessarily relates to a materiality that is to be conceived as an explanatory analytic, that of taking contingency, change and stability as historical markers. Scrutinizing the scientific visual culture, which the images and

16   Anne Secord, "Botany on a Plate: Pleasure and the Power of Pictures in Promoting Early Nineteenth-Century Scientific Knowledge," *Isis* 93:1 (2002); Banner Bill Morgan and Deam Hunter Ferris, "Photography as a Basic Research Tool," *Scientific Monthly* 69:5 (1949).
17   Secord, "Botany on a Plate," p. 29.

botanical imagery of the turn of the twentieth century share, and in which botanical illustrations served as visual evidence of plants and objects of nature, it is important to stress the "mutual interaction of speaker, audience, image and object that creates the social relations between producers and observers."[18]

More generally, the long history of botany acknowledges the significance of the premodern collection and circulation of *materia medica*. This became the principal material or matter of a colonial bio-prospecting, constitutive of the formation and differentiation of economic botany. As highlighted by the historian Richard Grove and conceived within the perspective of a "green imperialism," the *materia medica* deeply embodied a local epistemology, that later began to be replaced by a network of more universal botanical knowledge and more specifically by the universal taxonomic classification of botany following Linnaeus's modern classificatory system.[19] Grove posits an epistemic shift from the use of plants to the taxonomy of a universal knowledge that "makes invisible" the local cultural knowledge, that is knowledge about the uses of plants, the long-standing practice of their cultivation and broader cultural semantics, which hitherto had always been embodied and understood as botanical knowledge.[20] The errant botanical taxonomy of the Linnaean classificatory system, though, later became a synonym for a highly artificial classification procedure "in the sense that it derived from no detailed examination of plant morphology, which might reveal 'natural' affinities between distinct species."[21] Paul Carter further pinpoints that "It was based instead on a superficial comparison of a limited number

---

18   Ibid., p. 33.
19   Richard H. Grove, *Green Imperialism: Colonial Expansion, Tropical Island Edens, and the Origins of Environmentalism* (Cambridge: Cambridge University Press, 1995), p. 142.
20   See Londa Schiebinger, "Lost Knowledge, Bodies of Ignorance, and the Poverty of Taxonomy as Illustrated by the Curious Fate of *Flos Pavonis*, an Abortifacient," in Galison, *Picturing Science, Producing Art*, pp. 134–135.
21   Carter, *The Road to Botany Bay*, p. 19.

of characteristics. Once these characteristics had been defined for a type specimen, it simply became a question of *seeing* to what extent any new plant corresponded to it."[22]

Yet the drawings by Blaschka are meticulously prepared to represent different parts of the plant, its blossom and fruit, and in particular the reproductive parts, in a single layer by showing "'a complicated mechanism made up of simple parts' and [illustrating] the point with a gear-like diagram of a standard blossom."[23] However, as we are reminded by Lorraine Daston, "nineteenth-century botanists were skeptical about image-making procedures [...], in which plants left imprints on specially prepared paper, and the photograph, both of which registered the specifics of the individual plant at the expense of the general type."[24] With regard to the later Glass Flowers collection, for which these drawings served as preliminary studies, the scientific utility of Blaschka's meticulously detailed mimetic naturalist models has been called into question.[25] Moreover, with respect to the Blaschka glass collection and the drawings, it quickly became clear that "good botanical illustrations had their place but 'must never be used to the exclusion of fresh specimens or well-preserved dry ones'."[26] Although their scientific value was questioned, it was also quickly recognized that morphology, "the science of appearances, and the ability to fuse vision and judgment into a single trained faculty for making sense of the pied variety of organic forms" was a crucial methodology.[27] Blaschka considered the drawings and the glass models, displayed in the museum, which aimed to substitute botanical field work while serving as teaching aids for botanical classes at Harvard, to be more suitable media than photography.

22   Ibid., my emphasis.
23   Lorraine Daston, "The Glass Flowers," in *Things that Talk: Object Lessons from Art and Science*, ed. Lorraine Daston (New York: Zone Books, 2004), p. 243.
24   Ibid., pp. 227–228.
25   Ibid., p. 228.
26   Ibid., p. 245.
27   Ibid., p. 248.

By using the handicraft methods of the artisan he seemed to converge "with nature's own, and made nature superfluous."[28] This, nevertheless, relates to the predominant understanding of a universal knowledge of botany, for the local epistemic practices of plants and thus cultural matrices are made invisible. Yet, the rise of a modern universal botanical scientific knowledge, to which the Glass Flowers as idealized and detailed mimetic naturalist models correspond, seems to become constitutive of the loss of the cultural matrices of the plants' uses. This dichotomy is also negotiated on the level of visualization becoming thus a matter of representation. So the problem of representation may be framed in this way: "Are the procedures that determine everyday research praxis to be judged according to the same criteria as the final results, which are still to be reduced to magical concepts such as objectivity, rationality and logical rigor?"[29] Accordingly, materiality might be conceived as a way to grasp these manifold and complex procedures that are the foundation of knowledge, beyond the categories that reiterate the logic of representation. The question of representation turns one's attention to materiality as a more comprehensive and sensible analytic. As suggested by Hans-Jörg Rheinberger, "implicitly a *Preschool of Seeing* – as crisis and apotheosis of representation – has long been established as a component of scientific culture and praxis."[30] Ultimately, a series of questions emerge: What was the aim of opting for visualization in botany, particularly with regard to the simultaneously established US Department of Agriculture to which the United Fruit Company had affinities? How is the dichotomy of a universal botanical knowledge and the loss of cultural matrices manifested in visualization? What kind of materiality is put into effect? What are the prerequisites under which objects become visible in sci-

28   Ibid., p. 250.
29   Hans-Jörg Rheinberger, Michael Hagner, and Bettina Wahrig-Schmidt, eds., *Räume des Wissens: Repräsentation, Codierung, Spur* (Berlin: Akademie Verlag, 1997), p. 10, my translation.
30   Ibid., p. 11, my translation.

entific culture?[31] How do these images work in their specific contexts? What about the viewing and knowing, in which both scientific and cultural practices and productions are brought into consideration?[32] Following the idea of epistemic equivalence between vision and knowledge: "What do we know when we see?"[33] Corresponding to the desire to articulate a universal botanical knowledge, the Blaschka glass models become a kind of perfect simulacra of nature, while they simultaneously conceal the embedded cultural matrices and local epistemic knowledge. While pinpointing an entanglement of knowledge production and cultural contact, I consider photography as a cultural technique that relates to the operations or chains of operation as the historical and logical primaries of media concepts that emanate from them.[34] In doing so, I discuss in the following visualization and specifically the use of photography in botanical fieldwork, particularly on the USDA agricultural expeditions of the 1910s until the 1940s.

In the modern context, materiality overlaps, conceptually, with technology and techniques. The photographic practices of the USDA agricultural expeditions disclose an embodied technological knowledge that seems to correspond with the establishment of economic botany as scientific knowledge.[35] Notes from the field book by Wilson Popenoe, as a sort of agricultural text, reveal that the main objective of the USDA botanical expeditions was to conduct a land resources survey. He explicitly summarizes the aims of the USDA in a report in 1925 as follows:

31 Galison, *Picturing Science, Producing Art*, p. 1.
32 Ibid., p. 6.
33 Ibid., p. 13.
34 Bernhard Siegert, "Weiße Flecken und finstre Herzen. Von der symbolischen Weltordnung zur Weltentwurfsordnung," in *Kulturtechnik Entwerfen. Praktiken, Konzepte und Medien in Architektur und Design Science*, ed. Daniel Gethmann and Susanne Hauser (Bielefeld: transcript, 2009), p. 23.
35 See Bray, "Science, Technique, Technology," p. 320.

Fig. 4.2: "Ambato, Ecuador Jan 1921, Shipment of seeds and plants ready to start to Washington DC by parcel post." Black & white print, 4,5 x 6,5 inches; Photographer Wilson Popenoe. Popenoe Family Papers, Hunt Institute for Botanical Documentation, Carnegie Mellon University.

Two means of securing plant introductions are now employed by the Department, through the Office of Foreign Seed and Plant Introduction, in the Bureau of Plant Industry. They are: (1) agricultural explorers, who are sent out on special missions to obtain certain plants, or to collect promising plant material of all sorts in remote and little-known regions; and (2) correspondence with diplomatic and consular officers abroad, and with experiment stations of foreign governments, botanists, missionaries, and others.[36]

To this end, agricultural or plant explorers were systematically sent abroad to conduct tropical surveys: interestingly, the explorers' attention turned to local epistemologies of plants, determining plant exploration as a core activity and ground

36   Wilson Popenoe, "Foreign Service and Agriculture," *The American Foreign Service Journal* II:11 (1925), p. 366.

for economic botanical knowledge.[37] In the context of colonial knowledge production, botany constituted a key strategic scientific activity, thus acquiring significant geopolitical importance. Popenoe, botanist, agricultural explorer and a key figure in US economic botany in the first half of the twentieth century—along with many other explorers, such as David Fairchild, Paul Allen and Walter Hodge who were sent to the Caribbean, and Central and South America—searched for knowledge on tropical plants and fruits to enhance their commercialization with the USDA. Employed by the USDA and more specifically by the BPI, Bureau of Plant Introduction, Popenoe worked for the plant introduction programs of 1913–1915, 1917, 1919, 1920 and 1921.[38] The USDA was formally created in 1897, but had originally been conceived in 1862, and differentiated into many more specialized institutional and governmental agencies, such as the Bureau of Plant Introduction, which moved to the Office of Markets and Rural Organization, the Bureau of Animal Industry, and the Bureau of Soils. Interestingly, the United States had also been one of the pioneers in setting up "an embryonic Department of Agriculture in 1836 as a branch, significantly, of the Office of the Commissioner of Patents."[39] It seemed that agriculture and agronomy became notable statecrafts. Accordingly, also with regard to the USDA, "the production and circulation of agronomic knowledge by the state was a key technique of government."[40] The constant reorganization

37 Walter H. Hodge and Angela I. Todd, "Agricultural Explorers of the USDA's Bureau of Plant Industry, 1897–1955," *Huntia* 14:1 (2009), p. 31. Moreover, the USDA's official objectives, defined by its first director Isaac Newton, were: "1) collecting, arranging, and publishing statistical and other useful agricultural information; 2) introducing valuable plants and animals; 3) answering inquiries of farmers regarding agriculture; 4) testing agricultural implements; 5) conducting chemical analyses of soils, grains, fruits, plants, vegetables, and manures; 6) establishing an agricultural library and museum." Gladys L. Baker, *Century of Service: The first 100 years of the United States Department of Agriculture* (Washington: Centennial Committee, U.S. Dept. of Agriculture, 1963), p. 14.
38 Hodge, "Agricultural Explorers," p. 29.
39 Bray, "Science, Technique, Technology," p. 327.
40 Ibid.

213

Fig. 4.3: "Cartago, Colombia 11-17-20, Bamboo lumber drying on the river bank." Black & white print, 4,5 x 6,5 inches; Photographer Wilson Popenoe. Popenoe Family Papers, Hunt Institute for Botanical Documentation, Carnegie Mellon University.

and shifting internal structure of the USDA reflected, for instance, a narrowing of the focus of the BPI's activities. This institutionalization of agricultural operations certainly corresponds to the United States' long agricultural history. As early as 1898 "tropical surveying, cataloging and plant introduction were happening in response to the United States officially acquiring such widely separated territories as Puerto Rico and Hawaii,"[41] and as a reflection of a reordering of imperial powers. It was quickly acknowledged that "this accumulation of territories made the desire for agricultural knowledge and tropical crops research public and urgent,"[42] while establishing a preeminent role for US economic, and hence, tropical botany abroad.

41 Hodge, "Agricultural Explorers," p. 31.
42 Ibid.

Fig. 4.4: "Cartago, Colombia 11-17-20, Rio La Vieja at Cartago. The people on the river bank are catching the bamboo driftwood as it passes (high water)." Black & white print, 4,5 x 6,5 inches; Photographer Wilson Popenoe. Popenoe Family Papers, Hunt Institute for Botanical Documentation, Carnegie Mellon University.

In this respect, tropical surveying became a key activity in the context of knowledge production in economic botany and the agriculture industry, which had its apotheosis in the emergence of the figure of the agricultural explorer. Two aspects become thus pertinent when it comes to discussing materiality overlapping with technology and techniques: first, that of collecting plant material, and, second, the importance of field work, which takes place in the bio-contact zone. Both are to be conceived as epistemic practices and became central activities in economic or tropical botany. I shall point out here that collecting has been a common botanical practice since early colonial times, in particular with regard to the plants' medicinal use. It thus becomes important to frame this activity within that of ethnobotany, for which the uses of plants are important knowledge. As for tropical botany, these practices of collecting and field work have significantly shaped the scientificity

Fig. 4.5: "Laguna, avocado trees used for shade in a coffee plantation." Black & white print, 4,5 x 6,5 inches; Photographer Wilson Popenoe. Popenoe Family Papers, Hunt Institute for Botanical Documentation, Carnegie Mellon University.

Fig. 4.6: "Palin, Guatemala. Open air market under a giant Ceiba tree." Black & white print, 4,5 x 6,5 inches; Photographer Wilson Popenoe. Popenoe Family Papers, Hunt Institute for Botanical Documentation, Carnegie Mellon University.

of modern botanical knowledge production altogether, which under the aegis of the USDA and BPI was personified in the figure of the plant collector, incarnated as the agricultural explorer who searched for new plants and locally and culturally embedded knowledge. Popenoe's notes in his field book offer insights into how knowledge about the use and cultivation of the plants became the primary quest. This becomes especially pertinent when examining the photographic series of the USDA that collected, described and annotated the plants in detail and eventually established significant and extensive photographic archives at the core of the programs of plant introduction to the United States.

Notably, for the botanical survey Popenoe, as well as the other USDA agricultural explorers, extensively used photography to document the practices of surveying, collecting and nursing the plants, along with the most common uses they were put to by the local people, depicting techniques and technologies as practices that embody and codify botanical knowledge. As a research tool and furthermore as a visual inscription of knowledge, photography was systematically employed on the USDA botanical field expeditions to "remote and little-known regions."[43] As such, these practices seem to have quickly established a field praxis, to which photography corresponded by helping to constitute a bio-geographical imagination, incorporating the new territories into the Western orbit of knowledge and responding to the desire for agricultural knowledge, on the one hand, and, more importantly, encoding a visual knowledge of plant and local agricultural practices, on the other. A specific modern model of knowledge has been established that Francesca Bray rightly pinpoints as follows:

> Technology takes the universal knowledge generated by science and applies it systematically to specific transformations of matter, thus rendering the world in which we live more orderly, productive and convenient. [...] This model of the production and application of ideas about matter left little or no place for the kind of embodied knowledge characteristic of preindustrial production, what we might refer to as "craft" or "skill," knowledge embodied in techniques.[44]

So, during his agricultural surveys in Colombia and Ecuador in 1920 and 1921, Popenoe extensively used the photographic camera on his field trips, the photographs of which were systematically sent to the BPI, renamed the Office of Foreign Seed and Plant Introduction. But he also did so much earlier, during his Brazil and Cuba expeditions in 1914 and 1915 respectively. He not only expanded his noted observations with schematic drawings and long descriptions of location and soil characteristics, but also documented thoroughly, recording landscape and fruit samples neatly cut and displayed, following a more conventional botanical pictorial arrangement. As an agricul-

---

43   Popenoe, "Foreign Service and Agriculture," p. 366.
44   Bray, "Science, Technique, Technology," p. 322.

tural explorer and botanist he visually depicts the context and habitat of the plants, capturing their transplantation and local cultivation practices and exploring the bio-contact zone when searching for the plants' local epistemologies. These practices of transmitting and transplanting as epistemic practices, constitutive of botanical knowledge, relate to the technologies and techniques of grafting and drafting, which certainly reiterate a colonial and imperial production of botany, but more significantly relate to old practices of farming that are, at heart, a form of culturally embodied knowledge. In the context of this search, photography as media technology was systematically used by the agricultural explorers and generated a new visibility of the tropical world, which shaped the emergence of modern economic botany, whose plants' discourse networks and thus efficient institutionalization transformed agricultural lands into a "tropical landscape." So it is that the photographs taken by Popenoe disclose an agricultural gaze that offers not so much a "scientific" view but rather one that frames the cultural contact and uses of plants.

As search sites these agricultural lands defined, according to Popenoe's notes, areas of interest to collect and identify new specimens along the routes of already existing cultivations. Compared to the rather approximate and idealized representation of nature in Blaschka's drawings, photography makes visible here the broader field of a botanical gaze seeking the commodification of fruits and plants while emphasizing the techniques and technologies of farming, that is, following an understanding of techniques as highly skilled practices "that go into the material production of knowledge as well as the production of artefacts,"[45] but also of technologies as sets of practices, techniques, and institutions that are social-material networks. Considering textual, material or visual inscriptions, the photographic archives of the USDA thus work to encode means of farming and botanical knowledges to be absorbed

45   Bray, "Science, Technique, Technology," p. 320.

Fig. 4.7: "Brazil. Mandioca." Black & white print, 4,5 x 6,5 inches; Photographer Wilson Popenoe. Popenoe Family Papers, Hunt Institute for Botanical Documentation, Carnegie Mellon University.

as modern scientific knowledge. In particular contrast to the Blaschka drawings, seeing becomes "knowing-through-technology"; moreover, a kind of "indirect cognition," that is "Highly mediated, eliding into unbounded, less visual zones in which 'nature' is produced purely discursively, produces all the wonders of the universe that we no longer need to 'see' to believe."[46] Though we are not even really able to recognize the specific characteristics of the strawberry plant, because of the unspecific black and white photography, and must rely on the caption the pictures hold to recognize the fruit, the pictures communicate something more important here. They relate to the cultural contact and local epistemologies of the plants' cultivation, while simultaneously depicting the transformation of nature into agricultural land, binding this conversion into a material exchange process of value and commodity.

46   Galison, *Picturing Science*, p. 13.

Fig. 4.8: "Duenas, Guatemala, 1916. Indian women drying and shelling corn in front of their huts." Black & white print, 4,5 x 6,5 inches; Photographer Wilson Popenoe. Popenoe Family Papers, Hunt Institute for Botanical Documentation, Carnegie Mellon University.

What becomes elemental for the knowledge production of economic botany is thus another mode: that of circulation. In the age of mechanical reproduction photography, both as novel technological medium and with regard to the pictures as knowledge-objects in their own right, helped establish a new form of knowledge circulation. Photography as used in the context of the USDA tropical surveys seems to have had at least two significant impacts: making visible the bio-contact zone and the material exchange, which fostered the creation of the photographic archives along with the collection of plants and seeds that were sent to the USDA's BPI. From within the understanding of materiality as an analytic concept to examine the epistemic praxis of science and knowledge, following materiality herewith as an historical *a priori* that indispensably relates to the techniques themselves, circulation thus becomes constitutive of knowledge production. Photography became thus a complementary practice to collecting plants and specimens, and together they constitute the fundamental epistemic practices of botanical fieldwork. Plants and specimens were collected *in situ* and shipped as fragile things to the main botanical institutions, such as the botanical garden of Soledad or the material repositories of the BPI. For this purpose, the BPI established an efficient institutional network that backed the botanical activities and foreign agricultural operations abroad.[47]

Institutional networks are the backbone of knowledge production, while material culture is the *conditio sine qua non* of knowledge, which has been also discussed under the lemma of the material turn. Whereas Bruno Latour relates "context" to institutions, Michel Foucault refers to dispositives or networks. Moreover, Latour expands this reasoning towards the understanding of the knowledge object as an actor that necessarily participates in the production of knowledge. Acknowledging the material conditions of knowledge production, expanding it towards the techniques and technologies as semantics of a broader cultural context, we may ask what apparatus, operations and chains of operation, decisions and interventions, are materially involved. With respect to the USDA photographic archives, on the one hand, the pictures certainly adopt the language of scientific representations, being themselves knowledge-objects that participate in the production of knowledge, particularly on the level of bureaucracies. On the other, they establish a kind of traffic or material exchange, that of commodity, which seems to ground the very scientific activity of the BPIs agricultural operations. Following the idea of contingency as an historical marker, I argue for "the mutual mediation of culture and materiality" and, furthermore, for conceiving "culture [as] materially mediated, and materiality [as] mediated culturally."[48] Interestingly, as Bray underscores:

---

47 See David Fairchild, "Two Expeditions After Living Plants: The Allison V. Amour Expeditions of 1925–27, Including Two Voyages in the Especially Equipped Yacht Utowana," *Scientific Monthly* 26 (1928), p. 103.
48 Bill Brown, "Materialities of Culture," in *Cultural Histories of the Material World*, ed. Peter N. Miller (Ann Arbor: University of Michigan Press, 2013), p. 189.

Historians, anthropologists and sociologists of science now routinely treat sciences (at least sciences as they have emerged in the post-Renaissance West) as materially rooted practices in which the materiality both of the object of study and of its observation is intrinsic to the generation of knowledge. Techniques and skills are reestablished as an essential element in the generation of scientific ideas, a key dimension of experiencing, perceiving and knowing matter. [...] In other words, science is not just knowledge about matter; it is also knowledge that comes through matter. Techniques mediate dialectically between knowledge and matter. As such they are essential both to scientific investigation and to technological practice, underlining the epistemological continuities between the two domains.[49]

In the context of botany and agriculture, institutional practices drew on two important technologies, as previously discussed with regard to the representation of plantation economy as landscape: first, grafting, that is, transplantation and plant transfer, and, secondly, drafting, that is, the "plans and reproductive 'blueprints' for plantations' layout and machinery," to make of the lands an economic, political and aesthetic hybrid landscape.[50] More specifically, the cultural conversion into "tropical landscape" was brought forward through transplantation, the transfer of plants, seeds, machinery, commodities and humans, and through agriculture as "improved," "peaceful," "productive cultivation," a modern process of rationalization, transforming land into a "colonial landscape of utility."[51] Both technologies thus intrinsically intersect and complement each other and mutually make the colonial landscape of utility viable. Taking a cue from Bray again, technology is to conceive of a "material system in which tacit understanding and explicit science both play a role in naturalizing social

---

49   Bray, "Science, Technique, Technology," p. 323.
50   Casid, *Sowing Empire*, p. 30.
51   Ibid., pp. 28–31.

Fig. 4.9: "Guatemala City. Avocado seeds drying in the patio of the United Fruit Co." Black & white print, 4,5 x 6,5 inches; Photographer Wilson Popenoe. Popenoe Family Papers, Hunt Institute for Botanical Documentation, Carnegie Mellon University.

hierarchies and encoding cultural values."[52] Consequently, landscaping, as related to both technologies of drafting and grafting, becomes pivotal for the naturalization of the social hierarchies of the "tropical landscape" that is constituent to the plantation economy. This kind of codification of landscape has been envisioned as a textual and graphical inscription of scientific knowledge, whose representations Latour has more recently called "immutable mobiles." Bray interestingly pinpoints that it "applies equally to science now and in premodern societies, [...] to define science as textually or graphically inscribed knowledge." She underscores that in "the process of inscription the knowledge is often further encoded by translating it into a specialist technical vocabulary, verbal or visual. [...] Hence the drive in inscription to simplify, to homogenize, to produce representations of the nature of material processes

52   Bray, "Science, Technique, Technology," p. 324.

Fig. 4.10: "Mazatenango, Guatemala. Citrullus melocoton." Black & white print, 4,5 x 6,5 inches; Photographer Wilson Popenoe. Popenoe Family Papers, Hunt Institute for Botanical Documentation, Carnegie Mellon University.

Fig. 4.11: "Indian woman beside collection of Guatemala textiles." Black & white print, 4,5 x 6,5 inches; Photographer Wilson Popenoe. Popenoe Family Papers, Hunt Institute for Botanical Documentation, Carnegie Mellon University.

that are accepted as generally valid beyond the time and place of their production."[53]

With regard to economic botany and the USDA tropical survey, and a particular US-Latin American geo-cultural relationship, photography turns out to be one of the novel technologies, which accounts for drafting. Moreover, concerning this conversion Sekula points out elsewhere that photography "constitutes a uniquely privileged technical invention in its refusal or inability to dominate or transform the realm of nature. Photography would seem to offer an inherently preservationist approach to nature," unlike other technologies such as the railroad or the telegraph.[54] It therefore becomes pertinent to conceive photography as a medium that does not directly intervene in nature, but appropriates it by visually representing it as given, in the

53   Ibid.
54   Allan Sekula, "The Traffic in Photographs," *Art Journal* 41:1 (1981), p. 22.

way it abets this peaceful transformation of "nature" into an agricultural land and produces "nature" only discursively. Likewise, the pictures traffic a sort of ethno-botanical knowledge, which is transmitted, translated, circulated and materialized in the specimens and seeds of plants, but also made viable through the visual. Photography and economic botany thus share a mutual relationship backing each other's discourse and allowing for traffic and commodification. As such, photography in this context becomes a landscaping technique that is supported by various discourse networks from agriculture to tropical medicine, and helps realize this cultural conversion through a visually structured knowledge space. With regard to the management of the topographical space, it turns out that the inception of the photographic archives of the USDA correlates with the organization of such a homogenous space to manage the gigantic flow of data. Both photography as media technology and the archive belong to the order of cultural techniques, through which scientific expansion is efficiently structured. The chains of operation are thus pivotal for this transformation: first, the creation of a homogenous space, and, secondly, the creation of an archive that as an epistemic continuity corresponds to the botanical expeditions and surveys. Bray in her study rightly questions the "official strategies for producing agronomic knowledge added to the technical knowledge of farmers." She asks: "How did they select, encode and deploy knowledge, and for what ends, and how successfully could such encodings be decoded and rematerialized as techniques or artefacts? Were official inscriptions simply records of existing knowledge, or did official agronomists also create new forms of knowledge?"[55]

However, there seems to be another relevant aspect when it comes to grasping this conversion of "nature" into agricultural land and the effective realization of the US expansion. With regard to the field of botany, it seems that these photographs

---

55   Bray, "Science, Technique, Technology," p. 328.

"create a new domain of the visual, producing at the same time new viewing subjects to make sense of that domain,"[56] which is informed by the institutional network and respective bureaucracies.[57] This conversion seems to become viable because of one fundamental assumption of what has been conceived, in an occidental understanding of science, as objectivity. That this conception is highly problematic has been discussed elsewhere.[58] Because of photography's discursivity of "non-intervention" and "not verisimilitude," reflecting a mechanical objectivity as a dominant mode, the transformation of "nature" into peaceful and improved agricultural land takes place smoothly, efficiently and eventually invisibly.[59] The photographs of the USDA share this kind of discursivity, inasmuch as they seem to have largely informed the new bureaucracies or institutional networks of agriculture and tropical botany in the United States.

56 Galison, *Picturing Science*, p. 17.
57 See Lorraine Daston and Peter Galison, "The Image of Objectivity," *Representations* 40 (1992), p. 98.
58 See Lorraine Daston, and Peter Galison, *Objectivity* (New York: Zone Books, 2007).
59 Let me recall at this point that the photograph as a mechanical image became the emblem for all aspects of non-interventionist objectivity: "The photograph has acquired a symbolic value, and its fine grain and evenness of detail have come to imply objectivity; photographic vision has become a primary metaphor for objective truth. This was not because the photograph was necessarily truer to nature than hand-made images – many paintings bore a closer resemblance to their subject matter than early photographs, if only because they used color – but rather because the camera apparently eliminated human agency. Nonintervention, not verisimilitude, lay at the heart of mechanical objectivity, and this is why mechanically produced images captured its message best. Images had always been considered more direct than words, and mechanical images that could be touted as nature's self-portrait were more immediate still. Thus images were not just the products of mechanical objectivity; they were also its prime exemplars." Daston, "The Image of Objectivity," p. 120.

The Political Economy of Agriculture

> The garden, as a small space that amasses the various parts of
> the world into one place, represents one of the main functions
> of these other spaces [the heterotopias], the ability to bring
> together in one space multiple and seemingly incompatible
> sites. [...] The itineraries of landscape gardens [...] may operate
> as vehicles, which like the ships of imperial "exploration" and
> commerce, take us other places and give us spaces in which to
> dream, the heterotopias of island gardens. However, in inverting
> the imperial real, the heterotopias of imagined geography do not
> necessarily upset the structuring logic of imperial ideology. [...]
> the more general claim that the role of heterotopia may be to cre-
> ate another real space challenges us to rethink [...] the relation
> between the imagined and materialized domains of empire.[60]

In the media history of botany, the USDA photographs belong
to the technologies of drafting, which account for botanical and
agricultural practices, thus helping to form such a homogenous
space. Most pictures of the agricultural or tropical surveys, such
as the photographs by Popenoe, imagine landscape in terms of
agricultural improvement and envision a future rationalization
of space and an effective modern production of natural commodities and seeds as technological artifacts. The actual "scientific" value of the pictures may lie in the way they make this
potential landscape visible, in that they reproduce and constitute
landscape as "a cultural medium,"[61] while enhancing the conversion of land into a productive agricultural landscape. Ultimately,
the photographs as *media a priori* help to form the discourse of
economic botany on the level of both representation and institutional practice. I wish to underline, at this juncture, that the

---

60   Jill H. Casid, "Inhuming Empire: Islands as Plantation Nurseries and
Graves," in *The Global Eighteenth Century*, ed. Felicity Nussbaum (Baltimore:
The Johns Hopkins University Press, 2003), pp. 294–295.
61   Mitchell, *Landscape and Power*, p. 2.

pictures are primarily embedded in an institutionalized network that enhances agricultural knowledge production linked to state-sponsored research. It becomes pertinent with regard to the US context and its state driven agricultural activities, such as plant introduction and breeding programs abroad, to conceive of agriculture as statecraft, necessarily taking place within a geopolitical rationale. At least until 1935, the history of plant breeding is linked to a pattern of public institutional development, in which the USDA was an important player. The rise of agribusiness became vital afterwards and eventually replaced state intervention in agricultural research. Interestingly, the United Fruit Company gained its momentum as a protagonist of cutting-edge agricultural research.[62] Wilson Popenoe became a key figure not only because of his contributions to the field of tropical botanical research—during his years in Guatemala, between 1916 and 1924, he introduced key crops from the tropical sphere, such as the avocado, into US agricultural production and markets—but also because he served both the USDA, where he started to work as early as 1913, and the United Fruit Company, where he became the chief agronomist in 1925 and director of agricultural experiments. He also later managed the *Escuela Agricola Panamericana*, which was founded in 1941 by the United Fruit Company and directed by none other than Samuel Zemurray, and other prominent scientists and naturalists such as Thomas D. Cabot and Thomas Barbour.

Among the USDA agricultural explorers, who substantially contributed to the USDA photographic archives, we also find Paul Allen and Walter Hodge, who observed:

> Introduction of plants from one region to another, from the wild into cultivation, is as old as agriculture itself, and it will continue as long as man moves about the surface of the earth. The curious, the beautiful and the useful plants that have been found in all corners of the globe

---

62   Jack Ralph Kloppenburg, *First the Seed: The Political Economy of Plant Technology* (Madison: University of Wisconsin Press, 2004), pp. 13–14.

have been carried by man from place to place, some to find a new home and many to die either because of man's ignorance as to their needs or the plant's inability to withstand a different environment.[63]

Even in the early years of the USDA, plant and seed introduction became a primary concern, inasmuch as officers of the Foreign Service were asked to send back valuable seeds and plants from their missions abroad. Accordingly, plant introduction and seed distribution became the first agricultural activities, which were later formalized by the USDA. It thus becomes pivotal to my argument about agriculture as statecraft or, in the Foucauldian sense, as governmentality to stress again the federal concern with organizing this key economic sector of the introduction and distribution of plants and germplasm, and the constituent role of the photographic archives in this. It is from within this perspective of geocultural impetus that the metaphor "the world was my garden," as pronounced by David Fairchild, who was in charge of the Federal Plant Introduction unit between 1903 and 1928 and became the key figure in the design of this federal program, must be read.[64] Wilson Popenoe seems to have been his longtime protégé. At the headquarters of the USDA Plant Industry Station in Beltsville, Maryland, today, the Section continues to have a twofold purpose: the "introduction into cultivation of new plant materials from all parts of the world; and preliminary testing of this material for potential use by agriculture in the United States."[65] However, in the US self-perception of a *mission civilisatrice* for the "backward countries" has been present since the earliest "American and United Nations agricultural missions": "Besides supplying technological advice on agricultural problems, these groups, in order to improve the local economy, have been introducing standardized crop

63   W. H. Hodge and C. O. Erlanson, "Federal Plant Introduction: A Review," *Economic Botany* 10:4 (1956), p. 299.
64   Ibid., p. 302.
65   Ibid., p. 304.

Fig. 4.12: "Near Ambato, Ecuador Jan 1921. Close view of fruits of babaco."
Black & white print, 4,5 x 6,5 inches; Photographer Wilson Popenoe. Popenoe
Family Papers, Hunt Institute for Botanical Documentation, Carnegie Mellon
University.

varieties as replacements for the primitive indigenous types.
Thus our own technology is contributing to the loss of varietal
wealth from the ancient reservoirs of crop germplasm,"[66] advancing the loss of biodiversity and helping to install agricultural monoculture. Vis-à-vis the political economy of agriculture
and the birth of modern economic agriculture, which euphe-
mistically come to be called "tropical," it is clear that the State
became the principal framework for the accumulation of capital and the production of homogenous space. Already during
the previous centuries "tropical" botany and agriculture were
deployed as key sciences that shaped the colonial and imperial
impetus of all the European powers. Indigenous knowledge on
plants in the region has been systematically sought since the
eighteenth century (and even earlier), when the Spanish Royal
Botanical Expeditions explored the region as it was being shaped

66   Ibid., p. 310.

Fig. 4.13: "Ambato, Ecuador Jan 1921. The market – potatoes in the fore-
ground." Black & white print, 4,5 x 6,5 inches; Photographer Wilson Popenoe.
Popenoe Family Papers, Hunt Institute for Botanical Documentation,
Carnegie Mellon University.

by geopolitical interests. Old routes and circuits were therefore
significant as they became prerequisites for the production of
agricultural knowledge.

It was Popenoe again who was sent as an agricultural
explorer on an early plant-hunting mission to Brazil and Cuba
in the years 1914 and 1915, before becoming a leading expert
on Central American flora and fruits. What thus became a
remarkable feature was that the production of botanical knowledge was "to be in the field," inasmuch as the plant explorers
needed to undertake extensive and long-term field expeditions
to gather this type of embodied knowledge in the bio-contact
zone and to make the transfer of plants possible. It is noteworthy that the institutional network that supported the formation
of economic botany is well reflected in the biographies of the
plant explorers. As we follow the itineraries of the plant explorer
and botanist Paul Allen, we read about how the institutional
network of tropical botany was decidedly entangled:

Fig. 4.14: "Near Ambato, Ecuador Jan 1921, Watchman in strawberry field."
Black & white print, 4,5 x 6,5 inches; Photographer Wilson Popenoe. Popenoe
Family Papers, Hunt Institute for Botanical Documentation, Carnegie Mellon
University.

Fig. 4.15: "Near Ambato, Ecuador Jan 1921, Strawberry fields of Ganchi."
Black & white print, 4,5 x 6,5 inches; Photographer Wilson Popenoe. Popenoe
Family Papers, Hunt Institute for Botanical Documentation, Carnegie Mellon
University.

Fig. 4.16: *(no inscription).* Black & white print, 4,5 x 6,5 inches; Photographer Wilson Popenoe. Popenoe Family Papers, Hunt Institute for Botanical Documentation, Carnegie Mellon University.

He made his first trip to the tropics in 1934 [...] as student assistant and botanical collector, for the Missouri Botanical Garden. [...] returned to Panama in 1936 [...] this time as manager of the Missouri Botanical Garden's Tropical Station, to carry on the plant collecting for the Flora of Panama and later as superintendent of the Canal Zone Experimental Station, at Summit. With the beginning of the war, many botanists were needed as field technicians, to work on the stratigic [sic] wild products of rubber and quinine under the auspices of the Rubber Development Corporation. His work on rubber took him to the land of Bates and Spruce – the primative [sic] and extremely interesting indian country along the tributaries of the Oronoco [sic] and Amazon Rivers, in Colombia. After the war he returned to Panama and then to Cambridge, Massachusetts to complete a work on Panama's orchid taxonomy. His interests covered all phases of tropical plant work so, in 1948, he joined The United Fruit Company's Research Department to experiment with tropical timber trees and to do the field work for his publication "The Rain Forests of Golfo Dulce". Next he tried to return to the United States as Director of the Fairchild Tropical

Garden but, Florida just is not tropical, so he soon returned to The United Fruit Company's Escuela Agricola Panamericana, in Honduras, to teach until he was loaned to the Government of El Salvador to do a survey of their timber resources. In 1959 he again returned to The United Fruit Company as Director of their famous Lancetilla Experimental Station but almost immediately they decided to send him off in charge of their banana collecting expedition to the Far East. The purpose of this trip was to assemble a Far Eastern Reference Genetic Bank as a basis for breeding whose objective is the combining in one commercial banana variety of all possible desirable qualities—mostly disease resistance. Banana rhizomes and wealth of information were collected over a period of two years in the Philippines, Taiwan, North Borneo, Sarawak, Malaya, Singapore, Java and Bali with short stopovers in Thailand, Ceylon and the Herbaria at Florence and Kew for additional information. All of this helped to build up the world's largest collection of bananas for The United Fruit Company.[67]

It becomes clear when reading this biographical fragment that the United Fruit Company was significantly involved on at least two levels: first, with a supporting scientific infrastructure, such as experimental stations, botanical gardens, and agricultural schools but also within the discourse networks related to technology that fostered traffic and transfer, such as shipping, the telegraph, and the railroad; second, in the recruitment and exchange of human resources, inasmuch as many of the leading figures in botany and agricultural researchers were linked to the research units of the United Fruit Company and other leading institutions in the field, among them the USDA. Significantly, the United Fruit Company was engaged in a series of experimental and botanical research projects, not limited to the main fruit, the banana, but including all sorts of promising and useful tropical fruits, such as citrus, sisal, pasture, sugar cane, coconut, and cacao. It is also noteworthy that the

---

67   *Paul Hamilton Allen Papers, 1911–1963*, Hunt Institute for Botanical Documentation, Carnegie Mellon University, Pittsburgh.

Company participated in specific strategic scientific programs led by the USDA, such as the cinchona program of 1940, to which it loaned some territories it owned in Central America for the purpose of supporting experimental cinchona research, in addition to the loan of scientific researchers, including Popenoe.[68] The Lancetilla Experiment Station in Honduras, founded in 1925 by the United Fruit Company and directed by Popenoe, served as one among several branches of the Company's research department to study banana cultivation.[69] Popenoe notes, with regard to the cinchona program, that "It is therefore obvious that the agriculturist must devote little attention to the botanical classification of the material with which he works and much to its characteristics of growth and its economic value."[70]

This gaze at a range of potential natural commodities and the search for sites and cultivation is also framed in the photographic albums of the United Fruit Company that mirror the embodied scientific discourse and the *mise-en-valeur* of the Caribbean. Both kinds of pictures, those from the albums and those from the USDA, make the political economy of agriculture visually explicit in the way they focus on the material practices of farming and the use of plants, giving preference to the documentation of local epistemologies. The pictures are in this way a visual inscription of agricultural knowledge codified in a

---

68   Wilson Popenoe, "Cinchona Cultivation in Guatemala – A Brief Historical Review up to 1943," *Economic Botany* 3:2 (1949), p. 155.
69   Paul C. Standley, "Lancetilla Experiment Station," *Science* 68:1760 (1928), p. 265. Further: "There has been established at Lancetilla, also, the Serpentarium of the Antivenin Institute of America, maintained by the Tela Railroad Company [a United Fruit Company subsidiary], the Museum of Comparative Zoology of Harvard University and the H. K. Mulford Company. The purpose of the present note is to direct attention to the suitability of Lancetilla as headquarters for research work in the natural sciences [...]. The Tela Railroad Company has been generous in supplying to visiting scientists every facility for the performance of their work, and the director of the station is keenly interested in the assembling and publication of information regarding the fauna and flora of the region." Ibid., pp. 265–266.
70   Popenoe, "Cinchona Cultivation in Guatemala," p. 154.

systematic documentation series while constituting an important archive within a modern botanical machine. Further, the pictures, like other visual inscriptions, become pivotal for the creation of heterotopias, whose role "may be to create another real space [that] challenges us to rethink [...] the relation between the imagined and materialized domains of empire."[71] Thus, Lucile Brockway points out that it "is not any one society or empire, but the network emanating from the West that penetrated all societies, binding colonized to colonizers, and colonizers to each other."[72] This network is supported on the level of the visual, while enabling a cultural transfer. Recent research has oriented itself towards new differentiations of these transfer processes, focusing on the phenomenon of globalization and on the question of the cultural conditions of colonialism as a critique of the Occidental epistemic order, looking at different forms of knowledge and power.[73] Looking at patterns of appropriation and economic utilization of space that fostered a biogeographical interest in the world outside Europe as an expansion of the Occidental epistemic order, which has been identified as one of the principles of the geopolitical contention between the (former colonial) European powers.[74] Ultimately, the success and efficiency of Occidental expansion, including the United States, could not be explained through a military component alone, but also required lasting biological and ecological ones. I argue for considering this against the backdrop of the scientific expeditions and surveys within the history of spatialization to better grasp the construction, incorporation into the Occidental epistemic order and scientification of "tropical" Latin America and the making of tropical botany, due to the photographic images that become here an effective means. What institutional infrastructure and connectivity were

71   Casid, "Inhuming Empire," pp. 294–295.
72   Brockway, *Science and Colonial Expansion*; Crosby, *Ecological Imperialism*, p. 9.
73   Poole, *Vision, Race, and Modernity*.
74   See Brockway, *Science and Colonial Expansion*, p. 7.

Fig. 4.17: "Near Ambato, Ecuador Jan 1921, Small orchard of Mexican avocados at Pitula – believed to have been planted by the Jesuits at least 150 years ago." Black & white print, 4,5 x 6,5 inches; Photographer Wilson Popenoe. Popenoe Family Papers, Hunt Institute for Botanical Documentation, Carnegie Mellon University.

created? What significance do image processes have for knowledge production and circulation in the context of the political economy of agriculture?

Following these questions, I expand on one significant spatial figure and emergent modern institution: the botanical garden. As pointed out, botanical gardens are imagined and materialized domains of empire, realized at the crossroads of science, aesthetics, and economy, which feature the correspondence of space and landscape. They are small entities that assemble "the various parts of the world into one place [with] the ability to bring together in one space multiple and seemingly incompatible sites."[75] And, yet, they are a sort of enclave; enclosed and scientifically engineered spaces that artificially delimit nature's auspicious biodiversity and the economic promise

75   Casid, "Inhuming Empire," p. 294.

Fig. 4.18: "Near Ambato, Ecuador Jan 1921. One of the largest avocados groves in Ecuador – at Pingui." Black & white print, 4,5 x 6,5 inches; Photographer Wilson Popenoe. Popenoe Family Papers, Hunt Institute for Botanical Documentation, Carnegie Mellon University.

of accumulation of capital and knowledge. We mostly find in them a large section of those plants classifiable as economic botany, such as timber, fruits, vegetables and other crops. It becomes clear that they too are based on an economic rationality. Significantly, they belong to what I refer to as discourse networks, inasmuch as they help establish and institutionalize the material practices of landscaping: grafting and drafting. Along with the gardens as sites of experimenting and molding nature into something knowable and manageable, circulation and exchange define the rationale of economic botany and thus the transformation of land into an economically viable, aesthetic, and hybrid landscape. Two sites are particularly noteworthy for their role in configuring the Caribbean as a geocultural space giving shape to the rise of US tropical botany in the early twentieth century: the botanical garden at Soledad in Cuba, later known as the Atkins Garden of 1899, and Barro Colorado Island

Fig. 4.19: "Ambato, Ecuador Jan 1921. In the valley of the Rio Ambato; vine-yards on the slopes, fruit trees on the floor. The volcano Tungurahua in the distance." Black & white print, 4,5 x 6,5 inches; Photographer Wilson Popenoe. Popenoe Family Papers, Hunt Institute for Botanical Documentation, Carnegie Mellon University.

in Panama, founded in 1923.[76] Barro Colorado Island as a piece of "primeval tropical nature" was a by-product of the flooding of land for the Panama Canal, which was a major environmental and ecological transformation of the land into a "civilized" and manageable economic space. The botanical garden at Soledad also had its origins in an equally violent alteration of the land-scape related to the sugar industry and the modern plantation economy.

---

76   See here the study by Megan Raby, "Ark and Archive: Making a Place for Long-Term Research on Barro Colorado Island, Panama," *Isis: Journal of the History of Science Society* 106:4 (2015), where she examines the formation of US tropical botany within natural history and the prominent role of the island as an archive. See also Megan Raby, "Making Biology Tropical: American Science in the Caribbean, 1898–1963," (Ph.D. diss., University of Wisconsin-Madison, 2013).

Both are "highly mediated and managed sites" and, furthermore, scientifically engineered landscapes.[77] Significantly, one observable hallmark of this new science of botany is that, in terms of material practices, it becomes pivotal that collecting specimens goes hand in hand with the observation of nature, reflected broadly in the use of photography, that is, not only for documenting plants but also for depicting the practices of nursing, and the plant's uses and milieu. The historian of science and environment Megan Raby underscores that the "Research at [Barro Colorado Island] typified a broader shift from a concentration on collection to the integration of collection with extended observation of living organisms in nature" and that "the movement toward place-based research became a more conscious shift to long-term research," in which documentation became a crucial activity. Following on from this, this shift may also have created the pivotal role of photography, which was then extensively used on the agricultural and botanical field surveys, but also to document the botanical garden at Soledad. Like the collected plant specimens, the pictures were exchanged within the network and generously circulated between the different institutions, making the collected and documented data available within the scientific networks. In her study, Raby relates this shift towards long-term environmental research to the idea of the archive, suggesting a more profound, metaphorical understanding of natural history, that is, "the preservation of a past order for a future good, pretensions to completeness, and even sanctity."[78] I argue that the botanical garden, as an archive, projects and forecloses the transformation of land into an economically viable and hybrid landscape, becoming a distinctive temporal and spatial experimental site. Moreover, plantation economy created a specific, efficient and scientifically engineered landscape, which was similarly backed by small scientific sites such as botanical gardens. Raby further argues

77   Raby, "Ark and Archive."
78   Ibid.

242

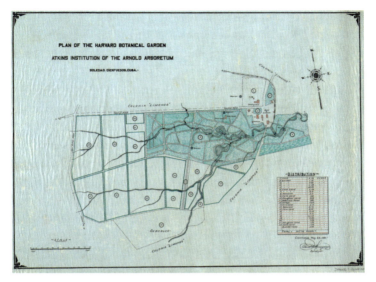

Fig. 4.20: "Plan of the Harvard Botanical garden-Atkins Institution of the Arnold Arboretum: Soledad, Cienfuegos, Cuba," May 8, 1933. Surveyor Oswaldo Binayarza, map, colored, 64 x 115 cm. Arnold Arboretum Horticultural Library Map Collection, Harvard University.

that "transforming the site into a scientific object also meant modifying it to make it accessible and observable, rather than maintaining the site unchanged."[79] Accordingly, the archive is related here to "the scientific practices and landscape transformations that made long-term research possible."[80] This is true with regard to Barro Colorado Island and the botanical garden at Soledad. Yet, I wish to extend this consideration to the landscape itself. The environment culturally altered through agriculture makes past material practices of landscaping accessible while linking them to other components, such as textual and visual inscriptions. It has been acknowledged that the archaeological-ethnological understanding of "nature," for instance as related to the Amazon basin, has never been a primeval one,

79   Ibid.
80   Ibid.

untouched or simply wild. Instead, it is an (agri)culturally modi-
fied past space that has become an archive of landscaping techniques that grasp the past and present interactions between
man and "nature."

Let me return to the botanical garden at Soledad, which is
situated at the crossroads of science and economy, constituting a particular site inside this institutional network of the
United Fruit Company. We find in the correspondence of the
agricultural explorers, particularly in Wilson Popenoe's, Walter
Hodge's and Paul Allen's papers, a well-articulated nexus of US
economic botany that unfolds between the United Fruit Company and the USDA and spans the diverse experiment stations,
the botanical garden at Soledad, and the botany and tropical
biology research departments of the academic complex, such
as Harvard University. The origins of the botanical garden at
Soledad are more than symbolic: originally part of the Atkins
sugar estates under Edward Atkins, a wealthy sugar plantation
owner and businessman from Massachusetts, it was primarily assigned to the research of sugar cane for the purpose of
commercialization. Formally evolving into a botanical garden
in 1899, backed by Harvard University and the botany department under the auspices of Oakes Ames and George L. Goodale,
the tropical botanical garden united both economic interests
and an academic vision.[81] Significantly, the garden was originally inseparably linked to the Cuban sugar industry and thus
to the darker history of slavery and forced African and Chinese
labor, characteristic of the plantation regime of the previous
centuries.[82] Atkins developed this estate that was the primary
plantation in Soledad together with other lands acquired later,
into one of the "most modern and progressively managed sugar

81   Marion D. Cahan, "The Harvard Garden in Cuba – A Brief History," *Arnoldia*
51:2 (1991), p. 22.
82   For the history of the plantation Soledad in Cuba see also the study by
Rebecca Scott, "A Cuban Connection: Edwin F. Atkins, Charles Francis Adams,
Jr., and the Former Slaves of Soledad Plantation," *Massachusetts Historical
Review* 9 (2007).

estates on the island."[83] As observed by Casid, again, "given the material conditions of the sugar plantation with its forced slave labor, to plant or impress imperial subjects with a new ideology of empire as cultivation rather than conquest, the colony required reimagining. This conceptualization was the island at a remove, the island as garden shifted from the plantation sites of slave labor on the colonized islands of the Caribbean to create [...] the *antiempire* of the island garden."[84] It is in this way that the botanical garden—as a colonial and bourgeois imagined and materialized site and, formalized, as an institution—realized its symbolic role, shaped by the plantation regime as a necessarily socio-economic hierarchical space.

The push towards scientific research was shaped by economic purposes that aimed to improve sugar cane and increase the disease resistance of the crops. Within the framework of the political economy of agriculture, the botanical garden at Soledad became a symbolically and materially realized heterotopian space and a promise of a future development of the "Tropics," backed by the discourse of tropicality. Shortly after the foundation of the Atkins Garden, many other plants and fruit trees were imported and experimented with for future cultivation and commodification, and the garden eventually became "one of the largest collections of tropical plants in the Western Hemisphere."[85] Among the crops successfully tested we find bananas, cocoa, coffee and rubber. Internal correspondence suggests that three crops became of particular interest to the United Fruit Company, namely banana, cocoa and sugar, and these were systematically improved and became an integral part of the agricultural activities on the Company plantations across the entire Caribbean. Between 1903 and 1926 the garden included a collection of eighteen Cuban-grown banana varieties,

---

83   Cahan, "The Harvard Garden in Cuba," p. 27.
84   Casid, "Inhuming Empire," p. 280.
85   Cahan, "The Harvard Garden in Cuba," p. 27.

and was thus one of the largest of its time.[86] The research program was further extended to include strategically important species of citrus fruits, which were cultivated on a trial basis, leading to the production and testing of "hundreds of hybrid mango seedlings."[87] Grasses, and large collections of palm and bamboo, were also among the botanical assemblages that formed one unified space of multiple and even incompatible sites.

It is noteworthy that in 1933 it was decided to dismantle the tropical greenhouses of the Harvard Botanical Garden in Cambridge to transfer the larger part of the material to Soledad.[88] The naturalist Thomas Barbour, keenly interested in economic botany, who was also the scientist who founded the Barro Colorado Island Laboratory, reports that it was, among many other botanists, Wilson Popenoe of the United Fruit Company who most frequently visited the botanical garden at Soledad and with the support of the Company made significant additions to the botanical assemblage and testing. Importantly, after the renaming of the institution as The Atkins Institution of the Arnold Arboretum, the main focus shifted from "commercial crops to the planting of tropical tree species imported from Florida, Jamaica, the East Indies, Australia, tropical Africa, and Central America."[89] It is remarkable that the botanical garden materialized these shifting economic interests within its collections, unquestionably reflecting the institutional network within the diversity of its interests. Ultimately, plants were transferred and transplanted intensively on the site that became not only a scientific object, but also, and perhaps even more so, a model for the conversion of the world into a garden, meticulously monitored and scientifically engineered: the garden was the testing ground for modern botanical knowledge production, thus fostering the commodification of landscape.

86   Ibid., p. 28
87   Ibid., p. 27.
88   Thomas Barbour and Helene M. Robinson, "Forty Years of Soledad," *The Scientific Monthly* 51:2 (1940), p. 145.
89   Cahan, "The Harvard Garden in Cuba," p. 29.

The garden mirrors here the coalescence between science and economy, to which the altered landscape seems to correspond, that of the site of human interaction with the environment. Indeed, the garden seems to be an imaginative figure, making the "Tropics" a viable space to be consumed at a global scale. Eventually, the botanical garden at Soledad belongs to the kind of replicas, "often on a giant scale, of the experimental station," into which unfavorable local conditions were transformed into a testing ground of the modern.[90] By laying the groundwork for the conversion of the world into a garden, bound to its politics of value, the very rationale becomes operative: science and economy with their specific sites of enclosure and control, the garden and the enclave, make the Caribbean a laboratory of the modern. Both as an archive and as an eternal promise of modernity, the garden as a wishful and materialized site simultaneously represents a past and a future that are inseparably grounded on destruction and creation. In a scientific manner, rather ingenuously, the botanist Elmer Drew Merrill reports:

> Since the garden is located in a region where most of the native arborescent vegetation has been largely destroyed, it is fortunate that a considerable tract of native forest is included. This area, a rocky outcropping known as the *seboruco*, is being maintained as a characteristic representation of native lowland Cuban forest. [...] Because of prolonged dry seasons, we thus have the opportunity of developing tropical plantings of those species that are more or less characteristic of those parts of Asia, Australia, Africa, Mexico, and South America which have somewhat similar climatic conditions; all of these regions have contributed extensively to the rapidly expanding plantings of Soledad. At the same time, with irrigation, it is possible to grow a great many tropical species that are adapted to regions of higher humidity and a greater or more evenly distributed annual rainfall.[91]

90   Bray, "Science, Technique, Technology," p. 326.
91   E. D. Merrill, "The Atkins Institution of the Arnold Arboretum, Soledad, Cienfuegos, Cuba," *Bulletin of Popular Information* 8:13 (1940), pp. 69–70.

In August 1961, with the Cuban Revolution, the garden as an US-American institution was abandoned, yet some of the transplanted plants still survive today. Nevertheless, whereas Barro Colorado Island continued to exist and evolved into a key institution for tropical research, it was the botanical garden at Soledad with its specific blend of economic interest and natural science that remained a significant site within the institutional complex and discourse networks of botany and agriculture at the crossroads of geopolitics. This was also articulated by the USDA and became its main rationale, insofar as "Gardens for testing new or little-known immigrant plants" were conceived as vital to the successful formalization of plant introduction to the United States.[92] Whereas the importance of the botanical garden or *hortus conclusus* as a symbolic figure of ordering space was acknowledged, the expansion of the network of tropical botany and agriculture was soon recognized as another urgency shared by elite circles. Intersecting with different routes and circuits as "tropical" crossroads of the world, the United Fruit Company, pondering on its own interests, understood early the importance of laying the groundwork for the reproduction of agricultural knowledge: the founding of the *Escuela Agricola Panamericana* or School of Panamerican Agriculture in Honduras in 1941 by the prominent and dubious figure, then head of the United Fruit Company, Samuel Zemurray, known as "Sam the Banana Man," as a higher education institution for agriculture, backed by a series of agricultural explorers and widely recognized naturalists, among them Popenoe, aimed at fulfilling this promise.

This is the larger narrative within which both photographic archives, that of the USDA and that of the Company, came into being. I argue that these archives are shaped by the emergent modern bureaucratic culture, while at the same time contouring the emergence of tropical botany. The botanical survey with its material practices of collecting and transferring plants

92   Hodge, "Federal Plant Introduction," p. 318.

configured this landscape as a scientific one: agriculture thus became a significant geopolitical modern science. Correspondingly, Casid notes:

> The acquisition of plants, transfer of vegetable commodities, and seeding of the ground were the founding, paternalistic gestures in the European formation of colonies [and the US expansion alike]. Inseminating appropriated land with transplanted seed was a material act, a staking of geopolitical claims that, as a privileged scene, attempted to perform the imaginative labor of converting conquest into something "sweet and humane."[93]

This certainly captures the nature of the political economy of agriculture experienced during the first half of the twentieth century under the protective influence of the USDA and expanding global companies, such as the United Fruit Company, along with the commodification and scientification of "nature."[94] Ultimately, the making of commodities and thus the introduction of seeds and plants created a powerful asymmetry and reproduced and reiterated a sort of "colonial" or imperial relationship between the "center" and the "peripheries." This has also been highlighted by Jack Kloppenburg in his study of biotechnology as one of the premises of the mode of capitalist production of space. He astutely points out:

> The flow of plant germplasm between the gene-poor and the gene-rich has been fundamentally asymmetric. This asymmetry is expressed on at least two dimensions. First, in purely quantitative terms, the core has received much more material that it has provided to the periphery. Second, in qualitative terms the germplasm has very different social characters depending on the direction in which it is moving. The

---

93   Casid, "Inhuming Empire," p. 279.
94   Marjory Stoneman Douglas, *Adventures in a Green World – The Story of David Fairchild and Barbour Lathrop* (Miami: Field Research Projects, 1973), pp. 2–3.

germplasm resources of the Third World have historically been considered a free good—the "common heritage of mankind" [...]. Germplasm ultimately contributing billions of dollars to the economies of the core nations has been appropriated at little cost from—and with no direct remuneration to—the periphery. On the other hand, as the seed industry of the advanced industrial nations has matured, it has reached out for global markets. Plant varieties incorporating genetic material originally obtained from the Third World now appear there not as free goods but as *commodities*.[95]

Science and the scientification of "nature," as I have shown, back this process of cultural conversion that is based principally on two interventions: on time and on space. Correspondingly, agriculture and in particular landscaping, with its techniques and technologies, constitute the transformation of the Caribbean into a modern chronotope, that is, that "Irregularities of time are minimized. [...] Space, too, is homogenized. Mountainsides are levelled, swamps drained and deserts irrigated till they bloom. This material technology is not unlimited in its powers to standardize local landscapes and climate."[96] Bray pinpoints that "The material technologies of industrial farming do more than simply apply the facts of normal agricultural science, they help turn them into harder facts by testing them against initially adverse conditions. And they give enormous mobility to their immutables (general principles of tillage, hybrid seeds) by transforming unfavourable local conditions into replicas [...]."[97] Following this, the Caribbean's transformation is by no means "a physical object, but a cultural one."[98]

---

95   Kloppenburg, *First the Seed*, p. 15. Kloppenburg argues that the Third World nations are today much more concerned with these patterns of flows of genes: "Through the medium of the Food and Agriculture Organization of the United Nations (FAO), developing nations are insisting that a 'new genetic order' be a part of the New International Economic Order." Ibid., p. 17.
96   Bray, "Science, Technique, Technology," p. 326.
97   Ibid.
98   Carter, *The Road to Botany Bay*, p. xxii.

Let me thus go back to the scientific circuits that are significant for my argument on the political economy of agriculture. I wish to recall some aspects of the historical account of this transformation of land into an agricultural landscape and the role of the USDA in that process. In 1887, the Hatch Act provided federal funds for the establishment of Agricultural Experiment Stations and articulated a "turning point in USDA history, 'the culmination of a long battle by the proponents of agricultural science to bring the financial power of the federal government to the aid of the nation's farming interests at the state and local levels.'"[99] Accordingly, "tropical surveying, cataloging and plant introduction were happening in response to the United States officially acquiring such widely separated territories as Puerto Rico and Hawaii in the 1890s." Importantly, as former agricultural explorer Walter Hodge notes, "Administrators, policy makers and the public" wanted to test the economic viability of these territories for future agricultural development.[100] So it was that the making of the "tropical" landscape went hand in hand with the expansion of agricultural and botanical surveys in the Caribbean and tropical Latin America, articulating a geopolitical interest in the region to which the radical environmental changes that accompanied the expansion of the United States towards the South corresponded. Moreover, these material practices of surveying, collecting data, documenting, preserving ecological sites and the cultural techniques of landscaping describe the realm of natural history, in which the knowledge production of botany and agriculture was deeply rooted. Botanical expeditions and surveys thus backed this kind of knowledge production, inasmuch as they helped contribute to the collection of plant species and specimens, in which both the photographic archives of the USDA and the botanical gardens and laboratories became constitutive components.

99   Hodge, "Agricultural Explorers," p. 31.
100 Ibid.

The pictures as scientific photography are determined by some "expectations of empirical science, topography, and record-keeping," as photography's discursive space.[101] Yet, as documents they belong to the discourse of conquering new spaces, while they are ascribed to a scientific practice, established during the second half of the nineteenth century as survey photography. Interestingly, Kelsey points out elsewhere that "When surveys emerged as ongoing bureaucratic programs administered by competing agencies, pictures were pressed into service as promotional materials, intensifying suspicions about the need to produce them at public expense. At the same time, as survey disciplines developed into scientific specialties, graphic practices became increasingly differentiated."[102] While the surveys of the American West of the second half of the nineteenth century can be characterized by the strong involvement of the government itself, towards the end of the nineteenth century and particularly during the first half of the twentieth century, this involvement was diminished and new private actors, such as transnational corporations, began to dominate the field of scientific expeditions. Without a doubt, the survey photography of the USDA determines a material practice that makes the institutional or organizational character of the production of photographic images particularly clear. Kelsey further observes with regard to the circulation of survey photography that "the value of photography for generating publicity had begun to trump its limitations as a tool of science" undermining the authority of texts.[103] However, more than a scientific tool, the photograph seemed to have adopted the form of knowing as being related to popular legibility: "While only the select few can appreciate the discoveries of the geologists, or the exact measurements of the topographers, everyone can understand a picture."[104] I under-

---

101 Kelsey, *Archive Style*, p. 77.
102 Ibid.
103 Ibid.
104 *New York Times* 1875, cited in ibid., p. 79.

score two main points here: first, the expeditionary culture of surveys, and, second, "the neglect of the internal workings of bureaucracies within the study of visual culture."[105] Within this specific context of the institutional and scientific entanglement of the USDA and the United Fruit Company, the production of survey photography took its specific forms and shapes. It is certainly the case, with regard to the USDA photographic archives, that ultimately "Making a picture seem like an archival record entailed making it seem uncontrived. Ensuring that visual pleasure registered as incidental required the suppression of aesthetic intent."[106]

The scientific circuits and this institutional embeddedness, however, significantly shaped the formation of techniques and technologies, such as the photographic archives that became the register of the abiding environmental and cultural conversion of the landscape. It is interesting that ultimately "specimen viability and the crop viability in their new environs were questions only answered in the long-term, as well as the even slower revelations of plants' uses. In addition to long-term industrial uses and pharmaceutical developments, plant disease resistances also continue to be discovered from plants collected by these early USDA plant explorers."[107] Whereas scientific circuits eventually materialized the biogeographical interest, endeavoring the *mise-en-valeur* of the globe, there was a simultaneous "emphasis on the nation as an agricultural whole, exacerbated by plunging national economies during the depression of the previous era" and an attempt to contextualize farming within "the concept of the nation as an agricultural unit rather than as a collection of sections, States, counties, communities, or individual farms."[108] Hodge further points out that this "mark of the Great Depression could be seen in the research plans

---

105 Ibid., p. 11.
106 Ibid., p. 82.
107 Hodge, "Agricultural Explorers," p. 36.
108 Ibid., p. 41.

of the USDA, as well as in its attention to a major constituent, farmers."[109] Interestingly, Hodge even suggests that "this USDA plan for conceptualizing the nation as a whole increased in its urgency with the outbreak of the World War II" and that "departmental planning anticipated the United States' 1942 entry in the war" while looking at the food supply and, in fact, food surplus of the pre-war years.[110] Thus, the aims of the agricultural and botanical surveys certainly reflect a transnational and geopolitical rationale.[111] In her study, Brockway similarly underpins that "the multinational corporation is the characteristic instrument of neocolonialist expansion in the world system," with its own scientific information and internal organs of research and development, such as private research firms, the university, or government agencies.[112]

The photographs that aimed at documenting the material practices of the ongoing surveys became thus constitutive of the fieldwork. This becomes particularly true when looking at the function of the visual inscriptions of agricultural knowledge on another botanical mission that reflects the ongoing process of institutionalization of tropical botany. Interestingly, Hodge underscores, "While food supplies topped the list of the USDA's priorities during World War II, two non-food USDA projects that coalesced at this time were those organized around *Cinchona*, the bark of which is the major source for the anti-malaria drug quinine, and *Hevea*, a source for rubber."[113] The so-called *Cinchona mission* (1943–1945), led by Francis Raymond Fosberg and William Campbell Steere, was organized under the direction of the Board of Economic Warfare. In the imperial mold of scientific exploration, "Botanical crews were dispatched to the back country of South America, particularly the Andes Mountains, the native habitat of Cinchona, in search of concentra-

109 Ibid.
110 Ibid.
111 See Baker, *Century of Service*, p. 274.
112 Brockway, *Science and Colonial Expansion*, p. 10.
113 Hodge, "Agricultural Explorers," p. 44.

tions sufficient for serving as a quinine source."[114] Interestingly, *Hevea* studies were implemented when the "United States lost 90% of its Pacific sources of natural rubber due to Japanese invasions."[115] Many botanists were thus sent with accompanying field teams by the USDA to the Caribbean, in particular Cuba, Haiti, the Dominican Republic, Panama, Costa Rica, Venezuela, Colombia, but even more so to Brazil and the Amazon Basin. They created a workforce in a colonial way, because "Many *Hevea*-heavy tropical locations were not populated by native people, so the field team would locate the rubber plants, build a camp site and then hire and transport native workers to assist with the rubber tapping. *Hevea* breeding programs were developed in Haiti and Costa Rica."[116] Hodge further underscores that the USDA tested "'almost every rubber-producing species in temperate as well as tropical America [...] for rubber possibilities."[117] Along with these botanical surveys, the broad and systematic use of photography was astounding when it came to documenting the surveying, collecting and nursing practices, eventually constituting them as landscaping techniques, backed by an emerging institutional network of experimental stations and other scientific circuits in the Tropics that involved craftsmanship and local knowledge in order to locate and cultivate both *Hevea* and cinchona. The species were thus collected *in situ* and shipped to the main botanical institutions. When possible, "a species that did not survive shipping could be collected and shipped again"; yet, "sometimes the responsible explorer had moved on and recollecting the specimen was not an option."[118]

114 Ibid.
115 Ibid.
116 Ibid.
117 Ibid., p. 45.
118 Ibid., p. 37. Fairchild notes: "The seeds of many tropical plants are very short-lived. If dried they die and if kept moist they germinate in a few days, so that the only way to send them is as seedlings in Wardian cases. From Singapore to Panama by the fastest mail route is today [1928] about two months and there are few things deadlier to tender young plants than salty spray. So that when a

Eventually, the botanical institutional network and its scientific circuits formed "nature" into a modern laboratory, as we have seen here in the case of the botanical garden at Soledad, and sparked the very idea of nature as a replica of a future landscape to be an archival repository of botanical knowledge. Significantly, it was the photographic archive that indexed the emergent altered landscape and thus became a tool that helped incorporate these new territories into a Western orbit of knowledge and into a modern political space. Moreover, the visual determines here an efficient mode of colonizing "tropical land," making it visible as "tropical landscape" and reproducing the very idea of tropicality at the heart of botany. Thus, the visualization and the visual inscriptions of agricultural knowledge sparked the production of the modern space, to which science and the commodification of nature correspond, during the first decades of the twentieth century.

Visual Epistemology and Botanical Matter

Within the media history of botany, one's attention turns to the interrelation of craft and science and to artisan epistemology, when it comes to discussing the interlacing of skills and knowledge in the context of the domestication of plants. "Such skills— sometimes referred to as crafts—" as observed by historian of science Pamela Smith, "grew out of a collective interaction with the material world."[119] She further underscores that "Some see the modern scientific and technological capability of human beings as essentially different from these earlier developments, but there is no reason to regard the present development and

delicate seedling of some especially valuable Oriental plant starts on a journey towards South America it has rather poor chances as a rule of arriving alive." Fairchild, "Two Expeditions After Living Plants," p. 112.
119 Pamela H. Smith, "The History of Science as a Cultural History of the Material World," in *Cultural Histories of the Material World*, ed. Peter N. Miller (Ann Arbor: University of Michigan Press, 2013), p. 213.

accumulation of techniques and knowledge by means of the natural sciences as radically different from the very long-enduring human engagement with the environment."[120] The term "craft knowledge" has been coined in this context. An underlying assumption is that of a founding materiality, which spans crafting techniques and technologies as *conditio sine qua non* of knowledge generally, but even more so of scientific knowledge. With regard to botany, and more specifically, in view of the tropical survey as the epistemic context in which the photographs were being produced, these pictures are to be conceived as technical images that are visual inscriptions of agricultural knowledge.[121] Yet, following the idea of "mechanical objectivity," botanical survey photography, as reflected with these pictures, shares the discourse of technicality, inasmuch as the pictures seem to record the different techniques of grafting to use and cultivate plants. As a sort of technical image, the photographs thus reflect a *visual epistemology* of economic botany, which searches for the different crafting skills as a material culture of plants and visually structures this new space of knowledge. How do these images work in their specific contexts? What about the viewing and knowing, in which both scientific and cultural practices and productions are brought into consideration? Or, "What do we know when we see?"[122]

Most of the BPI tropical survey photographs did not circulate widely outside the USDA and were mostly used as internal documents. Selected ones, though, were used in related botanical and scientific publications and USDA bulletins. The pictures were also carefully kept in the USDA records, forming the photographic archives that offer insights into the history of the

---

120 Ibid.

121 For "technical images" see Gabriele Werner, "Bilddiskurse. Kritische Überlegungen zur Frage, ob es eine allgemeine Bildtheorie des naturwissenschaftlichen Bildes geben kann," in *Das Technische Bild. Kompendium zu einer Stilgeschichte wissenschaftlicher Bilder*, ed. Horst Bredekamp et al. (Berlin: Akademieverlag, 2008), p. 30.

122 Galison, *Picturing Science*, p. 13.

collected plants and specimens of the tropical surveys. How-ever, to date, knowledge production and visual epistemology have been discussed predominantly in the context of botanical taxonomy, relating to the discourse of visual evidence.[123] As over-lapping worlds, that of an imperial administration and a natural science, namely botany, Bleichmar underlines a sort of shared *visual lingua franca*. As technical images, based on knowledge and observation of nature, sight became increasingly relevant to the question of representation. Nevertheless, Secord rightly warns "that part of the construction of scientific objectivity in the mid-nineteenth century resulted in the marginalization of sensory practices that involved aesthetic pleasure."[124] What is questioned here is therefore nothing less than the very concep-tion of visual evidence and, moreover, if we consider material-ity as an analytical concept, it becomes pertinent to examining a tactile knowledge, into which the scientificity of knowledge seems to always have already been culturally embedded. So it is, regarding the similarities between the sciences of botany and physiology, as Lorraine Daston points out:

> Although these two sciences occupied opposite extremes along the spectrum of wordiness, they shared a strong reliance on sensory acu-ity and bodily tact. The eye that could distinguish a dozen species of rhododendron at a glance or register minute changes in the percep-tion of light intensity; the hand that could quickly sketch a new species of fern in the field, or diagnose lead poisoning from the erratic rhythm of a pulse—such accomplishments had traditionally been the stock-in-trade of both botanist and physiologist. A comparison of the two disciplines will highlight how both wordy and wordless objectivities could unite in the suppression of bodily knowledge.[125]

123 See the discussion in Bleichmar, *Visible Empire*, p. 45.
124 Secord, "Botany on a Plate," p. 31.
125 Lorraine Daston, "Scientific Objectivity with and without Words," in *Little Tools of Knowledge: Historical Essays on Academic and Bureaucratic Practices*, ed. Peter Becker and William Clark (Ann Arbor: University of Michigan Press, 2001), pp. 264–265.

Notwithstanding, Daston conceives botany as a "wordy objectivity" and fails to fully recognize the visual as a primary sensory mode of botanical knowledge. She rightly underlines the often overlooked argument of "sensory acuity" and "bodily tact" with regard to epistemic practices that do involve "aesthetic pleasure" and are to be conceived as prerequisites of (scientific) knowledge. However, we ask why the privilege is given to vision as a dominant sensory activity. Taussig observes that "the very concept of 'knowing' something becomes displaced by a 'related to.' And what is troublesome and exciting, not only are we stimulated into rethinking what 'vision' means as this very term decomposes before our eyes, but we are also forced to ask ourselves why vision is so privileged, ideologically [...]."[126] Moreover, with regard to "mimetic machines" such as photographic cameras:

> These [...], to state the matter simplistically, would create a new sensorium involving a new subject-object relation and therefore a new person. In abolishing the aura of cult objects and artworks, these machines would replace mystique by some sort of object-implicated enterprise, like surgery, for instance, penetrating the body of reality no less than that of the viewer.[127]

Significantly, Taussig outlines here an understanding of materiality, which he anchors in the medium of photography, that frames this new relationship between the perceiver and the photographed (object) as the "copy *and* contact."[128] Accordingly, this "object-implicated enterprise" determines the cultural contact that penetrates "the body of reality no less than that of the viewer."[129] This aspect becomes important, for it underscores the understanding of photography as a cultural technique that

126 Taussig, *Mimesis and Alterity*, p. 26.
127 Ibid., p. 24.
128 Ibid., p. 21.
129 Ibid., p. 24.

is not necessarily reducible to vision alone. Against photography's discourse of objectivity, one's attention is turned rather to the images' autonomous laws that cheat the idea of intentionality and control by establishing their "true" meaning. Knowing as being related to and knowledge production are remarkably defined by bureaucratic cultures that set out what is pertinent and what not, defining a discursive materiality. As for the botanical survey photography, it becomes important that the epistemic contexts, in which the pictures were being produced, are related to the very institutional activities of the BPI and of foreign agricultural services such as the establishment of photographic archives, in order to organize a homogeneous space and to be able to record data. Vision as sensory acuity relates to photography as a means of spatial production, allowing for an economic expansion of which the botanical transfer became a constitutive part. The extensive use of the camera for the tropical surveys by the USDA plant and agricultural explorers and the produced, made and circulated visual botanical information is tied to what I conceive as visual epistemology.

Regarding the institutional formation of economic botany, visual epistemology seems to have a different function to that of visual evidence. That is, it becomes important to assume that knowledge is always already embedded into contexts and prerequisites, such as biological, social, historical, technical, or material ones. Framing visual epistemology in this sense, it becomes pertinent to conceive it as intrinsically tied to the bio-contact zone and the complex cultural interferences. Furthermore, visual epistemology is bound to an apparatus, such as of the USDA bureaucracy, in which photographic archives had a predominant role. Consequently, inquiring into the status of knowledge, the photographs become epistemic things that act upon the formation of an economic botany, entangled with that of a modern institutionalization of botany, for which the tropical survey and plant collection became key activities. As such, both the photographs and the archive are *media a priori* that form the homogeneous space necessary to organize data and register cultural difference, as discussed. In other words, "In this material form the dynamic materiality was seen from the inception of the archive as central to the expectations, understanding, and archival performance through which these photographs could come to have meaning."[130] Accordingly, the photographs as epistemic things are constitutive of reality. Yet, on the level of materiality and thingness, the importance lies in the difference between emphasizing mattering as opposed to signifying, to overcome the question of representation as a signifying discourse.

As Allan Sekula once remarked, "Although [...] photography is fundamentally related in its normative way of depicting the world to an epistemology and an aesthetics that are intrinsic to a system of commodity exchange [...], photography also needs to be understood as a simultaneous threat and promise in its relation to the prevailing cultural ambitions of a triumphant but wary western bourgeoisie."[131] This ambivalence of photography, of both partaking in constituting the "normative way of depicting the world" as well as potentially articulating a threat in "its relations to the prevailing ambitions," remains present when examining the pictures of the tropical surveys by the USDA. Meaningful in this particular institutional context for a given time, the use of photographs articulates a visual epistemology that is tied to the system of commodity exchange, inasmuch as they contour a knowledge bound to economic cycles of a capitalist production of space, in which vision acquires a predominant role. While the geopolitical importance of botany in the British Empire has been partially investigated, the case of botany in US-Latin American interrelations has not yet been fully understood. What I have argued for is to question the role of visualization in the sphere of transmitting, producing, communicating and making knowledge viable in the context of environmental changes, cultural transfer, and the commodity

130 Edwards, "Photographs: Material Form and the Dynamic Archive," p. 51.
131 Sekula, "The Traffic in Photographs," p. 22.

exchange. Correspondingly, the emergent modern visual culture in botany, to which the drawings by Blaschka as preliminary studies for the famous Glass Flowers and the numerous photographs of the USDA tropical survey belong, was deeply rooted in the institutionalization of botanical knowledge production and circulation. Subsequently, with regard to the communicative power of images, the visual was decisive in the formation of this modern botanical knowledge. Along with this there was a change of sensory apparatus shifting from the collected thing as the only reliable material source to the image, and, furthermore, the archival image that recorded, depicted, and even imagined the future altered landscape, thus claiming its role as an operative artifact. The discourse networks of botany wield the visual as materiality through which the new spaces of the Caribbean and further South are made accessible. As underscored by Sekula, "[...] we are not simply talking about a global political economy of signs, [but] we are [...] invited to imagine an epistemological treasure trove, an encyclopedia organized according to a global hierarchy of knowledge and power."[132]

However, whereas Daniela Bleichmar in her study underpins that visualization was successful in botanical taxonomy because it helped to identify plants for classification, she conceives the visual as ineffective in the field of economic botany, which deals with transplanting and reproducing plants outside their native habitat, in order to commercialize them as natural commodities.[133] The "unfulfilled promise" was to "deploy natural history in the service of the State," as was the case of the Spanish Royal Botanical Expeditions. She suggests the images did not become the desired effective technical and media devices to (re)produce knowledge based on the realness of a plant's chemical and thus material composition. As a result, this kind of visibility turned out to be a less powerful achievement than

132 Ibid.
133 Bleichmar, *Visible Empire*, p. 123.

expected in the geo-cultural battle.[134] In terms of a botanical imperial dominance this meant that material transplantation through collecting and reproducing could not easily be substituted. Accordingly, the image could not become a surrogate in the context of economic botany and the commercialization of crops as natural commodities. In the context of the Spanish Royal Botanical Expeditions, the visual was not sufficiently sustained by the other media devices that make up botany's discourse networks. However, Bleichmar's findings fall short of recognizing the powerful geopolitical potential of images in knowledge production that is based indubitably on the fickle status of knowledge. I argue that economic botany plays a crucial role in the capitalist production of space that remarkably embodied the cultural matrices and local epistemologies that enhanced the conversion of the world into a garden. It therefore spurred the efficient altering of the landscape and the environment of the Caribbean. Moreover, botanical survey photography, created by the USDA, reveals a new representational regime that supports the very conversion of land into a productive and commodifiable "tropical landscape."

Yet, "What do we know when we see?" The answer certainly remains elusive, for the USDA photographs as epistemic things faded out of focus, whereas Blaschka's globally acclaimed glass models remain a sort of perfect copy, though, "for the botanists, the models are too detailed to highlight the taxonomic characteristics of the plants; for the artists, meticulous verisimilitude and mismatch of form to medium signal kitsch. Connoisseurs of glassware appreciate the technical achievements of the Blaschka models, but as an artisanal dead end that inspired no styles or schools."[135] While the USDA photographs gain their meaning from within the embedded cultural contact and the material practices of the cultivation of plants made visible here as passages between matter and knowledge, the Blaschka

---

134 Ibid., p. 127.
135 Daston, "The Glass Flowers," p. 252.

drawings and glass models conceal them, for they become themselves an objectified nature in the search for a universal knowledge, inscribed into the discourse of natural history. Ultimately, the Blaschka drawings that embody the idea of taxonomic botanical knowledge belong to the knowledge order of the museum display, materialized in the glass models, revealing that these epistemic practices felt out-of-time. Rather, the unfashionable technique of glass modeling discloses a form of representation that seems to be an end in itself. Whereas the models seemed to have their *raison d'être* in the museum display, the photographs of the USDA archive were mostly kept as non-circulating and largely unseen objects, constitutive of the internal workings of bureaucracy. Eventually, this photography in correlation with the material collection of plants and specimens became a critical media device for establishing the discourse networks of economic botany.

After neglecting these surveying practices in botany in the last decades, it has been claimed more recently by James Miller, Dean and Vice President for science at the New York Botanical Garden, that: "Another renaissance of plant exploration is desperately needed to comprehensively inventory the plant species in these tropical forests that will be degraded or disappear in the next few decades. While protection of wild populations is clearly the ideal solutions for protecting biological diversity, it is also abundantly evident that at current rates of habitat loss, botanical gardens must play a key role in protecting threatened plant species."[136] Remarkably, though, with regard to recent currents in botany, botanical material in the form of plants, specimens and germplasm has regained its momentum and with it, in the face of growing sensitivity towards biological diversity and environmental change, so has plant exploration.[137]

136 Cited in Hodge, "Agricultural Explorers," p. 46.
137 See Peter Chapman, *Bananas: How the United Fruit Company Shaped the World* (New York: Canongate, 2007), pp. 22–23.

Yet, as scientists today "graft and clone, so the banana is dying, and a process that might have occurred anyway over the centuries has been greatly accelerated by the United Fruit and its kind. It took the fruit out of the jungle and turned a natural product into a 'commodity,' a thing of commerce and the mass market. As a result it appears unequal to the business of survival."[138] To conclude, from this perspective, the USDA tropical survey, from its very inception, seems to have supported a paradigm shift, based on the plant material, fostering the bureaucratic culture of economic botany. In turn, the photographic archives of the USDA seem to contour a knowledge paradigm by effecting a new transmedial sign system that relied in a similar manner on the visual and the collected material by imagining a new materiality, a surrogate of the real living plants and our environment, in which the picture eventually assumed the function of an operative artifact.

138 Ibid.

Chapter 4

Ethnographic Eyes and Archaeological Views

> In other words, can't we say that to give an example, to instan-
> tiate, to be concrete, are all examples of the magic mimesis
> wherein the replication, the copy, acquires the power of the rep-
> resented? And does not the magical power of this embodying
> inhere in the fact that in reading such examples we are thereby
> lifted out of ourselves into the images? [...] With this replica [...]
> we have mimesis based on quite imperfect but nevertheless
> (so we must presume) very effective copying that acquires the
> power of the original—a copy that is not a copy, but a "poorly
> executed ideogram" [...]. Sliding between photographic fidel-
> ity and fantasy, between iconicity and arbitrariness, wholeness
> and fragmentation, we thus begin to sense how weird and com-
> plex the notion of the copy becomes [...]. The ability to mime,
> and mime well, in other words, is the capacity to Other.[1]

Regarding the resurgence of the "primitive" in modernity, alongside the "revelation of the optical unconscious,"[2] it is significant
that the United Fruit Company deploys "mimetic machinery,"
such as the camera, producing both still pictures and films. This
"mimetic machinery" gives form to a powerful physiognomy
of the visual world while mirroring and concurrently shaping
corporate fantasies and self-perceptions. Whereas in the previous chapters I emphasize the non-documentary character of
photography, even arguing against the very faculty of mimetic
machines, in this chapter I use this concept to explore further
the complex cultural contact of the United Fruit Company in
Central America following, as Walter Benjamin once suggested
in his reflections on modernity, the resonating conceptual pair

1   Taussig, *Mimesis and Alterity*, pp. 16–19.
2   Ibid., p. 20.

of alterity and the "primitive." Within the larger framework of material culture, to which food as commodity produced by the Company indubitably belongs, the resurgent images that depict the Company's archaeological activities become of fore-most interest, inasmuch as they seem to complete the picture of the radical transformation of the material landscape in a long-lasting way.

It is common knowledge that companies were engaged in the business of collecting antiquities, and businessmen cre-ated the most impressively large private collections of artifacts, arts and other "contact goods."[3] Yet the resurgent images and objects of the United Fruit Company's cultural contact are less well known and reflect the archive's silences. In 1949 the Com-pany produced the film *The Maya Through the Ages*, directed by ethnologist and photographer Giles G. Healey. There are also other archaeological views, such as those materialized in the pictures collected for the Company photographic albums that show the archaeological site at Quirigua in Guatemala, marking it as a significant symbolic reference point. The archaeologi-cal site became a featured discovery, reflecting the Company's scientific engagement, out of para-archaeological rather than scientific curiosity. All this activity eventually had its material apotheosis in the largest private collection of Central Ameri-can Pre-Columbian artifacts, that of Minor C. Keith, one of the founders of the United Fruit Company. As a gift or long-nego-tiated acquisition his collection became the foundation of the Mesoamerican Cultures Collection and was later split between the Brooklyn Museum, the American Museum of Natural His-tory and the Metropolitan Museum in New York, which received the valuable Costa Rican gold work objects that were the object of the initial debate over whether such objects should be con-

3   I refer here in particular to the Pre-Columbian collection realized by Nelson Rockefeller, the importance of which for the conception of Pre-Columbian arts has been discussed by Joanne Pillsbury in "The Pan-American: Nelson Rock-efeller and the Arts of Ancient Latin America," *The Metropolitan Museum of Art Bulletin* LXXII:1 (2014).

sidered Pre-Columbian arts or antiquities. By looking at these resurgent images and collections of Pre-Columbian objects, I discuss the discursive boundaries between history, archaeology, and photography and examine the long-standing agency of the Company in shaping the material culture of "contact goods," and how that corresponds to the material culture of the food exchange as yet another embodied circuit of the politics of value. The collections of arts and artifacts, and the still and moving pictures, thus resonate around the historical beginnings of a modern material culture, intrinsically linked to agriculture insinuating the Company's self-legitimating rationale: as pictures they emerged as foundational images.

Let me thus turn to the mimetic as a distinct feature, in order to grasp the modern cultural contact embodied therein and to relate it to the mythical traits of fetishism and animism when discussing the collection and exchange of material objects in the very process of becoming commodities. Michael Taussig makes explicit that "to get hold of an object at very close range by way of its likeness, its reproduction" reflects that "contact and copy merge to become virtually identical, different moments of the one process of sensing; seeing something or hearing something is to be in contact with something."[4] This assumption becomes important, insofar as pictures as representations seem to mediate the cultural contact, which is often conflictive in its nature. Moreover, archaeological representations, more generally, "were means of reflecting on antiquity, on the sublimity of the passage of time and the fate of civilizations."[5] Yet, with regard to the excavated, collected and exchanged cultural objects, such as stones, pottery, jewelry, and even gold and silver work, we sense that this rather conflictive, hierarchized and eventually violent contact of the United Fruit

---

4   Taussig, *Mimesis and Alterity*, pp. 20–21.
5   Joanne Pillsbury, ed., *Past Presented: Archaeological Illustration and the Ancient Americas* (Washington D.C.: Dumbarton Oaks Research Library and Collection, 2012), p. 1.

Company in Central America is displaced unconsciously onto the level of representation of these objects that embody this contact through a kind of animation. Herein comes the "optical unconscious" that Walter Benjamin speaks about, to be examined on the level of the visual and with regard to the resurgent images. So, it is Taussig again who refers to the eye in particular, as an organ of tactility, through which we significantly relate to the world. He underscores: "Here is what is crucial in the resurgence of the mimetic faculty, namely the two-layered notion of mimesis that is involved—a copying or imitation, and a palpable, sensuous, connection between the very body of the perceiver and the perceived."[6] So, what is the nature of the connection between the perceiver and the perceived? How do the pictures mediate, represent, or displace the cultural contact? What does the "optical unconscious" reveal about this embodied contact and its violence?

The term "commodity fetishism" has been coined to speak about the displaced and invisibilized material regime. Following the argument of Taussig rereading Karl Marx, "such fetishization resulted from the curious effect of the market in human life and imagination, an effect which displaced contact between people into that between commodities, thereby intensifying to the point of spectrality the commodity as an autonomous entity with a will of its own."[7] Accordingly, it is important to emphasize the very nature of the displacement of men's labor into the commodity, becoming thus the form of the social relations. I argue that both activities, that of collecting archaeological objects and that of making natural commodities, are linked to the alteration of the environment and to the fact that the material landscape quintessentially embodies labor, as reflected in the labor-intensive agricultural operations and digging for ancient cultural objects. "The swallowing-up of contact

6   Taussig, *Mimesis and Alterity*, p. 21.
7   Ibid., p. 22.

we might say, by its copy," Taussig reminds us, "is what ensures the animation of the latter, its power to straddle us."[8] Moreover:

> We need to note also that as the commodity passes through and is held by the exchange-value arc of the market circuit where general equivalence rules the roost, where all particularity and sensuousity is meat-grindered into abstract identity and the homogenous substance of quantifiable money-value, the commodity yet conceals in its innermost being not only the mysteries of the socially constructed nature of value and price, but also all its particulate sensuousness—and this subtle interaction of sensuous perceptibility and imperceptibility accounts for the fetish quality, the animism and spiritual glow of commodities [...].[9]

Enter here the mimetic machines "to pump out contact-sensuousity": representations of the collected objects that reveal nothing less than the "optical unconscious" concealed in the "spectrality of commoditized world."[10] Accordingly, the pictures might become a means to unlock this labor conversion, materialized and encased in the commodities with their phantasmagorical potential and value-surplus, while articulating an "image sphere." I adopt this conception to define the displaced cultural contact materialized in the archive. It is best grasped as the oscillation of the conceptual pair of mimesis and alterity, inasmuch as the "ability to mime [...] is the capacity to Other."[11] In what follows, this will resonate with the archaeological views and ethnographic gazes embodied in the resurgent images of the United Fruit Company and its collected objects.

By looking at the ethnographic stills, film pictures and archaeological photographs, on the one hand, I scrutinize the displacement of the cultural contact and its visual resurgence

---

8   Ibid.
9   Ibid.
10   Ibid., p. 23.
11   Ibid., p. 19.

in the archives. On the other hand, I will consider the institutional entanglement that helped shape the very alteration of the material landscape, looking at the scientific engagement of the United Fruit Company and the other scientific institutions that were ultimately involved. I argue that this visual resurgence or image sphere, in addition to occupying varied discursive spaces, seems to offer insights into the media use and knowledge production of the United Fruit Company and ultimately the archaeological hustle and bustle of Central America at the time of the birth of American big business. The "archaeological reconnaissance" and the expansion of modern agriculture in this particular region dominated by the Company go hand in hand. It becomes important to remember once again, as emphasized by John Tagg elsewhere, that there is no historical consistency to photography or the status of photography, for technology is changeable with regard to its power relations: photography's practices depend on institutions and persons, who define the use of photography. Consequently, the history of photography has no unity but rather oscillates within a field of institutional spaces. We therefore need to study this field, not photography as such. Taussig thus warns that "Confined within the purity of its theater of operation, science can proceed calmly despite the violence of its procedure" and that, eventually, "[...] the scientific quotient of the eyeful opened up by the revelations of the optical unconscious is also an hallucinatory eye, a roller-coastering of the senses dissolving science and art into a mode of truth-seeking and reality-testing," following Benjamin who noted that "the achievement of the film [was] to extend our scientific comprehension of reality." Notwithstanding, "it is here, in this transgressed yet strangely calm new space of debris, that a new violence of perception is born of mimetically capacious machinery."[12] It is to this new space of debris that I will now turn.

12   Ibid., p. 32.

The Archaeological Expeditions to Quirigua

> An operation! (Hide your heads, ye speculator in up-town lots!)
> To buy Copan! Remove the monuments of a by-gone people
> from the desolate region in which they were buried, set them
> up in the "great commercial emporium" [New York City],
> and found an institution to be the nucleus of a great national
> museum of American antiquities![13]

Out of the confluence of contingencies relics of the past resur-
faced and shaped the political economy of American archaeology: the confluence of an early object-oriented understanding
of knowledge production, viewing the past as embodied in the
object as a privileged form of data, and of an entrepreneurship of business abroad, which within the larger framework
of geopolitics and philanthropy funded that object-driven
research. Moreover, with the foundation of anthropological
museums, such as, in this context, the American Museum of
Natural History and the Peabody Museum at Harvard University, the material culture and "lost civilization" of the Maya
resurged, marking and marked by a network of diverse actors
and institutions often foreign themselves to anthropology and
archaeology.[14] This mediation certainly involved a negotiation

13 John L. Stephens, 1841, cited in Curtis M. Hinsley, "In Search of the New
World Classical," in *Collecting the Pre-Columbian Past*, ed. Elizabeth Hill Boone
(Washington D.C.: Dumbarton Oaks Research Library and Collection, 2011),
p. 111.
14 Curtis Hinsley observes here: "Consular archaeology [...] enacted a complex of attitudes best described as 'imperial': that no significant distinction lies
between agencies of politics, business, and science in exotic regions, for they
are complementarily and coherently engaged in a single, multifaceted project of
metropolitan expansion, discovery/recovery, and consumption; that it is proper
for state-supported agents to aid in this process; and that removal (collecting)
of pre-Columbian material culture—originals or replicas—like other samples
of resources from the colonial periphery, is a legitimate, and perhaps obligatory
act, both for their preservation and for the cultural edification of metropolitan
audiences." Hinsley, "In Search of the New World Classical," p. 110.

273

Ethnographic Eyes and Archaeological Views

of "not-fully-comprehended cross purposes."[15] Yet, within this object-oriented impetus favoring collections, it seems important to understand cultural contact in the liminal space of objects and Others, and within that, the mediating role of images and representations. A first series of occurrences that supported the resurgence of Mayan antiquities and stimulated a broader interest in Mesoamerican archaeology is linked to the rediscovery of the archaeological site at Quirigua under the benevolent yet highly ambivalent influence of the United Fruit Company. It has been discussed in this context that, ultimately, "Insofar as support was forthcoming, it was facilitated by the fact that material objects served as both commodity and medium of exchange within the restricted political economy of anthropological research."[16] George Stocking further points out:

From the perspective of donors whose beneficence was sustained by success in the world of commodity production, palpable and visible objects could be seen as a return on investment, even if their aesthetic or utilitarian value was minimal by conventional cultural standards. From the perspective of anthropologists, the collection of objects for sale to museums was an important if somewhat tenuous means of capitalizing research on less marketable topics. Between them, at the center of the political economy of anthropological research, stood the museums, institutions premised on the collection and display of objects.[17]

It is certainly within this intermingling of interests and donors that such expeditions to and archaeological research in Quirigua, Guatemala, became at all possible, while determining a

15 George W. Stocking, "Philanthropoids and Vanishing Cultures: Rockefeller Funding and the End of the Museum Era in Anglo-American Anthropology," in *Objects and Others: Essays on Museums and Material Culture*, ed. George W. Stocking (Madison: University of Wisconsin Press, 1988), p. 12.
16 Ibid., p. 113.
17 Ibid., pp. 113–114.

274

focus on Mayan civilization and archaeology as a cultural and thus scientific topic. The famous Peabody Museum was able to make its mark, with a transition that is best grasped by the lemma "from shell-heaps to stelae," and established its distinction in the field by, "on the one hand, finding a subject of inquiry that would seem worthy of support to groups within the Boston and New England social and cultural elite; on the other hand, training a group of investigators who would be deemed worthy of support in the more professional environment that was beginning to develop within the national anthropological community."[18] Hence the increase in the study of ancient Maya civilization and the particular interest in Mayan antiquities to be collected for the Peabody Museum, and for other influential anthropological institutions, including those promoted by the Rockefeller philanthropies.[19] Certainly, there was an intellectual and to some extent institutional push towards the collection and study of objects in the formation of Mesoamerican archaeology.[20] Yet, other historical studies remind us with regard, for instance, to the Rockefeller philanthropies that "patterns of research" reflected "the dominant ideology of

18   Hinsley, "In Search of the New World Classical," p. 70.
19   I refer here to Stocking, "Philanthropoids and Vanishing Cultures." Stocking examines the intellectual and institutional pushes and confluences of important sponsors, such as the Rockefellers, in shaping the field of early anthropology and archaeology. Significantly, the Rockefellers had an important capital share in the United Fruit Company, being one of the most influential political families in the United States, known for their involvement in research and research programs, as reflected in the institutionalized Rockefeller philanthropies: the Rockefeller Institute for Medical Research, the General Education Board, the Rockefeller Foundation, and the Laura Spelman Rockefeller Memorial. In this milieu of philanthropy the United Fruit Company also took advantage of sponsoring a series of remarkable projects in Central America as a public service. See also Pillsbury, "The Pan-American."
20   Stocking underscores: "Within an evolutionist framework, human physical remains, archaeological finds, and contemporary material culture were the most ready means of graphically illustrating the development of mankind; and though they were not convenient for public display, even the texts collected by linguists had rather an 'object' character." Stocking, "Philanthropoids and Vanishing Cultures," p. 114.

corporate capitalist society or the class self-interest of its leading groups."[21] As "representatives of corporate capitalism or western colonialism," characteristic for many of the sponsoring organizations of that era, the United Fruit Company was involved in a series of important research activities in diverse fields, including Mesoamerica. In this confluence another factor might also have become important for understanding the United Fruit Company's engagement in research at the crossroads of knowledge production and geopolitics. It is noteworthy that, for instance, once the Rockefeller Trustees "accepted the view that human welfare could best be achieved by the advancement of knowledge," the charge of antiquarianism in anthropology was forsaken, "its very exoticism enhanced its appeal."[22] This vision might be suitable also to describe, at least partially, the United Fruit Company's engagement in archaeological research, and helps us to grasp its ambivalent nature.

Nevertheless, it is remarkable that the United Fruit Company not only became a financing body for archaeological research, but more importantly was deeply involved with the infrastructure and the archaeologists themselves. At least five of the prominent figures who laid the ground for a Mesoamerican archaeology that still resonates today were linked to the Company: Doris Stone, daughter of none other than Samuel Zemurray, Dorothy Popenoe, wife of Wilson Popenoe, Minor C. Keith, at the time the most important private collector of Mesoamerican antiquities, Victor Cutter, president of the United Fruit Company and also a private collector, and Giles G. Healey, the ethnologist, photographer and filmmaker hired by the Company. It is noteworthy with regard to Rockefeller's engagement in archaeology and anthropology that seemingly "What had sold the discipline to philanthropoids [...] was not so much its alleged practical colonial utility as its promise of

---

21 Ibid., p. 133.
22 Ibid., p. 137.

esoteric scientific knowledge."[23] Although obscure and even more ambivalent, this might, nevertheless, help illuminate my concern about the cultural contact and the relationship of the United Fruit Company to material culture, channeled through diverse material and scientific practices, veiled by the collecting of antique objects from other cultures.

To give a brief picture of that time before the First World War and between the two World Wars, it is important to stress that the institutional impact, more generally, had favored the funding of anthropological research linked to museum collections and "the study of the human past as it was embodied in collectible physical objects," fostering the biological and thus natural sciences.[24] It was certainly in this climate that the United Fruit Company and, more specifically, the associated archaeologists, ethnologists and collectors, developed an interest in Mesoamerican antiquities, underpinned by the search for a kind of "esoteric" or "exotic" knowledge. But I also ask if they might have been "interested in objects primarily as personal keepsakes of transcultural experience, brought back to decorate the walls of their homes, or to distinguish" themselves, an assumption that would allow for speculating about a more intimate relationship between oneself and oneself, miming the Other.[25]

This curiosity, both scientific and "exotic," is certainly reflected in the archaeological excavations financed by the United Fruit Company. Digging certainly became a primary activity within the quest for antiquities and the construction of archaeological objects of the lost Mayan civilization. Though the site of the Quirigua ruins with its important stonework, the stelae and marvelous zoomorphs, was known as early as 1843 through the travel descriptions by John L. Stephens and the drawings by the architect Frederick Catherwood, it was only later archaeologically investigated by the British explorer Alfred

23 Ibid.
24 Ibid., p. 141.
25 Ibid., p. 142.

Percival Maudslay.[26] In 1910, 1911, 1912 and 1914 a series of important archaeological excavations and long-lasting works were undertaken by the School of American Archaeology of the Archaeological Institute of America under the direction of Edgar Lee Hewett. This was made possible because in 1909 the United Fruit Company purchased land along the Montagua River that coincidentally included the ruins with its ancient objects. Through an arrangement in 1910 with Victor Cutter, then manager of the Virginia Division of the United Fruit Company, the Quirigua Park, a reservation of 75 acres surrounding the site's main group, was later set aside to be maintained in perpetuity as an archaeological monument: "It was decided to leave standing at Quirigua Park a small section of the forest —lofty mahoganies, giant *ceibas*, graceful cohunes, loveliest of all palms—as an example of the mighty tropical jungle which originally covered the entire valley."[27] More generally, "nature" was here perceived as threatening the ancient monuments and the future excavation of the site. The 1911 and 1912 archaeological expeditions were co-financed by the United Fruit Company, which had witnessed an interest in the archaeological site on their terrains in Central America newly purchased for future fruit plantations. Subsequently, the Company provided logistical support for the four archaeological expeditions and the beginning of the restoration of the ruins. The third expedition of 1912 saw the "important and, to the archaeologist, perhaps most congenial task of digging," whereas the expedition of 1914 aimed at collecting and securing casts of some finer sculptures for exhibition at

26   Joanne Pillsbury rightly underscores in this context that the "Archaeological illustration has received less attention than archaeological texts, yet the images have been equally or more influential. In this light, archaeological illustrations are the stealth operators of knowledge production. To treat them as transparent conveyors of visualized information is to overlook a critical aspect of how that information is organized, codified, perceived, and exchanged." Pillsbury, *Past Presented*, p. 3. With regard to Mesoamerican antiquities, the illustrations and photographs by Maudslay certainly had a predominant role.
27   Sylvanus G. Morley, *Guide Book to the Ruins of Quirigua* (Washington: Carnegie Institution, 1935), pp. 9–10.

the Panama-California Exposition at San Diego, California, in 1915.[28] So it is that accompanying archaeologist Sylvanus Morley remembers in his *Guide Book to the Ruins of Quirigua*:

> Thus Quirigua was the first Old Empire city I ever saw and while I have visited it many times since, for me it has never lost its original romantic thrill or its absorbing human appeal. [...] The great forest which formerly covered the river plain has been replaced by banana plantations of equal extent, and save for the lofty waving plumes of Quirigua Park this former mighty growth of tree and bush, creeper and vine is no more.[29]

Sylvanus G. Morley is known to have been one of the most ambiguous figures among the archaeologists co-sponsored and supported by the Company, inasmuch as he—among other prominent and famous archaeologists like Samuel Kirkland Lothrop, Herbert J. Spinden, John Alden Mason, who later worked with the Keith collection of Mesoamerican objects in New York, and the agricultural explorer Wilson Popenoe—became an important spy for the US Office of Naval Intelligence during the First World War.[30] The controversial spying activities of archaeologists are

---

28   Ibid., p. 12.
29   Ibid., pp. 14–15.
30   I refer here to Charles H. Harris and Louis L. Sadler, *The Archaeologist Was a Spy: Sylvanus G. Morley and the Office of Naval Intelligence* (Albuquerque: University of New Mexico Press, 2009), which reconstructs the prominent role of the archaeologist and spy Morley in recruiting among prominent US archaeologists and creating an intelligence network of espionage in Central America during World War I, and the subsequent involvement of the United Fruit Company. The spying activities of many archaeologists eventually led to the controversy surrounding the censure of the leading anthropologist Franz Boas by the American Anthropological Association over the prominent letter where Boas claimed that US archaeologists betrayed the discipline by hiding their spying activities in its name. See also David Browman, "Spying by American Archaeologists in World War I," *Bulletin of the History of Archaeology* 21:2 (2011), pp. 10–17. Spying activities of archaeologists have been also discussed by Paul Sullivan in *Unfinished Conversations: Mayas and Foreigners Between Two Wars* (Berkeley: University of California Press, 1991).

discussed elsewhere;[31] I wish, though, to highlight this activity as being a part of the discourse network that helped establish the archaeological activities of the United Fruit Company within a hierarchized Western knowledge production, in which both governmental or institutional actors and private entrepreneurs shared mutual yet ambivalent cross-purposes. The formation of the field of American anthropology in the early twentieth century is problematic, as its main feature might be that of "an ideological milieu befogged by evolutionary racialist assumption, [where] an object orientation often contributed to a degrading and distancing objectification of the 'Others' who had made the objects, and who were themselves literally objectified in museum displays."[32] Nevertheless, the engagement of the United Fruit Company may have laid the foundations for long-lasting archaeological research and institutions in the Central American countries themselves. This becomes particularly true with regard to the foundation of the National Museum of Costa Rica and the archaeological section brought into being by Doris Stone.[33] Still, as rightly underscored by George Stocking, "Be that as it may, there seems to have been some tendency for the more object- and museum-oriented anthropologists to be more closely identified with the dominant groups in American culture, and with the cultural ideology that justified their dominance."[34] This might also be true of the internal racial tensions and ideological struggles with regard to immigration that were experienced at the time, in particular in the West Indies and Costa Rica. Following this, digging for objects of ancient and other cultures became a major activity to assure preeminence in the prerogative of interpretation and to secure the

31 Sullivan, *Unfinished Conversations*; Harris and Sadler, *The Archaeologist Was a Spy*; Browman, "Spying by American Archaeologists in World War I."
32 Stocking, "Philanthropoids and Vanishing Cultures," p. 114.
33 E. Wyllys Andrews and Frederick W. Lange, "In Memoriam: Doris Zemurray Stone 1909–1994," *Ancient Mesoamerica* 6 (1995), p. 96.
34 Stocking, "Philanthropoids and Vanishing Cultures," p. 114.

alleged supremacy of one's own culture, whilst placing the Other's culture on display.

Out of the confluence of these diverse orientations emerged in the United States the "first specifically anthropological museum," namely the Peabody Museum of American Archaeology and Ethnology,[35] notwithstanding the various conceptual and institutional constraints to which it was subjected. Reflecting a common ideological alignment of the time, "it faced a strong predisposition in established Boston circles against the worthiness of 'primitive' peoples and their artifacts for the moral education of civilized nations."[36] This becomes important, for it was a number of bodies belonging to the well-established New England elites of the time, such as the board of the United Fruit Company, which gave contours to the archaeological views that formed a part of the self-determining cultural question. Collecting and buying collections from private collectors became an important practice, laying the foundations for the very activities of the museum. So, it might have been a welcome moment for those becoming collectors, such as Minor C. Keith and Victor Cutter, promoting the initiation of their own private collections of Pre-Columbian antiquities linked to the archaeological expeditions to Quirigua, Guatemala, and more generally to Costa Rica. It is noteworthy, with regard to the institutional endeavor, that "a viable alternative research focus was by then emerging which was at once culturally and professionally more respectable: the study of ancient Mayan civilization."[37] Promoting "the nature of the archeological prizes at stake in Central America," it thus became significant that the Peabody Museum's focus shifted from "shell-heaps to stelae." Out of this confluence emerged the United Fruit Company's interest in promoting the "great heritage of the region"

---

35 Curtis M. Hinsley, "From Shell-Heaps to Stelae: Early Anthropology at the Peabody Museum," in Stocking, *Objects and Others*, p. 50.
36 Ibid., p. 51.
37 Ibid., p. 70.

of Central America and a series of cultural and scientific programs in the field of public service.[38] In a similar way, Curtis
Hinsley in his study underscores that:

> Rather they were now the stelae and stepped pyramids of Copan, and
> later the gold and copal incense of Chichen Itza. If these were not in the
> direct lineage of European high culture, they were nonetheless clearly
> the products of the highest culture the New World had produced, as
> well as of a history steeped in romance. At last, Peabody archeology
> had found a subject that seemed comparable to that of the Mediter-
> ranean basin: a New World civilization worthy of a museum, worthy of
> investment, and worthy of study.[39]

In the light of self-perception and self-fashioning, the United
Fruit Company re-imagined its civilizing project as a great
modern enterprise in comparison with the Old Maya Empire
at Quirigua, where "perhaps as early as the dawn of the Christian era, groups of agricultural Indians occupied the region
and set about clearing the forest and planting the land with
corn."[40] Morley in his account of 1935 further remembers that
"more than a millennium later, a great modern corporation,
the United Fruit Company, seeking land suitable for growing another great food plant—the banana—cleared the valley
a second time and placed it under cultivation."[41] As the following images indubitably witness, the self-fashioning of the
Company reflects the corporation's fantasies of "civilizing" the
spaces wrested from nature while legitimizing its economic
expansion as a cultural project, underpinned in particular

38   *The Ruins of Zaculeu Guatemala*, 1953.
39   Hinsley, "From Shell-Heaps to Stelae," p. 71. It is remarkable that the first
archaeological program of the Peabody Museum was not only established with
a focus on Mayan archaeology, but also gave birth to a first generation of trained
Mayan archaeologists. Ibid., p. 72.
40   Morley, *Guide Book*, p. 15.
41   Ibid., p. 16.

Fig. 5.1: Jesse Nusbaum, "Excavation of Structure 6, Quirigua, Guatemala," 1910. Courtesy of the Palace of the Governors Photo Archives (NMHM/DCA), 061328.

by photography and archaeological knowledge production.[42] This certainly describes one dimension of the cultural depth of the alteration of the material landscape, wherein digging for ancient objects and planting became complementary or even corresponding activities.

Let me briefly illuminate my understanding of material culture, when discussing the United Fruit Company's potential relationship to it. Taking a cue from Arnold Bauer's study of goods and power in Latin America, I wish to draw attention to

---

42   In his account, Edgar L. Hewett writes: "In connection with the excavation a considerable work of repair and preservation has been accomplished; [...] It is a pleasure to state that the future preservation of Quirigua is assured, Mr. Minor C. Keith, of the United Fruit Company, having undertaken to fence the grounds and place a custodian in charge. This, I believe, is the first of the Central American ruins to be protected." Edgar L. Hewett, "The Excavation of Quirigua, by the School of American Archaeology," *International Congress of Americanists XVIII* (1912).

Fig. 5.2: Jesse Nusbaum, "Structure 5 from temple plaza during excavation, Quirigua, Guatemala," 1911. Courtesy of the Palace of the Governors Photo Archives (NMHM/DCA), 061084.

the core items of material life, which are "food, clothing, shelter, and the organization of public space."[43] It seems important to underline that digging for antiquities not only belonged to a sort of modern ritual relating to the ancient past, but also became a practice for organizing a modern public space mediated by and bound to material objects that circulated and were displayed. As an epistemic correlation, digging for artifacts relates to commodification, which was at stake with the alteration of the landscape bound to the capitalistic mode of production of space. Rightly, Hinsley further underlines that:

> Perennial uncertainty over legitimate claim to the land, and thus over the material patrimony, was an intolerable condition for an aggressively capitalistic culture; consequently it brought forth strenuous

43 Arnold J. Bauer, *Goods, Power, History: Latin America's Material Culture* (Cambridge: Cambridge University Press, 2001), p. xv.

effort at confirmation, through acquisition, removal, and propri-
etary display, of grounded, buried items: arrowheads, amulets and
bones, jungle-shrouded stelae, cenote jade and gold. The patrimo-
nial stewardship extended from Cincinnati to the hemisphere; thus
Pre-Columbian collections function as symbolic capital not only for
cosmopolitan status but for the legitimation of a grounded national
culture.[44]

Interestingly, in his study, Bauer identifies four "explanatory
schemes" for discussing material culture that become relevant
also for my argument: "supply and demand, or relative price;
the relationship between consumption and identity; the importance of ritual, both ancient and modern, in consumption; and
the idea of 'civilizing goods'."[45] Accordingly, he further underscores, "imitation, resistance, negotiation, and modification"
were brought forth in the practices of material culture. Following this, digging for antiquities—and photography—describe
in this context in a very precise way the contact society or the
cultural contact. I ask: Why do people acquire things and in
particular ancient objects? Still, Bauer reminds us, "the value
we attribute to an object may be largely determined by what it
means to us—by the degree to which it 'resonates with associations and meanings in our own minds.' [Goods] provide [...] the
material substance in rituals that help to create and maintain
social relationships—or, put another way, goods 'fix public
meanings'."[46] Thus, following the cultural contact, materialized in the scientific practices of digging for ancient objects, it
is manifest that Latin America became part of "the entirely distinct material regimes of the Spanish and Portuguese empires
and later, from the early nineteenth century, dependent upon
the powerful industrial countries of Western Europe and the

44   Hinsley, "From Shell-Heaps to Stelae," pp. 111–112.
45   Bauer, *Goods, Power, History*, p. xvi.
46   Ibid., pp. 3–5.

Fig. 5.3: Jesse Nusbaum, "Stela F, showing man cutting tree in background, Quirigua, Guatemala," 1910. Courtesy of the Palace of the Governors Photo Archives (NMHM/DCA), 060934.

United States."[47] I ask again: What value was attributed to the objects, besides the scientific one, in the context of these expeditions? For the United Fruit Company this is best reflected in the private collections of antiquities by Victor Cutter and Minor C. Keith, where the objects were seemingly of ethnographical and archaeological interest becoming objects of the transcultural contact.[48] While on the one hand the United Fruit Company—like many others US companies in this zone—maintained a colonial-like racist regime that was reflected in the organization of the plantation and its hierarchical organization of space and labor, on the other, it mediated and displaced this racist view in the exaltation and mystification of Indianness that became a prominent idea for a "lost ancient high civilization," allowing for the tendency to fetishize Pre-Columbian objects. This certainly happened because these objects were inserted into the circuits of consumption and identity, miming the Other. Consequently, Pre-Columbian objects became wishful and desired "civilizing goods" that had their impact on the relationship with the ancient past in US society but also in the host countries that fashioned the foundational myths of their own Indianness. It is within this larger framework that the expeditions to Quirigua, one of the most important sites of the "archaeological reconnaissance" of Central America, came into being, bringing together a series of other institutional sponsors such as the Carnegie Institution of Washington. Literally, digging—also a practice that cleared the jungle for future monoculture plantations—was the material practice of alteration of the landscape, thus allowing for its conversion into a modern and symbolic space, which was also materialized in the transfer of goods, such as food or Pre-Columbian objects, into other societies. This transformation primarily consisted of the conversion

---

47   Ibid., p. 7.
48   The notable private Pre-Columbian collection of Mesoamerican objects of Mrs. and Mr. Victor Cutter is today part of the Hood Museum of Art at Dartmouth College in Hanover, New Hampshire. The collection particularly consists of terracotta objects from Costa Rica, including the site of Quirigua.

Fig. 5.4: "Quirigua ruins." [Zoomorph P – 'The finest piece of aboriginal art in all the Americas.' Photographer: Valdeavellano; published in Popenoe 1950]; Gelatin silver process on paper. United Fruit Company Photograph Collection, Baker Library, Harvard Business School, Box 5.

of land into a productive landscape, which was bound symboli-cally and materially to a new value regime that enabled the very circulation of goods within the ritualized circuits of consump-tion and identity, mediating the social relationships and pub-lic meanings. Digging for the ancient objects of past cultures and civilizations became thus a part of this reorganization of modern landscape and, correspondingly, was a complement to agriculture and food production.

Moreover, digging for ancient objects subsequently allowed for the transformation of landscape, and its invasive material technique was photographed and documented in minute detail for the records of the Quirigua archaeological expeditions. To some extent, as previously discussed, these photographs might be conceived of as technical images or scientific pictures. It is remarkable the detail with which the archaeological site at Qui-

Fig. 5.5: "Quirigua ruins." Gelatin silver process on paper. United Fruit Company Photograph Collection, Baker Library, Harvard Business School, Box 5.

rigua is photographed and depicted as a Carnegie Institution archaeological endeavor. Yet, the United Fruit Company photographic albums only include two dozen pictures that show the Quirigua archaeological site and findings. I argue that these pictures belong to the Carnegie Institution expedition and might only have been included as copies in the Company albums at a later date. Four of them explicitly show the stelae of the archaeological park at Quirigua and are seemingly dated later. These were included in one album that predominantly features a touristic view of Guatemala, as they figure among other colonial sites in Guatemala City, Antigua and other places, subsequently depicting a touristic infrastructure.

At least six of the United Fruit Company album pictures were published elsewhere, by the United Fruit Company and in Wilson and Dorothy Popenoe's *A Guide to Quirigua. An Ancient Maya City* in 1950, and in Lilian Elliott's article "Quirigua," already

Fig. 5.6: "Glimpse of the ruins of Quirigua." [Photographer: Valdeavellano];
Gelatin silver process on paper. United Fruit Company Photograph Collection,
Baker Library, Harvard Business School, Box 5.

published in 1910 by the *Pan-American Magazine*. This characterizes the Company photographic archive as a site of diverse
picture collections, brought together from varied sources, defining it also as a sort of archival hodgepodge. The images that
depict the archaeological site and findings at Quirigua, later
to be turned into an archaeological park, seem to belong to
the documentary photographs shot during the scientific expeditions to Quirigua in 1910 and subsequent years. In 1912, it
was the student Earl Morris, assistant to Morley, who appears
to have so thoroughly documented the excavations at Quirigua.
Moreover, it was clear that Minor C. Keith was a frequent visi-
tor and possibly supervisor, also securing funds from the United
Fruit Company to segregate and protect the archaeological site
and the ongoing excavations. The picture series share a common feature here: they certainly document the ongoing invasive
operations to clear the jungle and the site and they insinuate

Fig. 5.7: "Quirigua ruins." Gelatin silver process on paper. United Fruit Company Photograph Collection, Baker Library, Harvard Business School, Box 5.

the duality of nature and culture. The pictures included in the Company albums highlight the ancient objects as cultural trophies, inasmuch as they orchestrate the adventurous character of finding and presenting the anthropomorphic stelae and the rediscovered site. They show the objects singled out, often heroically accompanied by a small group of alleged archaeologists or other expedition participants. Subsequently, the images orchestrate the findings in the way they capture a moment of artificial arrangement of the discovery, while consciously framing the ancient object as a cultural one within "wild" nature, yet bearing witness to the transcultural contact and adopting the pictorial gesture of taking possessing of an ancient unknown culture through its objects.

Archaeological photography has always depicted the human body as a feasible measurement and possible scale. However, what the album pictures mostly underline is the gesture of the white man taking possession of an indigenous cultural space.

On the level of the "optical unconscious," the pictures include insignia of the making of modern space, such as the emblematic cutting of old-growth trees. They seem to visually arrange the imagined chronotope in such a way that the ancient objects are assembled in a modern timeframe, literally stripping away the mighty and "mystic" ancient jungle to expose and make seen an ancient civilization. It is important to underscore here the traditional motives that are embedded and the gazes passed down in relation to the material culture of things past. Joanne Pillsbury interestingly points out of the visual history of scientific communication that, "Gradually over the sixteenth and seventeenth centuries, and with increasing fervor in the eighteenth century, ruins in Europe developed a new cultural purpose as a springboard for meditations on the merciless processes of time on all things human, including the inevitable rise and fall of civilizations."[49] Moreover, by the end of the nineteenth century, photography became the dominant means for archaeological documentations, especially with regard to the explorations of the New World.[50] Accordingly, the idea of photography was also linked to "appropriation, in one sense literally as a tool in grand-scale collecting" and "as implying rights and possession."[51] So we find here again, the ruins were extensively recorded, and were perceived "as models of engineering prowess, establishing a parallel between the great engineering achievements [for instance] of the Inca and the modern technology of the new railroads."[52]

Accordingly, the archival pictures seem to provide a form of self-assurance for the undertakings, insofar as they primarily index time within this transcultural exposure. By articulating a visual trace that unlocks the ancient space, photographing and digging became complementary ventures that work towards

---

49 Pillsbury, *Past Presented*, p. 7.
50 Ibid., pp. 26–27.
51 Ibid., p. 27.
52 Ibid., p. 28.

the exposure of this other cultural space. Subsequently, these pictures as copies, within a visual regime of mechanical reproduction, work on the mimicry of the Other enabling its possession, studying, collecting and displaying, while helping to contour the imagined white cultural supremacy. It has been criticized elsewhere that archaeology is the modern discipline that helps hierarchize ancient cultures as enclosed and dead, arranging them within past time while studying them as extinct time-space fostering the discourse of othering. Accordingly, archaeology has been conceived as a dispositive that defines our relationship to our haunting modernity.

Yet as both, copies and artifacts, photographs truly remain ambiguous, for they make the relationship with other cultures tangible. Nevertheless, they seem to become objects of sublimation of the embodied violence that seems to be the *conditio sine que non* of their existence. It is in this particular context of the United Fruit Company photographic archive and the scientific expeditions that the pictures obtain their *raison d'être,* embedding a powerful surplus-value that corresponds to commodity fetishism. Significantly, one characteristic of this photographic archive is that images that reflect ethnological interests or an ethnographic gaze make up a substantial portion of the albums. I argue that the images and image series that belong to this ethnographic gaze or the archaeological view of Quirigua define a secret (self)reflection on the part of the Company about the contact zone. They do not necessarily reflect on it critically, but they do reflect it as a photographic situation that contains the complex interferences of the cultural encounter. So, the images of the United Fruit Company photographic archive, which mirror an imperial gaze, do not only appropriate visually what they make seen as the Other, but they simultaneously contour the unseen as "unimagined communities," creating a sort of incidental meaning.

The Keith Collection or the Magic of the Company's Pre-Columbian Objects

> And what does such a compulsion to become Other imply for
> the sense of Self? Is it conceivable that a person could break
> boundaries like this, slipping into Otherness, trying it on for
> size?[53]

I have asked this question before with regard to the representation of plantation economy as landscape. Yet, it becomes
equally relevant to reexamine this landscape as it resurfaces in
the famous Keith collection of Mesoamerican antiquities and
within the "archaeological reconnaissance" of Central America
at the turn of the twentieth century. One of the most important
and precious collections known to archaeologists, today held by
the American Museum of Natural History in New York and the
Brooklyn Museum, originated in the Minor C. Keith collection
of antiquities, consisting mainly of stonework and pottery, but
also of copper, jade and gold objects, assembled during that
same period when the banana industry and its infrastructure
were being established in Costa Rica.[54] The story of the first gold
object discovered on the Mercedes plantations in the valley of
the Santa Clara River was often retold, and that presumably led
to more rigorous digging for ancient objects, as Keith used "his
unique opportunities [with the United Fruit Company] for the
satisfaction of his antiquarian penchant."[55] In the only compre-

53   Taussig, *Mimesis and Alterity*, p. 33.
54   Mason's report seems to be precise about the collection: "The Minor C.
Keith Collection originally consisted of 16,308 specimens, 15,427 of which were
recorded in the main catalogue and 881 in a special catalogue of gold and jade
ornaments. The majority of these, 8097 of the main collection and 874, virtually the entirety of the ornaments, were originally selected and deposited in
the American Museum, the remainder going to the Museum of the American
Indian, Heye Foundation, New York." John Alden Mason, "Costa Rican stonework; The Minor C. Keith collection," *Anthropological Papers of the American
Museum of Natural History* 39:3 (1945), p. 201.
55   Ibid., p. 199.

hensive report about the Keith collection at the Museum, former curator and archaeologist John Alden Mason writes:

> In the hitherto undeveloped and almost unexplored forests and jungles of eastern Costa Rica, the machete of the peon, clearing the land for banana plantations, and the shovels of the engineers, building rights-of-way and road-beds for the railroads, uncovered ancient cemeteries replete with admirable products of ancient and extinct civilizations. [...] Such unrifled cemeteries are as rare in America and as important to the Americanist as are untouched tombs of the Pharaohs to the Egyptologist. [...] He [Keith] was thus able to retain all the treasures, amounting to more than 10,000 pieces, in a single compact collection. The result was the acquisition of one of the largest, most important, and intrinsically most valuable homogeneous collections of American archaeology in the world [...]. In later years, Mr. Keith, his interest in Costa Rican archaeology whetted, employed other persons to excavate, and also purchased additional small collections from various parts of Costa Rica, from the central highlands, the southern area near the Panama border, and the northwestern section, mainly on the Nicoya Peninsula. Thus the collection was augmented until it contained more than 16,000 specimens.[56]

While, metaphorically or even literally, a "hurricane exposed [the grave's] contents to the modern eye,"[57] the archaeological objects started to be collected and to circulate outside of Central America, and to be displayed and become visible within a modern institutional network. Simultaneously, this seems to have encouraged Costa Rica's interest in its own cultural heritage and founding ancient material cultures. Interestingly, as the objects "represent birds, pumas, frogs, snakes, mythical gods," often in gold or gold encrusted, "most of them [...] have found their way into museums or private collections, [while] a few specimens, can still be found in antique shops in San

---

56   Ibid.
57   Stewart, *Keith and Costa Rica*, p. 161.

José where they are sold by weight."[58] But more importantly, as reported by Mason, the Keith collection "was brought gradually to [the United States] and until 1914 remained in [Keith's] country home at Babylon, Long Island, where it was catalogued and exhibited in part."[59] But what do the archaeological-anthropological operations such as those conducted by Minor C. Keith with the support of the United Fruit Company tell us about the modern Western relationship to ancient objects of other and even bygone cultures? What do they tell us about our relationship to material culture? How do the pictures of the archaeological excavations relate to the collected objects?

I argue that two cultural techniques are involved here and become important for understanding of the Company's relationship with material culture: first, *collecting* and, second, *displaying*. Both are bound to institutional practices, mainly those of the museum. Unfortunately, we can no longer find significant textual material that would help us understand and make explicit the provenience and circumstances in which the objects were found and their respective transfer to the museums.[60] Yet, through Keith, the Company certainly helped ensure that objects, plants, people, commodities, and cultural artifacts started to circulate efficiently within institutional networks. Consequently, in the social life of things, circulation and exchange create value and build value regimes that determine this contact as deeply transcultural. Again, as "exchange is not a by-production of the mutual valuation of objects, but its source,"[61] it is circulation that estab-

58   Ibid., p. 162.
59   Mason, "Costa Rican stonework," p. 199.
60   Interestingly, Mason reports here: "While the archaeologists will be ever grateful to Mr. Keith for the collection and preservation of this extraordinary material, they will equally regret that his foresight did not include the recording of details of the excavation data. Probably this was too much to expect of a busy pioneer. Apparently no notes were kept, and all scientific deductions must be based on an empirical study and comparison of the objects." Ibid., p. 200. Yet, it is assumed that there existed such reports of the recording details, which were lost under controversial circumstances.
61   Appadurai, *The Social Life of Things*, p. 56.

lishes the re-signification of objects, inasmuch as it integrates them into a circuit of economic and symbolic value. Accordingly, the concept of materiality may be used here to describe two inherent dimensions: first, materiality is linked to the object as a material thing that becomes the object of representation and embodies knowledge transfer while simultaneously reflecting a superimposition of codes. Second, the object's materiality is bound to institutional and social practices that determine its status and effect as well as its authority in the process of signification. Hence, it is of primordial importance that the United Fruit Company or Keith collected these artifacts and material objects that reflect the cultural contact, albeit in a highly problematic and asymmetrical way, as part of the process of digging, planting, and extracting: of economic enterprise and the material alteration of the landscape. Moreover, collecting objects from other times and spaces advances the chronotope underpinning the eternal promise of modernity, the integration of incompatible places and times into a homogenous and manageable space. "Slipping into Otherness, trying it on for size" thus becomes part of a defined and safe exercise that never seems to question the self, but displaces it towards the material object that is the sublimation of the subjugated and subaltern Other.

In the field of archaeology it remains noteworthy that the United Fruit Company, as part of the emergent institutional network that was beginning to support the social sciences, facilitated archaeological research in the United States and to an even greater extent in the host countries in the South, thus stimulating, in an ambiguous way, a sensibility towards these countries' cultural heritage. Some scholars suggest that this engagement was philanthropic, a benevolent engagement that resulted in the lasting development of archaeology.[62] Others are more prudent about it, for archaeology was a field in which

---

62   Stewart, *Keith and Costa Rica*; Diane K. Stanley, *For the Record. The United Fruit Company's Sixty-Six Years in Guatemala* (Guatemala City: Editorial Antigua, 1994).

diverse interests intersected and which eventually even became a geopolitical battleground.[63] Without going deeper into this discussion, I further develop Appadurai's argument about value regimes and the idea of exchange as a source of value in order to link it to the notion of fetishism that is inherent to the commodity exchange. I argue here for a broader understanding of economy as a culture of exchange. Interestingly, Georges Bataille once observed "that [magic] is part of an exchange system, that it is its cultural dimension which allows it to function as an exchange economy" with regard to the "irreducible surplus value, which he translated into the notion of expenditure."[64] Magic is certainly related to wonder, enchantment, or even the sacred, which re-emerges in different forms in modern life as an aesthetic experience. Could this give us a hint about the United Fruit Company's relationship to material culture, and more precisely, Keith's relationship to the ancient objects of other cultures? In another context I argued, with regard to the European expansion that stimulated the emergence of modern disciplines such as ethnology or sociology, that the "necessity to introduce new analytical and descriptive categories which aimed at describing the many new social phenomena in Europe and the outer-European world made clear that nothing less than European identity itself was negotiated and reformulated."[65] Significantly, with the apotheosis of the colonial expansion of European empires and the transference, particularly by the French and the British, of the anthropological fiction of "primitive society" onto tribal societies, a new general classification needed to be invented to deal with the diverse "artifacts brought to Europe through conquest, pillage, and

63   Sullivan, *Unfinished Conversations*; Harris and Sadler, *The Archaeologist was a Spy*.
64   Liliana Gómez, "The Urbanization of Society: Towards a Cultural Analysis of the Sacred in the Modern Metropolis," in *The Sacred in the City*, ed. Liliana Gómez and Walter van Herck (London: Continuum, 2012), pp. 39–40.
65   Ibid., p. 31.

collection zeal."[66] Relating the concept of magic to the idea of fetish became central to aesthetic theories, economics and politics alike in societies of mass consumerism.[67] This was because commodities acquired or exposed their nature as fetish within the process of exchange and circulation. Yet in that exchange and circulation there is a second, less explicit movement involved, which determines the creation of the modern value regime. This is related to the metropolis in a twofold way: to the urban metropolis as the center of intellectual and scientific production, understood as a dynamic economic nucleus; and to the asymmetrical relationship of "metropolis-periphery." This double discursive context certainly determines the struggle of disciplinary debates over key concepts such as the sacred, magic and fetish, that "dealt with an epistemological necessity to focus on the analysis both of the cultural modernization of European societies and urbanization, against a background of what Max Weber once called the 'disenchantment of the world', a formulation that for a long time shaped the imagination or dogma of the split between 'modernity' and 'magic'."[68] This is underpinned by the understanding that "every (archaic) society is based on violence and crime" and that modernity has always been opposed to this relation.[69] Accordingly, modernity is the attempt to be grounded in unequivocal reality and to construct the world according to comprehensive categories, such as economy versus sacrifice or sense versus madness.[70] So it was that labor and science as modern rationalities became strategies of disenchantment that aimed at constructing a continuous and homogenous space and time in order to avoid paradox,

---

66   Carlos Rincón, "Magisch/Magie," in *Ästhetische Grundbegriffe. Historisches Wörterbuch in sieben Bänden*, Band 3, ed. Karlheinz Barck et al. (Stuttgart: Metzler, 2001), p. 724, my translation.
67   Ibid.
68   Gómez, "The Urbanization of Society," p. 32.
69   Dietmar Kamper and Christoph Wulf, eds., *Das Heilige. Seine Spur in der Moderne* (Frankfurt am Main: Athenäum, 1987), p. 3, my translation.
70   Ibid.

antinomy, or even animism. Accordingly, *magic* became a part of the history of identity and mimicry determining an intrinsic relationship to modernity and modernization.[71] Interestingly enough, the reports of the archaeological excavations suggest a particular interest in the objects and sites related to religious and ceremonial rites. Without a doubt, the religious had always played a major role in archaeological and ethnological research, yet it is particularly striking that the United Fruit Company, as we shall see, emphasized this aspect in its own scientific engagement. The collection and displaying of objects became surrogates or substitutes for the magical and irrational. At the same time they constitute a modern economic rationality, in that the "accursed share" and the expenditure are controlled within a homogenous and disciplinary space, to which archaeology significantly contributed. As part of the performance of cultural identities, magic certainly allows for mimicking the Other, trying it on for size. Accordingly, the collected ancient artifacts and objects reflect the very materialization of the surplus value that cannot be fully embodied in the economic circuit of the Company. But as cultural Other they transform that expenditure into a symbolic capital in the form of being displayed. Within the play of transcultural exchange this cultural reconversion remains complex and open. Yet, this reconversion recreates the modern value regime set up with the plantation as discourse.

By creating a continuous and homogenous space, collecting and displaying ancient objects, situated at the unstable limit between the private and the public, become the material practices of archaeology, and serve here as another means of controlling the irrational eruptions of the objects as fetishes. Cultural techniques, such as collecting and displaying, relate to this economy in their attempt to tame magic as an irrational element, and contain it within economics. So it is of primary importance that the objects collected by Keith formed a private collection before being turned into a gift to the museums and becoming part of

71   Rincón, "Magisch/Magie," p. 730.

the public sphere in the United States, the metropolis. These material objects from past cultures certainly do not only underpin the construction of scientific objects within the discourse of archaeology, they also serve as cultural legitimation for taking possession of the space and time of the "periphery." Accordingly, they also become another type of commodity, alongside tropical fruits, belonging to the economic circuit defined by the complicated relationship "metropolis-periphery." Following the observations of the exchange as a source of value, I argue that the United Fruit Company intervened in the material landscape in at least two ways: both sowing seeds and collecting objects become irreducibly landscaping techniques, modeling space and time, helping to mold them into a modern chronotope defined by circulation and exchange and bound to the constant reproduction of cycles of marginality. Where science progresses and contributes to this type of accumulation of knowledge, the spatial production of the capitalist economy is assured. Accordingly, these two commodities shape the discourse of plantation by reproducing the binary of metropolis-periphery, inasmuch as on two different but intertwined levels of material culture they incorporate Central America into the orbit of Western knowledge and commodity exchange that is bound to the hegemony of capital and thus to magic. More so, it was the gold material in the objects that became the fetish of modernity and the capitalist economy.[72] Looking at the collected objects, made of gold, ceramic, and stone, which were later displayed in the museums, we might recognize here a sort of animation of these non-living inert things.[73] Relating to the metaphor and figure of the Gold

---

72 I refer here to *My Cocaine Museum* (Chicago: Chicago University Press, 2004) by Michael Taussig, where he retells, from the vantage point of the Gold Museum in Bogotá, the story of the suppressed material and political history of gold, namely that of slavery embodied and invisibilized in the collection and exhibition of Pre-Columbian gold as another Colombian commodity, besides cocaine, reflecting the violent foundation of the museum.

73 Alf Hornborg, "Animism, Fetishism, and Objectivism as Strategies for Knowing (or not Knowing) the World," *Ethnos: Journal of Anthropology* 71:1 (2006), p. 29.

Museum in Bogotá in Colombia, Taussig stresses the importance of making explicit that other hidden and concealed narrative and the violent nature of this kind of exchange and display:

> The walk through the Gold Museum is to become vaguely conscious
> of how for millennia the mystery of gold has through myth and sto-
> ries sustained the basis of money worldwide. But one story is missing.
> The museum is silent as to the fact that for more than three centuries
> of Spanish occupation what the colony stood for and depended upon
> was the labor of slaves from Africa in the gold mines. Indeed, this
> gold, along with the silver from Mexico and Peru, was what primed the
> pump of the capitalist takeoff in Europe, its primitive accumulation.
> [...] It seems so monstrously unjust, this denial, so limited and mean
> a vision incapable of imagining what it was like diving for gold in the
> wild coastal rivers, moving boulders with your bare hands, standing
> barefoot in mud and rain day after day, so unable to even tip your hat
> to the brutal labor people still perform today alongside the spirits of
> their parents and grandparents and of all the generations that before
> them had dug out the country's wealth.[74]

As Alf Hornborg points out, the animation of objects is "in fact
fundamental to fetishism, and fetishism [...] was central to modern capitalism," underscoring both the idea of the "ideological
illusion" of the capitalist political economy and a "condition
of phenomenological resonance."[75] So it is, Hornborg explains
in his reading of the genealogy of the concept of fetishism and
fetish, that "Every commodity produced for the market at some
point or points in its 'biography' [...] assumes the alienated,
shop-shelf condition we have referred to as 'signifier without a
signified'. Precisely in having been stripped of its original social
context, it is open to semiotic transformation. We have seen
how the disembedding of commodities can generate fetishistic

---

74   Taussig, *My Cocaine Museum*, p. x.
75   Hornborg, "Animism, Fetishism, and Objectivism," p. 29.

representations among consumers and producers alike [...]."[76] More importantly, with regard to the collection of ancient objects, "the fetishized objects are in some sense *constitutive*— not just misrepresentations—of accumulation."[77] It certainly becomes true that these objects, through being collected and displayed, were ascribed a significant role in mediating the cultural contact, that is, the play of the self and the Other, in which cultural identities always situated at the unstable limit between the private and the public need to be stabilized. Moreover, consider that these objects are not only fetishes of a primitive accumulation, but also help to sublimate the violent nature of clearing, digging, sowing seeds and creating a modern monoculture as a homogenous and thus manageable and aesthetic space that predominantly works towards the erasure of the animation of objects and the magic of commodities.

Foundational Images: *The Maya Through the Ages* (1949)

> Few would deny that illustrations have remarkable power: they take on an authority, an authority that at times overrides the original subject.[78]

It is thus important to examine another materialization of the United Fruit Company's cultural contact: the animation of pictures that depict and narrate the Company's archaeological curiosity and thus reflect its relationship to material culture in a broader sense. Furthermore, we are confronted with the copy of things and the question of how archaeology intervenes in the alteration of landscape and thus shapes the perception of this very same material alteration. Following the idea that exchange

---

76   Alf Hornborg, "Symbolic Technologies: Machines and the Marxian Notion of Fetishism," *Anthropological Theory* 1:4 (2001), p. 485.

77   Ibid., p. 490.

78   Pillsbury, *Past Presented*, p. 3.

creates value, what is at stake is, again, the very question of representation as the battlefield where material culture is negotiated and defined. It becomes thus helpful to introduce the term fetishism again, not so much as a descriptive ethnographical term, but rather as an abstract analytic concept, to grasp that relationship to material culture and speculate about the animation of the material related to it: the ancient objects and eventually the pictures that manifest the archaeological view and the ethnographical gaze. On an analytical level, in terms of cognitive processes, four main varieties of fetishism can be distinguished that might help us to better grasp this relationship: first, concretization; second, animation; third, conflation of signifier and signified; fourth, ambiguous power relations.[79] In the following I deploy fetishism as explanatory analytic, in order to examine the question of representation with regard to the animated pictures in the film *The Maya Through the Ages* (1949), and I examine the workings of visualization that seem to mediate the United Fruit Company's relationship to material culture.

Let me recall some of the circumstances that led to the making of this film: In May 1946, ethnologist and photographer Giles Greville Healey, at the time engaged in making a moving picture of Maya ruins and the "living Maya" for the United Fruit Company, "discovered" an important frescoed ruin named Bonampak in Chiapas, Mexico, while being guided by Lacandon Indians to the site. It was by no means a coincidence that the United Fruit Company owned vast terrains near to where the discovery was made. In February 1947, a Carnegie Institution expedition, led by Giles G. Healey and financed by the United Fruit Company, begun "to record and appraise the Bonampak discovery."[80] Already in 1945, Healey had started to prepare his

---

79 Hornborg, "Symbolic Technologies," p. 481.
80 Charles Morrow Wilson, "Backwards a Dozen Centuries," *Natural History* 56:8 (1947), p. 374. The discovery was also depicted and recounted in the United Fruit Company Annual Report of 1948, which dedicated an entire chapter to Healey including a double-sided color picture of the copy, the visual reproduction, of one of the Bonampak murals.

trip and scientific exploration to Chiapas and to meet with eth-nologist and archaeologist Karl Frey in order to be introduced to the region, where the Lacandon Indians, perceived as descen-dants of the Maya civilization, lived. This was the background to the making of a film on the "living Maya." Healey was commis-sioned by the United Fruit Company, which engaged Edmund S. Whitman and Charles Morrow Wilson as project directors. This project also appears to have been supported by the govern-ments of Guatemala, Honduras, and Mexico with the help of the National Institute of Anthropology and History of Mexico and the Carnegie Institution of Washington. Yet we know little about the United Fruit Company's intentions in making this film, as textual archival sources are scarce. The film, in color pictures, had an educational purpose and was originally intended for classroom instruction, but was never circulated after its comple-tion. The first part of the film presents an archaeological view. The archaeological sites of Copan, Chichén Itzá and Palenque are shown, thus animating the ancient stones and Maya ruins. The voice of the narrator, Vincent Price, tells the glorious story of the ancient Maya civilization, emphasizing their achieve-ments in architecture, astrology, the calendar, the numerical system and writing. The storyteller underlines the pictures' own narrative as a heroic one. Then, in the second part, the film fol-lows the "living Maya," the Lacandon Indians, and depicts other syncretic catholic religious practices in the small colonial city of San Cristobal de las Casas, representing the cultural contact between Spain and the Pre-Columbian civilizations, while pro-viding glimpses into artisan practices and everyday material cul-ture. This second part certainly reflects an ethnographical gaze.

Yet, as these two views coalesce, they suggest a genealogy from ancient Maya civilization culminating with the Lacandons, the idea of Indianness, and their great achievement in agricul-ture, the ancient cultivation of Indian corn. The film also depicts the cultivation of other plants, such as tobacco and cotton, and shows how these plants are used by the Lacandons. Interestingly, Healey used long image sequences showing the different family members of the Lacandon group he met, with close-ups of faces and facial expressions, revealing a racialized perspective. The Lacandons are purposefully posed and filmed by Healey. Importantly, Healey captures how and when corn is planted, showing the sowing of seeds, distributed in accordance with the rainy season. He suggests that the lives of the Lacandons are quintessentially organized around that cultivation, which seems to define the time and space of the ancient Maya civilizations in the way it relates to Pre-Columbian cycles of agriculture and their techniques. The narrative finally ends with glimpses into the secret religious ceremonies of the Lacandons that are presented as reminiscent of the spiritual life of the ancient Maya. Finally, Healey's discovery of the murals of Bonampak is shown and orchestrated as apotheosis of the cultural encounter between Healey (the United Fruit Company) and the "Indians" or the ancient civilization. Following this narrative, these animated pictures become the foundational fiction of goods and power that infuses the Company's self-fabricated myths. Moreover, in the figure of the "living Lacandon" as the "true" ancestor of the great Mayan civilization, the mimetic machinery helps the Company slip "into Otherness, trying it on for size,"[81] while relating to Mayan agriculture through an imagined and desired genealogy. Fetishism could be used here to describe the Company's relationship with the objects of Others and to material culture in the sense of the animation (of land) against the backdrop of the ambiguous and asymmetrical power relations that the pictures carefully conceal. The animated pictures seem to suggest that this landscape embeds a long-standing material alteration of space through the agriculture of previous civilizations, with the aim of culturally and symbolically legitimizing the Company's own modern undertakings.

Interestingly, in 1948, Healey recalls the expedition and himself photographing it as an adventure, framing the pictures as a sort of material result of this rare and spectacular cultural encounter:

81   Taussig, *Mimesis and Alterity*, p. 33.

Fig. 5.8: "Palenque, Chiapas." Black & white print, 21 x 26 cm, circa 1946. Giles G. Healey Negatives, Collection of Western Americana Photographs. Department of Special Collections, Princeton University Library.

This region has been visited in centuries past by military expeditions and zealous missionaries, these visitors did not change the Lacandon way of life and Catholicism is still unknown to them. Commercial ventures have had more effect: the booms (and failures) of the mahogany interests, in the 1890's, have given them steel axes, and the recent war boom on chicle has given them machetes and muzzle-loading shotguns. Lacandons of today are stone-age people who use the white man's steel. I first entered this region early in 1945 with guns and cameras. The guns, some of them cheap and old muzzle-loading flintlocks, I gave to the Lacandons. On other trips I brought in supplies of shot and powder. These gifts gave me a good trading position and I was successful in filming the daily life of the Lacandons and even their religion, at visits to their shrines, which are ancient Maya ruins. [...] When we approached, the ruins could hardly be discerned at a distance of fifty feet. We spent hours felling the smaller trees, and cutting lianas and undergrowth with machetes, so as to get enough throw for photography.[82]

Moreover, because of the circulation of these foundational images of Bonampak, it was quickly acknowledged that Healey had discovered the extraordinarily rare and well-kept Mayan murals inside one of the remote ruins. The discovery of 1946 was immediately received with great interest by scientific journals, and even more popular magazines, such as *Time* or *Life*. Yet other sources from members of the first expedition in 1945–1946 suggest that for Healey the photographic image had become a strategy to record and bear witness to this "planned" discovery of the Mayan murals, which later was even disputed and rectified with some grievance.[83] It has been described as a sort of "hunting with the camera."[84] Healey entered the jungle to meet the Lacandons and "document" their daily life. But how did he really relate to the Lacandons, as they used to live in the remote jungle? The compiler of his published Bonampak photographs, Charles Morrow Wilson, an official United Fruit Company historian, writes:

> To study and photograph these fast-vanishing people, Healey set out from his headquarters at San Cristobal las [sic] Casas, an old colonial town in the Chiapas mountains, near the Guatemalan frontier. He flew to the farthest outposts of the Miramar area and there, with a pack mule and an interpreter who spoke the little-known languages of these Indians, set out to find the white-robed, long-haired Lacandones. [...] After coming upon his first clans of Lacandones, Healey found them excessively camera shy. But when he brought out his fiddle and played waltzes, the Lacandones crowded about to listen and presently permitted him to photograph them.[85]

82 Giles G. Healey, "Oxlahuntun," *Archaeology* 1:4 (1948), pp. 129–130.
83 John Bourne, *Recollections of My Early Travels in Chiapas*, 2001.
84 Pinney, *Photography's Other Histories*, p. 13.
85 Morrow Wilson, "Backwards a dozen centuries," pp. 371, 378.

Fig. 5.9: "At Bonampak, J. Eric S. Thompson, renowned Carnegie epigrapher enters ruins with Lacandon Indians," circa 1946. Giles G. Healey Negatives, Collection of Western Americana Photographs, WC064. Department of Special Collections, Princeton University Library.

Certainly, the selected photographic series by Morrow Wilson shares an idealized view of the "original Indian." It reflects a hierarchical gaze, through which these images, both of the publications about the discovery of Bonampak and the animated pictures of the film, became foundational images of Indianness as the idealized Other. Moreover, through Healey's lenses, "nature" and landscape, the supposedly virgin jungle, are captured and made visible as primeval nature and as abundance. It is this primary aestheticized approach that characterizes Healey's gaze, the picture series of the film, and also of his still photographs. In this way, he self-fashioned himself as the photographer-discover of Bonampak. Furthermore, landscape seems here to be the *mis-en-scène* of his discovery and becomes a media dispositive, framing Indianness as an idealized "primitivism"

Fig. 5.10: "Lacondon man sitting before ruins of a sculpted stone at the Bonampak Site," circa 1946. Giles G. Healey Negatives, Collection of Western Americana Photographs. Department of Special Collections, Princeton University Library.

and "backwardness."[86] It might be significant, with regard to the discovery of the ruins, that his companions on the first expedition remembered him as a clumsy "ethnologist," who seemed not to be afraid of inventing any kind of tradeoff economy and gifts to persuade the people to be photographed, apparently using trustfulness and alleged naiveté in his favor.[87]

The photographic camera as a mimetic machine became here the technical device for the construction of the ethnological and archaeological study object, while concealing the truthful cultural contact and relationship between Healey and the Lacandons. Morrow Wilson writes later in his account: "For

86 Ibid.
87 Bourne, *Recollections*.

Fig. 5.11: "Lacandons, two men and a boy in the ruins of the central Maya temple at Bonampak, which remains their place of worship," circa 1946. Giles G. Healey Negatives, Collection of Western Americana Photographs, WC064. Department of Special Collections, Princeton University Library.

the first time we had a *true picture in color* of what the ancient Mayas actually looked like. Books and books have been written about them with only a slight indication of what they looked like and wore... and here on this wall was revealed for the first time *authentic evidence* of the glorious Mayas of the first empire period."[88] As noted elsewhere, in the context of archaeological and ethnological knowledge production the success of photography as an image technology, its rapid dissemination and absorption into manifold discourses of knowledge and power was certainly a consequence of its affirmative aspects.[89] With regard to the Bonampak discovery photography became a

---

88   Morrow Wilson, "Backwards a Dozen Centuries," p. 374, my emphasis.
89   See the discussion by Solomon-Godeau, "Wer spricht so?".

Fig. 5.12: Still picture from the film *The Maya Through the Ages*. 00:01:13, Reel 2; 45 min. sd., color, 16 mm. Script and editing, Kenneth Macgowan. Narration, Ralph Bellamy, Irving Pichel, Vincent Price. Filmed by Giles Greville Healey; United Fruit Company, 1949.

constitutive part in the discourse of evidence and history. Literally, it was through the lenses of Healey that Bonampak was re-discovered.

So it is that the photographs show the colored image of the murals of the ruins, the most sacred place in the living culture of the Lacandons, as a last mimetic copy. Symbolically, the Lacandon Indian is posed in front of the image and seems to contemplate or be afraid of that copy, as the Lacandon groups in this once remote region would soon vanish into oblivion.[90] Yet, again, it seems that photography is used here to intervene

90   The compiler of Healey's photographs, Charles Morrow Wilson, writes in 1947: "[Sr. Villagra, who represented the Mexican Government] states that the Bonampak find is such outstanding importance that the Mexican Government is faced with the choice of removing the paintings from the walls and preserving them for the ages to come, or building a landing field near the remote location so that all interested scientists may have access to the discovery. The other

Fig. 5.13: Still picture from the film *The Maya Through the Ages*. 00:15:13, Reel 2; 45 min. sd., color, 16 mm. Script and editing, Kenneth Macgowan. Narration, Ralph Bellamy, Irving Pichel, Vincent Price. Filmed by Giles Greville Healey; United Fruit Company, 1949.

in the time-space compression of the modern expansion, inasmuch as the image remains a visual leftover of an equally distant cultural encounter. But this cultural contact is framed by a different narrative that reflects the United Fruit Company's self-consciousness about its relationship to material culture. So, we read in the reports about another archaeological project, the ruins of Zaculeu, which the Company helped reconstruct in detail with great effort:

> The United Fruit Company expresses its social responsibility in Middle America through a number of programs in the field of public service. Included among these are the financing of agricultural schools, diversified crops, reforestation, and agricultural experimental projects.

temples must be protected from the weather and safeguarded from vandalism." Morrow Wilson, "Backwards a dozen centuries," pp. 374–375.

Fig. 5.14: Still picture from the film *The Maya Through the Ages*. 00:16:23, Reel 2; 45 min. sd., color, 16 mm. Script and editing, Kenneth Macgowan. Narration, Ralph Bellamy, Irving Pichel, Vincent Price. Filmed by Giles Greville Healey; United Fruit Company, 1949.

The Company also contributes to the better understanding between the Americas through the dissemination of knowledge concerning this fruitful area. The restoration of the ancient Maya city of Zaculeu in Guatemala is an outstanding example of United Fruit Company's research to help unearth and reveal to Middle America the great heritage of the region. The Company, with the approval of the Government of Guatemala, began work in February, 1946 in this one-time capital of the Mam Maya Kingdom of the pre-Columbian era. Upon completion, the site was restored to the people of Guatemala to become a national monument.[91]

Healey's lenses certainly reflect the Company's self-consciousness and the images became agents of modern knowledge production, while fashioning the Company's self-fabricated,

91   *The Ruins of Zaculeu Guatemala*, 1953.

314

Fig. 5.15: "Villagra, National Museum of Mexico reproduction of ancient Mayan frescoes discovered by Giles G. Healey at Bonampak ruins, Chiapas, Mexico." Black-and-white, 21 x 26 cm, circa 1946. Giles G. Healey Negatives, Collection of Western Americana Photographs. Department of Special Collections, Princeton University Library

culturally benevolent work. Moreover, it was the visual *mis-en-scène* of the Maya ruins and the archaeological site of Bonampak and earlier that of Quirigua, through which the Company invented a genealogical line, going back to these ancient civilizations, that culminated in the great modern agricultural endeavor and the Company's civilizing mission. I underline that "If our images of the world take such an active part in shaping it, we need to be more reflexive about the potential impact of the images we produce."[92] Accordingly, both the photographic camera and the scientific gaze conquered and appropriated future space and

92   Hornborg, "Symbolic technologies," pp. 480–481.

time, while efficiently fostering the transformation of land into an aesthetic and economically viable hybrid landscape.

But let me return at this point to my concern about representation, as it is related to the problem of cognitive processes and the concept of fetishism: What strikes me is that seemingly the images deployed by the United Fruit Company, including the pictures of the photographic archive and the film, do not necessarily reflect the purpose of scientific images. Rather it seems that they become in themselves objects of interest. With regard to the depicted archaeological sites, they even seem to become things, inasmuch as the pictures do not, as a matter of course, relate to some sort of outside or the signified, for they are mostly stripped of their broader context. So, it seems that the concept of fetishism, as related to cognitive processes, might be useful to designate this relationship as a conflation of signifier and signified. This underpins my reading of the image not so much as representation of something else but rather as a material reality as and of itself, that even as "an authority [...] overrides the original subject."[93] Following this, could we think of the Company's relationship to material culture, regarding ancient objects and agricultural commodities, as a fetishized form that efficiently displaces and invisibilizes the cultural contact as an unequal and asymmetrical exchange? Could we even think of the objects and eventually the images as fetishes or surrogates, as artificial replacements, for the time-space compression realized in a capitalist economy? It is certainly the case, with regard to the question of representation, as suggested by Hornborg, that this inherently unequal exchange, caused by digging, sowing seeds, and sending objects back to the metropolis, is carefully concealed and invisibilized.

Does the process of invisibilization even manifest an act of displacement that is no longer defined by the signifier-signified scheme and thus manifests a surrogate, that is, the conflation of signifier and signified? Accordingly, fetishism might be a

93   Pillsbury, *Past Presented*, p. 3.

helpful concept to designate this cognitive process or the relationship to the material negotiated by the pictures of the United Fruit Company. The film unquestionably invisibilizes the inherently unequal exchange by orchestrating an archaeological and thus scientific view. On the level of the visual this fetishized material relationship is displaced and eventually concealed. Interestingly, fetishism seems to be "'a cultural representation over which we have lost control.' Fetishes are symbols that have become masters of their authors."[94] Yet the "fundamental question is whether the fetish can or cannot be said to mystify or conceal some aspect of social reality."[95] Accordingly, the question remains open about whether "the representation is or is not *material.*"[96] Importantly, what Taussig suggests with regard to the Gold Museum is that there remains an irreducible "alienating split between people and the products of their labour" arguing for "a reification—in the form of a small part of it—of a wider context of real material relationships, such as flows of goods and services."[97] This distinction seems important for understanding that archaeological objects and natural commodities define the order of exchange value of both material culture and a capitalistic mode of production of space, inasmuch as they either visibilize or conceal the productive forces defining time as the unequal exchange of labor time and natural space as the unequal exchange of resources.[98]

So it is that the photographs of the archaeological objects as well as the animated pictures in the film become foundational images, insofar as they obscure the unequal exchange of time and space that binds the periphery to the center within the Western material regime of the United Fruit Company. As foundational images they further conceal and mystify the Company's fetishized relationship to material culture that is

---

94 Hornborg, "Symbolic Technologies," p. 482.
95 Ibid.
96 Ibid.
97 Ibid., p. 483.
98 Ibid., p. 486.

manifested in the collections of ancient objects and the altered landscape. Finally, as foundational images they veil this mystification at a representational level, eventually making it "an intrinsic aspect of the constitution of social reality."[99]

Animated Materiality

> Even before the political processes of modern nationalism defined it as such [...], material culture was, in a literal economic sense, "cultural property." The very materiality of the objects of material culture entangled them in Western economic processes of the acquisition and exchange of wealth. While many ethnographic objects were acquired by expropriative processes involving no element of exchange, many others were acquired by barter or purchase, so that the development of museum collections has always been heavily dependent on the commitment of individual, corporate, or national wealth [...]. And while the detritus of the shell heap has never been given a value commensurate with the labor expended in its recovery, its aesthetic-cum-economic valuation in relation to objects higher on the scale of "culture" has been a factor affecting the allocation of resources for its collection and preservation [...]. From the beginning, market processes have been potent influences on the constitution of museums as archives of material culture—the more so insofar as the objects therein have been regarded, or come to be regarded, as objects of fine art, rather than as artifacts [...].[100]

To this extent the unequal exchange relies on the animation of materiality, inasmuch as material objects are collected, circulated and displayed, forming potent knowledge institutions such as the museums as archives of material culture. The United

99 Ibid., p. 482.
100 Stocking, "Philanthropoids and Vanishing Cultures," pp. 5–6.

Fruit Company had its significant share in the institutionalization and beginnings of Mesoamerican archaeological research,
which became a political field controlled by manifold and often
disparate interests. These interests were carefully negotiated on
the level of representation, as is reflected in the film *The Maya
Through the Ages*, but also in the Company's involvement in the
foundational collection of Pre-Columbian objects initiated and
contributed to by Keith. Importantly, as Stocking underlines, "It
is not, however, simply a question of the ownership of 'cultural
property,' but also of who should control the representation
of the meaning of the objects in the Western category, 'material culture.'"[101] When discussing the United Fruit Company's
relationship to material culture, it is this representation of the
meaning of objects that is at stake. Epistemologically, representation is a constitutive part of the exchange of value and, moreover, of the politics of value, that the Company was incredibly
aware of. It thus becomes important to underscore, again, that
the Company's relationship to material culture is defined by
the "very materiality of the objects of material culture [that are]
entangled [...] in Western economic processes of the acquisition
and exchange of wealth."[102] In other words, "Time and space
can be approached as commoditized human resources that the
market [...] render[s] interchangeable, so that time can be converted into space and vice versa [...]."[103] So, in the way archaeology intervenes in the landscape and participates in its alteration
it becomes not only a landscaping technique, but even more so a
modern dispositive allowing for intervention into time.

Let us recall at this point with regard to knowledge production that "Foucault pointed out that initially magic and erudition belonged together and complemented each other until
the modern rationalization of the world removed the sacred
and magic as valid aspects of knowledge, since which time they

101 Ibid., p. 11.
102 Ibid.
103 Hornborg, "Symbolic Technologies," p. 488.

seem to have been dissolved by the modern sciences and have disappeared forever."[104] Against this backdrop, it is certainly true to view the collected Pre-Columbian objects as embodied knowledge conflating magic and erudition, though obscured and concealed. Moreover, on the level of representation, the collected and displayed objects displace the lived magic knowledge of "Indianness" and articulate a materially accumulative scientific knowledge that is fostered by early archaeology on Mesoamerica. Interestingly, the extensive use of copies instead of originals was common in the early period of the museum displays on Mesoamerican culture. Moreover, it was in this institutional context that photography achieved a predominant role in promoting archaeology and ethnography for the public.[105] Diana Fane, former curator of the Brooklyn Museum, underlines the use of photography here as follows:

> to "bridge the apparent gap between the aesthetics of the Old World and the New" by means of photography, beginning with appealing views of clay figurines "that are not burdensome by reason of detail and that relate to the human side of life," and gradually progressing to the "more complicated examples of Middle American Art." [...]. No photograph, however, could convey the power of the sacred architecture that Vaillant [curator at the American Museum of Natural History between 1927 and 1945] considered ancient Mexico's finest achievement. An image of the ruined structure [...] only showed the consequences of centuries of neglect and decay. The model of the temple [...], on the other hand,

104 Gómez, "The Urbanization of Society," p. 31.
105 Fane points out with regard to the reconstruction of other pasts: "Documentation and preservation were the primary goals of this archaeological program. The invention of photography only increased the incentive for taking molds by holding out the possibility of securing a truly comprehensive record of all the visual facts. The first photographers in both Egypt and Mexico also made squeezes. Impressions of significant surface finds were immediately sent back to museums for reproduction, study, and display, thus greatly increasing the quantity and quality of information available about ancient civilizations and significantly adding to museums' holdings." Diane Fane, "Reproducing the Pre-Columbian Past: Casts and Models in Exhibitions of Ancient America, 1824–1935," in Hill Boone, *Collecting the Pre-Columbian Past*, p. 150.

with its crisp outlines and decorative niches gave "an impression of the stateliness of the building before vegetation had begun its destructive action." Models allowed Vaillant to gain control over the ravages of time and the accidents of history. [...] Vaillant was not alone in recognizing the display value of reproductions. Ancient America has continually been represented and interpreted through the selective replications of its surviving monuments. In this process unique objects have become multiples and acquired new histories and associations.[106]

Yet the relation between models or copies and the originals seems to be even more complicated. From a curatorial point of view, the undertakings of displaying certainly reveal what Fane goes on to stress: "In an exhibition context, replicas become artifacts in their own right; each copy derives its meaning from other objects on view rather than from the lost or absent original."[107] As animated materiality, displayed copies and original ancient objects evolve an independent life mediating and concealing the violent nature of the inherent cultural contact. So it is that with regard to the contact zone, complex cultural interferences are determined by a cultural apparatus of work and bureaucracy, into which the *exchange* of value is embedded and in which displaying became a significant modern quest. Moreover, in this "prolonged cultural dynamic" it was "technological conquest and consumption" that were emphasized.[108] Importantly, "the technologies of representation, reproduction, and removal themselves became a public and self-conscious form of power celebration."[109] Hinsley underpins that "Drawing, daguerreotype, photograph, mold, cast—the constantly improving processes of

---

106 Ibid., p. 142–143. The use of photography to this end became particularly important in the context of early exhibitions in the United States, such as the 1893 Chicago World's Fair, the 1915 Panama-California Exposition in San Diego and the Brooklyn Museum's first Pre-Columbian exhibition in 1935. See Fane, "Reproducing the Pre-Columbian Past."
107 Ibid., p. 144.
108 Hinsley, "In Search of the New World Classical," p. 113.
109 Ibid.

image- and meaning-extraction from site to museum collection became themselves the subjects of image and heroic narrative. In effect they served to reinscribe the Euro-American narrative of technological progress and prowess by legitimating the process of ever more precise knowledge transfer."[110]

Accordingly, cultural orders and material regimes were stabilized by global actors such as the United Fruit Company. The Company was significantly engaged in shaping and molding the contact zone on various levels of material culture, in the way it engineered vision as a primary modality and fostered an animation of materiality to stabilize the hierarchical cultural order between oneself and the Other, between oneself and oneself. In other words, the collections of Pre-Columbian objects and these photographs became important in stabilizing the modern political space that was bound to the Western material regime and the principle of primitive accumulation. Christopher Pinney also relates to this when he suggests that it is by "abandoning the notion that photographic history is best seen as the explosion of a Western technology whose practice has been molded by singular individuals" in order to focus on the images' global dissemination and the local appropriation of the medium, thus emphasizing the idea of visual economy.[111]

Looking at these pictures, again, it becomes obvious that identities of the Self and the Other as an assumed unitary subject need to be questioned because the "subject is then overlain with artifact-mobilized identities."[112] As Pinney rightly reminds us, "the process of representation and presenting the 'world as picture,' as a domain susceptible to human actions, is fundamental to the constitution of the modern subject as a crucial starting point for theorizing the complex fields within which photography as (self-)representation might function."[113]

110 Ibid.
111 Pinney and Peterson, *Photography's Other Histories*, p. 1.
112 Ibid., p. 12.
113 Ibid., p. 13.

Yet photographs not only mediate the cultural contact, they also reflect it, while often disclosing a fetishized relationship to material culture. Accordingly, both the collected ancient objects and the pictures suggest that the invisible is not a "mere nothing, not a *tabula rasa* of the perception" but "a more or less countered space of imagination" and eventually a conscious and psychic displacement of our seeing.[114] The history of images is thus always an attempt at a visual transgression, a *mis-en-scène* by the act of non-showing of images.[115] But what these images and Pre-Columbian objects, which started to circulate back and forth, as animated materialities certainly implied is best captured as a modern material regime, inasmuch as:

> those who endeavored to *impose* consumption in Latin America, as well as those inhabitants of Latin America who *voluntarily* acquired certain goods, often came to think of themselves as part of an occidentalizing process. [...] But the scramble for identity, the need to redraw, or cross over, the lines of social relationships through the acts of visible consumption, are perhaps rather more intense in colonial and postcolonial societies where power and the reference for fashion are often established by foreigners, while the status and prestige of people within the colony or country are strongly influenced by the jigsaw-puzzle of class and ethnicity, the negotiation of which is made all the more important for its ambiguity.[116]

This dilemma of cultural identity is what is at stake when questioning the representation negotiated by the images and the collected ancient objects. This brings us back to the project of modernity, insofar as it frames the alteration of material landscape and our relationship to it, allowing for perceiving that "the social condition and technological accomplishments of

114 Peter Geimer, "Gegensichtbarkeiten," *Bildwelten des Wissens. Kunsthistorisches Jahrbuch für Bildkritik* 4:2 (2006), p. 41, my translation.
115 Ibid., p. 42.
116 Bauer, *Goods, Power, History*, p. 9.

'modernity' have been founded on a categorical distinction between Nature and Society," as pointed out by Hornborg when questioning animism and fetishism as epistemological and ontological categories.[117] "It is," he further underscores, "by drawing a boundary between the world of objects and the world of meanings that the 'modern' project has emerged. By, as it were, 'distilling' Nature into its material properties alone, uncontaminated by symbolic meanings or social relations, modernists have been freed to manipulate it in ways unthinkable in pre-modern contexts."[118] So, it is of primordial importance that the United Fruit Company, for better or for worst, was engaged in the modern project of collecting Pre-Columbian objects. Besides the fact that this fetishized relationship to material culture remains purposely concealed, the magic of these objects constitutes a part of modern knowledge production, unmasking in its antagonism that modernity is not completely rooted in scientific rationality or Reason, but disclosing modernity's significant share in the pre-modern.

117 Hornborg, "Animism, Fetishism, and Objectivism," p. 21.
118 Ibid.

Epilogue. Upheavals and the Resurgent Photographic Archive

> To articulate the past historically does not mean to recognize it "the way it really was" [...]. It means to seize hold of a memory as it flashes up at a moment of danger. Historical materialism wishes to retain that image of the past which unexpectedly appears to man singled out by history at a moment of danger.[1]

Civil Contract and the Materiality of the Image

Both the moment of danger and memory shape the question of representation, as they configure the banana massacre of 1928. By way of conclusion to this book, I will consider the massacre, which took place in the United Fruit Company plantations, as a topos for socio-political upheavals in Latin American history. I reread it against the backdrop of the archive as lieu of potential history, drawing on the concept of the civil contract of photography, as elaborated by Ariella Azoulay. In the way the photographic archive participates in the political, I wish to cast it as a point of departure for promoting human rights. In *The Civil Contract of Photography,* Azoulay anchors "spectatorship in civic duty toward the photographed persons [...] who, in turn, enable the rethinking of the concept and practice of citizenship."[2] She does so using the term "citizenship" in the analysis of the "act of photography or in understanding the ways in which some populations are more exposed to catastrophe than others."[3] Rethinking the political, in the way Azoulay suggests, it becomes a "space of relations between the governed, whose

---

1   Benjamin, "Theses on the Philosophy of History," p. 255.
2   Ariella Azoulay, *The Civil Contract of Photography* (New York: Zone Books, 2008), pp. 16–17.
3   Ibid., p. 17.

political duty is first and foremost a duty toward one another, rather than toward the ruling power."[4] Having the United Fruit Company photographic archive at hand, it becomes clear that the civil contract here refers to the "partner-participants in the act of photography"; Azoulay proposes to "extract [these] from the practices of both picture taking and the public use and display of photographs."[5] Thus, the archive's use today relies on an ontological-political understanding of photography, that implies the participation of the camera, the photographer, the photographed subject, the spectator to the photographic act, and photography's meaning.[6] As Azoulay underscores:

> The civil contract of photography assumes that, at least in principle, the governed possess a certain power to suspend the gesture of the sovereign power seeking to totally dominate the relations between us, dividing us governed into citizens and noncitizens thus making disappear the violation of *our* citizenship.[7]

This observation underlines my rereading of the United Fruit Company archive, against the background of the recently emerging claims for a judicial response to the role of corporate officials of the United Fruit Company's successor, Chiquita, in crimes against humanity.[8] In this final chapter I consider the banana massacre as a topos for socio-political upheavals in Latin American history, with the archival testimony, and the way it contours the question of representation. What Walter Benjamin argues in the opening quote is key here: to conceive representation not as an expression of something essential or

4   Ibid.
5   Ibid., p. 20.
6   Ibid., p. 23.
7   Ibid.
8   See the report by the International Human Rights Clinic, Harvard Law School, "The Contribution of Chiquita Corporate Officials to Crimes Against Humanity in Colombia. Article 15 Communication to the International Criminal Court" (Cambridge, Mass.: Harvard Law School, 2017).

archetypal that would reflect the quest for the persistence of culture, but rather as a symptom of something displaced. As an image-symptom the image's structure is a symptom, where latencies and crises, repetitions and differences, repressions and "après-coups" are intermingled.[9] Yet, the photographed subject and thus the "governed possess a certain power," as Azoulay suggests, to "suspend the gesture of the sovereign power"; this is the inherent potential power of the resurgent United Fruit Company photographic archive.[10] As a topos for socio-political upheavals, the banana massacre of 1928 in Ciénaga, on the Colombian Caribbean coast, is a symbol of powerful resistance and the struggle for human rights.

The moment of danger and memory serves as a vantage point for examining a series of images from the United Fruit Company photographic archive related to the events of the labor strike and massacre of 1928. As historical images they contest the more general convention of understanding them as documents. Rightly, we are reminded that if "we sever them from their phenomenology, from their specificity, and from their very substance" then we lower them to that status.[11] Having that in mind, I discuss the banana massacre, as narrated by Gabriel García Márquez in *One Hundred Years of Solitude*, against the reading of this photograph series. I argue that this particular series is contested by what later became the imaginings of Macondo, a fictitious archive that is created within the novel. Fiction functions here as a counter-semantic to the photographs and as a critical work of remembrance. Although the chemical-technical invention of photography once promised visibility, the photographic archive of the United Fruit Company makes the banana massacre invisible. Conversely,

---

9   See the discussion by Georges Didi-Huberman, *Confronting Images: Questioning the Ends of a Certain History of Art* (University Park: Pennsylvania State University Press, 2005), p. 261.

10   Azoulay, *The Civil Contract of Photography*, p. 23.

11   Georges Didi-Huberman, *Images in Spite of All: Four Photographs from Auschwitz* (Chicago: Chicago University Press, 2008), p. 33.

García Márquez's fiction potentially reinstates its visibility. Accordingly, the Company photograph series will be examined not as documents, inasmuch as the alleged documentary character consists of the visible result or the clear information they contain, but following the images' phenomenology, that is "everything that made them an event."[12]

On the theoretical level, one suggestion may be that literature does not primarily orient itself toward the mimetic and mnemonic potential that are aspects of the photograph understood as document, but instead toward the "pre-modern" and "magical" attributes that are comparable to the performative moment of the photographic act.[13] It is to this extent that a rereading of the banana massacre, of the Company photograph series, and of the novel's relation to the history in which its fictional reality is embedded becomes pertinent. I thus discuss the banana massacre from the double perspective of the two archives: one being the photographic archive of the United Fruit Company that includes pictures of the labor strike of 1928; the other being the fictitious archive created by the novel. I do not suggest that these two archives, the photographic and the literary, necessarily belong to each other, as they emerge as two very different narratives, at different times. Nevertheless, when read in parallel and simultaneously, the literary text and the photographic archive intersect, inasmuch as, regarding the banana massacre as a moment of danger and memory, they raise questions of testimony and of the image's materiality. I wish to speculate about the intimate relationship between photography and history and the photographic in literature. Georges Didi-Huberman reminds us that "[...] the image is the *eye of history*: its tenacious function of making visible. But also that it is *in the eye of history*: in a very local zone, in a moment of visual sus-

12   Ibid., p. 36.
13   Irene Albers and Bernd Busch, "Fotografie/fotografisch," in *Ästhetische Grundbegriffe. Historisches Wörterbuch in sieben Bänden*, Band 2, ed. Karlheinz Barck et al. (Stuttgart: J.B. Metzler, 2001), p. 550.

pense, as the 'eye' of the hurricane [...]."[14] However, whereas the novel by García Márquez was received worldwide in 1967 and made the banana massacre well known as a traumatic episode of Colombian history, the photographic archive of the United Fruit Company was only recently made even partially accessible, when twenty-eight of the pictures were circulated back to the Colombian Caribbean in 2008, to commemorate the massacre.[15] As such, my parallel reading aims to reflect upon the echoed and contested meanings and on the image's materiality at the interstice of the two archives, fictitious and real, in the mode of both the actuality and the remembrance of the event.

More generally, it is only recently that the concept of material has been discussed as an aesthetic category, and that materiality has been readdressed, particularly in literature, in terms other than those of an opposition between form and material. Literary scholars have been searching for a means of differentiating between dimensions of the material, such as the unexpressed, the implicit, and the concrete.[16] The question of materiality has made explicit the potential of types of texts, such as literary ones, in which objects and situations become semantically available while acquiring a conciseness that appeals to a particular imagination.[17] Thus a new conception of materiality emerged that is not included in the meaning of aesthetic signifiers.[18] When I speak of the materiality of the image, I do not refer to the picture as a material object, although it is also that. Rather I underscore the material process of the image event, which is related to the very process of knowing. This is also

14   Didi-Huberman, *Images in Spite of All*, p. 39.
15   Aviva Chomsky, "Making a Difference: Repatriating Photographs," *Revista. The Harvard Review of Latin America* VIII:2 (2009), p. 64.
16   Karl Ludwig Pfeiffer, "Materialität der Literatur?," in *Materialität der Kommunikation*, ed. Hans Ulrich Gumbrecht and Karl Ludwig Pfeiffer (Frankfurt am Main: Suhrkamp, 1988), p. 17.
17   Ibid., pp. 19–20.
18   Monika Wagner, "Material," in *Ästhetische Grundbegriffe. Historisches Wörterbuch in sieben Bänden,* Band 3, ed. Karlheinz Barck et al. (Stuttgart: J. B. Metzler, 2001), p. 882.

underlined by Azoulay with the concept of the civil contract of photography.[19] In other words, I refer to materiality in order to grasp the relationship between photography and history, taking the image not as an idea of synthesis, but conceiving it as "an act and not a thing."[20] Considering materiality in terms of historical materialism means understanding the image in the way once suggested by Walter Benjamin:

> The historical index of the images not only says that they belong to a particular time; it says, above all, that they attain to legibility [*Lesbarkeit*] only at a particular time. [...] The image that is read—which is to say, the image in the now of its recognizability—bears to the highest degree the imprint of the perilous critical moment in which all reading is founded.[21]

I argue that the United Fruit Company photograph series attains legibility in the light of the echoed and contested meaning of the fictitious archive created with *One Hundred Years of Solitude*, which made it the banana massacre, because it was the novel that first imagined it as such, configuring it as a topos for socio-political upheavals and as an unspoken trauma in Colombian history; as something which is displaced and remains as a symptom of the quest for persistence of culture. Accordingly, to examine the pictures is not related to the search for the photograph as fact, but rather to the function of testimony of the act of photography. The concept of testimony in photographic images reveals that the image cannot be simply evidence, since photographs need a critical examination to unlock such knowledge. Rather, testimony is situated beyond historicization and the logic of evidence, because the gesture of witnessing is fundamentally different to that of evidencing.[22] The United Fruit

19 Azoulay, *The Civil Contract of Photography*, p. 20.
20 Jean-Paul Sartre cited in Didi-Huberman, *Images in Spite of All*, p. 50.
21 Walter Benjamin cited in Didi-Huberman, *Images in Spite of All*, p. 89.
22 See the discussion by Heike Schlie, "Bemerkungen zur juridischen, epistemologischen und medialen Wertigkeit des Zeugnisses," in *Zeugnis und Zeugen-*

Company archival images articulate this very displacement: insofar as they configure a visibility that makes the massacre unseen, they conceal the violence. So their enduring significance may now lie in the importance of what a "careful reading can disclose about the unfolding of history in an ordinary [town] at a moment of terrible transformation."[23] What does it mean to look at the photograph series today, since the publication of García Márquez's novel in 1967, and in the light of the violent political turmoil Colombia has experienced since then? The massacre as a topos for socio-political upheavals "remains a contested site within national memory."[24] Today, the pictures gain a moment of legibility "in the now of its recognizability,"[25] amid calls for human rights and justice, and must therefore be reread against the backdrop of the two archives.

García Márquez's literary text depicts the historical event of the labor strike as a massacre, making the historical situation semantically available to a global readership while appealing to a particular imagination of historical reclamation. In the novel, the banana massacre turns out to be a key episode and "the highest point in García Márquez's extensive chronicle of Macondo."[26] In rereading the banana massacre in the light of the moment of danger and memory, I discuss how the novel intersects with the United Fruit Company photographic archive, along with other historical material that was used to mold the literary imagination of *One Hundred Years of Solitude*. García Márquez's creation of a fictitious archive raises pertinent

schaft. Perspektiven aus der Vormoderne, ed. Heike Schlie and Wolfram Drews (Munich: Wilhelm Fink, 2011), p. 26.

23   Darren Newbury, "Picturing an 'ordinary atrocity': The Sharpeville Massacre," in *Picturing Atrocity: Photography in Crisis*, ed. Geoffrey Batchen et al. (London: Reaktion Books, 2012), p. 209.

24   Ibid., p. 222.

25   Walter Benjamin cited in Didi-Huberman, *Images in Spite of All*, p. 89.

26   Gene H. Bell-Villada, "Banana Strike and Military Massacre: *One Hundred Years of Solitude* and What Happened in 1928," in *Gabriel García Márquez's One Hundred Years of Solitude*, ed. Gene H. Bell-Villada (Oxford and New York: Oxford University Press, 2002), p. 127.

questions about the other narrative created by the picture series relating to the strike in the banana zone that was included in the Company's photographic archive. Following García Márquez's fiction alongside the photographic archive, I unveil how the archives are configured by the banana massacre's descent into oblivion. Without a doubt, García Márquez's novel marked a turning point in the Latin American boom, significantly changing the reception of Latin American literature and the literature of the Global South. Furthermore, it was his novel that made the remembrance of the banana massacre possible at all, as it was an episode of Colombian history that had been mostly erased or forgotten until then. This could be because the novel is a complex semiotic product that amplifies itself infinitely through the reading process: meaning will be produced, not discovered, insofar as the novel's reception creates a social experience of reading.[27] Allowing for a receptive experience the literary text makes the "principle of self-recognition" particularly significant through the imagination of Macondo.[28] Following Walter Benjamin, the literary text does not articulate "the past historically [...] 'the way it really was'," but rather it seizes "hold of a memory as it flashes up at a moment of danger"; accordingly, it is from within this moment of danger that the text gains its legibility.[29] Again, with regard to the image's materiality, I maintain that because materiality is not comprised in the meaning of aesthetic signifiers, the focus now lies "outside" the text—in a similar vein to the archive—, allowing for a space in which meaning is contested by a different process of knowing, that is, the receptive experience. Put differently, I am interested "not in taking materiality as an irreducible, but in conducting a critical genealogy of its formulations" with regard to the literary text, on the one side, and the

27 Carlos Rincón, "Los límites de Macondo," *Teorías y poéticas de la novela: Localizaciones latinoamericanas y globalización cultural*, ed. Anabelle Contreras Castro (Berlin: Wissenschaftlicher Verlag Berlin, 2004), p. 21.
28 Ibid.
29 Benjamin, "Theses on the Philosophy of History," p. 255.

archive, on the other.[30] So it is that the image's materiality in the way I will explore it, both in the novel and with regard to the photographic archive, articulates the banana massacre as a place of memory and as political contestation. The banana massacre continues to challenge sight and seeing as forms of knowing, and to call for an ethics of seeing. Recent access to the archival photograph series has opened up this contestation: the point of departure is nothing less than the understanding of the photograph as a historical reflection.

The Banana Massacre and *One Hundred Years of Solitude* [31]

> The official version, repeated a thousand times and mangled out all over the country by every means of communication the government found at hand, was finally accepted: there were no dead, the satisfied workers had gone back to their families, and the banana company was suspending all activities until the rains stopped. [...] The search for and extermination of the hoodlums, murderers, arsonists, and rebels of Decree No. 4 was still going on, but the military denied it even to the relatives of the victims who crowded the commandants' offices in search of news. "You must have been dreaming," the officers insisted. "Nothing has happened in Macondo, nothing has ever happened, and nothing ever will happen. This is a happy town." In that way they were finally able to wipe out the union leaders.[32]

The December 6, 1928 labor strike in the *zona bananera* on the Colombian Caribbean coast was first fictitiously narrated by Colombian writers such as Álvaro Cepeda Samudio with *La casa*

---

30   Judith Butler cited in Wagner, "Material," p. 870, my translation.
31   This part is published in Spanish in a slightly different version in Liliana Gómez, "Residuos del archivo y el conflicto de las bananeras en Colombia: Figuraciones de violencia y contra-memoria en la literatura y la fotografía," *Iberoamericana* 19:72 (2019), pp. 81–103.
32   Gabriel García Márquez, *One Hundred Years of Solitude* (London: Penguin, 2007), pp. 315–316.

grande (1962), Erfaín Tovar Mozo with *Zig zag en las bananeras* (1964), Gabriel García Márquez with *Cien años de soledad* (1967) and Javier Auqué Lara with *Los muertos tienen sed. El drama de las bananeras* (1969). However, it was *One Hundred Years of Solitude* in particular that depicted the massacre as a significant event, giving shape to the fictitious Macondo and its tragic destiny. The banana strike is one of the key scenes that shape the novel and the reading of Macondo's decline as a metaphor for the experience of modernization: it is the key episode where history and fiction intersect, creating a wide variety of readings, as they are fantastically and even grotesquely interwoven.[33] In fact, there were different historical reasons for the real decline of the banana industry in the Magdalena region, which are depicted in the detailed descriptions of the downswing of Macondo that can be found in the diplomatic narrative reports, which circulated extensively between Colombia and the United States.[34] However, the literary text allows for an "epic of a forgotten people," within which the banana massacre seems to be the climax of the experience of modernization and constitutes "a true watershed not only in the history of our literature, but also in what has been called the Latin American 'imaginary'."[35] This becomes significant, inasmuch as the novel first created a place of memory in lieu of a national trauma, articulating an experience that was widely shared among a global readership. Moreover, it is this new literary quality of verisimilitude, that of narrating a fictitious reality recognized by the readership, that made the changing course of the 1960s a crucial moment for receiving these fictionalizations of actual events. The emerging sensibilities of the 1960s allowed for both the acknowledgment of the moderniza-

33 Bell-Villaga, "Banana Strike and Military Massacre," p. 129.
34 *Foreign Agricultural Service, Narrative Reports, Columbia,* 1943. See *Records of the Foreign Agricultural Service, Records of the Office of Foreign Agricultural Relations and its Predecessors, Correspondence and Narrative Reports, 1901–1958.*
35 Agustin Cueva, *Literatura y conciencia histórica en América Latina* (Quito: Planeta, 1993), p. 31, my translation.

tion of Colombia, predominantly through urbanization, and an openness to literature related to the experience of La Violencia.[36] This confluence in particular sparked the success of fictions such as *One Hundred Years of Solitude* and helped the banana massacre "to attain legibility [*Lesbarkeit*] only at a particular time." As such the receptive experience of the reader becomes a constitutive part of a moment of recognizability that "bears to the highest degree the imprint of the perilous critical moment in which all reading is founded."[37] Although other testimonial or journalistic depictions of the banana massacre of 1928—such as the reports by General Carlos Cortés Vargas or the congressional debate initiated by the charismatic liberal political leader Jorge Eliécer Gaitán—had already emerged in 1929, the incident was never officially recognized by the Colombian government of that time. The murder of Eliécer Gaitán by an assassin in 1948, was the final act that drove the incident and the laborers' history the rest of the way into oblivion. As we will see, this narrative of oblivion is also present in the United Fruit Company picture series. So it occurred that the spread of testimonies quickly became very limited. They briefly formed part of a political controversy in Colombia during a time of gridlocked debate between the Conservatives and the Liberals before they vanished altogether into oblivion. Again, it was García Márquez's novel that provided the literary portrayal of this significant historical event as a massacre.

The narrated massacre that García Márquez investigates in his fiction—himself and his family being from the neighboring town of Aracataca—was the outcome of unsuccessful negotiations between laborers from the United Fruit Company and nominated representatives. Certainly, one point of conflict

36   La Violencia refers to a historical period between 1948 and 1958 in Colombia, to frame the bipartisan violence of the time and the civil war, whose climax and cause was the assassination of the liberal political leader Jorge Eliécer Gaitán in Bogotá in 1948. In particular Colombian literature reflects this period in a critical and aesthetically original way.
37   Walter Benjamin cited in Didi-Huberman, *Images in Spite of All*, p. 89.

was that these representatives were alleged not to be from the United Fruit Company, and the Company declined to take any responsibility for the negotiations. Though historical studies began only much later to reconstruct the event, they remain unclear about the specific situation and relationship between the striking laborers and the Company. The laborers claim the Colombian army under General Carlos Cortés Vargas opened fire on the laborers because the laborers insisted that significant aspects of their demands be addressed. Yet the pivotal question of "What provoked the horrific killing spree?" still remains unanswered.[38] However, the darkest moment of the massacre, which articulates a feature that is common to many oppressive actions carried out during so-called States of Emergency, is that "The claim by the [Colombian army] that they opened the fire in response to a genuine and imminent threat posed by the protesters was never supported by the evidence."[39] This may be the most courageous predication of the literary text; García Márquez molds the "raw" material of history into a fictitious account and speculates on the omnipotent position the Company had over their laborers:

> The protests of the workers this time were based on the lack of sanitary facilities in their living quarters, the nonexistence of medical services, and terrible working conditions. They stated, furthermore, that they were not being paid in real money but in scrip, which was good only to buy Virginia ham in the company commissaries. José Arcadio Segundo was put in jail because he revealed that the scrip system was a way for the company to finance its fruit ships, which without the commissary merchandise would have returned empty from New Orleans to the banana ports. The other complaints were common knowledge.[40]

38   Newbury, "Picturing an 'ordinary atrocity'," p. 218.
39   Ibid.
40   García Márquez, *One Hundred Years of Solitude*, pp. 305–306.

The violent reaction to the laborers' strike undeniably reflected an expression of a new kind of relations between the laborers and the foreign transnational corporation, which operated almost as a state-within-a-state on the Colombian coast, where hired salaried laborers were deprived of many of their basic civil rights. In fact, the Company controlled almost every type of production and distribution resource in the banana zone: infrastructure for trains, telegraphs, drainage systems, and commissaries. At the beginning of the 1920s, the United Fruit Company enjoyed a monopoly, supported and highly subsidized by the Colombian government. In 1928, when the conflict broke out in the form of a well-organized strike by laborers, the Company asked for military protection from the Colombian government and an infantry regiment led by General Carlos Cortés Vargas was sent to Santa Marta on November 13, 1928. It is alleged that, as a reaction to the laborers' public plans to destroy the banana plantation, transportation and communication infrastructures, a telegram was sent to the representatives of the Ministry of Industry in Bogotá, which led to the General opening fire on the laborers. It remains unclear whether this telegram really existed, or whether Cortés Vargas fabricated the information. Nevertheless, the massacre as a topos for socio-political upheavals discloses a common pattern of that time that made it possible to turn the event of the labor strike into a massacre. Significantly, labor strikes became a form of resistance to the monopolistic and almighty presence of the United Fruit Company in Latin America. More notably, the Company's response was to make these upheavals ineffective and label them a communist threat, according to the rhetoric and politics of the "Red Scare."[41] These actions against strikes were widely

---

41   *Department of State, Bureau of Inter-American Affairs/Office of Middle American Affairs*: #A 1 1144. See *Subject Files, Textual Records from the Department of State, Bureau of Inter-American Affairs. Office of Middle American Affairs, 1947–1956*. This description of the "Red threat" clearly reflects the fears the United Fruit Company had fabricated even before the Cold War started. Labor conflicts and their depiction as communist-infiltrated upheavals represented a constant

backed by different governmental and semi-official networks in the Company divisions and beyond. It was not uncommon that "the government announced a State of Emergency, restricting further political demonstrations," facilitating the use of military force. Thus, although the crisis was seemingly short-lived, the consequences of the banana massacre were not.[42] García Márquez's novel responded to this by creating an imaginary space of contestation and historical reclamation. In 1929, the former General Carlos Cortés Vargas published his report *Los sucesos de las Bananeras* to describe his mission in the banana zone and argue the case for his violent "correction" of the strike. It seems that García Márquez used the report as a source of historical material for reimagining the massacre in his fiction. However, he did not use the historical material as an authentic form, molding it aesthetically instead, into a literary image that depicted the massacre as a hyperbolic and grotesque event that is the climax of the novel. Furthermore, he seems to have been aware of another report of the event, by Jorge Eliécer Gaitán.[43] In fact, these statements, presented to Congress by Gaitán, but only later published as a pamphlet in 1972, seem to be the ones that García Márquez transformed and incorporated into his fiction. García Márquez's maternal grandfather Márquez, then a town treasurer in Aracataca, was among the witnesses

confrontation and means of instrumentalization that underlies the United Fruit Company's politics.

42   Newbury, "Picturing an 'ordinary atrocity'," p. 219.

43   Jorge Eliécer Gaitán writes: "[Cortés Vargas] arrives that night with the army; before a sleepy multitude he reads the celebrated decree. The few who are awake cry out Long Live Colombia, and this pitiless and cruel man has a response to that cry: Fire! They begin to fire the machine guns, then, five minutes of rifle fire, the tragedy is complete. Many lives. Hundreds of lives fall to the murderous rain of bullets. The order was given by a drunken man. And it was not enough. Not content with having killed so many innocents, he orders the bayonet charge against the defeated multitude, against those who still cry out in pain from the floor, and there are scenes of incredible horror." Jorge Eliécer Gaitán, *El debate sobre las bananeras [cuatro días de verdad contra 40 años de silencio]* (Bogota: Centro Gaitán, 1988), p. 85, my translation.

to the congressional hearings.[44] This fact certainly creates a potential relationship between the eyewitness and the writer. Furthermore, it seems that García Márquez particularly molded Gaitán's eyewitnesses' story of the firing squad in the square into long narrative literary passages of the novel. In the way García Márquez configures these as key episodes in his fiction, he makes explicit another circumstance that later led to divergent readings of the massacre, namely the cruel involvement of the Colombian army in the United Fruit Company's battle against the Colombian laborers. Yet, *One Hundred Years of Solitude* remains particularly ambivalent and even opaque about it, while at the same time creating a place of memory for the darkest moment in Colombian history. García Márquez narrates:

> Martial law enabled the army to assume the functions of arbitrator in the controversy, but no effort at conciliation was made. As soon as they appeared in Macondo, the soldiers put aside their rifles and cut and loaded the bananas and started the train running. The workers, who had been content to wait until then, went into the woods with no other weapons but their working machetes and they began to sabotage the sabotage. They burned plantations and commissaries, tore up tracks to impede the passage of the trains that began to open their path with machine-gun fire, and they cut telegraph and telephone wires. The irrigation ditches were stained with blood. [...] The situation was threatening to lead to a bloody and unequal civil war when the authorities called upon the workers to gather in Macondo. The summons announced that the civil and military leader of the province would arrive on the following Friday ready to intercede in the conflict.[45]

Let me use this passage as a vantage point from which to re-read the documents and testimonial reports addressed by Gaitán. Through these eyewitnesses' reports Gaitán meticulously reconstructs the prehistory of the incident in his account,

---

44   Bell-Villaga, "Banana Strike and Military Massacre," p. 134.
45   García Márquez, *One Hundred Years of Solitude*, pp. 308–309.

demonstrating that the strike began in a peaceful fashion. He passionately cites the statement from the provincial government that witnessed the non-violent attitude of the striking workers: "We follow the lines and their branches, and in the stations we find multitudes of perfectly peaceful strikers. [...] As the liquor stores were closed, they all remained in their normal state."[46] So, how does the novel relate to the eyewitness and historical evidence? Understanding this relationship as a significant dimension of the materiality of literature, insofar as unseen objects and unspoken situations become semantically available through fiction, I further ask: How do testimony and literature relate to one another? And how do the images of the Company archive relate both to these testimonies and to García Márquez's fiction? Are they non-pictures, insofar as they are images without imagination? With regard to the event of the banana massacre, the army behaved as an independent body, seeming to favor the state of siege in order to be able to intervene without any directives from the Colombian government. In fact, the testimonies outline the hypothesis that different telegrams were sent to Bogotá in order to legitimate this state of siege, a situation that was favored by the United Fruit Company for their own aims of non-negotiation with the laborers. Furthermore, witnesses even suggest that the sabotage was not carried out by the workers, but instead by the United Fruit Company itself.[47] Several documents from Gaitán's report refer to this understanding of the strike. Obviously, this aspect of army involvement remains the most controversial and García Márquez seems to be prudent enough not to let the details speak for themselves. Instead, he incorporates this hypothesis through a hyperbolic literary transformation, creating an opacity that in itself becomes the means of understanding this key episode of the massacre. As Salman Rushdie once observed, magical realism is doubtlessly inscribed here within a concrete reality, as it "would be a mistake to think of Márquez's

46   Gaitán, *El debate sobre las bananeras*, p. 80, my translation.
47   Ibid.

literary universe as an invented, self-referential, closed system. He is not writing about Middle-earth, but about the one we all inhabit. Macondo exists. That is its magic."[48] This concrete reality is certainly also bound to and embodied in the two archives, the fictitious and the photographic. With regard to our concern about the testimony of the photographic archive, any visit to a document depository rightly reminds us "that an archive does not give memory that fixed meaning, that set image [...]. It is always—tirelessly—a 'history under construction whose outcome is never entirely perceptible'."[49]

I discuss the image of the past, the banana massacre, as it is remembered in *One Hundred Years of Solitude,* in order to look at it as a contested site within national memory. Literature works here as an alternative semantic to photography, while it operates as a critical work of remembrance in and of itself. Notably, the novel's meta-narrative is the way in which the text itself is self-reflexive about its materiality. Whereas photography is deployed as a modern device of evidence, in the novel it has been used as a means of investigating immaterial images, that is, what is not materialized as photographs, thus it is claimed as testimony rather than evidence. This interest in photography's dual nature of materialization and immateriality can also be found in the literary text itself, particularly with regard to the literary figure Melquíades and his experimentation with daguerreotype practices. As another important episode of the novel, it is clear that Melquíades serves here as a key figure for unlocking the novel's meta-narrative. Significantly, García Márquez narrates this episode as follows:

> [...] Melquíades had printed on his plates everything that was printable in Macondo, and he left the daguerreotype laboratory to the fantasies of José Arcadio Buendía, who had resolved to use it to obtain

---

48   Salman Rushdie, *Imaginary Homelands: Essays and Criticism 1981–1990* (London: Penguin Books, 1991), pp. 301–302.

49   Didi-Huberman, *Images in Spite of All*, pp. 98–99.

scientific proof of the existence of God. Through a complicated process of superimposed exposures taken in different parts of the house, he was sure that sooner or later he would get a daguerreotype of God, if He existed, or put an end once and for all to the supposition of His existence.[50]

Through these daguerreotype practices, Melquíades aims to "document" the little town of Macondo and to capture its transformations. Significantly, through these practices and Melquíades' laboratory the patriarch José Arcadio Buendía can connect to the story or genealogy of the Buendía family, which he will later be able to read in Melquíades' book. In this particular episode, José Arcadio Buendía tries to prove the existence of something as immaterial as God both scientifically and materially, ironically using photography here as an evidential device. At this point the novel reflects upon that very concept of testimony, inasmuch as it challenges the photograph as material evidence. This particular episode is full of irony because the photographic practices that aim at materializing God in the form of an image as a proof or evidence are reduced here to absurdity. Yet on the level of meta-narrative, the novel connects the material and the immaterial in a very intriguing way, inasmuch as the episode raises the question of the non-material and the idea of material in testimony as something that is not tangible to our senses. Testimony is thought of as a practice that involves a social and cultural situatedness that is constitutive of a social epistemology.[51] Consequently, testimony becomes possible through a receptive experience of readership, in which the meaning of both literature and the archival images are necessarily embedded. This episode is pivotal for my reading of the materiality of the image, inasmuch as it

50   García Márquez, *One Hundred Years of Solitude*, pp. 54–55.
51   Oliver Scholz, "Das Zeugnis anderer – Prolegomena zu einer sozialen Erkenntnistheorie," in *Erkenntnistheorie. Positionen zwischen Tradition und Gegenwart*, ed. Thomas Grundmann (Paderborn: Mentis, 2001), pp. 354–375.

provokes an understanding of the limits of photography as a producer of truthful images, challenging the idea of the image-document, or the value of the photograph as evidence. I argue that the novel, at its meta-narrative level, raises the question of testimony, reframing the unspoken and displaced historical incident of the banana massacre in Colombian history. Because there is a difference between the unattainability of the "image of God," that of the un-imaginable, and that of the massacre as an actively erased image, as both are collapsed onto one and the same plane of non-imageness, as an archival absence, and this is precisely the "magical-realist" effect of the juxtaposition of the two archives here.

In the early days, photography was often perceived as a procedure that seemed to indifferently reproduce greatly varying subjects and transfer them to a single material layer. Notably, originally classified as a mechanical reproductive process, photography was initially excluded from the arts.[52] Accordingly, it was believed that "photography shared a certain adaptability with synthetic materials, from cast iron to rubber to plastic, and like them it initially had to overcome the stigma of being a surrogate."[53] It is interesting, therefore, that whereas photography was excluded in the early positivist discourse of the arts, having been classified as an inferior material, in literature it seems to have been granted the status of a material capable of producing and capturing immaterial images. Valeria de los Ríos makes a pertinent point when she outlines that the apparition and the use of visual technologies in Latin American literature uses the phantasmagorical as a significant component to describe the relationship between literary fiction and the photographic image.[54] This is specifically true for García Márquez's fiction, inasmuch as the photographic appears here to be a layer

52 Wagner, "Material," p. 882.
53 Ibid., my translation.
54 Valeria de los Ríos, *Espectros de luz* (Santiago de Chile: Cuarto Propio, 2011), p. 15.

of self-reflection of a literary mediality, as a sort of a counter-part of literature "against which literature demarcates its own limitations and possibilities."[55] Moreover, in Latin American literature visuality has been contested and incorporated both on the level of the thematic and the rhetorical.[56] So photography in literature has become the materialization of the invisible,[57] as in the case of the fantastic, where it features as a kind of counter-semantic to the photographic, contrary to other forms of literary representation of the photographic image, and to the idea of *ekphrasis*—as a rhetorical correspondence of the two forms—that associates the photographic with a mimesis of the visible. Photography in literature, as Irene Albers notes, seems to be the medium that makes the invisible visible and gives the immaterial visions, hallucinations, and apparitions a material gestalt that may also be an *optique fantastique*; for example, what seems to be a literary fantasy becomes, as it did in the second half of the nineteenth century, the object of scientific or para-scientific matter.[58] This transposition makes photography an ambivalent, mysterious practice and object.[59] In the context of realistic and naturalistic discourses of photography, the photographic image is reduced to the aesthetic, understood here essentially as a copy or exact representation, while fantastic literature uses a concept of photography as a tracing medium that is associated with emotions, with the uncanny, and with simultaneous presence and absence, reality and non-reality.[60] I argue that it is the broader understanding of the photographic in literature that becomes pertinent here, for the discussion of the displaced banana massacre as an image of the past. What García Márquez's novel provokes is the recognition of a moment of danger and memory that challenges the very question of repre-

55   Albers, "Fotografie/fotografisch," p. 535, my translation.
56   de los Ríos *Espectros de luz*, p. 18.
57   Albers, "Fotografie/fotografisch," p. 543.
58   Ibid.
59   Ibid.
60   Ibid.: p. 544.

sentation. That is explored with the ambivalence of the invisible and the play with visibility in Melquíades' experiments with the daguerreotype in his alchemist's laboratory. Significantly, Melquíades has the pivotal function of a historian, as it is *he* who narrates and foretells both the history of Macondo and of the Buendía family.[61] In the novel, after the end of the inhabitants' collective state of oblivion that was caused by the plague of insomnia, Macondo recovers a new development. Not only is Melquíades the historian *sui generis*, through whom we might grasp a challenging conception of history and testimony, but he is also involved in the novel with the collective oblivion and the end of it, which symbolically articulates the silence around the unspoken banana massacre. So, on the level of the novel's self-reflexion, the rewriting of history is not intended as myth, but as an awakening, using the archive here in the modes of actuality and as a potential for a future reclamation. Both García Márquez's literary fiction and the photographic archive of the United Fruit Company provide resources for two different forms of memory, one displaced, the other actualized. They reconnect with the banana massacre as a fictional-historical event. Though I do not suggest that memory and archive are the same, nor that archive represents a metaphor for all forms of storage, it seems that there is a mutual affection between media, such as literature and photography, and different storage technologies relating to the "outside" of text or image. Rather, memory could be understood as a composite effect that stems from the open situation of the archive, in the sense that it is situated "always at the unstable limit between public and private, between the family, society, and the State, between the family and an intimacy even more private than the family, between oneself and oneself."[62] As has been pointed out with regard to the archival quality of Latin American literary modernity, the latter's "power

---

61   Lucila Inés Mena, *La función de la historia en "Cien años de soledad"* (Barcelona: Plaza y Janés, 1979), p. 157.
62   Jacques Derrida, "Archive Fever," p. 57.

to endow the text with the capacity to bear truth is shown to lie outside the text; it is an exogenous agent that bestows authority upon a certain kind of document" *not* "owing to the ideological structure of the period,"[63] I would argue, but instead owing to the potential of actuality of the archive as a non-linear source for remembrance, allowing for a materiality in which objects and situations once again become semantically available.

With regard to the novel and the plague of insomnia, the literary text not only addresses the difficulties of the work of remembrance against oblivion in a carnivalized form, but, as metafiction, archive, and simulacrum, it also deliberates on the concept of memory, unfettering it to make an alternative understanding possible.[64] The concept of archive in the literary text refers to a means of keeping the banana massacre from the oblivion of official silence, which materializes in the novel as the plague of insomnia. Following the trajectory of the novel, the plague happens long before the massacre occurs, however, it creates a kind of prediction and a cyclical repetition of events that is meaningful for the novel's time-structure. The idea of the archive's actuality is manifested through the cyclical time in the story of the Buendías. So it is that the text outlines a productive time-lapse as both prediction and repetition, which takes place at the interstice of memory and oblivion. As "myriad symmetries" between José Arcadio Buendía, Colonel Aureliano Buendía, and the strike's instigator, José Arcadio Segundo, these repetitions form intersecting cycles and symmetrical events to be read in the light of the banana massacre as the climax of the novel.[65] As a repetition of the story of the Buendía family, particularly that of the male protagonists, the novel creates a powerful fictitious archive that allows for a critical remembrance and an image of the past in a moment of

---

63   Roberto González Echevarría, "*One Hundred Years of Solitude*: The Novel as Myth and Archive," *Modern Language Notes* 99:2 (1984), p. 371.
64   Carlos Rincón, "Las artes de la memoria en la plaga de insomnio de Cien años de soledad," *Literatura y filosofía* 1:1 (2003), p.10.
65   Bell-Villaga, "Banana Strike and Military Massacre," p. 132.

danger. Significantly, following Derrida, it is the technique of repetition that determines the archive's economy. In fact, it is this very repetition that we conserve, and that the novel as a fictitious archive recreates.[66]

Let me turn, at this point, to photography once again. It seems that photography more generally reflects a twofold conception of materiality: firstly, the photograph as a visual artifact and material item; and secondly, the materiality of photography embedded in institutional and social practices that determine the photograph's status and effect, as well as bestowing upon it the authority necessary to give it meaning. As material objects, photographs are collected and archived. Potentially, photography creates a material and sensorial resource for understanding and studying a type of visual memory. We can clearly depict these photographic processes as *photomnemonics* in Melquíades' daguerreotype practices experimenting with the immaterial image. With regard to the oblivion, manifested as the most critical state of the plague of insomnia, the photographic process in the novel allows for perception, awareness of time, imagination and memory and can thus be taken as a counter-semantic to the photographic series of the Company archive. It becomes meaningful that the plague of insomnia coincides with the plague of the banana: as a key figure and a *deus ex machina*, Melquíades performs a magic act that puts an end to the plague of insomnia by giving the patriarch José Arcadio Buendía an unidentifiable drink. The plague of insomnia here is a metaphor for the collective oblivion into which the banana massacre evaporates, both on the level of the story and of the political and official silence that surrounded the historical incident in Colombia at the time. However, it is also a metaphor in the way it refers to the urbanization of Macondo and to the modern radical environmental and social transformations. The little village of Macondo becomes a modern town with railways, telephone, electricity and other modern inventions

66   Derrida, "Archive Fever," p. 14.

that are related to the plague of the banana—a radical urbanization process experienced in Colombia during the 1960s. In the novel, the patriarch José Arcadio Buendía's machine seems to work as a specialized model of *mnemotechniques* used against the manifestation of oblivion.[67] Significantly, this metaphor of insomnia is related to other metaphors, such as that of the daguerreotype, inasmuch as "every object or assemblage of objects [in the novel are] converted into 'memory machines' [...]; and, without doubt, it is related to a concept of literature as an antidote to oblivion [...] to recover and continuously recreate history in order to prevent us from being converted into a 'leaf storm without a past'."[68] Eventually, rescuing the image of the past, both metaphors configure and claim "a memory as it flashes up at a moment of danger."[69]

I have argued that this episode of self-reflexivity determines a key moment of the novel's intersection of history with literary imagination to potentially compose its fictitious archive. Moreover, I suggest that as foretelling and performative acts, Melquíades' daguerreotype practices challenge the historical oblivion and photographic invisibility of the banana massacre, to which José Arcadio Segundo later becomes the novel's only eyewitness as he repeats the Buendía family's cyclical experience of facing the firing squad. It is the very idea of seeing and, again, of testimony that is at the center of the novel's self-reflection. It challenges the photographic act as *photomnemonics*, as against the naive conception of photography as mimesis. Potentially, seeing, bearing witness and testifying are bound together here while articulating the novel's fictitious archive, a collective and shared memory, and thus the archive as a lieu to claim a potential history.

67   Rincón, "Las artes de la memoria," p. 24.
68   Cueva, *Literatura y conciencia histórica en América Latina*, p. 35, my translation.
69   Benjamin, "Theses on the Philosophy of History," p. 255.

The Resurgent Photographic Archive or the Ethics of Seeing

> Something—very little, a film—remains of a process of annihila-
> tion: that something, therefore, bears witness to a disappearance
> while simultaneously resisting it, since it becomes the opportu-
> nity of its possible remembrance. [...] It is a world proliferating
> with lacunae, with singular images which, placed together in a
> montage, will encourage *readability*, an effect of knowledge [...].[70]

Let me now turn to the photograph album of the United Fruit
Company archive labeled "Colombia," which includes the picture series related to the banana strike of December 1928. It
is noteworthy that the album does not highlight this specific
series, nor any other pictures. The embodied order is rather a
bureaucratic one, the pictures are collected and stored in an
album made up of thematic images related to the Colombia division, which reflect a sort of geographical imagination. Nevertheless, this picture series on the strike seems to classify all other
pictures as taken either before or after the incident, marking an
epistemic divide. As we are reminded when examining the relationship between history and photography, having these archival images at hand, the "image, and particularly photography as
a snapshot wrested away from the flux of constant movement,
as a distinctive sample of a lost reality, corresponds to what our
relationship with the past has become: a relationship of discontinuity governed by a mixture of detachment and approxima-
tion, radical distance and disconcerting confrontation."[71]

Among the album pictures we find a remarkable and noteworthy photograph. On the back of it the caption suggestively
states: "Native People – Family Group. Birth Control is unknown
here. Santa Marta, April 24, 1925."[72] At first glance, the picture

---

70 Didi-Huberman, *Images in Spite of All*, p. 167.
71 Pierre Nora cited in About, *Fotografie und Geschichte*, p. 10, my translation.
72 The suspicion about the concealment of the political is affirmed in particular with regard to this image, which has a secondary caption only added later,
glued into the album below the picture that states: "Native People – Family

Fig. 6.1: "Native People – Family Group. Santa Marta, April 24, 1925." On verso: "no. 299. Native People – Family Group. Birth Control is unknown here." Gelatin silver process on paper, 8 x 10 inches. United Fruit Company Photograph Collection, Baker Library, Harvard Business School, Box 31.

bears witness to an encounter in a quickly developing region that later came to be known as Macondo, a buzzing and rich contact zone. As we are informed, the image is a portrait of "native people" in Santa Marta in the Colombian Caribbean, dated 1925. We do not know much about the photographer, who was most likely a hired photographer from the region who worked for the Company. But the image's composition and the aesthetics certainly suggest a professional gaze. It shows a family of laborers in front of their house, posed and arranged to compose

Group. Santa Marta, April 24, 1925." It conceals the original message, as the caption on the picture's back informs us: "Birth Control is unknown here." It seems that there might have been a (post-) awareness, a (later) perception of the political realm of this message, configured in the interstices between the image and the caption, so that purposely this kind of incidental meaning came to be somehow controlled.

the image: In the center is the mother, the female worker who is ascribed a certain reproductive logic. However, she and the rest of the family members do not seem to be subjugated to this logic, nor do they appear to be disempowered. Rather, her expression is almost heroic, resisting the photographic gaze. She holds her baby in her arms with a sense of dignity and self-reliance, staring at the photographer. This picture is particularly remarkable, though, because it seems to persuade the viewer aesthetically, becoming almost iconic. Whereas the other album pictures remain bureaucratic, this one articulates a defined moment of reclamation. It is this particular image's meaning, as recalled by Aviva Chomsky, that was immediately recognized by Colombian workers from the region, inasmuch as the picture pertains to the history of the families, whose images are still alive, allowing for a disconcerting confrontation but also for a closer touch with the event, articulating a dynamic process of remembrance.[73] It might even be a photograph of resistance, containing the possibility of alternative semantics articulated against the omnipotent Company, challenging the image's relationship with the past. Significantly, this photograph seems to articulate the lacunae of the Company photographic archive, inasmuch as all the other pictures express a visual negligence to make seen exactly what occurred in the divisions. This picture is one of very few that allows political agency to be wrested away from the visual apparatus, through the facial expressions, the subtle gestures and "unconscious" postures of those the Company rather acciden-

73   Aviva Chomsky recalls here: "A few years later, I was researching United Fruit for my dissertation, and was met with a wall of silence when I tried to contact the company to gain access to its records. Several other scholars including Philippe Bourgois, Marcelo Bucheli, and Jorge Giovannetti, have managed to access UFCO papers in scattered locations (in Panama, Colombia, and Cuba, respectively). But company headquarters insist that the records have been officially destroyed and are not available to scholars. [...] We selected 28 images from the UFCO collection Colombia albums. Some of the photographs show the company's operations and facilities, some show the workers, and some show the results of the 1928 strike, uprising and massacre. Many company buildings were destroyed during the conflict, and the destruction was meticulously documented." Chomsky, "Making a Difference: Repatriating Photographs," p. 64.

tally photographed. With regard to the otherwise invisibilized banana massacre, as we shall see, a visibility and presence are articulated that claim for remembrance and potential history. Perhaps even the eyewitness to a coming massacre. Significantly, Didi-Huberman reminds us in another context that:

> [...] the witnesses themselves use up all their energies by attempting to tell, to pass on, to make something understood [...]. That is, to offer to the community [...] words for their experience, however defective or disjointed such words might be with respect to the experienced real. "It is a matter of telling the truth such as it can be transmitted from one man to another, of reestablishing the mediating function of language."[74]

Certainly, this picture makes seen those who would later be involved in the labor strike that turned into the banana massacre, inasmuch as it recognizes those who might speak up. Is this picture just an accidental image that slipped into the Company albums?

In the photograph album "Colombia" a series of pictures offer a glimpse of life in the Colombian division and are related to the labor strike of 1928 in one way or another. Read chronologically, they are mostly dated 1929 and aim to visibilize activities such as the construction of the commissary or other Company buildings and facilities, for instance, the hospital in García Márquez's home town of Aracataca. As readers today, we may be able to grasp from these images the visual imagination of the past, of how the laborers lived when demanding better living conditions in the context of the labor strike that evolved into the deadly conflict. One picture shows a 12-room camp at Indiana, dated October 10, 1928 before the banana massacre occurred. Although the pictures purposefully do not show any traces of violence, they depict desolate housing and conditions and raise the pivotal question of the ethics of seeing as informed by our knowledge of the massacre. They conceal the violent incident inasmuch as they make

---

74   Didi-Huberman, *Images in Spite of All*, p. 103.

Fig. 6.2: "Aracataca, hospital, Colombia, Dec. 30, 1929." Gelatin silver process on paper, 8 x 10 inches. United Fruit Company Photograph Collection. Baker Library, Harvard Business School (olvwork719199).

seen the "normal" operations of the Company in the Colombian division. This picture, "Commissary under construction, Sevilla, Colombia, May 8, 1929," shows the construction of a new commissary after the labor strike and the sabotage of the former commissary. Read in a sequence it suggests that this commissary is being constructed because the other was destroyed.

Among other means of communication, besides these pictures, we find narrative reports sent by the diplomatic representatives to U.S. authorities that describe the organization of the Colombian division of the United Fruit Company.[75] They circulated crucial economic and hence political information, to which the pictures seem to correspond, in that they visually

75   See *Records of the Foreign Agricultural Service, Records of the Office of Foreign Agricultural Relations and its Predecessors, Correspondence and Narrative Reports, 1901–1958*.

Fig. 6.3: "Commissary under construction, Sevilla, Colombia, May 8, 1929."
Gelatin silver process on paper, 8 x 10 inches. United Fruit Company Photograph Collection. Baker Library, Harvard Business School (olvwork719192).

"document" this internal organization of the emergence of a
modern space. The Company pictures embody this modern
bureaucratic language also in the form of the caption. It is thus
significant that diplomatic communication between Colombia and the United States explicitly deals with labor strikes as
socio-political upheavals that were closely monitored, as we
find, for instance, in the many narrative reports of the Foreign
Agricultural Service.[76] Nevertheless, the meaning of these photographs, randomly collected for the albums, remains obscure
and, at first glance, stripped of any political connotation.

So, let me turn to those pictures that were taken by the Company and included in the album to document the "revolution,"
as it is referred to by the Company when describing the destruc-

76   Ibid.

354

Fig. 6.4: "Retail commissary interior view from west end, Santa Marta, Colombia, Feb. 21, 1929." Gelatin silver process on paper, 8 x 10 inches. United Fruit Company Photograph Collection. Baker Library, Harvard Business School (olvwork719190).

tion caused by the striking laborers in the banana zone. They are images of sabotage, I argue, and as such form the main visual argument. The photograph series, dated December 10, 1928, shows the infrastructure, buildings and other facilities, as well as the commissaries and railway tracks that facilitated the operations of the Company. Significantly, the images suggest an erasing of violence or, let us be more precise, of the violent reaction of the military, because they only show the damages incurred by the Company's facilities.[77] These pictures do *not* show the massacre as the violent event depicted in García Márquez's novel. We find photographs of a destroyed commissary, the ruins of

77   See also the discussion by Coleman, "The Photos That We Don't Get to See," pp. 104–136.

Fig. 6.5: "Mdse. Bodega, exterior view Cienaga, Colombia, March 14, 1929."
United Fruit Company Photograph Collection. Baker Library, Harvard Business School (olvwork719161).

engineers' quarters or wrecked telephone lines along the railway tracks that transported the many banana railway cars, all representing acts of violence against the company and eventually forming a legal inventory of the damages. Apparently, some of these December 10th images, taken just a few days after the incident, only started to circulate outside of the photographic archive at a much later date.[78] For instance, the photographs

78   Some of the archival images were used in other historical studies about the Colombian Caribbean to illustrate the infamous massacre and the social conflict between the laborers and the foreign transnational corporation, in the period after the publication of the novel in 1967, when a timid process of historical reconstruction had begun. I refer here to the first critical historical reconstruction by Judith White in *Historia de una ignominia La United Fruit Co. en Colombia* (1978). She particularly takes account of the role of the workers' union in the strike and the evolution of the incident, but also of the asymmetrical relationship between the United Fruit Company and the Colombian laborers. Also, the studies by Catherine LeGrand helped to raise historical awareness of the

Fig. 6.6: "12 room laborers' camp, Indiana, Colombia, Oct. 10, 1928." Gelatin silver process on paper, 8 x 10 inches.United Fruit Company Photograph Collection. Baker Library, Harvard Business School (olvwork719282).

of the destroyed commissary and dispatchers' office and the ruins of the engineer's quarters were published in *Los sucesos de las bananeras* by General Carlos Cortés Vargas. The question remains: What kind of violence should they make seen? Do they aim at legitimating the violent intervention of the military with which the United Fruit Company was involved? Or, do they even help reimagine the labor strike as a massacre? However, these

banana massacre as a significant and forgotten event in Colombian history. LeGrand located new and overlooked archival sources for Caribbean history and the presence of the United Fruit Company in Colombia. See Catherine LeGrand, "Campesinos y asalariados en la zona banarera de Santa Marta (1900–1935)," (1983); "El conflicto de las bananeras," (1989); "Living in Macondo: Economy and Culture in a United Fruit Company Banana Enclave in Colombia," (1998); "Historias Transnacionales: Nuevas interpretaciones de los enclaves en América Latina," (2006), and Catherine LeGrand and Adriana Corso, "Archivos notariales e historias regionales: Nuevas fuentes para el estudio de la zona bananera del Magdalena," (2004).

Fig. 6.7: "Sevilla commissary and dispatchers office after Sevilla [sic] caused by revolution. Colombia. Dec. 10, 1928." Gelatin silver process on paper, 8 x 10 inches. United Fruit Company Photograph Collection. Baker Library, Harvard Business School (olvwork719206).

images have to be read along with their captions as a textual source, as the Company's attempt at illustration and eventually the images' posthumous archival meaning. And yet, the inscriptions inside the album may offer a different narrative of the historical incident. They speak of the incident not as a massacre but as the absence of it. In this photograph, no. 621, "View of cut and wrecked telephone lines like many others after the revolution, COLOMBIA, Dec. 10, 1928," there is a small figure carrying a gun and posing as a type of watchman—it is the only possible suggestion of a violent incident captured by the light of photography. Otherwise, the image remains quite technical and seems to aim at recording "objectively," predominantly "documenting" the damages supposedly inflicted in an act of sabotage by the laborers. As images of sabotage the photographs display an orchestrated absence of the massacre; they distinctively conceal it.

Fig. 6.8: "No. 620. Ruins of Engineers quarters and mess – Sevilla – after revolution. Colombia. Dec. 10, 1928." Gelatin silver process on paper, 8 x 10 inches. United Fruit Company Photograph Collection. Baker Library, Harvard Business School (olvwork719212).

So far, I have assumed the notion of the visible as opposed to the concept of the visual, or regime of perception. Indeed, the question of visibility becomes one of knowledge and knowing about the event. As such, it seems to be pivotal when it comes to discussing the materiality of the image: to this end it is interesting to consider what Didi-Huberman observes elsewhere when he notes that, for instance, a fresco will "[...] become visible [...] because something on it has managed to evoke or 'translate' for us more complex units, 'themes' or 'concepts,' [...] stories or allegories: units of knowledge. At this moment, the perceived fresco becomes really, fully visible—it becomes clear and distinct as if it were itself making explicit. It becomes *legible.*"[79] This unit of knowledge might be the massacre as a topos for the

79   Didi-Huberman, *Confronting Images*, p. 13.

emergent modern political space that we are able to recognize today in these images. Moreover, it is García Márquez's novel that reimagines the crushing of labor strike as the massacre, and it is only then that it becomes fully visible and legible. Put differently, these units of knowledge claim an ethics of seeing, inasmuch as "[the aesthetics] doesn't imply that [photography] 'save those that it shows' [...]: it is not about exculpating the actors of history [...] but, rather, about opening sight itself to a start-up of knowledge and to an orientation of ethical choice."[80] Accordingly, Didi-Huberman further suggests a very intriguing distinction regarding the visible, when he states that "if we are to make sense of this expression—'the unconscious of the visible'—we must turn not to its opposite, the invisible, but to a phenomenology that is trickier, more contradictory, more intense also—more 'incarnate.' It is this that the visual event, the visual symptom, tries to designate."[81] I ask: What does this image series make visible? What do the pictures tell us about the United Fruit Company's knowledge of the event and about our knowledge today? To what extent do we have to use our imagination to make these images speak? Didi-Huberman rightly claims that the archival image is "an indecipherable and insignificant photographic printing so long as I have not established the relation—the imaginative and speculative relation—between what I see here and what I know from elsewhere."[82] As some of the pictures of the Company photographic archive circulated back to the Colombian Caribbean to be seen by the former laborers' families, they form part of a public reclamation that helps us to unlock the images' meaning today and provokes us "to suspend the gesture of the sovereign power" with the empowerment of the photographed, as they claim the archive not as the past, but as the commons.[83]

80   Didi-Huberman, *Images in Spite of All*, pp. 178–179.
81   Didi-Huberman, *Confronting Images*, p. 29.
82   Didi-Huberman, *Images in Spite of All*, p. 112.
83   Azoulay, *The Civil Contract of Photography*, p. 23.

Fig. 6.9: "View of cut and wrecked telephone lines like many others after the revolution, COLOMBIA, Dec. 10, 1928." Gelatin silver process on paper, 8 x 10 inches. United Fruit Company Photograph Collection. Baker Library, Harvard Business School (olvwork719209).

Looking carefully at these pictures, one is convinced that some pictures were erased from the archive or never included, particularly because the Company seemed to use these pictures to shed a positive light on its operations abroad, deploying them for a legitimating cause. Accordingly, we will obviously not find any pictures that would have made seen the violent incident of the strike, which might lead to the emergence of the concept of massacre. It goes without saying that those pictures neither exist as archival images nor were included in the albums. Yet, I am following a different reading here: in Gaitán's argument, the telegrams and reported testimonies of eyewitnesses suggest that the laborers' attitude during the strike was peaceful, postulating the hypothesis that the acts of sabotage against company facilities were self-inflicted and even orchestrated by United Fruit Company employees or related outside parties in order to legitimate the military intervention. To "sabotage the sabotage," as García Márquez's fiction reimagines, the picture series visualizes the act of sabotage in order to show the damages inflicted.[84] The pictures certainly do not show who destroyed the facilities; they remain purposefully opaque about it. Significantly, the question of why these photographs of the sabotage were taken on December 10, 1928, although the incident occurred on December 6th, also remains obscure. Considering this, I suggest that the images do not document the incident at all, but instead they seem to aim to illustrate another narrative, that of the sabotage against the Company: they are images of sabotage, partaking as such in the persistent Company and thus official discourse.

Whereas García Márquez's fiction reimagines and makes visible the many corpses that were brought to the sea by train to be rejected like bananas, imagining José Arcadio Buendía as the only survivor and eyewitness, the United Fruit Company photographs purposely conceal any corpses. At this point, the two archives diverge greatly, but simultaneously contest the Company images' meaning when superimposed with one another. To this end it becomes important to remind ourselves that "[...] the photographs are most disturbing because they demand to be viewed as a sequence, retaining the rawness of each moment of capture, rather than resolving into a single iconic image."[85] This sequence, further, demands that we read these photographs with regard to the banana massacre and make use of them within an ethics of seeing, because the way the images were used by the Company as images of sabotage was an "act of political appropriation."[86] Yet the most crucial question concerning the losses and the victims in the banana massacre remains unanswered and calls for political reclamation. Significantly, this picture series reveals the dominant feature of the archive, that is, the non-representation of atrocity and violence. With regard to testi-

---

84   García Márquez, *One Hundred Years of Solitude*, p. 308.
85   Newbury, "Picturing an 'ordinary atrocity'," p. 219.
86   Ibid., p. 222.

mony and evidence the discussion on how photographic images work when they deal with violence and even genocide is rather wide-ranging. For instance, photography has been conceived as an efficient instrument to conceal or even entirely erase the atrocities committed by the State through a "'civilized' visuality," outlined by Jens Andermann as a history of violence in relation to the nation-building of Argentina in the nineteenth century. Andermann demonstrates how the visual efficiently makes violence and genocide invisible through "disappearing acts."[87]

Photographs, such as the following one (Fig. 6.10), accompanied internal Company memos as means of communication to provide visual information about certain political events. The picture captioned "View of Engineering Office – Asst. Div. Engrs' residence in background. Erasmos Coronel's grave right foreground – hat on top" clearly states the Company's interest in following up on the incident, even remarking on Erasmos Coronel, a leading figure in the organization of the laborers' strike. From within the marginal text of the caption that indicates where to look, traces of a corpse are at least reimagined in this picture, and the corpse in question is that of one of the strike leaders. The picture here eventually re-inscribes itself into a heroic gesture and one of sensationalism, i.e. an eager gaze on captured history. The meaning of the image is outlined by the performance between the caption and the photograph.[88]

87   See the discussion by Jens Andermann, *The Optic of the State: Visuality and Power in Argentina and Brazil* (Pittsburgh: University of Pittsburgh Press, 2007).
88   With regard to the banana massacre a very interesting memo has been published by Philippe Bourgois. We read: "March 8, 1929: The attached photograph shows the five of the principal leaders in the recent disturbances in the Colombian Division. Their names are as follows: [Check mark] No.1 Bernardino Guerrero. No. 2 Nicanor Serrano. No. 3 P.M. del Rio. No. 4 Raúl Eduardo Mahecha. [Check mark] No. 5 Erasmo Coronel [...]. No. 1 was secretary to Mahecha, the leader, and is now serving a term of fourteen years, seven months in the federal penitentiary in Tunga. No. 5 was killed in the fighting at Sevilla. Nos. 2 and 3 were simple laborers and were practically only figureheads in the organization. No. 4 Mahecha, was the brains of the entire outfit and is one of the most dangerous communist leaders in this country. He fomented the oil field strike in 1924 and last year was the leader of a bad strike in the coffee region in the interior. He

Fig. 6.10: "View of Engineering Office – Asst. Div. Engrs' residence in back-ground. Erasmos Coronel's grave right foreground – hat on top." Gelatin silver process on paper, 8 x 10 inches. United Fruit Company Photograph Collection. Baker Library, Harvard Business School (olvwork719214).

Regarding this intimate relationship between caption and photograph, it becomes significant that violence is concealed in the image itself, yet reimagined in the Company archive's writing. In particular, these pictures of the destruction of Company facilities that imagine the damages caused by the sabotage from the strike of 1928 serve as documents in favor of controlling the strike by any means necessary and serve as a post-legitimization of the "correction" of the strike. The images and furthermore

came to Ciénaga about August of 1928 and immediately started fomenting the movement which culminated in the disturbance of December 6th. He is an ex-army captain, has a remarkable personality and undoubted genius for organiza-tion. At the time the strikers were fired on in Ciénaga he fled and it is known that he was wounded in one leg. Since then he has disappeared completely and it is now reported in the press that he has escaped to Costa Rica." Cited in Bourgois, "One Hundred Years of United Fruit Company Letters," pp. 136–138.

Fig. 6.11: "Ruins of M & S bodega and Residence for Mdse. Employees after revolution. COLOMBIA, Dec. 10, 1928." Gelatin silver process on paper, 8 x 10 inches. United Fruit Company Photograph Collection. Baker Library, Harvard Business School (olvwork719215).

the Company photographic archive seek to reproduce the existing order of knowledge and its inscribed hegemonic power. To a certain degree, it might be obvious to speak of the Company's photographic practices as instrumentalizing the images for this purpose, but there is also a more nuanced understanding of photography here that relates back to my initial concern about materiality, which challenges the very idea of representation that governs the lettered order of historiography.[89] Significantly, photography questions this order. To explore this further, it seems that the photographic image reflects materiality as the "copy *and* contact" between the perceiver and the photo-

89   See my discussion in Gómez-Popescu, "Towards a History Through Photography."

graphed.[90] Following this, the terms identification, representation and expression are too easily ascribed to the photograph: we may decipher the meaning of the photograph as copy and contact, the "powerful and obscure in the network of associations" between the perceiver, the photographer, and the photographed subject.[91] Yet, this relationship of copy and contact remains open and becomes meaningful and readable only in a moment of danger and memory. Eventually, photography tells us about the eye and the sense of sight as used knowledge. It tells us about modes and means of perception and the bodily involvement of such contact. The Company's pictures articulate this particularly clearly with regard to a new spatial order. Accordingly, mimetic machines like photographic cameras not only challenge the social practice of photography, but also the conception of photography as a "record of reality" and the notion of any documentary tradition inherent to photography.[92]

More generally, the predominance of vision predates photography, at least in Western epistemologies. The visual world has already been deeply ingrained in Western culture through other imaging techniques and apparatuses, of which photography becomes a kind of automatic transcript. Yet, the widespread use of cameras determines the crucial role of photography in the creation of an imperial knowledge and, I argue, grounds the economic expansion of the United Fruit Company. In this sense, at least with regard to the image series of the Company archive, the photographs are deployed as evidence or proof when selected for the album. Vision not only informs the economic expansion of the United Fruit Company, but this sensory modality has also become the means of controlling labor unrest as socio-political contestations to modernization. This is evident in the image series from the Company's photographic archive, which mediates the laborers' strike as a discourse of

90   Taussig, *Mimesis and Alterity*, p. 21.
91   Ibid.
92   See Tagg, *The Burden of Representation*.

sabotage and violence against the Company, through which the incident as a massacre is shamelessly concealed. Yet, this is profoundly contested, making the resurgent archive an important medium for claiming dissonant narratives, and disputed truth, as performed by García Márquez's text. Today, the photographs seem also to echo the recent investigations into the contribution of corporate officials of Chiquita—formerly the United Fruit Company—to crimes against humanity. Possibly they become part of the presentation of the case to the International Criminal Court.[93] In my considerations, both the photographic archive and fiction are potential resources in calling for human rights. Historians today mostly view the United Fruit Company photographs for the purpose of illustrating the Company's history, and as such, the pictures are implicitly given the status of an objective documentation of what is seen. Yet, surprisingly, it seems that even historians resort to García Márquez's fiction in order to discover unknown or overlooked details about the banana massacre and its uncounted victims: one of the many obscure details is the exact number of people killed, as eyewitnesses, testimonies and historical documents differ greatly. Of course, the Company photographs remain silent about this important detail, as they follow its concealment. However, literature here fulfills some of the social tasks of creating a fictitious and "worlding" archive, critically addressing the lacunae of historiography: García Márquez's fiction reimagines that number that oscillates between the politics of oblivion and memory, eventually allowing for a critical work of remembrance. As a key fictional scene he narrates:

> "There must have been three thousand of them," he murmured.
> "What?"
> "The dead," he clarified. "It must have been all of the people who were at the station."

93 International Human Rights Clinic, Harvard Law School, "The Contribution of Chiquita Corporate Officials to Crimes Against Humanity in Colombia."

The woman measured him with a pitying look. "There haven't been any dead here," she said. "Since the time of your uncle, the colonel, nothing has happened in Macondo." In three kitchens where José Arcadio Segundo stopped before reaching home they told him the same thing: "There weren't any dead." He went through a small square by the station and he saw the fritter stands piled one on top of the other and he could find no trace of the massacre.[94]

As I have argued, with *One Hundred Years of Solitude* García Márquez reimagines the historical incident of the labor strike as a massacre, and challenges Colombian official history, by rescuing it from a silence and from the metaphorical plague of insomnia, a "nightmare that impedes sleep and dissolves out of the memory any remembrance."[95] Thus literature becomes a contested site of testimony, challenging the fickle status of evidence and truth through a process of social epistemology that involves a participating readership and testimony in the production of its meaning. Through different magical constructions throughout the story of the Buendía family, García Márquez configures an archive that goes beyond the lettered order of historiography, using literature as a counter-semantic to photography as an alleged record of reality. On the level of meta-narrative, the novel thus challenges the concepts of both archive and memory. Although the United Fruit Company photographs outline a memory place in their obscure interior that might transcend the images' discourse of concealment and the disappearance of violence, it is in the interstices of the two archives that the photographs' meaning is contested and amplified. Today, through a rather silent re-appropriation of some of the images from the Company's photographic archive, circulating only recently among former laborers and their families, the receptive experience of readers and viewers will help the mean-

94   García Márquez, *One Hundred Years of Solitude*, pp. 313–314.
95   Rincón, "Las artes de la memoria en la plaga de insomnio," p. 4, my translation.

ing of these photographs to be recognized and re-appropriated as a political act of remembrance and revision. So, it becomes urgent to follow up on what Arcadio Díaz Quiñones critically underlines elsewhere, that "perhaps today we should reflect on what this external view point [which determines the modes of subjectification] meant for the later self-recognition and self-representation of the old and new colonies."[96] This implication of seeing and re-appropriating becomes pivotal, because the pictures have begun to circulate back to the Caribbean and beyond.

So let me conclude this reading of the photographs, as they call for an ethics of seeing, insofar as this picture series holds a special place in the Company photographic archive. When I first found the series of photographs related to the labor strike and thus the banana massacre in the United Fruit Company photographic albums, I found the visual event they outline to be suspect, as the pictures seemed rather to give contours to the "unconscious of the visible" as something displaced and concealed, which I have been confronted with already in the fictitious archive in *One Hundred Years of Solitude.* They seemed to articulate something, which was not yet articulated, namely a symptom that had become an expression of something displaced. It became clear that memory and remembrance are not at all stable processes and that the two archives articulate this unstable limit between the private and the public, negotiated in the act of displacement. Moreover, in the form of the literary imagination doubts began to materialize around this official version of the banana massacre that had allowed the historical event to remain a significant lacuna in Colombian historiography for so long. However, following the echoing meanings between the two archives, particularly in regard to the silence surrounding the massacre and García Márquez's secret re-visiting of historical records, it became clear to me that the United Fruit Company photographs that overlap with García Márquez's

96   Díaz Quiñones, "El 98: La guerra simbólica," p. 181, my translation.

literary fiction are to be read as model of historical reflection that challenges the lettered order of historiography. What Didi-Huberman suggests thus becomes important again: "What we should learn, [...] is to manage the mechanism of images so as to know what to do with our sight and with our memory." Moreover, he punctuates that the "ethical dimension does not disappear in images [...]. So it is a *question of choice*: in the face of every image we have to choose whether, or how, to make it participate in our knowledge and action. We can accept or reject this or that image; take it as a consoling object or as a worrying object; make it ask questions or use it as a ready-made response."[97] Following this, it must be that "In this courage alone [...] resides the capacity of the image to save the real from its cloak of invisibility. [...] the courage to know becomes a source of action."[98] Finally, this is the crucial dimension of the images, which remain open to be contested, that is the materiality of the image within a social epistemology. Consequently, these images of the resurgent archive call for an ethics of seeing and the use of our knowledge for action: this may be the need for circulation of the pictures outside of the Company photographic archive and back to the communities in the Colombian Caribbean, so we can learn to see and remember atrocities against humanity and the environment, such as those committed within the plague of the banana and manifested as a plague of insomnia, in order to see and remember the humanity of the victims.

The Struggle for Human Rights

In the aftermath of this resurgent photographic archive, once the United Fruit Company ceased its operations in 1970 to become first the United Brands Company and then in 1984 the globally well-known Chiquita Brands, these residual archival images

97 Didi-Huberman, *Images in Spite of All*, p. 180.
98 Ibid., p. 178.

become part of a discourse and narrative of human rights. In the light of the search for truth about the atrocities committed, the recurrent massacres, murders of union leaders, forced displacements, and continued payment of paramilitary forces, in which the fruit companies have been involved in the Colombian region of Magdalena since the late 1980s, in March 2007 Chiquita, as a corporation, was found guilty in the U.S. federal court of engaging in "illegal transactions with the [paramilitary group] AUC [United Self-Defence Forces of Colombia]" following an investigation by the U.S. Department of Justice.[99] In May 2017, this investigation was expanded to include the role of Chiquita corporate officials in crimes against humanity, and a detailed communication and request were sent to the International Criminal Court.[100] In the light of this other narrative of the search for truth, the resurgent archival images of the United Fruit Company are contested by the massacre that happened in the context of the banana strike of 1928, and is still not recognized, but which, as a topos for socio-political upheavals, is recurrent in the history of the fruit companies in Colombia. The United Fruit Company photographic archive, read against the grain, thus becomes a lieu of visual reclamation for a potential history and, in its aftermath, a critical remembrance of the historical violence of its foundations. As in 1928 with the plague of insomnia and persistent historical amnesia, the crimes committed against the laborers and Colombian union leaders were never legally addressed, nor has any other investigation been undertaken to look into the involvement of the Company. Yet, the resurgence of the photographic archive and thus the archive itself "take [...] place at the place of originary and structural breakdown of said memory,"[101] and call for truth and reparations.

99   International Human Rights Clinic, Harvard Law School, "The Contribution of Chiquita Corporate Officials to Crimes Against Humanity in Colombia," p. 4.
100 Ibid.
101 Derrida, "Archive Fever," p. 14.

Following the recently published report by the International Human Rights Clinic, examining the "Chiquita Papers,"[102] as a preliminary legal investigation into the relationship between the United Fruit Company successor Chiquita and the atrocities committed in the banana zones of Colombia between 1997 and 2004, independently recognized by different state and human rights organizations, the participation of the United Fruit Company in the banana massacre of 1928, which was never investigated or proven, could now be symbolically contested by legal mechanisms under the eyes of an international community. As an unresolved past, the new search for justice could eradicate the opacity of this long history of violence and human rights violations by the fruit companies in Colombia, through the continued funding of paramilitary groups as entities that operated on behalf of the economic interests of the banana industry by maintaining a regime of oppression and cycle of violence, a repeated history, that has been foretold by *One Hundred Years of Solitude*.[103]

The Human Rights Clinic report suggests a further investigation into the union worker killings is needed. We read: "Chiquita's payments to the AUC occurred against a backdrop of historical violence against labor organizers in Colombia, particularly violence against unions in the banana-growing regions."[104] The report further states that the absence of "strike activity on banana plantations was due to paramilitary efforts."[105] As part of the cycle of violence, grounded in the very foundations of the United Fruit Company with its radical environmental and social

---

102 Referring here to "an archive created and recently updated with documents obtained through public action by the National Security Archive at The George Washington University." International Human Rights Clinic, Harvard Law School, "The Contribution of Chiquita Corporate Officials to Crimes Against Humanity in Colombia," p. 10.

103 International Human Rights Clinic, Harvard Law School, "The Contribution of Chiquita Corporate Officials to Crimes Against Humanity in Colombia," p. 45.

104 Ibid., p. 44.

105 Ibid.

transformations, land dispossession and forced displacement became recurrent means for the violent implementation of vast plantations, that were contested by upheavals in the region. The report addresses how paramilitary groups "utilized forced displacement on Afro-Colombian land to support economic development plans ('megaprojects') which included 'acquir[ing] lands illegally for plantations and cattle ranching'," an observation that is based on both human rights organizations' witnesses and paramilitary testimonies, which formed the evidence for the investigation to be led by the International Criminal Court.[106] The crimes against humanity, as looked at in the recent Chiquita trials, are part of a larger untold history of radical environmental changes brought by the United Fruit Company to the region. Obviously, the recent legal initiatives frame the more recent decades of violence and crimes against humanity and the environment, and the same cannot be said of the banana massacre in 1928, which has not been looked at juridically. Nevertheless, I argue that the United Fruit Company photographic archive forms part of this larger narrative brought up by the recent Chiquita trials: the never-addressed crimes, committed against both humanity and the environment, in which the United Fruit Company was involved, are part of a deeply embedded cycle of historical violence. How can (historical) justice for the laborers and union leaders killed during the 1928 massacre and their families be addressed today? As I have shown, the photographic archive embodies its own latencies of revolt and contestation. It also forms part of this civil contract for a future reclamation; as a resurgent photographic archive it is inscribed into a larger narrative of testimony, a claim for human and environmental rights.

As argued, testimony is not the same as proof or evidence, specifically in legal settings. It necessarily requires the authenticated response of a recipient, because its strength lies in the self-responsible work on "certainty," with regard to the resurgence

106 Ibid., p. 42.

of the photographic archive, that is, what Jacques Derrida conceived as *"méta-témoignage,"* referring to the phenomenon of
how "'poetic' witnessing also reflects the being of testimony."[107]
As consignation, the archive seems to outline a figuration of
what can be told and seen, of what can be voiced and visibilized,
of what is to come. In the way the photographs are situated as
archival images at the unstable limit between public and private
and because of their foundational relationship to the future,
they allow for a potential history that can imagine and reclaim
the United Fruit Company laborers as historical agents. Accordingly, a future reclamation and a reception of the photographs
as signs of becoming become possible, allowing for a new civil
imagination and a claim for human rights. In the way the photographs belong to a larger visual archive of the Caribbean, we
recognize today the long imperial genealogy of environmental
degradation. Following this, the United Fruit Company photographs may help to disclose the embodied imperial genealogies
of upheavals as an ecological media history, manifested in the
many toxic injustices, dispossession of land, forced displacement of peoples, murders of laborers and union leaders, all
of which is still ongoing today. The pictures as visual leftovers
and imperial debris offer the potential for future generations
to articulate a claim for justice. Significantly, Giorgio Agamben
underlines an important relationship between the archive and
testimony as follows:

> The archive is thus the mass of the non-semantic inscribed in every
> meaningful discourse as a function of its enunciation; it is the dark
> margin encircling and limiting every concrete act of speech. Between
> the obsessive memory of tradition, which knows only what has been
> said, and the exaggerated thoughtlessness of oblivion, which cares
> only for what was never said, the archive is the unsaid or sayable
> inscribed in everything said by the virtue of being enunciated; [...] that

---

107 Schlie, "Bemerkungen zur juridischen, epistemologischen und medialen
Wertigkeit des Zeugnisses," p. 28, my translation.

is, as the system of relations between the unsaid and the said in every act of speech, between the enunciative function and the discourse in which it exerts itself, between the outside and the inside of language.[108]

While Agamben conceives of the archive as inscribed in language, that is, of the unsaid and sayable, with regard to the photographic archive I wish to punctuate the quality of the archive's speech act that allows for a space between "obsessive memory" and the "thoughtlessness of oblivion." Following this, we should note what Ann Laura Stoler has underscored elsewhere as imperial debris, with its ruins and the processes of ruination, as it continues to exert its influence today as a post-colonial presence, and possible legal aftermath. Understanding the archive as situated between the unsaid and the sayable, it becomes the site where imperial debris is overtly articulated, bearing witness to the "uneven temporal sedimentation in which imperial formations leave their marks."[109] Moreover, Stoler encourages us "to ask how empire's ruins contour and carve through the psychic and material space in which people live and what compounded layers of imperial debris do to them."[110] Reading these archival images helps us to understand what Stoler has called the "residual or reactivated imperial practices" that we can witness today in the material and visual leftovers of forms of violence and other residual repositories of meaning.[111] Yet, we are still "wrestling with the task of seeing, with acts of violation for which there are no photographs able to document bodily exposures and intrusions of space."[112] Both the captions and the photographs that constitute the archive at the limit of the unsaid and sayable belong to the bureaucratic culture of the colonial and thus imperial production of space. As violence is

108 Giorgio Agamben, *Remnants of Auschwitz: The Witness and the Archive* (New York: Zone Books, 1999), p. 144.
109 Stoler, *Imperial Debris*, p. 2.
110 Ibid.
111 Ibid., p. 4.
112 Ibid., p. 3.

not represented and possibly not even archivable as such, today we may only relate to it in the visual leftovers and residues that have left "their bold-faces or subtle traces [...] in which contemporary inequities work their way through them," and which we perceive and sense in the archive as meta-testimony.[113] Though manifested and imagined as a peaceful environmental transformation in the photographic archive, labor was used as a violent regime of control, contested by the many upheavals. This is certainly true of this photographic series on the labor strike or banana massacre of 1928, where labor is not directly represented, but is, I argue, eye-witnessed, and transmitted through a media process, inasmuch as labor seems to be visually subordinated to the plantation economy, in the same way that the photographs carefully conceal the violence of the environmental changes and the move to a man-made monocultural landscape. Interestingly, Agamben further suggests that:

> In opposition to the archive, which designates the system of relations between the unsaid and the said, we give the name *testimony* to the system of relations between inside and the outside of language, between the sayable and the unsayable in every language—that is, between a potentiality of speech and its existence, between a possibility and an impossibility of speech. [...] Precisely because testimony is the relation between a possibility of speech and its taking place, it can exist only through a relation to an impossibility of speech.[114]

Now, what becomes pertinent to my concern about testimony in the photographic archive is that testimony is the potentiality "that becomes actual through an impotentiality of speech; it is [...] an impossibility that gives itself existence through a possibility of speaking."[115] This possibility of speaking, I argue, forms the horizon shared by the archival images, which neces-

113 Ibid.
114 Agamben, *Remnants of Auschwitz*, p. 145.
115 Ibid., p. 146.

sarily claim the engagement of a potential history. The archival images depict the possible agents of the labor strike, who do not raise their own voices but remain silent in the archive. They are nevertheless part of testimony, in Agamben's sense, inasmuch as they bear "witness to the taking place of a potentiality of speaking through an impotentiality alone," as witnessing relates to authority not because of a "factual truth, a conformity between something said and a fact or between memory and what happened, but rather on the immemorial relation between the unsayable and the sayable."[116] Importantly, Agamben argues, this "authority of the witness consists in his capacity to speak solely in the name of an incapacity to speak."[117] What the pictures eventually bear witness to is the violent labor regime, with its many crimes committed against humanity, that is experienced within the plantation economy of the United Fruit Company, and which continues today, as evidenced by the recent "Chiquita Papers." I argue that this is the pivotal momentum through which the pictures become a political act of potential re-appropriation, and eventually a legal claim, as "Testimony thus guarantees not the factual truth of the statement safeguarded in the archive, but rather its unarchivability, its exteriority with respect to the archive—that is, the necessity by which, as the existence of language, it escapes both memory and forgetting."[118] As visual leftovers, the photographs are bound by the civil contract to the political as they confer on the archive the potential figuration of future meaning and reclamation. Embodying a view of its exteriority, they nevertheless recover an internalized experience that belongs to the witnesses alone, embodying the complex semantic situations of imperial experience and its material and psychic sedimentations. Likewise, this contestation is "contained" in the photographic series that subverts the discourse of modernization

---

116 Ibid., p. 158.
117 Ibid.
118 Ibid.

and haunts "our 'true' reality as a specter of what might have happened, conferring on our reality the status of extreme fragility and contingency, [that] implicitly clashes with the predominant 'linear' narrative forms of [historiography]."[119] Reading the United Fruit Company photographic archive means thus to read it against the grain: in this way the archive configures a potential voicing and makes seen new historical agents for unexpected future alliances, foregrounding the potentiality of testimony.

119 Slavoj Žižek, "Everything You Always Wanted to Know about Schelling (But Were Afraid to Ask Hitchcock)," in *Schelling Now: Contemporary Readings*, ed. Jason Wirth (Bloomington: Indiana University Press, 2005), p. 39.

Bibliography

(Anonymous), *La masacre en las Bananeras, 1928: documentos, testimonios* (Bogota: Ed. Los Comuneros, 1965)

The Ruins of Quirigua (Washington: Carnegie Institution, 1934, III: pp. 150–156)

About, I. and Clément Chéroux, *Fotografie und Geschichte* (Leipzig: Institut für Buchkunst, 2004)

Adams, F. U., *Conquest of the Tropics: The Story of the Creative Enterprises Conducted by the United Fruit Company* (Garden City, N.Y.: Doubleday and Page, 1914)

Agamben, G., *Remnants of Auschwitz: The Witness and the Archive* (New York: Zone Books, 1999)

Albers, I., and Bernd Busch, "Fotografie/fotografisch," in *Ästhetische Grundbegriffe. Historisches Wörterbuch in sieben Bänden*, Band 2, ed. Barck, K. et al. (Stuttgart: J.B. Metzler, 2001: pp. 494–550)

Aliano, D., "Curing the Ills of Central America: The United Fruit Company's Medical Department and Corporate America's Mission to Civilize (1900–1940)," E.I.A.L. Estudios Interdisciplinarios de América Latina y el Caribe 17:2 (2006): pp. 35–59.

Andermann, J., *The Optic of the State: Visuality and Power in Argentina and Brazil* (Pittsburgh: University of Pittsburgh Press, 2007)

Andermann, J., "Tournaments of Value: Argentina and Brazil in the Age of Exhibitions," *Journal of Material Culture* 14:3 (2009): pp. 333–363

Andermann, J., "Memories of Extractivism: Slow Violence, Terror, and Matter," *Journal of Latin American Cultural Studies* 29:4 (2021): pp. 1–18.

Anderson, W., *Colonial Pathologies: American Tropical Medicine, Race, and Hygiene in the Philippines* (Durham: Duke University Press, 2006)

Anderson, W., "Immunität im Empire. Rasse, Krankheit und die neue Tropenmedizin, 1900–1920," in *Bakteriologie und Moderne. Studien zur Biopolitik des Unsichtbaren 1870–1920*, ed. Sarasin, P. et al. (Frankfurt am Main: Surhkamp, 2007: pp. 462–495)

Andrews, E. W. and Frederick W. Lange, "In Memoriam: Doris Zemurray Stone 1909–1994," *Ancient Mesoamerica* 6 (1995): pp. 95–99

Appadurai, A., ed., *The Social Life of Things: Commodities in Cultural Perspective* (Cambridge: Cambridge University Press, 1986)

Appadurai, A., *Modernity at Large: Cultural Dimensions of Globalization* (Minneapolis, University of Minnesota Press, 1996)

Arendt, H., *Elemente und Ursprünge totaler Herrschaft. Antisemitismus, Imperialismus, Totalitarismus* (Munich: Piper, 1986)

Arnold, D., *The Problem of Nature. Environment, Culture and European Expansion* (London: Blackwell, 1996)

Azoulay, A., *The Civil Contract of Photography* (New York: Zone Books, 2008)

Azoulay, A., *Civil Imagination: A Political Ontology of Photography* (London: Verso, 2015)

Azoulay, A., *Potential History: Unlearning Imperialism* (London: Verso, 2019)

Azoulay, A., "Archive," http://www.politicalconcepts.org/archive-ariella-azoulay/ (accessed October 2021)

Baker, G. L., *Century of Service: The first 100 years of the United States Department of Agriculture* (Washington: Centennial Committee, U.S. Dept. of Agriculture, 1963)

Bakhtin, M., *Chronotopos* (Frankfurt am Main: Suhrkamp, 2008)

Balibar, É. and Immanuel Wallerstein, *Rasse – Klasse – Nation. Ambivalente Identitäten* (Hamburg: Argument-Verlag, 1990)

Barbour, T., and Helene M. Robinson, "Forty years of Soledad," *The Scientific Monthly* 51:2 (1940): pp. 140–146

Barthes, R., *Image, Music, Text* (New York: Hill and Wang, 1977)

Batchen, G., *Photography's Objects* (Albuquerque: University of New Mexico Art Museum, 1997)

Bauer, A. J., *Goods, Power, History: Latin America's Material Culture* (Cambridge: Cambridge University Press, 2001)

Bell-Villada, G., "Banana Strike and Military Massacre. One Hundred Years of Solitude and What Happened in 1928," in *García Márquez's One Hundred Years of Solitude*, ed. Bell-Villada, G. (Oxford: Oxford University Press, 2002: pp. 127–138)

Benjamin, W., "Theses on the Philosophy of History," *Illuminations* (New York: Schocken Books, 1969: pp. 253–264)

Besser, S., "Pathographie der Tropen: Literatur, Medizin und Kolonialismus um 1900," (Ph.D. diss., Amsterdam School for Cultural Analysis, 2009)

Bleichmar, D., *Visible Empire: Botanical Expeditions and Visual Culture in the Hispanic Enlightenment* (Chicago: Chicago University Press, 2012)

Bolaños, B. and Mario Casanueva, eds., *El giro pictórico. Epistemología de la imagen* (Barcelona: Anthropos, 2009)

Bolton, R., *The Contest of Meaning: Critical Histories of Photography* (Cambridge, Mass.: MIT Press, 1989)

Borsdorf, U. and Sigrid Schneider, "A Mighty Business: Factory and Town in the Krupp Photographs," in *Pictures of Krupp: Photography and His-*

tory in the Industrial Age, ed. Tenfelde, K. (New York: Philip Wilson Publishers/Palgrave Macmillan, 2005: pp. 123–158)

Bost, D., "Una vista panorámica de las respuestas literarias a la huelga de las bananeras de 1928," *Revista de Estudios Colombianos* 10 (1991): pp. 11–24

Bourdieu, P., *Photography. A Middle-brow Art* (Stanford: Stanford University Press, 1990)

Bourgois, P., *Ethnicity at Work: Divided Labor on a Central American Banana Plantation* (Baltimore: The Johns Hopkins University Press, 1989)

Bourgois, P., "One Hundred Years of United Fruit Company Letters," in *Banana Wars: Power, Production, and History in the Americas,* ed. Striffler, S. and Mark Moberg (Durham: Duke University Press, 2003: pp. 103–144)

Bourguet, M.-N. and Christophe Bonneuil, eds., *De l'inventaire du monde à la mise en valeur du globe : botanique et colonisation, fin 17e siècle – début 20e siècle* (Saint-Denis: Société française d'histoire d'outre-mer, 1999: pp. 322–323)

Bourne, J., *Recollections of My Early Travels in Chiapas,* 2001

Brannstrom, C., ed., *Territories, Commodities and Knowledges: Latin American Environmental History in the Nineteenth and Twentieth Centuries* (London: Institute for the Study of the Americas, 2004)

Bray, F., "Science, technique, technology: Passages between matter and knowledge in imperial Chinese agriculture," *The British Society for the History of Science* 41:3 (2008): pp. 319–344

Brenna, B. and Mari Hvattum, eds., *Routes, Roads and Landscapes* (Surrey: Ashgate, 2011)

Brockway, L. H., *Science and Colonial Expansion: The Role of the British Royal Botanic Gardens* (New Haven: Yale University Press, 2002)

Browman, D. L., "Spying by American Archaeologists in World War I (with a minor linkage to the development of the Society for American Archaeology)," *Bulletin of the History of Archaeology* 21:2 (2011): pp. 10–17

Brown, B., "Materialities of Culture," in *Cultural Histories of the Material World,* ed. Miller, P. (Ann Arbor: University of Michigan Press, 2013: pp. 187–196)

Browne, J., "A Science of Empire: British Biogeography Before Darwin," *Revue d'histoire des sciences* 45:4 (1992): pp. 453–475

Bucheli, M., *Bananas and Business: The United Fruit Company in Colombia, 1899–2000* (New York: New York University Press, 2005)

Buchloh, B. and Robert Wilkie, eds., *Mining Photographs and Other Pictures, 1948–1968. A Selection from the Negative Archives of Shedden Studio, Glace Bay, Cape Breton* (Halifax: Press of the Nova Scotia College of Art and Design, 1983)

Bunz, M., "Die Ökonomie des Archivs – Der Geschichtsbegriff Derridas zwischen Kultur- und Mediengeschichte," *Archiv für Mediengeschichte* 6 (2006): pp. 33–42

Cahan, M. D., "The Harvard Garden in Cuba – A Brief History," *Arnoldia* 51:2 (1991): pp. 22–32

Caraffa, C., "From 'Photo Libraries' to 'Photo Archives': on the Epistemological Potential of Art-historical Photo Collections," in *Photo Archives and the Photographic Memory of Art History*, ed. Caraffa, C. (Munich: Deutscher Kunstverlag, 2011: pp. 11–44)

Carter, P., *The Road to Botany Bay: An Exploration of Landscape and History* (New York: Knopf, 1987)

Casid, J. H., "Inhuming Empire: Islands as Plantation Nurseries and Graves," in *The Global Eighteenth Century*, ed. Nussbaum, F. (Baltimore: The Johns Hopkins University Press, 2003: pp. 279–295)

Casid, J. H., *Sowing Empire: Landscape and Colonization* (Minneapolis: University of Minnesota Press, 2005)

Chapman, P., *Bananas: How the United Fruit Company Shaped the World* (New York: Canongate, 2007)

Chomsky, A., *West Indian Workers and the United Fruit Company in Costa Rica, 1870–1940* (Baton Rouge: Louisiana State University Press, 1996)

Chomsky, A., and Aldo Lauria-Santiago, eds., *Identity and Struggle at the Margins of the Nation-State: The Laboring Peoples of Central America and the Hispanic Caribbean* (Durham: Duke University Press, 1998)

Chomsky, A., "Making a Difference: Repatriating Photographs," *Revista. The Harvard Review of Latin America* VIII:2 (2009): p. 64

Cloward, D. J., *Schools in Bananaland: The Role of the United Fruit Company in Education in Middle America* (Boston: 1965)

Colby, J., *The Business of Empire: United Fruit, Race, and U.S. Expansion in Central America* (Ithaca: Cornell University Press, 2011)

Coleman, K. P., and Daniel James, *Capitalism and the Camera: Essays on Photography and Extraction* (London: Verso, 2021)

Coleman, K. P., and Daniel James, "Capitalism and the Limits of Photography," *Photography and Culture* 13:2 (2020): pp. 149–156.

Coleman, K. P. "The Photos That We Don't Get to See. Sovereignties, Archives, and the 1928 Massacre of Banana Workers in Colombia," in *Making the Empire Work: Labor and United States Imperialism*, ed. Bender, D. E. and Jana K. Lipman (New York: New York University Press, 2015: pp. 104–136)

Coleman, K. P., "A Camera in the Garden of Eden," *Journal of Latin American Cultural Studies* 20:1 (2011): pp. 63–96

Coleman, K. P., *A Camera in the Garden of Eden: The Self-Forging of a Banana Republic* (Austin: University of Texas Press, 2016)

Corbus Bezner, L., *Photography and Politics in America: From the New Deal into the Cold War* (Baltimore: The Johns Hopkins University Press, 1999)

Cortés Vargas, C., *Los sucesos de las bananeras. (Historia de los acontecimientos que se desarrollaron en la zona bananera del Departamento de Magdalena, 13.11.1928–15.3.1929)* (Bogota: Ediciones Desarrollo, 1979)

Crary, J., *Techniques of the Observer: On Vision and Modernity in the Nineteenth Century* (Cambridge, Mass.: MIT Press, 1990)

Crosby, A. W., *Ecological Imperialism: The Biological Expansion in Europe, 900–1900* (Cambridge: Cambridge University Press, 1993)

Cueva, A., *Literatura y conciencia histórica en América Latina* (Quito: Planeta, 1993)

Cutter, V., "Caribbean Tropics in Commercial Transition," *Economic Geography* 2:4 (1926): pp. 494–507

Daston, L. and Peter Galison, "The Image of Objectivity," *Representations* 40 (1992): pp. 81–128

Daston, L., and Peter Galison, *Objectivity* (New York: Zone Books, 2007)

Daston, L., "Scientific Objectivity with and without Words," in *Little Tools of Knowledge: Historical Essays on Academic and Bureaucratic Practices*, ed. Becker, P. and William Clark (Ann Arbor: University of Michigan Press, 2001: pp. 259–284)

Daston, L., "The Glass Flowers," in *Things that Talk: Object Lessons from Art and Science*, ed. Daston, L. (New York: Zone Books, 2004: pp. 223–256)

de los Ríos, V., *Espectros de luz* (Santiago de Chile: Cuarto Propio, 2011)

Deeks, W. E., *Malaria: Its Cause, Prevention and Cure* (Boston: United Fruit Company, 1925)

Derrida, J., "Archive Fever: A Freudian Impression," *Diacritics* 25:2 (1995): pp. 9–63

Derrida, J., *Mal d'archive. Une impression freudienne* (Paris: Galilée, 1995)

Derrida, J., *Limited Inc.* (Vienna: Passagen-Verlag, 2001)

Díaz Quiñones, A., et al., eds., *El Caribe entre imperios: coloquio de Princeton* (Río Piedras: Facultad de Humanidades, Departamento de Historia, Universidad de Puerto Rico, Recinto de Río Piedras, 1997)

Díaz Quiñones, A., "El 98: La guerra simbólica," in *Culturas imperiales. Experiencia y representación en América, Asia y África*, ed. Salvatore, R. and Renato Ortiz (Rosario: Beatriz Viterbo Editora, 2005: pp. 165–183)

Didi-Huberman, G., *Confronting Images: Questioning the Ends of a Certain History of Art* (University Park: Pennsylvania State University Press, 2005)

Didi-Huberman, G., *Bilder trotz allem* (Munich: Wilhelm Fink, 2007)

Didi-Huberman, G., *Images in Spite of All: Four Photographs from Auschwitz* (Chicago: Chicago University Press, 2008)

Dinius, O. and Angela Vergara, eds., *Company Towns in the Americas: Landscape, Power, and Working-Class Communities* (Athens: University of Georgia Press, 2011)

Drale, C., "The United Fruit Company and Early Radio Development," *Journal of Radio and Audio Media* 17:2 (2010): pp. 195–210

Ebeling, K. and Stephan Günzel, eds., *Archivologie. Theorien des Archivs in Wissenschaft, Medien und Künsten* (Berlin: Kunstverlag Kadmos, 2009)

Echeverri-Gent, E., "Forgotten Workers: British West Indians and the Early Days of the Banana Industry in Costa Rica and Honduras," *Journal of Latin American Studies* 24:2 (1992): pp. 275–308

Edwards, E., ed., *Anthropology and Photography, 1860–1920* (New Haven and London: Yale University Press with the Royal Anthropological Institute, 1992)

Edwards, E., *Raw Histories: Photographs, Anthropology and Museums* (New York: Berg, 2001)

Edwards, E., "Photographs: Material Form and the Dynamic Archive," in *Photo Archives and the Photographic Memory of Art History*, ed. Caraffa, C. (Munich: Deutscher Kunstverlag, 2011: pp. 47–56)

Edwards, E., *The Camera as Historian: Amateur Photographers and Historical Imagination, 1885–1918* (Durham: Duke University Press, 2012)

Elliott, L. E., "Quirigua," *Pan-American Magazine* X:2 (1910): pp. 71–75

Fairchild, D., "Two Expeditions After Living Plants: The Allison V. Amour Expeditions of 1925–27, Including Two Voyages in the Especially Equipped Yacht Utowana," *Scientific Monthly* 26 (1928): pp. 97–127

Fairchild, D., *The World Was My Garden: Travels of a Plant Explorer* (New York: Scribners Sons, 1943)

Fane, D., "Reproducing the Pre-Columbian Past: Casts and Models in Exhibitions of Ancient America, 1824–1935," in *Collecting the Pre-Columbian Past*, ed. Hill Boone, E. (Washington D.C.: Dumbarton Oaks Research Library and Collection, 2011: pp. 141–176)

Farley, J., *Bilharzia: A History of Imperial Tropical Medicine* (Cambridge: Cambridge University Press, 2003)

Föhl, A., "On the Internal Life of German Factories – Industrial Architecture and Social Context at Krupp," in *Pictures of Krupp: Photography and History in the Industrial Age*, ed. Tenfelde, K. (New York: Philip Wilson Publishers/Palgrave Macmillan, 2005: pp. 159–180)

Foucault, M., *Discipline and Punish: The Birth of the Prison* (New York: Vintage Books, 1979)

Foucault, M., *La naissance de la biopolitique. Cours au Collège de France, 1978–1979* (Paris: Éditions du Seuil, 2004)

Gaitán, J. E., *El debate sobre las bananeras [cuatro días de verdad contra 40 años de silencio]* (Bogota: Centro Gaitán, 1988)

Galison, P. and Caroline Jones, eds., *Picturing Science, Producing Art* (New York: Routledge, 1998)

García Márquez, G., *Cien años de soledad* (Bogota: Grupo Editorial Norma, 1997)

García Márquez, G., *One Hundred Years of Solitude* (London: Penguin, 2007)

García Márquez, G., *Leaf Storm* (London: Penguin, 2008)

Geimer, P., "Gegensichtbarkeiten," *Bildwelten des Wissens. Kunsthistorisches Jahrbuch für Bildkritik* 4:2 (2006): pp. 33–42

Gómez, L., "Un caso de archivo fotográfico. Economía visual de la circulación de mercancías, cuerpos y memorias," in *Relaciones caribeñas. Entrecruzamientos de dos siglos. Relations caribéennes: entrecroisements de deux siècles*, ed. Gómez, L., and Gesine Müller (Frankfurt am Main: Peter Lang, 2011: pp. 109–131)

Gómez, L., "The Urbanization of Society: Towards a Cultural Analysis of the Sacred in the Modern Metropolis," in *The Sacred in the City*, ed. Gómez, L. and Walter van Herck (London: Continuum, 2012: pp. 31–51)

Gómez, L., "Residuos del archivo y el conflicto de las bananeras en Colombia: Figuraciones de violencia y contra-memoria en la literatura y la fotografía," *Iberoamericana* 19:72 (2019): pp. 81–103

Gómez-Popescu, L., "Towards a History Through Photography. An Introduction," *E.I.A.L. Estudios Interdisciplinarios de América Latina y el Caribe* 26:2 (2015): pp. 7–16

Gómez-Popescu, L., "Epilogue. Archive Matters," *E.I.A.L. Estudios Interdisciplinarios de América Latina y el Caribe* 26:2 (2015): pp. 95–103

Gómez-Popescu, L., "La Masacre de las Bananeras: la imagen fotográfica y la literatura," in *Imaginando América Latina: historia y cultura visual, siglos XIX a XXI*, ed. Schuster, S. and Óscar Daniel Hernández Quiñones (Bogotá: Editorial de la Universidad del Rosario, 2017): pp. 23–57

González Echevarría, R., "*One Hundred Years of Solitude*: the novel as myth and archive," *Modern Language Notes* 99:2 (1984): pp. 358–380

Gorgas, W. C., *Sanitation in Panama* (New York: Appleton, 1915)

Graham, R., et al., eds., *The Idea of Race in Latin America, 1870–1940* (Austin: University of Texas Press, 1990)

Grove, R. H., *Green Imperialism: Colonial Expansion, Tropical Island Edens, and the Origins of Environmentalism* (Cambridge: Cambridge University Press, 1995)

Guillory, J., "The Memo and Modernity," *Critical Inquiry* 31:1 (2004): pp. 108–132

Hannig, J., "Photographs as a Historical Source," in *Pictures of Krupp: Photography and History in the Industrial Age*, ed. Tenfelde, K. (New York: Philip Wilson Publishers/Palgrave Macmillan, 2005: pp. 269–288)

Harpelle, R., "Racism and Nationalism in the Creation of Costa Rica's Pacific Coast Banana Enclave," *The Americas* 56:3 (2000): pp. 29–51

Harris, C. H. and Louis R. Sadler, *The Archaeologist was a Spy: Sylvanus G. Morley and the Office of Naval Intelligence* (Alburquerque: University of New Mexico Press, 2003)

Healey, G. G., "Bonampak," *Archaeology* 1:1 (1948): pp. 30–31

Healey, G. G., "Oxlahuntun," *Archaeology* 1:4 (1948): pp. 129–133

Healey, G. G., "The Lacanja Valley," *Archaeology* 3:1 (1950): pp. 12–15

Herlinghaus, H., *Violence Without Guilt: Ethical Narratives from the Global South* (New York: Palgrave Macmillan, 2009)

Hewett, E. L., "The Excavation of Quirigua, by the School of American Archaeology," *XVIII. International Congress of Americanists* (1912)

Hill Boone, E., ed., *Collecting the Pre-Columbian Past* (Washington D.C.: Dumbarton Oaks Research Library and Collection, 2011)

Hinsley, C. M., "From Shell-Heaps to Stelae: Early Anthropology at the Peabody Museum," in *Objects and Others: Essays on Museums and Material Culture*, ed. Stocking, G.W. (Madison: University of Wisconsin Press, 1988: pp. 49–74)

Hinsley, C. M., "In Search of the New World Classical," in *Collecting the Pre-Columbian Past*, ed. Hill Boone, E. (Washington D.C.: Dumbarton Oaks Research Library and Collection, 2011: pp. 105–122)

Hirsch, M., *Family Frames: Photography, Narrative, and Postmemory* (Cambridge, Mass.: Harvard University Press, 1997)

Hirsch, M. and Diane Taylor, "The Archive in Transit. Editorial Remarks," *E-misférica* 9:1–2 (2012)

Hodge, W. H., "Hunting Cinchona in the Peruvian Andes," *Journal of the New York Botanical Garden* 45 (1944): pp. 32–43

Hodge, W. H., "The Plant Resources of Peru," *Economic Botany* 1:2 (1947): pp. 119–136

Hodge, W. H., "Wartime Cinchona Procurement in Latin America," *Economic Botany* 2:3 (1948): pp. 229–257

Hodge, W. H., "Notes on Peruvian Cinchonas," *Botanical Museums Leaflets, Harvard University* 14:6 (1950): pp. 137–155

Hodge, W. H. and C. O. Erlanson, "Federal Plant Introduction: A Review," *Economic Botany* 10:4 (1956): pp. 299–334

Hodge, W. H. and Angela I. Todd, "Agricultural explorers of the USDA's Bureau of Plant Industry, 1897–1955," *Huntia* 14:1 (2009): pp. 23–50

Hornborg, A., "Symbolic Technologies: Machines and the Marxian Notion of Fetishism," *Anthropological Theory* 1:4 (2001): pp. 473–496

Hornborg, A., "Animism, Fetishism, and Objectivism as Strategies for Knowing (or not Knowing) the World," *Ethnos: Journal of Anthropology* 71:1 (2006): pp. 21–32

Hugill, P. J., *Global Communications since 1844: Geopolitics and Technology* (Baltimore: The Johns Hopkins University Press, 1999)

Hull, M., *Government of Paper: The Materiality of Bureaucracy in Urban Pakistan* (Berkeley: University of California Press, 2012)

International Human Rights Clinic Harvard Law School, "The Contribution of Chiquita Corporate Officials to Crimes Against Humanity in Colombia. Article 15 Communication to the International Criminal Court," Cambridge, Harvard Law School, 2017, http://hrp.law.harvard.edu/wp-content/uploads/2017/05/2017-05-18-Communication-0845.Pdf (last accessed 16.10.2019).

Jaguaribe, B. and Maurício Lissovsky, "The Visible and the Invisibles: Photography and Social Imaginaries in Brazil," *Public Culture* 21:1 (2009): pp. 175–209

Joseph, G., Catherine LeGrand, and Ricardo Salvatore, eds., *Close Encounters of Empire: Writing the Cultural History of U.S.-Latin American Relations* (Durham: Duke University Press, 1998)

Kamper, D. and Christoph Wulf, eds., *Das Heilige. Seine Spur in der Moderne* (Frankfurt am Main: Athenäum, 1987)

Kelsey, R., *Archive Style: Photographs and Illustrations for U.S. Surveys, 1850–1890* (Berkeley: University of California Press, 2007)

Kemp, M., "'Implanted in our Natures': Humans, Plants, and the Stories of Art," in *Visions of Empire: Voyages, Botany, and Representations of Nature*, ed. Miller, P. (Cambridge: Cambridge University Press, 1996: pp. 197–229)

Kepner, C. D. and Jay Henry Soothill, *The Banana Empire: A Case Study of Economic Imperialism* (New York: The Vanguard Press, 1935)

Kepner, C. D., *Social Aspects of the Banana Industry* (New York: Columbia University Press, 1936)

Kinzer, S., *In the Shadow of State and Capital: The United Fruit Company, Popular Struggle, and Agrarian Restructuring in Ecuador, 1900–1995* (Durham: Duke University Press, 2002)

Kittler, F. A., *Grammophon, Film, Typewriter* (Berlin: Brinkmann & Bose, 1986)

Kittler, F. A., *Discourse Networks, 1800/1900* (Stanford: Stanford University Press, 1990)

Kittler, F. A., "Aufschreibesysteme 1800/1900. Vorwort," *Zeitschrift für Medienwissenschaft* 6 (2012): pp. 117–126

Kloppenburg, J. R., *First the Seed: The Political Economy of Plant Technology* (Madison: University of Wisconsin Press, 2004)

Koch, M. and Christian Köhler, "Das kulturtechnische Apriori Friedrich Kittlers," *Archiv für Mediengeschichte* 13 (2013): pp. 157–165

Latour, B., "Visualization and Cognition: Thinking with Eyes and Hands," *Knowledge and Society: Studies in the Sociology of Culture Past and Present* 6 (1986): pp. 1–40

LeGrand, C., "Campesinos y asalariados en la zona banarera de Santa Marta (1900–1935)," *Anuario Colombiano de Historia Social y de la Cultura* 11 (1983): pp. 235–250

LeGrand, C., "El conflicto de las bananeras," *Relaciones Internacionales, Movimientos Sociales* 3 (1989): pp. 183–218

LeGrand, C., "Living in Macondo. Economy and Culture in a United Fruit Company Banana Enclave in Colombia," in *Close Encounters of Empire: Writing the Cultural History of U.S.-Latin American Relations*, ed. Joseph, G., Catherine LeGrand, and Ricardo Salvatore (Durham: Duke University Press, 1998: pp. 333–368)

LeGrand, C. and Adriana Corso, "Archivos notariales e historias regionales: Nuevas fuentes para el estudio de la zona bananera del Magdalena," *Huellas: Revista de la Universidad del Norte* 31 (2004): pp. 158–209

LeGrand, C., "Historias transnacionales: nuevas interpretaciones de los enclaves en América Latina," *Nómadas* 25 (2006): pp. 144–155

Lüdtke, A., "The Faces of the Workforce. Portraits of Labour," in *Pictures of Krupp: Photography and History in the Industrial Age*, ed. Tenfelde, K. (New York: Philip Wilson Publishers/Palgrave Macmillan, 2005: pp. 67–88)

Lynch, M. and Steve Woolgar, eds., *Representation in Scientific Practice* (Cambridge, Mass.: MIT Press, 1988)

Mason, J. A., "Costa Rican stonework: The Minor C. Keith collection," *Anthropological Papers of the American Museum of Natural History* 39:3 (1945): pp. 193–317

Mason, R., "The History of the Development of the United Fruit Company's Radio Telegraph System," *Radio Broadcast* 1 (1922): pp. 377–398

Massalongo, M., "Bild und Zeugenschaft. Erkenntnis und Gedächtnis im Zeitalter des Zeugen," in *Nachleben und Rekonstruktion. Vergangenheit im Bild*, ed. Hagner, M. and Peter Geimer (Munich: Wilhelm Fink, 2012: pp. 176–205)

Matz, R., "Gegen einen naiven Begriff der Dokumentarfotografie," *European Photography* 6 (1981): pp. 6–12

Matz, R., *Industriefotografie. Aus Firmenarchiven des Ruhrgebiets* (Essen: Museum Folkwang, 1987)

Matz, R., "Works photography – an attempt at the collective view," in *Pictures of Krupp: Photography and History in the Industrial Age*, ed. Tenfelde, K. (New York: Philip Wilson Publishers/Palgrave Macmillan, 2005: pp. 289–304)

McCreery, D., "Wireless Empire: The United States and Radio Communications in Central America and the Caribbean, 1904–1926," *South Eastern Latin Americanist* XXXVII 1 (1993): pp. 23–41

Mena, L., "La huelga de la compañía bananera como expresión de lo 'real maravilloso' americano en Cien Años de Soledad," *Bulletin Hispanique* 74 (1972): pp. 379–405

Mena, L., *La función de la historia en "Cien años de soledad"* (Barcelona: Plaza y Janés, 1979)

Merrill, E. D., "The Atkins Institution of the Arnold Arboretum, Soledad, Cienfuegos, Cuba," *Bulletin of Popular Information* 8:13 (1940): pp. 64–74

Miller, J. S., "Racing Against the Clock: The Urgent Need for a Renewed Renaissance of Plant Exploration," *Public Guard* 21:4 (2006): pp. 5–6

Mitchell, W. J. T., ed., *Landscape and Power* (Chicago: Chicago University Press, 2002)

Morgan, B. B. and Deam Hunter Ferris, "Photography as a Basic Research Tool," *Scientific Monthly* 69:5 (1949): pp. 306–311

Morley, S. G., "Excavations at Quirigua, Guatemala," *National Geographic Magazine* 24:3 (1913): pp. 339–372

Morley, S. G., *Guide Book to the Ruins of Quirigua* (Washington: Carnegie Institution, 1935)

Morley, S. G., *The Ancient Maya* (Stanford: Stanford University Press, 1946)

Morrow Wilson, C., *Ambassadors in White: The Story of American Tropical Medicine* (New York: Henry Holt and Company, 1942)

Morrow Wilson, C., "School of Pan American Agriculture," *The Scientific Monthly* 59:1 (1944): pp. 29–36

Morrow Wilson, C., "Backwards a Dozen Centuries," *Natural History* 56:8 (1947): pp. 370–378

Morrow Wilson, C., *Empire in Green and Gold: The Story of the American Banana Trade* (New York: Henry Holt and Company, 1947)

Newbury, D., "Picturing an 'ordinary atrocity': The Sharpeville Massacre," in *Picturing Atrocity: Photography in Crisis*, ed. Batchen, G. et al. (London: Reaktion Books, 2012: pp. 209–224)

Nixon, R., *Slow Violence and the Environmentalism of the Poor* (Cambridge, Mass.: Harvard University Press, 2011)

Nye, D. E., *Image Worlds: Corporate Identities at General Electric, 1890–1930* (Cambridge, Mass.: MIT Press, 1985)

Olmi, G., *L'inventario del mondo: catalogazione della natura e luoghi del sapere nella prima età moderna* (Bologna: Il Mulino, 1992)

Ortega, J., "The Discourse of Abundance," *American Literary History* 4:3 (1992): pp. 269–385

Peard, J., *Race, Place, and Medicine: The Idea of the Tropics in Nineteenth-Century Brazilian Medicine* (Durham: Duke University Press, 1999)

Pfeiffer, K. L., "Materialität der Literatur?," in *Materialität der Kommunikation*, ed. Gumbrecht, H. U. and Karl Ludwig Pfeiffer (Frankfurt am Main: Suhrkamp, 1988: pp. 15–28)

Pillsbury, J., ed., *Past Presented: Archaeological Illustration and the Ancient Americas* (Washington D.C.: Dumbarton Oaks Research Library and Collection, 2012)

Pillsbury, J., "The Pan-American: Nelson Rockefeller and the Arts of Ancient Latin America," *The Metropolitan Museum of Art Bulletin* LXXII:1 (2014): pp. 18–27

Pinney, C., and Nicholas Peterson, eds., *Photography's Other Histories* (Durham: Duke University Press, 2003)

Poole, D., *Vision, Race, and Modernity: A Visual Economy of the Andean Image World* (Princeton: Princeton University Press, 1997)

Popenoe, D. H., "Some Excavations at Playa de los Muertos Ulua River, Honduras," *Maya Research* 1:2 (1934): pp. 8–81

Popenoe, D. H., "The ruins of Tenampua, Honduras," *Smithsonian Report* (Washington: Smithsonian Institution, 1935: pp. 559–572)

Popenoe, W., "Foreign Service and Agriculture," *The American Foreign Service Journal* II:11 (1925): pp. 365–269, 390

Popenoe, W., "The Human Background of Lancetilla," *Unifruitco* (August 1931): pp. 19–25

Popenoe, W., "Cinchona on Guatemala," *Tropical Agriculture* 18:4 (1941): pp. 70–74

Popenoe, W., "Banana Culture around the Caribbean," *Tropical Agriculture* 18:1 (1941): pp. 8–12

Popenoe, W., "The Development of Inter-American Cooperation in Agriculture," *Bulletin of Pan American Union* 15:7 (1946): pp. 362–374

Popenoe, W., "Cinchona Cultivation in Guatemala – A Brief Historical Review up to 1943," *Economic Botany* 3:2 (1949): pp. 150–157

Popenoe, W. and Dorothy Hughes Popenoe, *A Guide to Quiriguá, An Ancient Maya City* (United Fruit Company, 1950)

Pratt, M. L., *Imperial Eyes: Travel Writing and Transculturation* (London: Routledge, 1992)

Putnam, L., *The Company They Kept: Migrants and the Politics of Gender in Caribbean Costa Rica, 1870–1960* (Chapel Hill: University of North Carolina Press, 2002)

Raby, M., "Making Biology Tropical: American Science in the Caribbean, 1898–1963," (Ph.D. diss., University of Wisconsin-Madison, 2013)

Raby, M., "Ark and Archive: Making a Place for Long-Term Research on Barro Colorado Island, Panama," *Isis: Journal of the History of Science Society* (2015)

Rancière, J., *The Politics of Aesthetics* (London: Continuum, 2004)

Rankin Bohme, S., *Toxic Injustice: A Transnational History of Exposure and Struggle* (Oakland: University of California Press, 2015)

Reif, H., "'The worker's well-being and domestic happiness'. Works Life Beyond the Factory Gates in Photography at Krupp," in *Pictures of Krupp: Photography and History in the Industrial Age*, ed. Tenfelde, K. (New York: Philip Wilson Publishers/Palgrave Macmillan, 2005: pp. 105–122)

Rey, R., "Espèces, espaces: la biogéographie sans frontières," *Revue d'histoire des sciences* 45:4 (1992): p. 375–388

Rheinberger, H.-J., Michael Hagner, and Bettina Wahrig-Schmidt, eds., *Räume des Wissens: Repräsentation, Codierung, Spur* (Berlin: Akademie Verlag, 1997)

Richards, T. H., *The Imperial Archive: Knowledge and the Fantasy of Empire* (London: Verso, 2003)

Rincón, C., "Magisch/Magie," in *Ästhetische Grundbegriffe. Historisches Wörterbuch in sieben Bänden*, Band 3, ed. Barck, K. et al. (Stuttgart: Metzler, 2001: pp. 724–759)

Rincón, C., "Las artes de la memoria en la plaga de insomnio de Cien años de soledad," *Literatura y filosofía* 1:1 (2003): pp. 3–36

Rincón, C., "Los límites de Macondo," *Teorías y poéticas de la novela: Localizaciones latinoamericanas y globalización cultural*, ed. Contreras Castro, A. (Berlin: Wissenschaftlicher Verlag Berlin, 2004: pp. 13–74)

Rosenberg, E., *Spreading the American Dream: American Economic and Cultural Expansion, 1890–1945* (New York: Hill and Wang, 1982)

Rosengarten, F., *Wilson Popenoe: Agricultural Explorer, Educator, and Friend of Latin America* (Lawai, Kauai, Hawaii: National Tropical Botanical Garden, 1991)

Rossi-Wilcox, S. M. and David Whitehouse, eds., *Drawing Upon Nature: Studies for the Blaschkas' Glass Models* (Corning: Corning Museum of Glass, 2007)

Rushdie, S., *Imaginary Homelands: Essays and Criticism 1981–1990* (London: Penguin Books, 1991)

Said, E., *Orientalism* (New York: Pantheon Books, 1978)

Said, E., *Yeats and Decolonization* (Derry: Field Day, 1988)

Salvatore, R., "The Enterprise of Knowledge: Representational Machines of Informal Empire," in *Close Encounters of Empire: Writing the Cultural History of U.S.-Latin American Relations*, ed. Joseph, G., Catherine LeGrand, and Ricardo Salvatore (Durham: Duke University Press, 1998: pp. 69–104)

Salvatore, R., ed., *Culturas imperiales. Experiencia y representación en América, Asia y África* (Rosario: Beatriz Viterbo Editora, 2005)

Schäffner, W., "Verwaltung der Kultur. Alexander von Humboldts Medien (1799–1834)," in *Interkulturalität. Zwischen Inszenierung und Archiv*, ed. Rieger, S., Schamma Schahadat, and Manfred Weinberg (Tübingen: Narr, 1999: pp. 353–366)

Schäffner, W., "Los medios de comunicación y la construcción del territorio en América Latina," *História, Ciências, Saúde – Manguinhos* 15:3 (2008): p. 811–826

Schiebinger, L., "Lost Knowledge, Bodies of Ignorance, and the Poverty of Taxonomy as Illustrated by the Curious Fate of *Flos Pavonis*, an Abortifacient," in *Picturing Science, Producing Art*, ed. Galison, P. and Caroline Jones (New York: Routledge, 1998: pp. 125–144)

Schiebinger, L., *Plants and Empire: Colonial Bioprospecting in the Atlantic World* (Cambridge, Mass.: Harvard University Press, 2004)

Schlesinger, S., and Stephen Kinzer, *Bitter Fruit: The Untold Story of the American Coup in Guatemala* (Garden City, N.Y.: Doubleday, 1982)

Schlie, H., "Bemerkungen zur juridischen, epistemologischen und medialen Wertigkeit des Zeugnisses," in *Zeugnis und Zeugenschaft. Perspektiven aus der Vormoderne*, ed. Schlie, H. and Wolfram Drews (Munich: Wilhelm Fink, 2011: pp. 23–29)

Scholz, O., "Das Zeugnis anderer – Prolegomena zu einer sozialen Erkenntnistheorie," in *Erkenntnistheorie. Positionen zwischen Tradition und Gegenwart*, ed. Grundmann, T. (Paderborn: Mentis, 2001: pp. 354–375)

Schubert, P., *The Electric Word: The Rise of Radio* (New York: Macmillan, 1928)

Schwoch, J., *The American Radio Industry and its Latin American Activities, 1900–1939* (Urbana: University of Illinois Press, 1990)

Scott, R. J., "A Cuban Connection: Edwin F. Atkins, Charles Francis Adams, Jr., and the Former Slaves of Soledad Plantation," *Massachusetts Historical Review* 9 (2007): pp. 7–34.

Secord, A., "Botany on a Plate: Pleasure and the Power of Pictures in Promoting Early Nineteenth-Century Scientific Knowledge," *Isis* 93:1 (2002): pp. 28–57

Sekula, A., "The Traffic in Photographs," *Art Journal* 41:1 (1981): pp. 15–25

Sekula, A., "Photography between Labour and Capital," in *Mining photographs and other pictures, 1948-1968. A selection from the negative archives of Shedden Studio, Glace Bay, Cape Breton*, ed. Buchloh, B. and Robert Wilkie (Halifax: Press of the Nova Scotia College of Art and Design, 1983: pp. 193–268)

Serena, T., "The Words of the Photo Archive," in *Photo Archives and the Photographic Memory of Art History*, ed. Caraffa, C. (Munich: Deutscher Kunstverlag, 2011: pp. 57–71)

Serje, M. R., *El revés de la nación. Territorios salvajes, fronteras y tierras de nadie* (Bogota: Universidad de Los Andes, Facultad de Ciencias Sociales, Departamento de Antropología / CESO, 2005)

Shuttack, G. C., *Tropical Medicine at Harvard* (Boston, Mass.: Harvard School of Public Health, 1954)

Siegert, B., "Weiße Flecken und finstre Herzen. Von der symbolischen Weltordnung zur Weltentwurfsordnung," in *Kulturtechnik Entwerfen. Praktiken, Konzepte und Medien in Architektur und Design Science*, ed. Gethmann, D. and Susanne Hauser (Bielefeld: Transcript, 2009: pp. 19–47)

Smith, N., *Uneven Development: Nature, Capital, and the Production of Space* (Athens: University of Georgia Press, 2008)

Smith, P., "The History of Science as a Cultural History of the Material World," in *Cultural Histories of the Material World*, ed. Miller, P. (Ann Arbor: University of Michigan Press, 2013: pp. 210–225)

Smith, P., Amy Meyers, and Harold Cook, eds., *Ways of Making and Knowing: The Material Culture of Empirical Knowledge* (Ann Arbor: The University of Michigan Press, 2014)

Snyder, J., "Territorial Photography," in *Landscape and Power*, ed. Mitchell, W. J. T. (Chicago: Chicago University Press, 2002: pp. 175–202)

Solomon-Godeau, A., "Wer spricht so? Einige Fragen zur Dokumentarfotografie," in *Diskurse der Fotografie. Fotokritik am Ende des fotografischen Zeitalters*, ed. Wolf, H. (Frankfurt am Main: Suhrkamp, 2003: pp. 53–74)

Soluri, J., *Banana Cultures: Agriculture, Consumption, and Environmental Change in Honduras and the United States* (Austin: University of Texas Press, 2005)

Spinden, H. J., "In Quest of Ruined Cities: How the Scientific Explorer Penetrates the Dense Tropical Forests of Central America in Search of New Evidence of a Vanished Civilization," *Scientific American* (February 1928): pp. 108–111

Standley, P. C., "Lancetilla Experiment Station," *Science* 68:1760 (1928): pp. 265–266

Stanley, D. K., *For the Record: The United Fruit Company's Sixty-Six years in Guatemala* (Guatemala City: Editorial Antigua, 1994)

Stepan, N., *Picturing Tropical Nature* (Ithaca: Cornell University Press, 2001)

Stephens, J. L., *Incidents of Travel in Central America, Chiapas, and Yucatan* (London: John Murray, 1843)

Stewart, W., *Keith and Costa Rica: A Biographical Study of Minor Cooper Keith* (Alburquerque: University of New Mexico Press, 1964)

Stocking, G. W., "Philanthropoids and Vanishing Cultures: Rockefeller Funding and the End of the Museum Era in Anglo-American Anthropology," in *Objects and Others: Essays on Museums and Material Culture*, ed. Stocking, G. W. (Madison: University of Wisconsin Press, 1988: pp. 112–145)

Stoler, A. L., "Making Empire Respectable: The Politics of Race and Sexual Morality in 20th-Century Colonial Cultures," in *Imperial Monkey Business: Racial Supremacy in Social Darwinist Theory and Colonial Practice*, ed. Breman, J. (Amsterdam: VU University Press, 1990: pp. 35–70)

Stoler, A. L., *Race and the Education of Desire: Foucault's* History of Sexuality *and the Colonial Order of Things* (Durham: Duke University Press, 1995)

Stoler, A. L., *Along the Archival Grain: Epistemic Anxieties and Colonial Common Sense* (Princeton: Princeton University Press, 2009)

Stoler, A. L., *Imperial Debris: On Ruins and Ruination* (Durham: Duke University Press, 2013)

Stoneman Douglas, M., *Adventures in a Green World – The Story of David Fairchild and Barbour Lathrop* (Miami: Field Research Projects, 1973)

Stott, W., *Documentary Expression and Thirties America* (Chicago: Chicago University Press, 1986)

Striffler, S. and Mark Moberg, eds., *Banana Wars: Power, Production, and History in the Americas* (Durham: Duke University Press, 2003)

Sullivan, P. R., *Unfinished Conversations: Mayas and Foreigners Between Two Wars* (Berkeley: University of California Press, 1991)

Tagg, J., *The Burden of Representation: Essays on Photographies and Histories* (Minneapolis: University of Minnesota Press, 1993)

Tagg, J., "The pencil of history," in *Fugitive Images: From Photography to Video*, ed. Petro, P. (Indianapolis: Indiana University Press, 1995: pp. 285–304)

Taussig, M., *Mimesis and Alterity: A Particular History of the Senses* (New York: Routledge, 1993)

Taussig, M., *My Cocaine Museum* (Chicago: Chicago University Press, 2004)

Tenfelde, K., ed., *Pictures of Krupp: Photography and History in the Industrial Age* (New York: Philip Wilson Publishers/Palgrave Macmillan, 2005)

Thompson, K. A., *An Eye for the Tropics: Tourism, Photography, and Framing the Caribbean Picturesque* (Durham: Duke University Press, 2006)

Todd, A., "Biographies of the Agricultural Explorers of the USDA's Bureau of Plant Industry, 1897–1955: Part 1, A–F," *Huntia* 14:1 (2009): pp. 51–86

Trachtenberg, A., *Reading American Photographs: Images as History, Mathew Brady to Walker Evans* (New York: Hill and Wang, 1989)

United Fruit Company, *Annual Report to the Stockholders of the United Fruit Company* (Boston: United Fruit Company, 1900–1967)

United Fruit Company, *Quarantine Tour of Central America and Panama by Health Authorities as Guests of the United Fruit Company* (1906)

United Fruit Company, *Annual Report* (Boston: Medical Department, United Fruit Company, 1912–1931)

United Fruit Company, "Proceedings of the International conference on health problems in tropical America," *International conference on health problems in tropical America* (Kingston, Jamaica: United Fruit Company, 1924)

Vismann, C., *Files: Law and Media Technology* (Stanford: Stanford University Press, 2008)

Vogl, J., "Medien-Werden: Galileis Fernrohr," *Archiv für Mediengeschichte* 1 (2001): pp. 115–123

Wagner, M., "Material," in *Ästhetische Grundbegriffe. Historisches Wörterbuch in sieben Bänden,* Band 3, ed. Barck, K. et al. (Stuttgart: Metzler, 2001: pp. 866–882)

Wengenroth, U., "Photography as source of the history of labour and technology," in *Pictures of Krupp: Photography and History in the Industrial Age,* ed. Tenfelde, K. (New York: Philip Wilson Publishers/Palgrave Macmillan, 2005: pp. 89–104)

Werner, G., "Bilddiskurse. Kritische Überlegungen zur Frage, ob es eine allgemeine Bildtheorie des naturwissenschaftlichen Bildes geben kann," in *Das Technische Bild. Kompendium zu einer Stilgeschichte wissenschaftlicher Bilder,* ed. Bredekamp, H. (Berlin: Akademieverlag, 2008: pp. 30–35)

White, J., *Historia de una ignominia. La United Fruit Co. en Colombia* (Bogota: Ediciones Presencia, 1978)

Williams, J., *The Rise of the Banana Industry and Its Influence on Caribbean Countries* (Worcester, Mass.: Clark University,1925)

Winkler, H., "Prozessieren. Die dritte, vernachlässigte Medienfunktion," *Media Theory in North America and German-Speaking Europe* (Vancouver: University of British Columbia, 2010)

Winthrop-Young, G., *Kittler and the Media* (Cambridge: Polity Press, 2011)

Woodbury, R. B. and Aubrey S. Trik, *The Ruins of Zaculeu of Guatemala (Vol. 1–2),* (United Fruit Company, 1953)

Woodger, E., "Wilson Popenoe, American horticulturist, educator and explorer," *Huntia* 5:1 (1983): pp. 17–22

Yates, J., "The Emergence of the Memo as a Managerial Genre," *Management Communication Quarterly* 2:4 (1989): pp. 485–510

Zanetti, O. and Alejandro García, *United Fruit Company: un caso del dominio imperialista en Cuba* (Havana: Editorial de Ciencias Sociales, Instituto Cubano del Libro, 1976)

Žižek, S., "Everything You Always Wanted to Know about Schelling (But Were Afraid to Ask Hitchcock)," in *Schelling Now: Contemporary Readings*, ed. Wirth, J. (Bloomington: Indiana University Press, 2005: pp. 31–44)

Archives and Archival Sources

Botanical Garden in Cuba, Director's Correspondence, 1898–1946, Harvard University Archives, Cambridge

Central American Expedition (Honduras, Guatemala) Record, 1891–1911, Peabody Museum of Archaeology and Ethnology, Harvard University, Cambridge

Everett C. Brown Papers, 1919–1921, Special and Area Studies Collections, George A. Smathers Libraries, University of Florida, Gainesville

Giles G. Healey Negatives, 1946, Indians of Chiapas, Mexico, Film Negatives Collection, Manuscripts Division, Department of Rare Books and Special Collections, Princeton University Library, Princeton

Oliver G. Ricketson, Jr. Collections, Papers and Photographs, 1920–1941, Peabody Museum of Archaeology and Ethnology, Harvard University, Cambridge

Papers of Oakes Ames, 1901–1950, The Arnold Arboretum of Harvard University, Cambridge

Paul Hamilton Allen Papers, 1911–1963, Hunt Institute for Botanical Documentation, Carnegie Mellon University, Pittsburgh

Popenoe Family Papers, Hunt Institute for Botanical Documentation, Carnegie Mellon University, Pittsburgh

Records from the Department of State, Bureau of Inter-American Affairs. Office of Middle American Affairs, 1947–1956, Department of State, Bureau of Inter-American Affairs/Office of Middle American Affairs, National Archives II, Maryland

Records of the Atkins Garden and Research, 1899–1954, The Arnold Arboretum of Harvard University, Cambridge

Records of the Foreign Agricultural Service, Records of the Office of Foreign Agricultural Relations and its Predecessors, Correspondence and Narrative Reports, 1901–1958, National Archives II, Maryland

Records of the Foreign Agricultural Service, Correspondence and Narrative Reports, 1949–1976, National Archives II, Maryland

Records of the Foreign Agricultural Service, Still Pictures, Photographic Negatives, 1942–1953, National Archives II, Maryland

Record of the Office of the Director; American Museum of Natural History, 1934–1936, Special Library Collections, Brooklyn Museum, New York

Record of the Office of the Director, Wise, John (legal-size folder), 1934–1935, Special Library Collections, Brooklyn Museum, New York

Richard Pearson Strong Papers, 1911–2004, Center for the History of Medicine, Countway Library, Harvard Medical School, Cambridge

Leopold and Rudolf Blaschka Archive, Corning Museum of Glass, New York

The Archives of Rudolph and Leopold Blaschka and the Ware Collection of Blaschka Glass Models of Plant, Harvard University, Cambridge

The Maya Through the Ages (1949), directors: United Fruit Company; Whitman, E. S. and Charles Morrow Wilson, Giles G. Healey (film), Harvard Film Archive, Harvard University, Cambridge

The Papers of Victor Macomber Cutter (1881–1952), Dartmouth College, Hanover

Thomas Barbour Papers, 1902–1946, Harvard University Archives, Harvard University, Cambridge

United Fruit Company – New York, Textual Records from the Department of Agriculture. Agricultural Research Administration. Bureau of Entomology and Plant Quarantine. Division of Foreign Plant Quarantine, 1927–1951, National Archives II, Maryland

United Fruit Company Papers, Philippe Bourgois Private Collection

United Fruit Company Photograph Collection, 1891–1962, Baker Library, Harvard Business School, Cambridge